Security, Conflict and Cooperation in the Contemporary World

Series Editors
Effie G. H. Pedaliu
LSE Ideas
London, UK

John W. Young
University of Nottingham
Nottingham, UK

The Palgrave Macmillan series, Security, Conflict and Cooperation in the Contemporary World aims to make a significant contribution to academic and policy debates on cooperation, conflict and security since 1900. It evolved from the series Global Conflict and Security edited by Professor Saki Ruth Dockrill. The current series welcomes proposals that offer innovative historical perspectives, based on archival evidence and promoting an empirical understanding of economic and political cooperation, conflict and security, peace-making, diplomacy, humanitarian intervention, nation-building, intelligence, terrorism, the influence of ideology and religion on international relations, as well as the work of international organisations and non-governmental organisations.

More information about this series at
http://www.palgrave.com/gp/series/14489

Morten Heiberg

Spain and the Wider World since 2000

Foreign Policy and International Diplomacy
during the Zapatero Era

Morten Heiberg
Department of English, Germanic
and Romance Studies
University of Copenhagen
Copenhagen, Denmark

Security, Conflict and Cooperation in the Contemporary World
ISBN 978-3-030-27342-2   ISBN 978-3-030-27343-9   (eBook)
https://doi.org/10.1007/978-3-030-27343-9

This Palgrave Macmillan imprint is published by the registered company Springer Nature
Switzerland AG
The registered company address is: Gewerbestrasse 11, 6330 Cham, Switzerland

PREFACE

This book is primarily based on interviews with His Excellency Miguel Ángel Moratinos, who served as Spain's Foreign Minister from 2004 to 2010. It also takes into account the precious oral accounts of other ministers, most notably that of Prime Minister José Luis Rodríguez Zapatero, vice ministers and key diplomats.

Regardless of the immense historical value of these testimonies, historians much prefer written contemporary sources over later oral testimonies, and whenever there is a disagreement between these two types of sources, they tend to go with the written ones. This author is no exception to the rule. For this reason, I boldly asked a number of the people involved in this book project if they would share with me their personal notes. I am truly grateful to those who did. This material, which is not explicitly quoted in the book, has served the important purpose of qualifying my interviews and ensuring that the direction of my interpretation is substantially correct.

Occasionally, I refer in my footnotes to "private information given to the author". This information, which was given to me on the premise of anonymity, is by no means vital to my historical interpretation of the Zapatero era, yet it does offer important texture which allows us to better understand how the political processes were shaped and what happened inside "the machine room" of Spanish and international politics. Not to share this insight with readers would, in my opinion, have been to fail. When I have anonymously attributed an exact quotation or a particular view to a specific person, for example a minister or a diplomat, that information may stem from the person in question or from somebody with an intimate knowledge of the political process.[1] Only on one occasion has this type of private information been of paramount importance to my interpretation, namely in the chapter on the Carmona coup, where I have used one particular anonymous source to strengthen one of my main arguments, namely that Spain and the United States supported Carmona's undertakings as long as they were staged as happening within the formal boundaries of the Venezuelan Constitution. This was of course only done after careful consideration concerning the validity of the information in question. Perhaps future editions of this book can be more explicit about the origin of each piece of information.

Finally, I owe a comment regarding the expression "The Moratinos files", which I have chosen as the title for the author's personal archive which holds the interviews and sources gathered for this book. The name chosen is merely meant to pay tribute to a former foreign minister who finds it important that he and his fellow foreign policy actors from the Zapatero government contribute to scholarship, and more generally, to the historical memory of Spain.

Copenhagen, Denmark   Morten Heiberg
2019

---

[1]Cf. the principles for the use of anonymous sources laid out by Bob Woodward in his most recent book. See: Bob Woodward, *Fear. Trump in the White House* (London, New York, Sydney, Toronto, New Delhi: Simon & Schuster, 2018), "Note to the Reader".

ACKNOWLEDGEMENTS

This book would never have come into being had it not been for the important initiative taken by Miguel Ángel Moratinos, who in early 2016 kindly asked me if I would consider writing a historical analysis of the foreign policy of the Zapatero government. I was of course honored and profoundly grateful to receive this unique offer. Since then, the many hours we have spent together sorting out the chronology and the inner dynamics of Spanish foreign policy have left me with nothing but keen memories of a man of intellect, dialogue, an extraordinary capacity for work and, not least, a profound will to change the world for the better. Moreover, I'm very grateful for the fact that he never tried to interfere with my interpretations. His only concern was to get the chronology and the facts right, and of course to offer his perspective.

Likewise, I'm very grateful to the distinguished Spanish historian and former diplomat, Professor Emeritus of the Complutense University of Madrid, Ángel Viñas, who encouraged me to undertake this complex endeavor. Throughout the entire process, Viñas patiently commented on the manuscript and on my use of sources, which turned out to be rather complex. To collaborate with him has been one of the greatest privileges of my career. I'm also very indebted to Ambassador Agustín Santos Maraver, who worked closely with Moratinos and from 2008 was his chief of staff. He answered all sorts of questions—at any given hour—besides generously sharing with me his unique knowledge of Spanish foreign affairs.

Whereas Moratinos, Viñas and Santos Maraver may have given the initial impetus to this project, it was the Carlsberg Foundation which generously provided me with a one-year 'Semper Ardens' research fellowship, thereby enabling me to spend thousands of working hours in Madrid. I am truly indebted to this magnificent patron of the arts. I'm also grateful to the University of Copenhagen which accepted my absence during more than two semesters, and not least to my dear colleagues in the Spanish Department who kindly covered my teaching obligations during the same period.

Besides Moratinos, I am truly indebted to the following ministers and vice ministers in the Zapatero government who found the time in their busy schedules to talk to me: Prime Minister José Luis Rodríguez Zapatero, First Deputy Prime Minister María Teresa Fernández de la Vega and Vice Minister for Development Leire Pajín. I'm further indebted to the former President of the Region of Andalucía, Manuel Chaves, who also served as president of the PSOE and later as minister in the Zapatero Government. Former Foreign Minister of Denmark, Dr. Per Stig Møller, kindly offered me his opinion on the Spanish-UN initiative, the Alliance of Civilizations, and on how Madrid assisted the Danish Government during the so-called Cartoon Crisis of 2005–2006. I would also like to thank the CEO and chairman of Repsol, Antonio Brufau, who kindly offered me his view of the Socialist government and its policies toward Bolivia and Venezuela. Further, I am indebted to Professor Julián Santamaría of the Complutense University of Madrid, who shared with me his unique knowledge of Spanish voting patterns prior to the 2004 general elections.

A number of Spanish diplomats provided me with their expert view of foreign affairs. I'm indebted to the former chief of staff from 2004 to 2008, Javier Sancho, who offered precious insight into the actions of the first Zapatero government. Furthermore, I owe my gratitude to the present chief of staff, Camilo Villarino, who in his former capacity as EU negotiator gave me his personal view of the Spanish bargaining position vis-à-vis the Treaty of Nice and the constitutional treaty. José Eugenio Salarich, former general director of foreign policies for Asia and the Pacific, generously provided me with his insights into the Asian policies of the Zapatero government. I'm also grateful to Juan Antonio March, former ambassador to the Russian Federation, who explained to me the dynamics of the evolving European crisis with Russia. Ambassador José Pons, former general director of foreign policy for Europe and

North America, lent me his sharp reflections on the Gibraltar question. Neither can I easily forget the many times that Moratinos' personal secretary, Ms. Ainhoa Camacho, assisted me and my family during my prolonged stays in Madrid. For this, I am deeply grateful.

Finally, I want to express my gratitude to Dr. Manuel Sanchis i Marco, Associate Professor of Applied Economics at the University of Valencia and a former employee of the European Commission. He generously shared with me his deep insights into the origins of the Spanish financial crisis. His incisive comments greatly improved Chapter 9 of this book. I'm also indebted to Dr. Irene Fernández-Molina, lecturer in International Relations at the University of Exeter, who kindly shared with me her deep knowledge of Moroccan foreign policy. The same applies to Dr. José Magone, Professor for Global and Regional Governance at the Berlin School of Economics, who critically reviewed the entire manuscript and pointed out numerous inconsistencies. Likewise, I'm truly grateful to Associate Professor Regin Schmidt and Associate Professor Mogens Pelt (both of the University of Copenhagen), who also read the entire manuscript and made several extremely useful suggestions. The remaining errors and incongruities can only be blamed on the author.

The book is dedicated to Elias and especially Mathias, who at the age of six was unmercifully enrolled in the Italian State School in Madrid in order for his father to write this book. Not even once did you complain. I shall never forget.

Copenhagen   Morten Heiberg
2019

CONTENTS

CHAPTER 1

Introduction

It was around nine in the morning, and the cell phone was ringing inces-
santly. Having celebrated until late into the night the end of a successful
election campaign, the sound of a beeping phone was not what Miguel
Ángel Moratinos particularly wanted to hear. Nevertheless, the internationally renowned Spanish diplomat got on the phone. "There has been a
series of explosions, a terrorist attack against the Madrid railway system. You
must come to Madrid at once."[1] The voice at the other end belonged to
José Luis Rodríguez Zapatero, the leader of the Socialist party, the PSOE,
who within a few weeks would also be the new prime minister of Spain.
For security reasons, all public transport had been shut down following
the terrorist attack, and in order to get from his constituency in Córdoba
to Madrid, Moratinos had to persuade some local party members to drive
him the nearly 400 kilometers to the Socialist headquarters in Calle Ferraz.
General elections were only three days away.

When Moratinos arrived in the capital on the evening of Thursday 11
March 2004, he had already received abundant information through private channels indicating that the terrorist attack was Al Qaeda's work.[2] It
was also clear that it was the most vicious assault against the West since

[1] Moratinos Files: Interview, Miguel Ángel Moratinos.
[2] Ibid.

© The Author(s) 2019   1
M. Heiberg, *Spain and the Wider World since 2000*,
Security, Conflict and Cooperation in the Contemporary World,
https://Doi.org/10.1007/978-3-030-27343-9_1

11 September 2001 and the worst in the recent history of Spain. Ten bombs had exploded simultaneously in four different local trains in Madrid between 7.37 and 7.41 a.m., and it later transpired that, all in all, 191 people had died and 1841 had been wounded.[3] In spite of the fact that the perpetrators had used the well-known Al Qaeda technique of simultaneous bomb attacks, the Spanish Conservative government under José María Aznar's leadership immediately pointed to Euskadi Ta Askatasuna (ETA), the Basque terrorist group, as being responsible for the massacre. By so doing, the Conservative Partido Popular (PP) effectively decoupled the disaster in Madrid from Islamic terrorism and thus also from the government's commitment to the US military intervention in Iraq, which the Socialist opposition had strongly opposed during the election campaign. Moratinos was a member of Zapatero's shadow cabinet and one of the main architects behind the Socialists' electoral promise to pull the Spanish contingent of troops out of Iraq. The next three days witnessed what has widely been described as a massive political cover-up by the Conservative government, who to the surprise of many observers lost the general elections on Sunday 14 March.[4]

Many aspects remain obscure, not only of this tragic event, but of the almost Copernican turn that Spanish foreign policy took after the bomb attacks. Was it truly Al Qaeda, who won the elections for the PSOE and triggered a shift in Spanish foreign policy? This was definitely a widespread view among both Spanish and foreign observers, especially those of Conservative stamp.[5] To the more objective observer, though, it looked at least as if the new Socialist government was determined to do more or less the opposite of their Conservative predecessors in almost every field. In fact, a number of important questions can be raised with regard to the immediate and longer-term objectives of the Zapatero government, which came to dominate Spanish politics for nearly eight years and in many ways transformed the country during that period.

[3]Fernando Reinares, ¡Matadlos! Quién estuvo detrás del 11-M y por qué se atentó en España (Barcelona: Galaxia Gutenberg, 2014), 8. Based on the written sentence of the Audiencia Nacional, No. 65 of 2007.

[4]Cf. Sect. 2.2 of this book.

[5]Cf. Tim Hames, "The Spanish Elections: A Landslide Win for Bin Laden", The Times, March 16, 2004. https://www.thetimes.co.uk/edition/news/the-spanish-elections-a-landslide-win-for-bin-laden-rnp707rvc7n.

However, before broaching such questions, it is necessary to briefly reflect on the political handling of the bomb attack, which has been subjected to contrasting interpretations. A crucial question remains as to why the Socialist opposition party was so well-informed of who the perpetrators behind the terrorist attack were, while José María Aznar's Conservative government claimed that it was not. On the day of the bombing, the Socialist leadership had few if any doubts about the authorship of the attack, yet on the very same afternoon, Prime Minister Aznar personally called the editors-in-chief of different newspapers to reassure them that ETA was the culprit, just as the Spanish Foreign Ministry contacted the UN Security Council in order to obtain a formal condemnation of the Basque separatist group.[6] To fully understand the degree to which the Conservative government was willing to defend the ETA narrative, one must take into regard all the crucial information to the contrary that was carefully collected by the Socialist party from its international sources, among others from Middle East intelligence agencies, and loyally passed on to the PP government, who however ignored it. This part of the history of the bomb attack has been left untold until this very day.

This study also hopes to provide a more nuanced understanding of the election campaign, which contrary to widely held beliefs saw the Conservative PP in grave difficulties long before Al Qaeda committed its hideous crime. While the PSOE was effectively mobilizing its potential voters, a crisis of confidence had occurred in the relationship between the PP and its electorate. The Conservative leadership was perfectly aware of the risk of failure, but never openly admitted that this was the case. In other words, this study seriously puts to the test the common claim that the Al Qaeda bomb attack won the elections for the PSOE. Thus, the first chapters are primarily concerned with the national and international legitimacy of the new Socialist government, as this played a major role in its potential to effectively apply a new foreign policy.

Seen from an international perspective, the immediate Spanish withdrawal of the Spanish forces from Iraq was probably the most controversial

---

[6] José Manuel Romero, „El desconcierto del Gobierno sobre la autoría del atentado," *El País*, March 13, 2004. https://elpais.com/diario/2004/03/13/espana/1079132404_850215.html; "Security Council Condemns Madrid Terrorist Bombings, Urges All States to Join Search for the Perpetrators," *United Nation Security Council*, Resolution 1530, adopted unanimously, March 11, 2004. https://www.un.org/press/en/2004/sc8022.doc.htm. See Chapter 2 for further information.

action of the new government, as it openly defied the foreign policy and the security doctrine of the Bush administration. In her memoirs, Condoleezza Rice claims that the new Spanish prime minister simply "reversed course, precipitously withdrawing Spanish forces from Iraq and causing tensions in our relationship that were never overcome."[7] True, the Bush administration certainly made the Zapatero government sweat in the following months, yet the fact remains that it did little more than that. Come spring 2005, this book holds, the bilateral working relations were essentially back on track. However, the fact that Madrid could turn its back on Washington almost scot-free clearly upset several US allies. The successful withdrawal of troops inspired new hopes within the anti-war movements in many countries, not least in Australia and Japan, two of America's most important allies in the world.[8] Was the world's last remaining hegemon loosening its grip on its allies? And if so, who would then govern the world?

It is important to stress that the decision to pull its forces out of Iraq was only one in a series of new Spanish initiatives concerning European, Latin American, African as well as Asian affairs, where the Zapatero government markedly changed the foreign policy course of Spain. What is indeed noteworthy of Zapatero's nearly eight years in power, is his government's proactive engagement in multilateral attempts to resolve international conflicts which were of no direct material concern to Spain and also largely considered the reserved domain of the major players of international politics. Yet, what did the Socialist government think it could actually achieve by getting involved in a long series of complex multilateral processes, the outcome of which was very uncertain indeed?

To answer this question satisfactorily, it is important to pay proper attention to the broader international context in which the new Spanish foreign policy was formulated. At the beginning of the millennium, there were strong countercurrents challenging the neoconservative foreign policy doctrine of the United States. To increase security and prosperity at home, the new Spanish Socialist government reasoned in 2004, one could no longer rely exclusively on unilateral measures, Cold War alliances or a "Spain first"

[7] Condoleezza Rice, *No Higher Honor: A Memoir of My Years in Washington* (New York: Broadway Books, 2011), 203.

[8] On several occasions, the Australian prime minister, John Howard, had to reject calls by either the Stop the War Coalition (StWC) or the Australian Greens for troops to withdraw immediately from Iraq. Cf. "Spain stands alone on Iraqi pullout," *ABC*, March 16, 2004. http://www.abc.net.au/news/2004-03-16/spain-stands-alone-on-iraqi-pullout/152288.

approach, as pronounced by Prime Minister Aznar prior to the 2000 general elections. The world was rapidly transforming—no one knew exactly into what—but surely the developments abroad, even in the most distant corners of the world, could no longer be ignored when they had the potential to bring about fundamental change at home. The terrorist attack in 2004 was just one example of this trend. The immediate aftermath of the terrorist attack saw many new trials, among others a refugee crisis with people suddenly arriving in thousands onto Spanish shores from central Africa or even from as far away as Bangladesh. Without marked changes to Spain's traditional foreign policy, the government reasoned, it could not expect to bring such situations under control. The main question, though, was how to handle these challenges most effectively.

What was also important for the PSOE's multilateral commitment was probably the weight of history. For most of the twentieth century, Spain had been incapable of controlling its own destiny in the international system, and the first democratic Socialist governments led by Felipe González (1982–1996) had worked overtime to reverse exactly this trend. In fact, among Zapatero's foremost advisors in foreign affairs were former diplomats who had been actively involved in some of the most important revisions of Spanish foreign policy during the era of democratic transition after General Franco's death in 1975. The first UCD center-right governments had managed to tackle some of the most pressing problems of Spain's foreign relations, the most important being the question of Spain's membership of NATO in 1982. However, the arduous task of rebalancing the uneven relationship with the United States and obtaining Spanish membership of the EC was left entirely in the hands of the PSOE, who won a landslide victory in the general elections of 1982.[9]

Interestingly, nearly all the notes and reports written by Spanish foreign policy advisors in this period recommended new undertakings that could secure a much higher degree of autonomy for democratic Spain in the international system. Although torn over the wisdom of joining NATO, they all agreed on the necessity of increasing Spain's multilateral engagements, as an isolated Spain would be too vulnerable to cope with the machinations of the great powers.[10] In diplomatic circles, there was still a vivid memory

[9]Morten Heiberg, *US-Spanish Relations After Franco. Will of the Weak*. vol of Harvard Cold War Studies Book Series (Lanham, MD: Lexington Books, 2018), 196–197.

[10]Ibid., xiii.

of Spain's complete international isolation after World War II followed by a long period of submission to US Cold War interests. In 1953, Spain had in fact accepted the installation of US military bases across Spain under the most humiliating terms.[11] Importantly, the dictatorship's gradual integration into the international economy during the late 1950s and 1960s did not imply that Spain would become a member of the European Economic Community, as formally requested by Spain in 1962.[12] New efforts to join the EC were made again in 1964, but it was only in 1970 that a commercial agreement between the parties was struck. This new deal implicitly maintained that membership would have to wait until after Franco's death.[13] For the very same reason, European integration became one of the most important foreign policy goal in democracy, together with a revision of defense relations with the United States.

The accession of Spain to the EC in 1986 and the agreement of 1988 to reduce the US military presence in Spain laid the groundwork for a new ambitious foreign policy, which enabled Spain to increase its international weight after the end of the Cold War. Spain took the natural lead in Europe's dealings with Latin America, while it also provided crucial logistic support in the war against Hussein in 1991. In its capacity as provisional head of the presidency of the European Union (EU) in 1995, Madrid also gave impetus to a new collaboration with Washington, which ten years later would be presented by the Zapatero government as a model for how Europe could positively reshape its relations with the United States. Importantly, this newfound relationship with Washington also meant that when the conservative PP finally gained power in 1996, the PSOE did not oppose

[11] As Dean Rusk and Robert McNamara coolly reminded President Kennedy in 1963: "…Spain has allowed us to use these bases for practically any purpose the US deemed necessary…This lack of restraints makes our bases in Spain particularly valuable whether in time of peace, increased tension or war." Cit. in ibid., 25.

[12] Despite positive signals from Konrad Adenauer in particular, the European left effectively barred the inclusion of Spain through a serious of initiatives, among others the so-called Birkelbach report of 1962 presented by the West German Socialists of the European Parliamentary Assembly. The message was that if Spain wanted to join the European family, the dictatorship would have to be dismantled first. Cf. Antonio Muñoz-Sánchez, *Von der Franco-Diktatur zur Demokratie. Die Tätigkeit der Friedrich-Ebert-Stiftung in Spanien* (Bonn: Dietz, 2013), 21. On the anti-communist affinities between West Germany and Spain, see Carlos Sanz Díaz, "España y la República Federal de Alemania (1949–1966): política, economía y emigración, entre la guerra fría y la distensión" (PhD Diss., Universidad Complutense de Madrid, 2005).

[13] Angel Viñas, "Años de Gloria. Años de sombra, tiempos de crisis," in *40 años con Franco*, ed. Julián Casanova (Barcelona: Crítica, 2015), 90–91.

the PP's decision to make Spain participate in NATO's integrated military structures.[14] However, during his second term as prime minister José María Aznar drew Madrid much closer to Washington at the expense of a deeper collaboration with Spain's closest European partners.[15]

For sure, after 2001 Prime Minister Aznar increasingly used both history and geography to defend his decision to reposition Spain alongside the UK in an imagined "Atlantic Europe" which hailed special bonds to the Americas. In his view, instead of leaning on France and Germany, Spain should have tried to use its privileged position vis-à-vis Latin America to mediate between their interests and those of the United States, the only true guarantor of Spanish and European security.[16] In many ways, his friend, and subsequent ambassador to the United States, Javier Rupérez, sums up what Aznar's political project had been all about. The ambassador uses the famous photo of Aznar, President Bush, and the British prime minister, Tony Blair, in the Azores, just hours prior to the intervention of Iraq in March 2003, as a metaphor for the importance that Aznar's Spain had gained in the international arena. Crucially, one had to go back centuries in

---

[14] After the landslide victory of the PSOE in the general elections of 1982, Prime Minister Felipe González redefined Spain's membership of NATO through a referendum in 1986. In fact, the PSOE had vigorously campaigned against the Spanish adhesion to the Alliance in 1982, but inherited from the UCD a de facto membership which could not have been realistically undone. By striking a new bilateral agreement with Washington in 1988, he also managed to diminish the US military presence in Spain significantly, and—from a Spanish view—clarify the conditions of US employment of the remaining military facilities in Spain. Cf. Angel Viñas, *En las garras del águila: Los pactos con Estados Unidos, de Francisco Franco a Felipe González* (Barcelona: Crítica, 2003), 500; Heiberg, *US-Spanish Relations After Franco*, 185–187.

[15] This summary owes to Charles Powell, *El amigo americano. España y Estados Unidos: de la dictadura a la democracia* (Barcelona: Galaxia Gutenberg, 2011), 637–644; Viñas, *En las garras del águila*, 505–510; Ibid., "Los pactos con los Estados Unidos en el despertar de la España democrática, 1975–1995," in *España y Estados Unidos en el siglo XX*, ed. Lorenzo Delgado and Maria Dolores Elizalde (Madrid: CSIC, 2005). See also Heiberg, *US-Spanish Relations After Franco*, 199–200. For a short, yet very useful overview of Spanish foreign policy after 1975, see Juan Carlos Jiménez Redondo, *De Suárez a Rodríguez Zapatero. La política exterior de la España democrática* (Paracuellos de Jarama: Editorial Dilex, 2006).

[16] Celestino Arenal, *Política exterior de España y relaciones con America Latina. Iberoamericanidad, Europeización y Atlantismo en la política exterior español* (Madrid: Fundación Carolina, 2011), 313, 324–325, 367.

time to find a similar moment in history when a Spanish leader was instrumental in taking such an important international decision.[17] Likewise, in numerous interviews, memoirs and diaries, politicians and diplomats close to the PP have stressed the unique relationship forged between Aznar's government and the Bush administration, and how Spain in its transatlantic relationship was able to punch far above its weight.[18] The White House willingly opened its doors to Aznar, and Bush listened to "Spain's visionary leader," as no other US president had done before him.[19] Spain had indeed become a power to be reckoned with.[20]

Jorge Dezcallar, former head of the Spanish intelligence services under Aznar, provides a more down-to-earth explanation for the US–Spanish rapprochement. He believes Tony Blair simply exploited Aznar's bad relationship with French President Jacques Chirac, sending the Spanish prime minister straight into the arms of President Bush.[21] Condoleezza Rice provides an entirely different claim, however, namely that it was the early US support of Spain's fight against Basque terrorism that created the bond.[22] Whatever the exact reason, Aznar no doubt tried to use the special relationship to establish Spain as a significant power in the international arena. His government's actions in Venezuela, which are subjected to scrutiny in one of the following chapters, bear witness to this strategy.

In other words, when Zapatero seized power in 2004 he tried to formulate a new foreign policy which on the one hand should be radically different from that of his conservative predecessor, José María Aznar, who after eight consecutive years in office had decided not to run for a third term in office and instead leave the party leadership in the hands of Mariano

[17] Javier Rupérez, *La Mirada sin ira. Memoria de política, diplomacia y vida en la España contemporánea* (Córdoba: Almuzara, 2016), 309.

[18] This view has also been accepted by some scholars. Cf. Cristina Crespo Palomares, *La alianza americana. La estrategia antiterrorista española y las relaciones hispano-norteamericanas (1996–2004)* (Madrid: Catarata, 2016).

[19] George W. Bush, *Decision Points* (New York: Crown Publishers, 2010), 246.

[20] It has even been argued that Spain under Aznar became a "revisionist" state in the sense that it coveted more than it currently possessed. Cf. David García Cantalapiedra, "Spanish Foreign Policy, the United States and *Soft* Bandwagoning," in *Contemporary Spanish Foreign Policy*, ed. David García Cantalapiedra and Ramón Pacheco Pardo (Abingdon & New York: Routledge, 2014), 94.

[21] Jorge Dezcallar, *El anticuario de Teherán. Historias de una vida diplomática* (Barcelona: Península, 2018), 564.

[22] Rice, *No Higher Honor*, 203.

Rajoy. On the other hand, the new Socialist government was expressing its awareness or concern of the fact that no country or cluster of countries seemed to be governing the world. The unilateral policies of the United States were failing, other aspiring hegemonic groups of the international system were clearly unable to apply their recipes either, and even though the idea of multilateralism was praised by a majority of nations, the same international actors were often quite incapable of establishing effective concerted mechanisms of collaboration. Yet this uncertain scenario also created new opportunities for Spain.

Zapatero's government wanted to offer what they saw as a more realistic vision of what Spain actually was. Although Spain had much to offer Europe and the rest of the world, it certainly did not have the financial strength of Germany, nor the military muscle of France and the UK. Spain was *not* a power in that sense, but it could realistically exercise or even increase its own influence if it proactively engaged in multilateral collaborations. The new Socialist government, therefore, chose to abandon Spain's hitherto unconditional Spanish support for the unilateral policies of the United States and instead engage in a series of multilateral collaborations—whether in international organs like the UN, spearheading EU policies in Central America, or working closely with two or three other nations to resolve specific international issues in North Africa, Asia or the Middle East. This vision was also in line with a more general theoretical belief among a growing number of experts of international relations, namely that some kind of multilateral global governance structure was going to replace the traditional foreign policy hitherto based on "national interest." The common foreign and security policies of the EU were but one example of this trend. Of course, larger countries would still continue, at least to some degree, to pursue goals that were distinct from joint policies, yet the scope to pursue narrow national interest was clearly shrinking, while multilateralism, particularly because of the possibility of greater risk sharing, was clearly the way forward.[23]

It is against this background that the new foreign minister, Miguel Ángel Moratinos, and his closest collaborators developed a new strategic concept

---

[23] Magone, José M., *Contemporary European Politics. A Comparative Introduction* (New York: Routledge, 2011), 581. On the role of the EU see José M. Magone, *The New World Architecture. The Role of the European Union in the Making of Global Governance* (New Brunswick, NJ: Transaction, 2006).

called "effective multilateralism" or "*multilateralismo eficaz.*"[24] Importantly, this new approach—inspired by the European Security Strategy adopted in 2003—also foresaw increased collaboration with several of the world's emerging powers, but above all it was envisaged that Spain would work alongside different players of international politics, big and small, and in regions where Spain did not traditionally have a strong foothold.[25] When Spain acquired the chairmanship of the OSCE in 2007, it chose to engage with Georgia, not only to solve the grave crisis in that country, but also because it offered the opportunity to work closer with the Russians.[26] In addition, as the Indian government was not prioritizing collaboration with Spain, Madrid opted instead for more collaboration with Islamabad, hoping that when New Delhi learned that Spain was proactively engaging with Pakistan, India would surely reshuffle its priorities in Spain's favor.[27] It is also within this context that we should understand the Spanish government's launching of an Alliance of Civilizations in 2004, a UN initiative aiming for a more equilibrated globalization based on dialogue and cooperation and, not least, mutual respect for diversity in order to avoid cultural conflict. Not only did this new alliance offer the possibility of decreasing tensions with the Muslim world in the aftermath of the Madrid attacks, it also held out new opportunities of international collaboration with Spain in the forefront.

This strategy also explains Spain's urgent request for a reform of the UN, especially of its Security Council where the permanent members could block any majority decision. In addition, the new government called for the reorganization of the G8 intergovernmental political forum into a more representative organ which would include Spain itself as well as the emerging economies of Africa and Asia. The PSOE government was wagering that in the twenty-first century "influence" would in many circumstances be a more efficient instrument than "power." Nevertheless, the new government may well have politically underestimated the fact that its multilateral

---

[24] Moratinos thoroughly explained the concept in his interventions before the Spanish Parliament on May 19, 2004. Cf. *Diario de Sesiones del Congreso de los Diputados, Comisiones, Asuntos Exteriores, Año 2004 VIII Legislatura Núm. 24, Sesión núm. 2*, May 19, 2004. http://www.congreso.es/public_oficiales/L8/CONG/DS/CO/CO_024.PDF.

[25] On the 2003 European Security Strategy and its influence on Spanish multilateralism see David García Cantalapiedra, "Spanish Foreign Policy," 97.

[26] Moratinos Files: Interview, Javier Sancho.

[27] Moratinos Files: Interview, José Eugenio Salarich.

and highly collaborative approach to foreign affairs also made it an easy target for its domestic political opposition. In fact, the PP made tireless efforts to portray Zapatero's new leadership as eagerly seeking compromise in the European arena, in contrast to Aznar's tough negotiating, just as they lamented the fact that the PSOE was incapable—essentially due to ideological affinities—of putting its foot down when confronted with unreasonable demands from autocratic third-world Socialist leaders. The PP effectively labeled both Zapatero and Moratinos as "friends" of Hugo Chávez, Evo Morales and the Castro brothers, a campaign based on well-known arguments to which neither the Spanish nor the international press was insensitive.

In an editorial of 20 October 2009, *the Wall Street Journal* described the Spanish foreign minister as "Havana's man in Europe", adding the following reflection: "Consider Mr. Moratinos a trend-setter in the age of Obama, as the U.S. president's own overtures to Castro (not to mention to Iran, Burma and now Sudan) follow a distinctly Moratinian philosophy. This holds that engaging dictators will yield better results than offering succor to their dissidents, and that tyrants and terrorists are somehow more malleable than their brutality suggests."[28] Such international affirmations were in turn used by the Spanish right to further question the Zapatero government's sound judgment. In response, Moratinos argued that unlike his own government, the former executive had not even obtained the release of one political prisoner in Cuba.[29] As we shall see throughout this book, instead of engaging critically with the new foreign policy concept, the opposition used the "soft" foreign policy approach of the PSOE government to expose its alleged weaknesses, although Spain's influence in the international arena under Zapatero was actually on the rise. The simple fact that a major US daily would write editorials complaining about Spain's Cuban policies and Obama's "Moratinian" behavior was probably in itself testimony to such increasing influence.

One thing is the polemical nature of politics. Another question is how to objectively measure the achievements of the Zapatero government's new approach in the international arena. It is, of course, very difficult to formulate an objective baseline against which we may measure the success of

[28] "Castro's Man in Europe," Editorial, *Wall Street Journal,* October 20, 2009. https://www.wsj.com/articles/SB10001424052748704500604574484923135150240.

[29] Luis Ángel Sanz, "'The Wall Street Journal': Moratinos es el 'hombre de Castro en Europa'," *El Mundo,* October 21, 2010. http://www.elmundo.es/elmundo/2009/10/21/espana/1256145330.html.

the PSOE. Accordingly, this study first and foremost applies the foreign policy goals set by the party itself as a benchmark of its success.[30] And, to the extent that the Socialists did or did not succeed in their endeavors, this book examines the reasons why. Finally, it also tries to assess the precise impact of the new foreign policy in order to better comprehend Spain's overall significance as an international actor during the period of Socialist government from 2004 to 2011. This book argues that the PSOE government, at the end of the day, was able to exercise positive influence on a number of international issues. To take one example which will be discussed at length in this book, it is doubtful whether there would have been such an important political opening from the Cuban regime toward the United States, had it not been for the strenuous efforts of the Spanish government.

The PSOE government's proactive multilateral approach to foreign affairs, and its recurrent emphasis on the relationship between domestic and foreign affairs, has inspired this historian to apply a dynamic analytical approach. On the one hand, the Spanish foreign policy of the new millennium is used throughout the book as a prism to better comprehend a world in rapid transformation. On the other hand, developments in other parts of the world are used to better understand how globalizing trends affect today's Spain. Thus, the ambition of this study is to offer a new international history of contemporary Spain, a narration "for a less national age" in which specific phenomena, events and processes related to Spanish policy choices are more clearly situated in their global contexts.[31] Accordingly, the study examines how the Spanish government reacted to a series of challenging cases, in which domestic changes interconnected with global transformations. To this end, it offers a tour de force of no less than four continents, and the studied cases can be said to be entangled in the fundamental restructuring of the world—to use Sebastian Conrad's useful expression.[32]

---

[30]Cf. the well-pondered methodological considerations in Tuomas Forsberg and Antti Seppo, "The Russo-Georgian War and EU Mediation," in *Russian Foreign Policy in the 21st Century*, ed. Roger E. Kanet (Houndsmill, Basingstoke, Hampshire: Palgrave Macmillan, 2011), 124.

[31]Sebastian Conrad, *What Is Global History?* (Princeton, NJ: Princeton University Press, 2016), 5, 116.

[32]Ibid., 9, 12. See also Conrad's chapter four for a more elaborate discussion.

CHAPTER 2

Terror in Madrid

2.1   Rising Star

Zapatero's ascent to power happened after a difficult period when the PSOE had been forced back into opposition. The defeat in 1996 to the Conservative PP, headed by José María Aznar, had put a sudden end to nearly fourteen years of Socialist reign. Without doubt, the feeble performance of the economy, the social protests against PSOE's labor market reforms, and above all, the increasing number of political and economic scandals had worn down the government, and the previously so charismatic leader Felipe González was no longer able to respond convincingly to all the accusations made against his party. The Socialist defeat in 1996, albeit by a narrow margin (38.8% of the votes and 156 seats in Parliament for the Conservatives, and 37.6% and 141 seats for the Socialists), also marked the beginning of the end to González's leadership of the party. His resignation from the post as General Secretary happened at the 34th Party Congress on 20 June 1997. Still, González remained a highly influential figure in the party in the years to come.[1]

---

[1] This brief summary of Zapatero's early career owes to the lucid biographical article written by Roberto Ortiz de Zárate. Cf. Roberto Ortiz de Zárate, "José Luis Rodríguez Zapatero." Online biography series of CIDOB (Barcelona Centre for International Affairs). http://www.cidob.org/biografias_lideres_politicos/europa/espana/jose_luis_rodriguez_zapatero.

© The Author(s) 2019   13
M. Heiberg, *Spain and the Wider World since 2000*,
Security, Conflict and Cooperation in the Contemporary World,
https://doi.org/10.1007/978-3-030-27343-9_2

Many in the party saw the subsequent appointment of Joaquín Almunia as party secretary as a sign of renewal despite the fact that he enjoyed
the support of Felipe González , former ministers, regional leaders (the
so-called *barones*) and important executives within the party. However,
behind the apparent unity, the party was deeply divided into factions. In
actual fact, Almunia lost the upcoming primary elections to become the
party's candidate for prime minister by a large margin to José Borrell, who
in the end declined to accept the role.[2] Borrell's refusal was not only due to
the fact that he did not have the support of the party leadership. He had also
been affected by the judiciary problems of two of his former collaborators.
In the 2000 general elections, the PSOE performed even worse than in
1996. Almunia immediately resigned, and as an interim solution, Manuel
Chaves, President of the Region of Andalucía, agreed to assume the post
until a new federal congress could decide on the future leadership. After
Almunia's defeat, Zapatero began to move politically in order to strengthen
his candidacy. The 39-year-old member of parliament representing León
did not explicitly adhere to any of the existing factions. During the 1990s,
Zapatero had slowly gained influential posts in parliament, just as he had
ably consolidated his own powerbase in León by curbing the local influ-
ences of Alfonso Guerra, the PSOE's historic number 2. From early on,
Zapatero had shown an extraordinary capacity for reconciling ideological and personal differences, while steadily creating consensus around his
own political aspirations to become a future leader. After five consecutive
reelections to the parliament, Zapatero, who was quite unknown to the
larger public, felt ready to make a bid for the leadership against the party's
favorite, the ten-year-older José Bono.[3]

Zapatero had gained the support of *Nueva Via* (New Way), a group of
reformers wanting to contribute to a more profound reform of the PSOE's
policies and party structure.[4] The project was clearly inspired by Tony
Blair's Third Way and also the *Neue Mitte* (New Center) of the German
Social Democratic Chancellor Gerhard Schröder. Thus, Zapatero clearly
distanced himself from the classic social democratic positions of the French
Prime Minister Lionel Jospin. Zapatero spoke of the need for a new left and

[2] Anna Bosco, "The Long Adiós: The PSOE and the End of the Zapatero Era," in *Politics
and Society in Contemporary Spain: From Rajoy to Zapatero*, ed. Bonnie N. Field and Alfonso
Botti (New York: Palgrave Macmillan, 2013), 24.

[3] Ortiz de Zárate, "José Luis Rodríguez Zapatero."

[4] Bosco, "The long Adiós," 25.

highlighted the impact of modernity in his political discourse. In a book of interviews, he praised Blair's capacity to renovate traditional working class-based socialism while calling for tax reductions at the same time.[5] In other circumstances, he made numerous references to multiculturalism and to a society that was radically changing in view of the ongoing IT revolution. He also emphasized that women should take a more active part in politics, just as he stressed the need to invest more in research and development. Zapatero also defended private initiative as the engine of the Spanish economy, but questioned the free market's ability to regulate itself. In other words, he opted for globalization with a human face. His critics argued that it was difficult to tell if these were just words or if they contained any real substance.[6] Importantly, he laid the groundwork for what came to be known as "citizens' socialism": He called for a series of reforms ranging from improved social rights, the reform of several regional statutes of autonomy, a new peace process with ETA, reforms on divorce, abortion, same-sex marriage and religious education, to compensation for the victims of the civil war and of Francoist atrocities.[7]

At the 35th Congress, Zapatero won a narrow victory by nine votes against José Bono leaving two other strong female contenders, Matilde Fernández Sanz and Rosa Díez far behind. His victory was a great surprise in that he did not enjoy the support of any of the PSOE's so-called families or the party apparatus.[8] Allegedly, Alfonso Guerra had voted for Zapatero merely in order to block Bono's rise to power and in the hope of having a say in Zapatero's future leadership. Contrary to the expectations of the veterans of the party, however, Zapatero immediately barred the major political factions from any automatic participation in the new twenty-five-man-strong party commission. For his new political project, Zapatero chose a number of trusted collaborators. It was a group of ambitious, yet to some extent less experienced politicians, who were not associated with the former leadership.[9]

[5] Julia Navarro, *El Nuevo socialismo. La visión de José Luis Rodríguez Zapatero* (Barcelona: Temas de Hoy, 2001), 20.

[6] Ortiz de Zárate, "José Luis Rodríguez Zapatero."

[7] Bosco, "The long Adiós," 26.

[8] Ibid., 25.

[9] Ortiz de Zárate, "José Luis Rodríguez Zapatero."

Moratinos's affiliation with the PSOE had been formalized in 2000, the year when Joaquín Almunia lost the general elections and was replaced by Zapatero. Moratinos was then stationed in Cyprus as EU Special Representative for the Middle East Peace Process, a position he had held since 1996. He had decided to become a member of the party, not in order to obtain a specific role, but mainly to contribute to the renewal of Spanish Socialist thinking. He held various meetings and contacts with the different secretary-generals until the victory of Zapatero, whom he met in Ferraz in 2000 together with his assistant, Bernardino León. The meeting was intended to last for only half an hour, but they ended up talking for two whole hours about Morocco, the Mediterranean and Europe. Obviously, the two bonded well.[10]

When Moratinos met Zapatero in 2000, the latter was highly concerned about the Conservative government's confrontational line toward Morocco. Later on, with the support of Moratinos, Zapatero decided to travel to Morocco and pay a visit to Mohammed VI, despite the fact that the relationship between Rabat and Madrid was at a historical nadir. On 19 December 2001, Zapatero met the recently appointed Moroccan king in Rabat and Prime Minister Abderrahman El Youssoufi—also a member of the Socialist International—in an attempt to unblock the diplomatic crisis. Suffice to mention, the meeting took place much to the chagrin of the Spanish Conservative government. However, during the crisis that arose from the occupation of Parsley Island (in Spanish *Islote de Perejil*) by a group of Moroccan gendarmes in July 2002, Zapatero supported Aznar's dispatch of troops to the island. Aznar's military response may have been inspired by fear that the occupation of this minuscule territory was a way of testing Spain's resolve to defend Ceuta and Melilla, the two Spanish enclaves on the Moroccan coast.[11] It is also possible that it was not the two enclaves that were in Moroccan sights, but rather the less significant islands of Alborán and Chafarinas, or that the incident pointed to purely domestic motives, as the king's control of foreign policy had allegedly been

[10]Moratinos Files: Interview, Moratinos.

[11]Charles Powell, "A Second Transition, or More of the Same? Spanish Foreign Policy Under Zapatero," in *Politics and Society in Contemporary Spain. From Rajoy to Zapatero*, ed. Bonnie N. Field and Alfonso Botti (New York: Palgrave Macmillan, 2013), 152.

challenged by members of the government.[12] Equally important, however, was Zapatero's criticism of the Conservative government for not having informed him in advance of a decision that implied the risk of escalation. It was the worst crisis between the two countries since the Green March in 1975 when Morocco occupied Spanish Western Sahara. From this moment on, Zapatero would ceaselessly denounce the majority government's unilateralism and systematic disregard for parliament.[13]

In July 2003, Moratinos returned to Spain after having completed his mission in Cyprus. He wished to continue to work in international diplomacy and to obtain a new mission within the United Nations. Aznar's Conservative government had promised him a post in international diplomacy, but allegedly vetoed his representing Spain in the United Nations. Upon his arrival in Madrid, Moratinos visited Zapatero again in July 2003. This time Zapatero asked him straight out if he would be prepared to join the Foreign Affairs Team in Ferraz, which was drafting the foreign policy section of the electoral program for the upcoming general elections in 2004. Moratinos was asked to put his services at the disposition of Manuel Marín, who had been the President of the European Commission for a short period following the demise of the Jacques Santer Commission in 1999. Upon his return from Brussels, Marín had been appointed secretary of international relations of the PSOE, a position from which one could expect to become foreign minister in a future PSOE government. Moratinos was asked to work mainly on the Mediterranean, the Near East and North Africa, all areas of which he had an intimate knowledge. All Moratinos's friends advised him against this uncertain career move—as did the political analysts of the time, convinced as they were that Mariano Rajoy of the PP would easily win the elections and that Zapatero would soon become yesterday's news.

Despite the ideological and generational differences within the PSOE, everyone was extremely dedicated and united in the belief that the elections could actually be won. The entire party possessed a very strong will to return to power, something which helped create the dynamics and the unity needed for this purpose.[14] However, the frictions and differences

---

[12]Aznar reveals in his diaries that the Spanish intelligence services were unable to provide any information whatsoever on the incident. Cf. José María Aznar, *El compromiso de poder. Memoria II* (Barcelona: Planeta, 2013), 68.

[13]Ortiz de Zárate, "José Luis Rodríguez Zapatero."

[14]Moratinos Files: Interview, Moratinos.

of opinion were still very visible underneath the surface. In this context, it is important to stress the influence that Felipe González still exercised within the party—also with regard to foreign policy issues. Marín was clearly under the influence of González, and so were the two high-profile party members Luis Yáñez-Barnuevo García and Máximo Cajal. Yáñez had built his political career as a member of Felipe González's entourage in Seville. He later became González's foreign policy advisor and had been a key player in the important recognition of Israel in 1986.[15] Cajal, an experienced diplomat, was especially renowned for his successful renegotiation of the US-Spanish base agreements in 1986–1987, a turning point in Spain's relationship with the United States.[16] In other words, around 2004, Felipe González could still count on the loyal services of highly influential and experienced people in foreign affairs.

In contrast to the *Felipistas*, Moratinos soon identified a different trend within the PSOE, which he describes as more "progressive" and "innova-tive" compared to the somewhat older guard, who in his view were more inclined to preserve status quo on a number of key issues. The group around Leire Pajín, born in 1976, represented the connection between civil society and different NGOs that Moratinos was looking for. Clearly positioned as a more left-wing, Catholic freethinker, Moratinos found his natural allies in this environment when it came to new ideas for moderniz-ing PSOE's foreign policy program. In his view, the *Felipistas* represented a more traditional foreign policy approach, mainly concerned with the re-Europeanization of Spain's foreign policy, whereas he was determined to define a new international identity for Spain—more in tune with the global challenges of the twenty-first century. In this, Moratinos' ideas coincided with those of Zapatero. In the end, the electoral program on foreign policy came to reflect very much Moratinos' and Zapatero's continuous encoun-ters with people representing civil society, ranging from NGOs to scholars from the universities, who to a large extent agreed with the necessity to change the concept of Spain's foreign relations.[17]

On the one hand, the new foreign policy design that was in the making clearly rejected Aznar's vision of a "special relationship" with the United

---

[15] Cf. Francisco Villar, *La Transición exterior de España: del aislamiento a la influencia (1976–1996)* (Madrid: Marcial Pons, 2016), 136.

[16] See Heiberg, *US–Spanish Relations After Franco*, 174–189.

[17] Moratinos Files: Interview, Moratinos.

States and consequently also Aznar's support for the invasion of Iraq. This way of thinking was very much in line with the traditional Socialist foreign policy doctrine which since the 1980s had aimed to reach a better equilibrium in Spain's relationship with the United States. It is widely agreed that Washington had successfully reduced Francoist Spain to a US satellite and that it was one of Felipe González's greatest achievements to have reversed this situation.[18] On the other hand, new ideas arose in the Socialist International around 2000, namely that globalization was now eroding traditional distinctions between foreign and domestic policies and that the values professed at home (peace, justice, solidarity, social cohesion, tolerance, secularism, etc.) should now also identify one's country abroad. This implied that greater significance should also be attached to soft power instruments.[19] From this moment on, a number of debates along these lines took place within the party. Another important question was the new treaty on the European constitution, where Almunia, Solbes and Barón followed the line of Marín, who, as mentioned, had briefly served as President of the European Commission. However, the perhaps biggest electoral issue of all was without doubt the withdrawal of Spanish troops from Iraq.

The in many ways fruitful dialectics between the *Felipistas* and *Progresistas* (as Moratinos defines the two factions) would soon develop into a personal struggle between Marín and Moratinos, two highly qualified candidates for the position of new foreign minister in the case of a Socialist victory. They were never enemies, but in politics there can only be one winner, something which naturally leads to fierce competition. Marín was absolutely convinced that he was going to be the new foreign minister, not only because of his experience in the Commission, but also because González backed his candidacy.

On certain issues, however, Moratinos tended to agree more with the *Felipistas* than with the *Progresistas*. Both factions agreed on the necessity of withdrawing from Iraq, but the latter were much more inclined toward an immediate withdrawal. Moratinos—in accordance with Yáñez—made different proposals in the Council of the Wise, all of which stressed the

---

[18] This is a main thesis in Heiberg, *US–Spanish Relations After Franco*, and Viñas, *En las garras del águila*.

[19] On the use of soft power in Spanish diplomacy, see: Alberto Priego Moreno, "Spanish Soft Power and Its Structural (Non-Traditional) Model of Diplomacy," in *Contemporary Spanish Foreign Policy*, ed. David García Cantalapiedra and Ramón Pacheco Pardo (Abingdon and New York: Routledge, 2014), 48–63.

need for more time to diplomatically negotiate the withdrawal with the Americans. His suggestion was eventually adopted in the following way: Spanish troops would be withdrawn from Iraq by 30 June 2004 if by then the UN had not adopted a new resolution that would hand over authority of the mission in Iraq to the United Nations (something which was judged unlikely due to Russian and Chinese resistance in the Security Council).

There were also vivid discussions regarding the relationship with Western Sahara and Morocco. Leire Pajín and other junior members argued in favor of more support and solidarity with the marginalized Sahrawi people living in Western Sahara and demanded a more critical position toward Morocco. In contrast, Moratinos' experience as a diplomat with special insight into North Africa made him more inclined to a pragmatic approach, i.e., reiterating Spain's principal concern with the Sahrawis and their suffering, and—above all—reinstalling a relationship of trust with Morocco. As we shall see further on, Aznar had challenged Morocco on a number of issues and both the *Progresistas* and the *Felipistas* wished to urgently reestablish dialogue and cooperation with Rabat. One can certainly speculate as to whether the tragic events of 11 March 2004 might actually have been avoided or reduced in scale had there been better working relations between the two countries. The fact was that the perpetrators were mainly from Maghreb countries, especially Morocco, and collaboration was probably not sufficiently organized due to the overall worsening of communications between the two countries.

Official aid to developing countries was also subject to heated discussions. NGOs affiliated with the party were campaigning for a considerable rise in the official contribution of the Spanish state to 0.7% of GNP. This was seen as totally irresponsible by the economists in the PSOE, who advised against stating an exact amount. With the support of Moratinos, Leire Pajín fought to take a large step forward on this issue. Very close to the beginning of the election campaign, an important meeting was held in the PSOE on this question, and Zapatero personally committed himself to doubling development aid from 0.23 to 0.5% in order to finally arrive at 0.7%.[20] During this phase, Moratinos was kept in the dark by Zapatero about the fact that he wanted him to appoint the rather inexperienced Pajín as Head of International Cooperation, a vice minister position, in fact, within the

---

[20]Moratinos Files: Interview, Leire Pajín.

Foreign Ministry. She served remarkably well in that position and gave a strong impetus to Spain's development policies.[21]

Moratinos' mission in Cyprus ended on 30 June 2003. In the preceding weeks, he had experienced a lot of pressure from the European Commission and from George Papandreou, the Minister of Foreign Affairs of Greece, which was currently holding the presidency of the Council of Ministers. They all wanted him to continue for one more year in order to have sufficient time to find a proper replacement. Moratinos ignored the request, as he was both exhausted and—as it turned out—seriously ill. When Moratinos went back to Madrid on 1 July 2003, he soon met with Zapatero. Although Moratinos had agreed to join the Foreign Affairs Team in Ferraz, he would, however, spend most of July and August recovering in a hospital in France. In September, he went to see Zapatero again and presided over meetings with his team in Ferraz.

In September, Zapatero asked him to run in the general elections, but Moratinos politely declined the offer as he wanted to continue working in international diplomacy. UNICEF, in particular, had caught Moratinos' interest. Aznar not only respected him, but allegedly also owed him a favor. However, the relationship between the two had changed after the attack on the Twin Towers in 2001 and especially after the invasion of Iraq in 2003. Moratinos sensed that the Conservative government was now less inclined in his favor, as Aznar did not make any special effort to comply with his wishes.[22] In contrast, the former Spanish-UN Ambassador Inocencio Arias claims that the Conservative government did raise the matter of Moratinos' candidacy for a top post on several occasions with Kofi Annan.[23]

From September 2003, Zapatero insisted several times through his right hand, José Blanco, that Moratinos should run for parliament. Moratinos discussed the proposal with his family but declined the offer. He was still determined not to enter politics. Nevertheless, his feelings were gradually beginning to change. For one, he had come to appreciate Zapatero very much as a person, just as he was becoming increasingly fond of the political

[21] Moratinos Files: Interview, Moratinos.

[22] Ibid.

[23] "Lo que sí sé que no es cierto, en absoluto, es que el gobierno anterior cameleara o no se emplease de verdad con la candidatura de Moratinos para un alto cargo en la ONU. Lo hicieron, y muy a fondo, tanto la ministra Palacio como Aznar, y soy testigo de excepción." Cit. in Inocencio Arias, *Confesiones de un diplomático. Del 11-S a 11-M* (Barcelona: Planeta, 2006), 319.

program which was being prepared in Ferraz. Another determining factor was the encounter with Aznar's Spain upon his return from Cyprus. Spain had changed for the worse under Aznar, and Moratinos found the majority government "superficial," "arrogant" and "authoritarian" (clearly a reference to Aznar's alleged disregard for parliament). He also found a tense and divided country. It was not the Spain he wanted for future generations and he felt a need to contribute to change this.

On 28 December 2003, Moratinos received a surprise call from Zapatero while he was in Segovia with a group of foreign friends. Once more he declined Zapatero's request to run for parliament. But in order to win him over, Zapatero then offered him a post in the Party's Council of the Wise ("Comité de notables") as Foreign Policy Advisor. Moratinos immediately accepted. This committee may roughly be considered a shadow cabinet, but Moratinos did not perceive the nomination as a sign that he was going to be the new foreign minister in case of a Socialist victory in the upcoming 2004 general elections.[24] In fact, Zapatero outwardly stressed—probably also to calm uneasy party members—that the committee was "... not a premise for a future government," which would include both members of his own generation and those of the 1982 generation.[25]

Right after Zapatero had made the names of his council public, Moratinos received a call from Aznar's Vice Minister and Secretary of State for Foreign Affairs, Ramón Gil-Casares, who expressed the government's outrage that Moratinos had opted for Zapatero. According to Gil-Casares, the PP had always considered Moratinos a nonpartisan actor within Spanish diplomacy.[26] Aznar furiously called Jorge Dezcallar in the CNI saying "¿Has visto a tu amiguito?" ("Have you seen your little friend?").[27] It is not unlikely that the PP was also uneasy about Moratinos joining the Socialist ranks in view of the upcoming elections. Foreign policy issues, particularly the Middle East, were going to be high on the agenda due to the Spanish military presence in Iraq and Aznar's highly contested pro-Bush policies.

In January 2004, Zapatero called Moratinos again and finally convinced him to run for parliament as well. Subsequent discussions were mainly

---

[24] Moratinos Files: Interview, Moratinos.

[25] "Zapatero Unveils 10-Member Team to Help Bring Socialists to Moncloa," *El País* (English edition), January 9, 2004.

[26] Moratinos Files: Interview, Moratinos.

[27] Dezcallar, *El anticuario de Teherán*, 105.

concerned with which constituency to assign to Moratinos. Madrid was soon ruled out as the local party branch had never shown a keen interest in Moratinos' services, even though he was a native Madrilenian. When Manuel Chaves, President of the Region of Andalucía, heard that Moratinos was looking for a constituency he immediately offered him the chance to run as number one in Almería. However, due to Spain's eternal conflicts with Morocco over agricultural issues, in which Almería farmers play an important role, Moratinos thought it better not to accept this offer. His concern was that it might harm his warm and efficient diplomatic relations with Morocco. Chaves then offered him the opportunity to run as number two in Córdoba. This was a perfect match because of the city's history. Córdoba is widely perceived as a symbol of "*convivencia*," a melting pot of Christian, Muslim and Jewish cultures.[28]

Why was Zapatero looking Moratinos' and not Marín's way? First, there was clearly a personal issue. Moratinos and Zapatero bonded well. Even after seven difficult years together in government, their relations remained warm, as can also be seen from Zapatero's handwritten letter to Moratinos in 2010 after Moratinos had stepped down as minister. Second, Zapatero simply identified more with Moratinos's approach to foreign affairs, which on paper offered a new foreign policy design which strongly appealed to his generation. Other factors may well have played a role: In 2004, rumor had it that Zapatero was a little intimidated by Marín's experience and allegedly feared that he would not have been easy to manage. During his election campaign in Córdoba, Moratinos read in the newspapers that if his party won, he would be the new foreign minister. This information was filtered to the press in a period when Moratinos also sensed a real change in the power relations within the party. Whenever there was an important meeting on foreign policy issues, Zapatero sent Moratinos to represent the party, not Marín, something which of course increased tension with the *Felipistas*. On 10 March 2004, the last day of the election campaign, Zapatero decided that Moratinos should present PSOE's foreign policy program at the Círculo de Bellas Artes in Madrid. Up until the very last minute, however, Marín tried to convince Zapatero that it should be him carrying out

---

[28] Moratinos Files: Interview, Moratinos. Cf. José Luis Rodríguez, "Miguel A. Moratinos 'Número 2' del PSOE al congreso: 'Quiero sacudir a Códoba en sentido positivo'," *Diario Córdoba*, January 18, 2004. http://www.diariocordoba.com/noticias/cordobalocal/miguel-a-moratinos-numero-2-psoe-congreso-quiero-sacudir-cordoba-sentido-positivo_100693.html.

this prestigious task, or—if this failed—that Marín and Moratinos should do the presentation together.

Moratinos' nomination was still an uphill struggle, however, due to pressures from those forces still supporting Marín. One can certainly understand Marín's frustrations. He had for a long time been first in line, and then in the summer of 2003, Moratinos appeared out of nowhere and grabbed "his" position. In essence, politics is not only about having the right ideas, which often serve as mere justifications. "Essentially, it is either you or me"—as Moratinos sums it up ("La política al final es el 'yo' o el 'otro'.").[29] Instead of becoming the foreign minister, Marín became President of the Congress of Deputies.

2.2   Massacres and Manipulations

Right after the bomb attacks on 11 March 2004, Prime Minister José María Aznar's Conservative government made a decision that would have a deep impact on the forthcoming elections: to publicly give prominence to one lead in the police investigation concerning the possible perpetrators of the murderous attacks. Thus, official statements during 11 March pointed immediately to ETA, the Basque terrorist organization, as the obvious perpetrator of this hideous crime. To be truthful, these statements loyally reflected the general belief among police forces and the intelligence services minutes after the attack. During the following hours, however, the forces subordinate to the Ministry of the Interior gradually received information that would seriously question the truthfulness of this immediate assumption. Furthermore, Arnaldo Otegi, leader of the political branch of ETA, Batasuna, immediately denied any Basque involvement, pointing instead to groups related to the "Arab resistance."[30] This statement was issued in response to the Basque President, Ibarretxe, who had stated early in the morning that it might have been ETA.[31]

Later in the day, Al Qaeda-related leads began to appear. Nevertheless, the government continued to give the impression that ETA was the

[29]Moratinos Files: Interview, Moratinos.

[30]"Otegi asegura que ETA no está detrás de 'esta masacre'," *El País*, March 12, 2004, referring to statement of Otegi the day before. http://elpais.com/diario/2004/03/12/espana/1079046070_850215.html.

[31]The wording of Ibarretxe's statement can be found in Anjel Rekalde et al., ed., *11-M. Tres días que engañaron al mundo* (Tafalla, Spain: Txalaparta, 2004), 178.

most plausible perpetrator. At 13:30, Foreign Minister Ana Palacio called Inocencio Arias, then Spanish ambassador to the United Nations, to urge for UN condemnation of the presumed ETA attack. At 5 p.m., she sent a note to the Spanish ambassador claiming that the Ministry of the Interior had confirmed that ETA was responsible for the attack. This immediately led the UN Security Council to condemn "in the strongest terms the bomb attacks in Madrid, Spain, perpetrated by the terrorist group ETA on 11 March 2004."[32] ETA was thus being held responsible, both nationally and internationally, and—one might add—the government's rationale behind the urgent wish for UN condemnation of ETA may well have been related to the upcoming elections on Sunday 14 March. Otherwise, it is difficult to understand the government's actions since the incoming pieces of evidence were clearly showing that the ETA lead was a dead end. Furthermore, the government could easily have waited a while longer before contacting the UN Security Council. In fact, on 16 March, Arias had to send a remorseful letter to a truly irritated Security Council claiming that the Spanish government had acted in good faith.[33]

Interestingly, the unequivocal condemnation of ETA made by the Spanish Ministry of the Interior, the foreign minister, and later in the day by the UN Security Council was not repeated by King Juan Carlos, when he addressed the nation three hours later in a televised speech at 8:30 p.m. This was probably not only due to the king's excellent instinct for politics, but also to developing events. The emergence of new evidence gradually made it clear that one should not a priori exclude the involvement of other terrorist groups in the attack. At 7 p.m., the Minister of the Interior, Ángel Acebes had expressed certain doubts about the authorship of the attack when he revealed that a small stolen van had been found in Alcalá de Henares which contained detonators and tapes with recorded verses of the Koran. Only a few minutes later, the Arab newspaper *Al Quds Al Arabi* made public that it had received a letter from Al Qaeda claiming responsibility for the

---

[32] "Security Council Condemns Madrid Terrorist Bombings, Urges All States to Join Search for the Perpetrators," *United Nation Security Council*, Resolution 1530, adopted unanimously, March 11, 2004. https://www.un.org/press/en/2004/sc8022.doc.htm.

[33] "España da explicaciones a la ONU por responsabilizar a ETA de los atentados de Madrid," *Noticias ONU*, March 16, 2004. https://news.un.org/es/story/2004/03/1031421.

attack.[34] Nevertheless, during Friday the government still continued to publicly consider ETA as the most plausible perpetrator, although they let it be understood that the authorities were still investigating a broad spectrum of possibilities. For the very same reason, Aznar came under attack from José Blanco, party secretary of the PSOE, who insisted that "there are well-founded suspicions concerning the implication of international terrorism," without, however, mentioning Al Qaeda or revealing his source for this information.[35] In this way, he allowed the Conservative government to keep defending the ETA position for the time being. An Internet article published by Spanish newspaper *El País* at 16:06 hours on Friday not only reported the PSOE's position. It also highlighted that the leading Catalan politician Josep-Lluís Carod-Rovira agreed with Blanco in accusing the government of "hiding and delaying information" on the assaults. The article also reported Carod-Rovira's demand that Aznar should clarify before election day whether Al Qaeda was behind the massacre or not.[36] The political pressure was clearly building on Aznar's government.

One of the most criticized elements of the crisis management was the behavior of the Spanish state television, TVE, which uncritically began running documentaries on the history of ETA violence—even on Saturday, just before Sunday's elections were about to begin. Many people felt afterward that they had been set up by Aznar, and on Saturday, the Secretary of the Socialist Party, Alfredo Pérez Rubalcaba, stated on national television that the Spaniards deserved a government that did not lie to them.[37] This statement was to have a considerable impact.

There has been much speculation as to why the Conservative government stuck to a narrative that in the long run was unsustainable. Perhaps, it was believed that unequivocal condemnation of ETA might secure popular backing and make people forget the PP's extremely unpopular support for George W. Bush's interventionism in the Middle East. Another plausible

---

[34] "Cuatro atentados simultáneos causan una matanza en trenes de Madrid," *El País*, March 12, 2004. http://elpais.com/diario/2004/03/12/espana/1079046001_850215.html.

[35] "Aznar insiste en que 'no se descarta' ninguna hipótesis en los atentados de Madrid," *El País*, March 12, 2004, 16:06 hours. http://elpais.com/elpais/2004/03/12/actualidad/1079083025_850215.html.

[36] Ibid.

[37] Luís R. Aizpeolea, "Toda la oposición acusa al Gobierno de manipular y ocultar información," *El País*, March 14, 2004. https://elpais.com/diario/2004/03/14/espana/1079218841_850215.html.

concern was that the revelation of a murderous Al Qaeda attack against Madrid's railway system might raise questions about the very raison d'être of Aznar's political alliance with George W. Bush, as it had not protected Spain and might affect the general elections negatively. Much has been written about the 11 March bomb attacks and the government's alleged disinformation campaign, but it clearly exceeds the limits of this chapter to go through all the details of this debate. What is important to stress, however, is that the Spanish judiciary carefully reconstructed the chain of events and also deflated the conspiracy theory launched by the Spanish newspaper *El Mundo* and eagerly followed by *Libertad Digital* that ETA had some kind of hidden hand in the attacks.[38] Nevertheless, two important and correlated aspects of the "11-M," as this tragic event is called in Spanish, probably need some reconsideration: The information made available to the Spanish intelligence services (CNI) and the PSOE respectively from 11 to 14 March. In other words, how did the political opposition know full well by early Thursday afternoon that Al Qaeda was the most plausible perpetrator, and the Spanish secret service claimed that it did not? Interestingly, on the day of the attack, Zapatero had also received information from a source on Wall Street through an economist that he knew well. The unequivocal message of this conversation was that everybody on Wall Street said that Al Qaeda was behind the attack. In the evening, Moratinos confirmed the same supposition on the basis of far more reliable sources. Allegedly, Felipe González had also picked up information during Thursday that the culprit was Al Qaeda.[39]

In the foreword to his diaries, José María Aznar rejects any wrongdoing, and in the entry for 11 March, he responds to all the criticism that was raised in this period. One might argue, however, that the former prime minister is remarkably precise in his diaries, taking into account that they are supposed to have been written during the fog of 11 March. He simply goes through all the main arguments of the political opposition and the press and responds to them—one by one. Why bother to construct in his diaries

---

[38] Cf. Jaime Ignacio del Burgo, "Informe: ETA y el terrorismo islamista," *Libertad Digital*, undated. https://www.libertaddigital.com/suplementos/pdf/InformeDelBurgo.pdf.

[39] Moratinos Files: Interview, Zapatero. According to the diary of José Bono, future Minister of Defense, also Felipe González knew around 1300 hours on 11 March that the ETA path was wrong and pointed to Islamic fundamentalism. Cf. José Bono, *Diario de un ministro. De la tragedia del 11 M al desafío independista catalán* (Barcelona: Planeta, 2016), entry for March 11.

a complete and perfect political defense of the government's dispositions on the very day of the attack, when the outcome of the events and the effect of the opposition's criticism—also from a political perspective—were still uncertain? And did he really have the time to do that on 11 March? Regardless of the truth, historians should always be critical of such precise assertions in a diary about such a sensitive issue, published years later by a former prime minister doubtless eager to improve his public image.[40] Moreover, the memoirs by Jorge Dezcallar, who was head of the joint intelligence service, CNI, at the time of the attacks, clash with those of Aznar. He underlines how the secret services were systematically kept in the dark by Aznar's government during 11–14 March. These two publications are additionally interesting in light of Moratinos' revelations.

Following Zapatero's direct orders on the morning of Thursday 11 March, Moratinos immediately began calling numerous contacts in the Middle East and North Africa, especially the heads of various intelligence services, who unanimously pointed in the same direction: They possessed intelligence indicating that Al Qaeda was behind the attacks. Accordingly, the PSOE leadership knew by Thursday evening—at the very latest—what the truth was most likely to be: Al Qaeda-linked groups were the perpetrators, not ETA. This was the very same conclusion that the Spanish judiciary arrived at after years of thorough investigation.[41]

When I critically asked Moratinos, why Zapatero personally stayed quiet about this for nearly forty-eight hours until Saturday, the day before the elections, he pointed to tactical considerations. He further stressed that Zapatero's defensive strategy clashed with that of Rubalcaba, who wanted to come out into the open and denounce the government.[42] In my view, Zapatero may well have thought it wise to let Aznar's plot thicken by letting the public gradually realize that it was being deceived by the government. This would double the boomerang effect of Aznar's decision to stick with the ETA narrative. Such a rationale would also explain Blanco's statements during Thursday to Friday to the press: He was clearly critical of the government's handling of the investigation, yet he also understated what the PSOE actually knew about the perpetrators, and it wasn't until Saturday

---

[40] The diaries concerning 11M are published as a part of his memoirs. See Aznar, *El compromiso del poder*, 291–315.

[41] Reinares, *¡Matadlos!*, passim.

[42] Moratinos Files: Interview, Moratinos.

afternoon that Zapatero called the Minister of the Interior to inform him that he knew that Al Qaeda was behind the attack. After this, there was no honorable retreat for the PP government. The background for this call was that on that very Saturday Zapatero had received information about Al Qaeda-related arrests from a crucial source that was *not* Spanish but a "European authority." In that precise moment, he decided to call Acebes, the Minister of the Interior, who confirmed that arrests were being made as they spoke, but that he did not want to give further details.[43]

Zapatero does not reject my thesis that the PSOE in these crucial hours applied a strategy of silence, i.e., to let the PP deal publicly with its own inconsistencies, manipulations and contradictions, but he stresses two important factors. First of all, the Basque leader, Ibarretxe, had not ruled out ETA's involvement in his early statement on 11 March. This clearly complicated the picture. More convincingly, Zapatero claims that his actions were also motivated by the desire not to deepen the divide in Spanish society. He stresses that it was a dramatic situation with nearly two hundred deaths. It was thus of paramount importance during the last remaining hours before election day to get the situation under control. The divide created by the PP government was already deep enough as it was. For the same reason, the PSOE had nothing to do with the people gathering in protest outside the headquarters of the Conservative PP in Calle Génova. According to his information, they were actually people belonging to the group around Pablo Iglesias of today's *Podemos* party. Zapatero was subjected to severe pressure from his own party to go public that day, yet he decided against it as he did not want to create more tension.[44]

The PSOE was not the only major force being held in the dark by the Conservative government. According to Dezcallar, then Head of the CNI, the joint Spanish intelligence services were systemically manipulated by their own government throughout 11–14 March. The CNI was allegedly caught in a trap set up by the Ministry of the Interior in collusion with the prime minister's office: In order to be able to sustain the ETA story, the government wanted to keep the secret services in the dark as long as possible with regard to the police's ongoing investigations which were now clearly pointing away from ETA and toward Al Qaeda. This meant that the CNI was excluded from the crisis cabinet meetings and not duly informed

---

[43] Moratinos Files: Interview, Zapatero.
[44] Moratinos Files: Interview, Moratinos.

of the important fact that the type of explosives used by the perpetrators was not the one usually employed by ETA. On the contrary, the CNI was erroneously led to believe that the type found was actually the one ETA normally used for sabotage. This meant that as late as 15:51 on Thursday the CNI would still continue to give prevalence to ETA as the possible perpetrator in a written note.[45]

The same kind of deception of the CNI repeated itself on Saturday afternoon, when Dezcallar, after much pressure, was finally received by the Minister of the Interior, Ángel Acebes, and his Vice Minister, Ignacio Astarloa. At this point, the latter two already knew that the suspicion of ETA was wrong since important detentions had been made at 4 p.m. of those who had sold telephone cards to the terrorists. Furthermore, three Moroccans and two Spanish suspects had been arrested. Yet according to his own account, Dezcallar was not informed of this. This is consistent with the fact that the political opposition also only learned about the arrests from foreign sources. Right after the meeting, Dezcallar was contacted by Alfredo Timermans, spokesperson of the Moncloa, who demanded in the name of the prime minister that he deny a press story running on *Cadena Ser*. The press story claimed that the CNI was now exclusively focused on Islamic terrorism—the truth was apparently that the CNI was now favoring the path of Islamic terrorism but had not completely abandoned other possibilities.[46]

The order from the prime minister's office led to the publication of a communiqué of the CNI which was picked up by Europa Press at 19:53 stating that "It is not exact and does not make any sense that we have completely abandoned one line of investigation in favor of another or others, as stated on Cadena SER."[47] A few minutes later, however, the Ministry of the Interior made the arrests public, something which made the CNI look completely ridiculous. What had happened in the meantime was that Zapatero, as already mentioned, had called the Minister of the Interior to call his bluff. After this, the ETA narrative could no longer be upheld. In turn, when the political scandal concerning the alleged cover-up exploded, the Aznar government immediately blamed the CNI, which according to

[45] Jorge Dezcallar, *Valió la pena: una vida entre diplomáticos y espías* (Barcelona: Península, 2015), 278.

[46] Ibid., 290.

[47] Ibid., 291.

the government had continued to give the highest importance to the ETA lead, thus omitting that it was the government itself that had given the false lead to the CNI.

In sum, in Dezcallar's interpretation, the CNI had been fooled twice: First, it had been constantly manipulated by the government. Second, when the government got into trouble, the CNI became the scapegoat for the government's own manipulations.

Dezcallar's version seems credible, but to what extent can we actually be sure that the CNI was only a victim? Without doubt, the CNI had legitimate reasons for feeling manipulated. Yet serious questions could certainly also be raised about the quality of the work of the CNI, as it failed to consider properly all the information it had received from Moratinos' foreign contacts. The background for this was—as mentioned—that from Thursday to Friday Moratinos had intense discussions with Rubalcaba and Zapatero about what to do with the information he had gathered from his intelligence sources abroad. Rubalcaba and Zapatero disagreed about when to go public. Rubalcaba wanted to do it on Friday, whereas Zapatero wanted to wait, probably in order to have further confirmation. In the last resort, Zapatero decided that the information should only be handed over to the CNI, which was also the correct thing to do.

So, apparently, the CNI continued to uphold the ETA path in spite of the new information that had been put at its disposal. Dezcallar's memoirs show—perhaps contrary to the author's intention—how easy, extremely easy, it was for two or three cabinet members to manipulate the entire Spanish intelligence community, which had already failed utterly by not preventing the bomb attacks. Yet to say that the services were kept completely in the dark from 11 to 14 March is not entirely sustainable in view of Moratinos' revelations.

The secret services may well have been manipulated by the government, but the CNI certainly failed to take the information made available to them by the PSOE into proper consideration. The case of 11-M is, at the very least, revealing of a malfunctioning intelligence system which was not as capable as it should have been of active information gathering and critical assessment. Furthermore, how had the PSOE through a few telephone calls been able to assert the truth so accurately while the CNI had not? Certainly, it was not helpful that diplomatic relations between Morocco and Spain were not back on track. This also had serious consequences at the level of cooperation in such vital security matters. Still, for this very reason, the CNI should have paid greater attention to Moratinos' information as he was able to use channels that were apparently closed to the CNI. It so happened that the CNI's foreign activities were primarily centered on Iraq. The service had simply not reformed itself in view of the threat from a wider spectrum of Islamic fundamentalists, just as the CNI had no direct relationship of trust with the heads of the various intelligence branches in the Middle East. Where the CNI might speak to number four in the intelligence service of some Arab country, Moratinos had a strong and confidential relationship with the heads of the intelligence services in the entire region. It is probably also fair to say that the CNI was "affected" by the overall theory of the government, namely that ETA was the culprit.[48] In the end, Moratinos treated Dezcallar clemently and offered him a post as ambassador to the Holy See.[49] Surely not the job Dezcallar had hoped for, but still a position as ambassador. In 2008, he was promoted to the important post of ambassador to the United States, a job much more in line with his diplomatic qualifications.

If any doubts still remain as to the biased analysis of the PP government, it will suffice to read a later report sent by the new Socialist Minister of Defense, José Bono, to Zapatero on 10 May 2004. In it, Bono argued that it was impossible that the government of Aznar could have had rational doubts about the authorship of the attack on the day it took place because one year prior to this tragic event the government had received precise warnings. In February 2003, the Ministry of the Interior was informed that due to the Spanish position on Iraq, Spain was still exposed to terror threats, also because Al Qaeda had explicitly threatened Spain. Furthermore, in November 2003, the same Ministry was warned that Allekema Lamari, one of the perpetrators of the bombing, might conduct an imminent violent action. Lamari had been set free in June 2002, eighteen months prior to 11-M, despite having been sentenced to fourteen years of prison for belonging to a violent armed group. Three days prior to the bombing, on 8 March, the same Ministry was alerted to the "dangerousness and fanaticism of Allekema Lamari, and to his decision to carry out an attack in Spain." Moreover, the reliability of the information and the graveness of the threat had been stressed to the Ministry of the Interior. Against this background, it is hard to understand how the Minister of the Interior on the same day of the bombing—at precisely 1:15 p.m.—was able to pronounce, "ETA

[48] Moratinos Files: Interview, Moratinos.
[49] Dezcallar, *Valió la pena*, 312

has reached its objective."[50] Fifteen minutes earlier, Aznar had called the editor in chief of *El País* to say that he was absolutely convinced ETA was behind the attack. Even after the finding of the van in Alcalá de Henares which clearly linked the attack to radical Islamism, and after the doubts expressed by Acebes in the evening, Aznar called the newspaper again at 8:45 p.m. saying that he was still convinced that ETA was responsible.[51]

With hindsight, one should not be too surprised or scandalized by the government's move. Elections were three days away, the situation in Spain was complete chaos, contrasting information was circulating, and the ETA theory could plausibly be defended in view of ETA's long history of violence (even though the attack on 11 March was out of tune with the kind of violent actions which had normally been undertaken by ETA since 1968).[52] However, to pull it off successfully, the ETA story had to be backed, or at least not questioned, by government agencies and the press. Keeping government agencies under control was difficult enough, but probably the least problematic exercise. Keeping the press and the opposition at bay was far more difficult. It implied that it would actually be possible to control the news stream and the information available to the political opposition. If we accept this conspiratorial thesis, this was probably the single greatest mistake by the government, which in the fog of 11 March overlooked that the opposition had excellent connections to the Middle East. Moratinos would easily be able to find out if the attack was in any way linked to the Arab world. Aznar must also have deeply underestimated the power of the new social media which would spread news and rumors with the speed of light and without the usual filters applied by newspapers and state television. Incredibly, he must have overlooked the fact that Islamic groups usually claim public responsibility for the attacks they conduct.

It is true that no direct link between the bomb attacks and the intervention in Iraq has ever been established by the Spanish judiciary. On the contrary, it is not unlikely that the perpetrators had their mind set on some kind of attack in Spain several months before the US intervention in Iraq,

[50]Bono, *Diario de un ministro*, 85.

[51]José Manuel Romero, "El desconcierto del Gobierno sobre la autoría del atentado," *El País*, March 13, 2004. https://elpais.com/diario/2004/03/13/espana/1079132404_850215.html.

[52]One exception being the Hipercor bombing of 1987 with 21 dead and 30 wounded. Cf. Paddy Woodworth, *Guerra sucia, manos limpias. ETA, el GAL y la democracia española* (Barcelona: Crítica, 2002), 158.

and—as it is well known—an Al Qaeda-related group had actually planned a new attack on the Barcelona subway in 2008, long after Spain had withdrawn from Iraq. Nevertheless, Iraq certainly served as a fig leaf for the 11 March attack. In fact, a few months after the military intervention, on 18 October 2003, bin Laden had mentioned Spain as a legitimate target through Al-Jazeera.[53] The day after bin Laden's talk, the date "11/3" in combination with the year 1921 was used by one cell member in Brussels to buy a prepaid telephone card, perhaps as a reference to the date of the future Madrid attack. The year might have been an allusion to the Sura 21 of the Koran.[54] What is probably also true—as previously stated—is that the heavily understaffed and underfinanced Spanish intelligence services had been far too focused on Iraq and probably lost sight of other crucial security risks linked to North Africa. At least, this was the immediate assertion of the new Zapatero government which took office on 18 April.

2.3   Al Qaeda's Victory?

The PSOE won the general elections with almost five percentage points and nearly one and a half million more votes than the PP, obtaining, however, only sixteen more seats than its adversary. In comparison, when the PP won a much narrower one-point victory in 2000, it obtained a similar advantage in seats. Moreover, with nearly one million votes more than the Socialists in 2004, the PSOE actually gained twenty-nine fewer seats than the PP did in 2000.[55] In other words, the Spanish voting system clearly favors the PP, which is very strongly represented in the countryside and in smaller provincial towns where it takes far less votes to obtain a seat in parliament. A candidate running for election in a major town can easily require more than 100,000 votes to be elected, whereas a candidate in less populated areas may win with roughly 30,000 votes.[56] Seen from this perspective alone, the victory of the PSOE came as a surprise to many. The PP had been leading in the polls for a long period and the electoral system was clearly beneficial to them. According to the Conservative newspaper *El Mundo*, the

[53] Reinares, *¡Matadlos!*, 160–163, 227–241.

[54] Ibid., 79–80.

[55] Julián Santamaría, "El azar y el contexto. Las elecciones generales de 2004," *Claves de razón práctica*, vol. 146 (2004): 28.

[56] José M. Magone, *Contemporary Spanish Politics*, second edition (New York: Routledge, 2009), 135.

government of José María Aznar had been extremely confident of victory on 10 March, the day before the terrorist attack: "They knew from all the opinion polls that four days later they would win the elections."[57]

By referring to such "objective facts," it was easy for politicians, intellectuals and opinion makers close to the PP to more or less openly pronounce that it was Al Qaeda and not the Spanish people who had decided the outcome of the general elections of 14 March, which the Socialists won by a large margin. This view echoed a widespread feeling among Anglo-American politicians, who were also backed by Rupert Murdoch's media outlets. "The Spanish elections: a landslide win for bin Laden"—read one of the headlines of *The Times* on 16 March 2004.[58] Moreover, members of the PP continued to defend the ETA narrative, but in the following months added yet more dubious claims about the existence of a plot in which the PSOE, the Spanish judiciary, and both the Spanish and the Moroccan intelligence services had secretly colluded.[59] As late as 2006, *El Mundo* published an article by the American Hispanist Stanley Payne claiming that Zapatero had been elected by international terrorism.[60] In actual fact, the newspaper was gradually damaging its own reputation by defending beyond reason the ETA story, which had been almost immediately abandoned by both the Spanish police and the intelligence and security services. In several feature articles, *El Mundo* made the implausible claim that ETA was somehow involved in the bombings and that the Spanish authorities were now covering their tracks.[61] Spanish right-wing revisionist Pío Moa took this view even further in his column in *Libertad Digital* when he claimed that he could not find any moral reason which would have prevented a sector of the PSOE from organizing or encouraging the massacre. He added, however, one major impediment: "the Socialist leaders would not have dared to make such an extreme provocation, knowing that sooner or later these

[57] Fernando Múgica, "Los agujeros negros del 11-M," *El Mundo*, April 23, 2004.

[58] Article already cited in the preface to this book.

[59] Rafael García Pérez, "España en un mundo en cambio: A la búsqueda de la influencia internacional (1986–2010)," in *La Política exterior de España. De 1800 hasta hoy*, ed. Juan Carlos Pereira (Barcelona: Ariel, 2010), 721.

[60] "El entreguismo de Zapatero," *El Mundo*, March 27, 2006. I'm indebted to Ángel Viñas, who gave me the reference.

[61] See, for example, Fernando Múgica, "Los agujeros negros del 11-M," *El Mundo*, April 23, 2004. http://www.elmundo.es/elmundo/2004/04/19/enespecial/1082356558.html.

actions would have come out into the open." He ended his reasoning in the following way. "Let's put it like this. Could it have been the PSOE? In my opinion, yes, of course. Was it, in reality? We do not know, and hopefully it was not. But our society needs to know."[62]

If anything, these statements serve to illustrate Zapatero's main point, namely how divided Spanish society had become, and—one might add— the degree to which opinion makers would say anything to make their case that the PSOE government was illegitimate, knowing full well that there was an insatiable audience for such views. Indeed, facts and nuances were not in high demand. Accordingly, Prime Minister Zapatero was careful in his future interventions never to link the terrorist attack in Madrid to the war in Iraq in order not to further increase the level of tension in Spanish society.[63] Instead, the new majority in the parliament constituted an inquiry commission which was clear in its conclusions, as was the judiciary process that followed: ETA was not responsible. It was Islamic terrorism, and the perpetrators, apart from the seven terrorists who had already blown themselves up during a shoot-out with the police in Leganés after the attack, were exemplarily convicted.[64]

In strict political terms, though, the terrorist attack turned out to be a disaster not only for the badly beaten PP, but also for the new PSOE government. The PSOE always felt that there was a dark cloud hanging over them. Would they have won the elections without the terrorist attack? Regardless of the futility of many of these claims, it is, however, an undisputable fact that many opinion polls made public *prior* to the elections showed that the PP had an advantage, and that the final result of the elections gave the Socialists a solid victory of nearly five points. Thus, it is unquestionable that in the last week from 7 to 14 March voter intentions had somehow been affected. In the end, the PSOE won by 42.59%, to 37.71% for the PP. Compared to the last elections, the PSOE had gained three million more votes. What were the reasons? And what was the actual impact of the bomb attacks?

---

[62] Pío Moa, "Hipótesis sobre el 11-M," *Libertad Digital*, August 8, 2006. http://www.libertaddigital.com/opinion/pio-moa/hipotesis-sobre-el-11-m-32772/.

[63] Moratinos Files: Interview, Zapatero.

[64] Reinares, *¡Matadlos!*, 34. The documents of the sentence of the Audiencia Nacional are reproduced on several newspaper sites, including that of *El Mundo.* http://www.elmundo.es/documentos/2004/03/espana/atentados11m/sentencia/sentencia_pdf.html.

It is widely recognized that Spain has more potential center-left than right-wing voters, yet the key problem for the PSOE was always to rally the voters. There were in fact a significant number of center-left voters who had stopped voting during the previous two elections, most notably in the year 2000.[65] For the same reason, the PP had opted for an overall defensive campaigning strategy aiming to discourage PSOE sympathizers from voting.[66] However, ten days prior to the elections, Zapatero's own contacts on the streets were convinced that potential PSOE voters had been sufficiently mobilized so as to win the elections. In the days prior to the general elections, mobilization was reported to be "spectacular," and Zapatero actually knew that the latest polls indicated the possibility of a victory for the Socialists. In fact, the nationally renowned sociologist Julian Santamaría, who carried out polls for the Catalan newspaper *La Vanguardia*, called Zapatero on Sunday 7 March with extremely good news. He revealed that the PSOE was leading by two points ("Estáis dos puntos por encima").[67] Depending on the method used for the poll, it showed everything from a two-point lead for the PSOE to a one-point loss. In an article published in the Catalan newspaper the same day, called "Empate técnico" (technical draw), he further stated his case. The dynamics were clear: The PSOE was rapidly gaining votes at the expense of the PP, which was why the two-point lead was judged to be plausible. This had been confirmed by recent polls over the last months which showed that the comfortable PP lead of the year before was dramatically shrinking.[68]

In a scientifically exhaustive analysis at a later date, Santamaría extrapolated a series of interesting facts and trends from the many opinion polls made by the leading institutes from 2000 to 2004. In the year 2000, the difference between the two political parties in expressed voter intentions was 10.3 percentage points in the PP's favor. In 2001, it had fallen to 4.4 and the year after to 3.8 points. In 2003, the PSOE had a one-point lead. If we

---

[65] Santamaría, "El azar y el contexto," 38.

[66] Víctor Sampedro, Óscar García Luengo, and José Manuel Sánchez Duarte, "Agendas electorales y medias de comunicación en la campaña de 2004," in *Elecciones Generales 2004*, ed. José Ramón Montero, Ignacio Lago, and Mariano Torcal (Madrid: Centro de Investigaciones Sociológicas, 2007), 62, 115.

[67] This phone call is confirmed independently by both. Moratinos Files: Interview, Zapatero; Santamaría.

[68] Julián Santamaría, "Empate técnico," *La Vanguardia*, March 7, 2004.

take into account sympathies expressed toward the two parties, the advantage of the PSOE in 2003 was at least three points.[69] However, by January 2004, the PP had recovered strength in the opinion polls, which foresaw a Conservative victory of anything from six to eleven points. Importantly, one element indicated that the relationship of force was actually much more balanced. People sympathizing with the PSOE by far outnumbered those in favor of the PP, an element that was gradually reflected in the opinion polls of February 2004. A further reason for optimism was that a series of important indicators were now favoring the PSOE. Rajoy was becoming more unpopular, while Zapatero's popularity was on the rise. People still thought that the PP would win, but the number of interviewees who desired a Socialist victory outnumbered the PP by four points. 43% of the interviewees were in favor of a Socialist victory, whereas 38% were inclined toward the Conservative party. Two studies made by NOXA in March indicated 42–43% to the Socialists and 36–37% to the PP, very close to the final result of the elections.[70]

The marked shift in the tendencies of the voters was of course also noted by the analysts in the PP, who alerted the leadership. In mid-February—just after a book launch—Santamaría was summoned by a small group of clearly concerned PP leaders, including Javier Arenas (the vice prime minister), who asked if he could confirm that the PP was likely to lose, to which Santamaría nodded affirmatively.[71] To my knowledge, no PP leader has publicly recognized that they actually knew once month prior to the elections that the party was in dire straits and even likely to lose.

The tendency in the polls no doubt indicated a possible PSOE victory before 11 March, but how do we then measure the effect of the bomb attack and the PP's handling of the crisis? Without doubt, when reading all the different books, articles, interviews and newspaper accounts regarding the period from 11 to 14 March, it remains clear that the centrifugal forces of civil society were somehow unleashed against the government from Friday to Saturday. But what were they reacting to? The bomb attacks for sure, but increasingly they also perceived the government's actions as essentially a cover-up, and the PSOE ably exploited PP's false moves to its own end. Friday 12 March saw some of the greatest public demonstrations in the

[69] "El azar y el contexto," 36–37.
[70] Ibid., 37.
[71] Moratinos Files: Interview, Santamaría.

history of democracy in Spain, and millions took to the streets denouncing terrorism, many were reproving ETA but condemnations of Al Qaeda were now also frequently being voiced.

Numerous studies have been made into the effects and possible influence of the social media from 11 to 14 March. One mentions that in this period Internet traffic increased by 5% and that more than two million people visited online newspapers between 8:00 and 15:00 hours on Thursday 11 March.[72] This was actually five times higher than the regular number of users. On 12 and 13 March, mobile messages and emails were used by thousands of demonstrators who gathered around PP's headquarters in Calle Génova 13 to show their disagreement with the way in which the executive had managed the situation. One of the messages which began to appear on the screens of people's mobile phones was:

> "Aznar gets away scot-free? They call it day of reflection and Urdaci is working? Today 13 March at 6PM PP Headquarters C/Génova 13. Silence. For the sake of truth. Pass this message on!"[73]

As can be seen, the text—which did *not* emanate from the PSOE—not only criticized the government, but also the media. Urdaci was then head of Spanish national television (TVE), and in the anonymous author's view, an important part of the disinformation campaign was due to TVE's continuous linking of the terrorist attack to ETA. The incident showed the importance of a new phenomenon, the SMS, as a means of social and political mobilization. Furthermore, 11-M showed the influence of new alternative media platforms such as *Nodo50* and *Indymedia* which ably challenged the silence of traditional media.[74]

In spite of the political turmoil and the massive public protests following the bomb attacks, the statistical data provided by the CIS after the elections presented a somewhat different picture. They indicated that only six percent of the interviewees decided to vote following the bomb attacks even though they had originally decided not to, and less than four percent

---

[72] Eva Herro Curiel, "Periodistas y redes sociales en España. Del 11M al 15M (2004–2011)" (Ph.D. diss., Universidad Carlos III de Madrid, 2013), 147–148.

[73] "¿Aznar de rositas? ¿Le llaman jornada de reflexión y Urdaci trabaja? Hoy 13-M a las 18 horas sede PP C/Génova 13. Sin partidos. Silencio. Por la verdad.¡Pásalo!", cit. in Herro Curiel, "Periodistas y redes sociales en España," 148.

[74] Ibid., 48–149.

of the interviewees declared that they had changed their votes (although it is not documented in what direction they changed their political preference). Interestingly, these tendencies are roughly the same as the ones registered during the previous elections and the effect of the bomb attack is thus likely to have been very limited.[75] Several studies have confirmed this supposition: The available, albeit incomplete data concerning this aspect of the 2004 elections do not sustain the interpretation that the bomb attacks were in anyway decisive.[76] True, the general elections saw a very high level of voter participation, yet such turnout was in no way exceptional as the important general elections of 1977, 1982 and 1996 go to show.[77]

Politicians know their voters, Zapatero told me, and his feeling had all along been one of victory. His personal impression was that the PP was paying a high price for its alleged authoritarian style, its manipulation of public television and not least its foreign policy deference to Washington—in stark contrast to the will of the people. The fact that the Conservative leader Rajoy did not even want to engage in public debate with Zapatero further strengthened the Socialists' position. Rajoy simply could not or would not answer the following questions: What are you doing to public television? What are you going to do about the Prestige affair in Galicia? And what are you doing in Iraq? The last question was not just about pacifism or interventionism. Above all, Zapatero argues, it was a matter of whether Spanish "sovereignty" was being infringed. This interpretation, which may certainly be described as a partisan view, actually coincides with one scientific analysis, which also refers—among other factors—to the Prestige affair and the war in Iraq as issues which influenced voters in the PSOE's

---

[75] "… en general, esos datos refuerzan la impresión de que la incidencia del atentado fue muy limitada y en línea con las preferencias previas." Cit. in Santamaría, "El Azar y el Contexto," 39.

[76] As underlined in a sociological study of 2007: "… los cambios ocasionados por acontecimientos imprevistos y traumáticos como los atentados terroristas masivos del 11-M no parecen haber transformado ni radical ni generalizadamente las preferencias electorales de los españoles." Cit. in José Ramón Montero and Ignacio Lago, "Del 11-M a 14-M: terrorismo, gestión del gobierno y rendición de cuentas," in *Elecciones Generales 2004*, ed. José Ramón Montero, Ignacio Lago, and Mariano Torcal (Madrid: Centro de Investigaciones Sociológicas, 2007), 201. See also Julián Santamaría, "Las elecciones generales de 2004 en su contexto," in *Elecciones Generales 2004*, ed. José Ramón Montero, Ignacio Lago, and Mariano Torcal (Madrid: Centro de Investigaciones Sociológicas, 2007), 62.

[77] Joan Font and Araceu Mateos, "La participación electoral," in *Elecciones Generales 2004*, ed. José Ramón Montero, Ignacio Lago, and Mariano Torcal (Madrid: Centro de Investigaciones Sociológicas, 2007), 167.

favor.[78] Another study points to the PP's confrontational policy toward the so-called peripheral nationalisms. In fact, the majority of the votes lost during the elections were not lost in Madrid, where the bombings had taken place, but in Catalonia, Basque Country and Andalucía, where 440,000 of the nearly 700,000 votes lost came from. In sum, a good argument can be made that the origins of the defeat predated the attack.[79]

Seen from Ferraz, the situation was more complex, though. Certainly, the PSOE knew during the hectic last days of the election campaign that the party was likely to win. Yet after the bomb attack, there was a widespread fear that Aznar—known to be a very cunning politician—would be capable of exploiting the events of 11 March to his own ends and thus sabotage the momentum that the Socialists had been gaining throughout the campaign. Thus, the PSOE leadership was initially shocked not only by the devastating bomb attacks, but also by their potential effects on the electorate. They feared that Aznar would embrace the opposition and call for national unity, thus leaving literally no space for Zapatero to promote his own policies. By sticking to the ETA story, however, Aznar provided the opposition with a breathing space and unexpected room for independent political action to discredit the government's actions that it would otherwise never have obtained. As mentioned, the single greatest fear in Ferraz was that Aznar would publicly "embrace" the opposition, which would be roughly the same as suffocating it.[80]

If anything, the election results, as well as all the polemics and the political turmoil surrounding the bomb attacks, showed that Spanish society was deeply divided, and that the new government should not underestimate the immediate and longer-term effect of the massacre. Two weeks after the attacks, public frustrations were still very visible. No better example of this exists than the official funerals of the victims which took place in the Cathedral of La Almudena on 24 March. On this occasion, Zapatero asked Moratinos to accompany him as one of the PSOE's formal representatives. The mourning families of the victims sat in the middle of the Cathedral

---

[78]Santamaría, "El Azar y el Contexto," 33–36.

[79]Moratinos Files: Carlos Iribarren Valdés, "Elecciones generales y cambio de gobierno en España." Undated analysis of the elections sent personally to Miguel Ángel Moratinos from the *Ebert Stiftung*, Madrid. The analysis can also be found on several Internet sites. The findings of this study roughly correspond to those of the other studies already cited in this chapter.

[80]Moratinos Files: Interview, Moratinos.

weeping, while all the official Spanish and international representatives sat at the sides. The ceremony was conducted by the Conservative Archbishop of Madrid, Antonio María Rouco Varela, and according to news coverage at the time, a father of one of the victims shouted out loud just before the Archbishop was about to begin his service, "Mr. Aznar, I hold you responsible for the death of my son" (*"Señor Aznar, le hago responsable de la muerte de mi hijo"*).[81] Moratinos heard even stronger words being used toward the end of the ceremony. A clearly shaken Aznar went to the altar together with his wife, Ana Botella, to take communion, when someone suddenly shouted "Assassin!"[82]

[81] "Emocionado adiós a las víctimas del 11-M en La Almudena," *El Mundo*, March 25, 2004.

[82] Moratinos Files: Interview, Moratinos.

CHAPTER 3

Breaking the Shackles

3.1 Leaving Iraq

"What is the time difference between here and Washington?" Zapatero asked while he was standing in a corner of the Zarzuela Palace together with Moratinos and his Majesty King Juan Carlos 1. It was around noon on 18 April, and the government had just been sworn in. "Six hours," Moratinos replied. The prime minister then gave him the following instructions, "When it's 8–8:30 in the morning in America, tell Colin Powell that at 5:30 p.m. [Central European Time] the Spanish government will announce the immediate withdrawal of Spanish troops from Iraq."[1] In this way, the Americans were given roughly three hours warning. To understand just how controversial Zapatero's decision was, one has to go back in time, more precisely to 24 March, the day of the funerals in the Almudena Cathedral.

The PSOE had actually used the occasion of the state funerals to meet with a series of foreign representatives, among others the US Secretary of State Colin Powell, the British Prime Minister Tony Blair, the French President Jacques Chirac and the German Chancellor Gerhard Schröder. To this end, a small reception room had been organized for the PSOE in the Spanish Parliament, and Moratinos was present both as an interpreter and a collaborator. In fact, right after the elections on Sunday, Zapatero had

[1] Moratinos Files: Interview, Moratinos.

© The Author(s) 2019   43
M. Heiberg, *Spain and the Wider World since 2000*,
Security, Conflict and Cooperation in the Contemporary World,
https://doi.org/10.1007/978-3-030-27343-9_3

asked Moratinos to become his right hand in foreign affairs, but did not tell him explicitly that he was going to be the new foreign minister. It was only later that Moratinos found out that Zapatero had been under pressure to appoint Marín, or alternatively Javier Solana as the new foreign minister. The latter also had ministerial ambitions since he was allegedly tired of his post in Brussels as High Representative for the Common Foreign and Security Policy of the European Union and wanted to return to Spain. One source indicated to me that the Americans allegedly exercised considerable pressure on the PSOE to avoid Moratinos.[2] I have, however, been unable to confirm this claim. If true, it might have been due to the US consideration that they would feel more comfortable with Solana, whom they were used to dealing with—Solana having been Secretary-General of NATO between 1995 and 1999.

It goes without saying that the Spanish withdrawal from Iraq was high on the agenda on 24 March. After meeting with his Spanish counterpart, Tony Blair made a public declaration saying that the decision to withdraw was entirely up to the new and democratically elected Spanish government. The British press speculated, however, that Blair had actually tried to persuade Zapatero that Spain should remain part of the coalition in Iraq and that their concerns could be met.[3] The truth was that no British pressure was applied during their conversation. This is interesting given Blair's unequivocal support for President Bush and his previous efforts to draw Spain closer to the Anglo-American alliance. The Spanish side simply told Blair in a very calm and undramatic tone of the need to withdraw by 30 June if the UN had not obtained a full mandate in Iraq by this date.[4] The meetings with Gerhard Schröder and Jacques Chirac were, of course, even more positive. Not only were they pleased with the new Spanish position on Iraq, which coincided with their own, but they literally embraced Zapatero and invited him to join them at the heart of the European project. The Spanish Socialist leader could in this regard not have hoped for a better reception. Both Schröder and Chirac, in fact, had bad memories of Aznar since the

[2] Moratinos Files: Private information.

[3] "Madrid Memorial for Bomb Victims," *BBC News*, March 24. http://news.bbc.co.uk/2/hi/europe/3562993.stm.

[4] Moratinos Files: Interview, Moratinos.

former Spanish prime minister had challenged the Franco-German consensus on several important issues.[5] Most importantly, the meeting with Colin Powell went surprisingly smoothly. It was agreed that once the new government was in place, the new foreign minister should go to Washington and negotiate the withdrawal of Spanish troops, possibly on 21 April. The two parties did not go into details, however. In this way, Spain would, as promised, inform the Americans beforehand of any vital decision concerning the withdrawal, and the Americans would somehow be involved in the process.

Seen against this background, it is therefore understandable that the Americans were outraged when they suddenly learned on 18 April that the Spanish had given them only a few hours' notice of the withdrawal and also refused to enter into real negotiations about it. By acting thus, the new Spanish government failed to comply with its initial promise, and—above all—it also left the Americans with virtually no time to influence Zapatero's decision. When Moratinos called Colin Powell in the afternoon of 18 April to communicate the Spanish decision, he was first met with complete silence on the other end. Then Powell quietly said: "I'm extremely disappointed." Little more was said during their conversation. Powell felt deceived.[6]

How did it come about that the Spanish government suddenly changed its course and what were the consequences of this decision for the future US-Spanish relationship? Prior to the elections, there had been much debate in the PSOE about the withdrawal from Iraq. Although the party was united in its belief of the necessity of withdrawing, there were differences of opinion as to the speed of this operation. In contrast to many younger left-wing party members, Moratinos actually agreed with the *Felipistas* on the need to proceed with the utmost care. It so happened that the great difficulties experienced with the Americans after the PSOE's first victory in the general elections in 1982 were still in the back of the minds of Moratinos and the *Felipistas*.[7] Under Felipe González's leadership, the PSOE had been agitating against NATO for years, yet after the landslide victory in the general elections of 1982 the party found itself not only in government, but also as a de facto member of the NATO alliance—a deal which had been struck by the former UCD government during its

[5] Ibid. See also Aznar, *El compromiso del poder*, 43–48, 67, 270–274.
[6] Moratinos Files: Interview, Moratinos.
[7] Ibid.

last months in office. Thus, González had to find a new formula that on the one hand respected the will of the electorate and on the other did not upset the United States and other NATO allies.[8] For exactly this reason, Moratinos argued in 2004 that time was essential to be able to negotiate the withdrawal diplomatically. The rationale was that Zapatero should have time to explain the withdrawal and also appeal to a US sense of democracy and respect for a government that had won the elections on the legitimate promise to withdraw its troops from a war it did not believe in. Against this view, it was argued that the United States might apply pressure if given time.[9]

One of the new cabinet members who strongly favored an immediate withdrawal from Iraq was actually the new minister of defense, José Bono. On 5 April, Bono had already told Donald Rumsfeld that Spain would indeed withdraw and that to remain would be complicated as the PSOE had made a solemn promise to the Spanish people. He mentioned that 75% of the Spanish people were in favor of the withdrawal and that it was likely to happen without having to wait for a new resolution in the Security Council, as the PSOE judged it unlikely that the United Nations would take military charge in Iraq. He further said that the withdrawal might happen very shortly and that Rumsfeld would be the first foreign leader to know the exact date.[10] Rumsfeld reacted to this by saying that every nation can make sovereign decisions and that Spain could decide whatever it wished, but Spain would be the only country to leave Iraq. Spain would have to carry that burden. He also confirmed Bono's suspicion that the United States would never leave the initiative in Iraq to the UN.[11] The meeting was tough, but Bono nevertheless agreed to keep Rumsfeld informed of future Spanish decisions, something that he was, however, unable to comply with.

Bono's diaries give the impression that the decision to immediately withdraw, formally put into effect on 18 April, was more or less taken in practice before he went to Washington on 5 April. Nevertheless, it is not certain that

---

[8]Cf. Heiberg, *US-Spanish Relations After Franco*, 145–164.

[9]Moratinos Files: Interview, Moratinos.

[10]Bono, *Diario de un ministro*, entry for April 5, 2004.

[11]Ibid.

Bono's statement to Rumsfeld fully reflected the views of the Spanish government as a whole. According to Moratinos, an immediate withdrawal was probably still only under serious consideration. Accordingly, it may well be that Bono was stepping somewhat out of line with his instructions since he was known for pushing hard with the other ministers *in spe* for an immediate withdrawal.[12] In actual fact, Zapatero decided after Bono's trip to ignore the Pentagon and deal with the matter directly through Moratinos and the Department of State instead. He may well have opted for this solution not only because of Rumsfeld's hostile behavior, but also because Moratinos had solid working relations with Colin Powell.

In a sense, Moratinos and Bono are both right. The truth was that Zapatero was firm in his decision to withdraw immediately, yet the overall problem was how to execute the withdrawal without jeopardizing the safety of the Spanish troops. This dilemma was significant for the announcement of the exact date of withdrawal. It was complicated because the decision had to be taken against the Americans, who on the other hand had to facilitate the withdrawal. Zapatero soon realized that the US position was very hostile, yet he sensed that the sooner Spain got out of Iraq the better. What was needed, though, were guarantees of an operational kind that the Spanish troops would be able to leave without having to fear for their lives. Hence, there were discussions as to the right strategy: the more "polite" version of Moratinos, who insisted on a negotiated solution with the Americans, or the instant application of the decision as desired by Bono and others. The exact date of the withdrawal was probably only confirmed very close to Zapatero's intervention in the Cortes on 15 April.[13]

In his speech during the investiture debate in the Spanish Parliament, Zapatero was in the beginning surprisingly unspecific about the question of the withdrawal of Spanish troops from Iraq, despite the fact that no less than four parliamentary groups, including the PP, had asked him to address the issue.[14] Probably as a special concession to the left-wing party, *Izquierda Unida* (IU), whom Zapatero depended on to obtain a majority in parliament, he waited until midnight, when in a special address to

[12]Moratinos Files: Interview, Moratinos.

[13]Moratinos Files: Interview, Zapatero. See also Javier Rupérez, *Memoria de Washington. Embajador de España en la capital del imperio* (Madrid: La esfera de los libros, 2011), 310.

[14]*Cortes Generales, Diario de sesiones del Congreso de Los Diputados, Pleno y Diputación Permanente, Año 2004, VIII Legislatura, Núm. 2, Sesión plenaria núm. 2, celebrada el jueves, 15 de abril de 2004*, 20–21.

party leader Gaspar Llamazares he expressed his government's unequivo-cal accord with the PSOE's electoral promise. He not only reiterated the promise to withdraw at some time before 30 June, but also stressed that the security situation was worsening in Iraq. When reading the text of his intervention today, it remains clear that Zapatero sincerely wanted to termi-nate the operation in Iraq as soon as possible. He just could not be specific about the date in order not to jeopardize the lives of the Spanish soldiers in Iraq.[15]

Our understanding of this crucial Spanish decision would be incomplete without examining the national and international context during which it matured. The war was extremely unpopular with the Spanish population, and Zapatero's decision to maintain his electoral promise would therefore strengthen the credibility of his government at a difficult moment, when the PP and the conservative press, at home as well as abroad, were ques-tioning the legitimacy of his leadership. As hoped for, when Zapatero's decision was made public, the immediate public reaction was overwhelm-ingly positive. An opinion poll made between 22 and 27 April revealed a ten-point lead for the PSOE over the PP, while the evaluation of the execu-tive was also extremely positive, with only 5.7% thinking it had done badly or very badly (1.2%).[16] This certainly boosted the legitimacy of the govern-ment. Internationally, there were also sound arguments for reconsidering Spain's involvement in a military mission that several political and military observers described as hopeless, as the security situation in Iraq seemed to be on the verge of collapse. February 2004 had actually witnessed the high-est number of coalition casualties since the invasion in March 2003 and many were being killed in suicide attacks, while the Iraqi security forces were experiencing ceaseless onslaughts. By the end of March, when the exact date of the Spanish withdrawal was being discussed, some two hun-dred attacks against Iraqi citizens were being registered on a weekly basis, and in April, attacks by the Jaysh al-Mahdi (JAM) in Basra suddenly esca-lated. In Fallujah, a ferocious response from the Sunni community arose in

[15] *Cortes Generales, Diario de sesiones del Congreso de Los Diputados, Pleno y Diputación Permanente, Año 2004, VIII Legislatura, Núm. 2, Sesión plenaria núm. 2 celebrada el jueves, 15 de abril de 2004*, 85.

[16]"El PSOE aventajaba en más de 10 puntos al PP un mes después de las elecciones gen-erales del 14-M," *El Mundo*, May 14, 2004. http://www.elmundo.es/elmundo/2004/05/13/espana/1084457219.html.

consequence of a US offensive that had followed the murder of four security contractors. Without doubt, the deterioration of the security situation in Iraq, together with revelations of the abuse of Iraqi detainees in the Abu Ghraib prison, marked a negative turning point in Iraq.[17]

To make matters worse, the CNI was receiving information stemming from the Shia community of Muqtadā al-Ṣadr saying that an attack on Spanish troops might be imminent. As it was extremely important for the government that Spain's retreat be an honorable one, Zapatero felt an urgent need to act. Furthermore, there was the fear that growing foreign pressures might jeopardize the entire operation. Spain could in no way withdraw under humiliating circumstances where the Spanish contingent experienced heavy losses. Zapatero therefore discussed the issue vigorously with several people in the government. There was also another factor which probably also had an impact on the government's decision, namely all the people who had gathered on 14 March outside the Socialist headquarters in Calle Ferraz, shouting "No nos falles" ("Don't let us down") with explicit reference to the war in Iraq.[18] To be unable to comply with this major electoral promise was simply not an option, so in view of the incoming intelligence Zapatero took the decision to anticipate the withdrawal. It was not a decision that Moratinos applauded as he wanted time to settle the question with Washington diplomatically, but with hindsight he recognizes that Zapatero's political instinct was right. Had they waited, the withdrawal might have been impossible to effectuate.[19] The day after Zapatero's intervention in the Cortes on 16 April, Bono told the Italian Prime Minister Silvio Berlusconi, "We'll be leaving immediately."[20]

Although very supportive of the decision to withdraw, Bono soon found himself in trouble because of Zapatero's decision to cut off communications with Rumsfeld and handle the case through foreign ministry channels instead. This led to new friction in the Spanish government as Bono was left alone to explain to the US Secretary of Defense why he had not been able

[17]Cf. *The Report of the Iraq Inquiry: Executive Summary* (London: House of Commons, July 6, 2016), 96. https://assets.publishing.service.gov.uk/government/uploads/system/uploads/attachment_data/file/535407/The_Report_of_the_Iraq_Inquiry_-_Executive_Summary.pdf.

[18]Moratinos Files: Interview, Moratinos; Zapatero.

[19]Moratinos Files: Interview, Moratinos.

[20]Bono, *Diario de un ministro*, entry for April 16, 2004.

to comply with what had been agreed on 5 April, i.e., that Rumsfeld would be the first to know about the Spanish decision. Tensions with Bono were already running high because Zapatero wanted to reform the CNI and put it under his direct control. However, during the first hectic days of the new Socialist government, Bono threatened to resign if this decision was put into effect. Eventually, Zapatero gave in.[21] Dezcallar was ousted from the CNI, and Bono allowed to place one of his trusted aides as the new head of the security and intelligence services. It should be recalled that in spite of the fact that Zapatero was the undisputed leader of the PSOE, the two main factions of the party, those who were closer to Felipe González and those belonging to the *Nueva* Via, were coexisting in a delicate equilibrium.[22]

On 19 April, Zapatero called Bush, who according to some sources strongly criticized the Spanish decision and even warned Spain against taking further steps which would give false comfort to terrorists.[23] In Zapatero's recollection, the tone was somewhat different. The first thing Bush said to him was that he was disappointed by the Spanish decision. In turn, Zapatero underlined the great democratic tradition of the United States, the role of the founding fathers of the American constitution and the obligation for politicians to comply with the will of their people. In other words, his strategy was to say that the Spanish decision was inspired by the important democratic values that the US had taught the world and that no modern statesman could ignore. Suffice it to say that President Bush was in no way impressed by Zapatero's democratic discourse. In essence, "coldness" is the word chosen by Zapatero to describe the attitude of the otherwise polite US President. The continued US use of its Spanish bases for the war in Iraq was never debated between them.[24] As everyone in Spain knows, the US base at Rota plays a crucial role for the US in the Middle East—in times of war as well as in times of peace.

Zapatero's decision meant that a lot of explaining had to be done in order to win back the trust of the US government. For the same reason, Moratinos' meeting in the State Department with Colin Powell, scheduled

---

[21] Moratinos Files: Private information.

[22] Bosco, "The Long adiós," 30.

[23] Cited in Glen Segell, *Axis of Evil and Rogue States: The Bush Administration 2000–2004* (London: Glen Segell, 2005), 274. See also Rupérez, *Memoria de Washington*, 309.

[24] Moratinos Files: Interview, Zapatero.

for 21 April, now had a completely different agenda, namely to justify Spain's sudden withdrawal. Moratinos later learned from a US government official that the visit to Washington had come very close to being suspended. Moratinos was only informed prior to the meeting that there would be no joint press briefing and that the State Department would not offer lunch as originally planned. In the end, Powell, with whom Moratinos had a good relationship, decided to offer him lunch but the joint press briefing remained suspended.[25]

To understand Powell's more accommodating approach, one should probably also recall that the US secretary of state had openly expressed some remorse about the fact that the United States had failed to obtain a UN resolution that would have given the invasion the kind of legitimacy that several Western leaders were crying out for. The coalition of the willing may well have included forty-nine nations as underlined by President Bush, yet to its critics the invasion still rested on shaky legal grounds as fundamental disagreement in the Security Council over Iraq's lack of compliance with Resolution 1441 persisted throughout the spring of 2003. Kofi Annan explained in a later interview from 2004, that seen from the UN Charter the war was illegal.[26] Only ten days after the invasion, Colin Powell was surprisingly frank in an interview with *The New York Times* about the failure of the US government to obtain international legitimacy for its actions, "Here is the bottom line of the story. That resolution went down, and it was seen as a defeat, and it was a defeat."[27]

On the other hand, both US and Spanish critics of the PSOE's plans to withdraw its forces reiterated that the Spanish troops now operating in Iraq were actually covered legally by the UN Council Resolution 1483 of 22 May 2003 which recognized "the specific authorities, responsibilities, and obligations under applicable international law of these states as occupying powers under unified command (the "Authority").[28] In this context,

---

[25] Moratinos Files: Interview, Moratinos.

[26] Ewen MacAskill and Julian Borger, "Iraq War Was Illegal and Breached UN Charter, Says Annan," *The Guardian*, September 15, 2004. https://www.theguardian.com/world/2004/sep/16/iraq.iraq.

[27] US Department of State, Archive: "Interview by the New York Times, Secretary Colin L. Powell, Washington, DC, March 29, 2003." http://2001-2009.state.gov/secretary/former/powell/remarks/2003/19171.htm.

[28] *UN Security Council Resolution*, 1483, May 22, 2003. https://documents-dds-ny.un.org/doc/UNDOC/GEN/N03/368/53/PDF/N0336853.pdf?OpenElement. The

we may also mention Resolution 1511 of 16 October which defined the terms of the US-led occupation.[29] In the critics' view, it was only in these circumstances that Spain was deploying its 1300 soldiers to Iraq. Neither had Spain participated in any military action in March 2003. It had only offered humanitarian aid during the occupation.[30]

This legal position is certainly defendable but what the PSOE reacted to in 2004 was not the subsequent UN resolutions, which merely recognized—in accordance with well-established principles of international law—the de facto authority of the occupying power. The PSOE denounced that the occupation in March 2003, strongly supported by Aznar, had come about without the consent of the Security Council of the United Nations—in explicit breach of Chapter 7, article 39 of the UN Charter and in contrast to the will of the vast majority of the Western population.[31] In Spain, no less than 91% opposed the war.[32] The UN should take control or Spain would pull out. As stated by the PSOE in the 2004 election program:

> Spain's participation in the war and occupation of Iraq has constituted the clearest expression of rupture with our model of foreign policy. The time passed has demonstrated that it was not only an illegal war, it was based on an accumulation of deliberate falsities and lies with regard to the risks of weapons of mass destruction, which did not exist, and to the connections between the Iraqi regime and Al Qaeda, which have also been proven false.[33]

text had been drafted by the US government and was being sponsored by both Spain and the United Kingdom.

[29] *Un Security Council Resolution*, 1511, October 16, 2003. http://www.un.org/en/ga/search/view_doc.asp?symbol=S/RES/1511(2003).

[30] Cf. Rupérez, *La mirada sin ira*, 310.

[31] Cf. UN Charter, Chapter 7, article 39: "The Security Council shall determine the existence of any threat to the peace, breach of the peace, or act of aggression and shall make recommendations, or decide what measures shall be taken in accordance with Articles 41 and 42, to maintain or restore international peace and security." http://www.un.org/en/sections/un-charter/chapter-vii/.

[32] Pilar Marcos, "El 91% de los españoles rechaza la intervención militar en Irak, según el CIS," *El País*, March 28, 2003. See https://elpais.com/diario/2003/03/28/espana/1048806001_850215.html.

[33] PSOE, *Merecemos una España mejor. Programa Electoral. Elecciones Generales* (Madrid: PSOE, 2004), 23. See http://web.psoe.es/source-media/000000348500/000000348570.pdf.

As documented by the later official British report on the Iraqi war, the United States had in reality committed itself to a timetable for military action which was radically different from the timetable and processes for inspection agreed by the Security Council.[34] Whether or not there were weapons of mass destruction in Iraq was apparently irrelevant. The United States demanded a regime change in Iraq and accordingly defended the military intervention on the basis of the existing resolutions 1441 and 687 and 678.[35] This fact also meant that Aznar had his hands completely tied. If he truly wanted to position Spain closer to the United States, he had no choice but to follow the plans and the time tables outlined by President Bush. As can be seen from the minutes of Aznar's meeting with Bush from 22 February 2003—filtered in its totality to the press in 2007—there was virtually no room for maneuver for Aznar. President Bush had already made his mind up:

> Saddam Hussein will not change and will continue to play. The time has come to get rid of him. It is like that … Saddam Hussein is not disarming. We have to catch him right now. We have shown an incredible degree of patience so far. Two weeks left. In two weeks we will be militarily ready. I think we will get the second resolution. In the Security Council we have the three Africans [Cameroon, Angola and Guinea], the Chileans, the Mexicans. I will talk to all of them, also to Putin, naturally. We will be in Baghdad at the end of March. There is a 15% chance that at that time Saddam Hussein is dead or gone.[36]

So, one month prior to the intervention, effectuated during the night of 19–20 March 2003, Bush had already told Aznar behind closed doors that the war was inevitable, although he also said that he was not insensitive to the fact that the war plans caused grave domestic problems for Tony Blair, just as he did not ignore the fact that millions of people had recently demonstrated in several cities in Spain against the impending war. "We

---

[34] *The Report of the Iraq Inquiry*, Executive summary, 51. http://www.iraqinquiry.org.uk/media/246416/the-report-of-the-iraq-inquiry_executive-summary.pdf.

[35] US Department of State, Archive: "Interview by the New York Times, Secretary Colin L. Powell, Washington, DC, March 29, 2003." http://2001-2009.state.gov/secretary/former/powell/remarks/2003/19171.htm.

[36] "Acta de la conversación entre George W. Bush y José María Aznar, Crawford, Tejas, 22 de febrero de 2003," *El País*, September 26, 2007. https://elpais.com/diario/2007/09/26/espana/1190757601_850215.html.

need you to help us with public opinion," Aznar said. To comfort him, Bush explained that the scope of the new resolution would be tailored to his needs. However, Bush utterly failed to deliver on this promise. The two Latin American countries mentioned in the quote, Chile and Mexico, which according to Bush could be won over, did not give into either Spanish or American pressures. They further found it quite inappropriate that Spain had tried to influence sovereign national decision-making processes about going to war or not. By traveling to Mexico City and Santiago to persuade them, Aznar actually compromised the relative autonomy that had characterized Spain's Latin American policies since the mid-1970s.[37]

In his memoirs, President Bush bluntly describes the kind of treatment he was subjected to by his two Latin American colleagues, Vicente Fox and Ricardo Lagos. Bush told Fox that he should not be seen to be supporting the French. Fox replied that he would think it over. An hour passed, when the embassy suddenly called Condoleezza Rice to tell her that Fox had been hospitalized. In Bush's own account, "I never did hear from him again on this issue," and as his memoirs reveal he had no better luck with Lagos.[38] Yet, as claimed by Powell, the resolution, which was essentially a political favor extended to Blair and Aznar, came to nothing, but the war went ahead as planned.[39] This also explains why Aznar was bound to ignore the arguments of international law if he truly wanted to position Spain alongside Britain and the United States. He actually decided against the reports issued by the head of the international legal department of his own foreign ministry, who warned that to legally apply military force against Iraq would require explicit authorization from the UN Security Council.[40]

A further argument in favor of withdrawal was that Aznar had never convincingly explained the connection between his support for the invasion of Iraq and Spain's national interests, and the bomb attacks in Madrid

---

[37] Manuel Iglesias-Cavicchioli, "A Period of Turbulent Change: Spanish-US Relations Since 2002," *The Whitehead Journal of Diplomacy and International Relations*, vol. 8 (Summer/Fall, 2007): 3.

[38] Bush, *Decision Points*, 246–247.

[39] US Department of State, Archive: "Interview by the New York Times, Secretary Colin L. Powell, Washington, DC, March 29, 2003." https://2001-2009.state.gov/secretary/former/powell/remarks/2003/19171.htm.

[40] Ernesto Ekaizer, "El último informe que pidió Exteriores antes de la guerra de Irak consideró ilegal la intervención," *El País*, December 13, 2005. See https://elpais.com/diario/2005/12/13/espana/1134428404_850215.html. Cf. Iglesias-Cavicchioli, "A Period of Turbulent Change," 4.

doubtless raised serious questions as to the wisdom of neglecting other, and perhaps more imminent, security threats from North Africa. Certainly, Aznar's unnuanced statement about Spain being a Euro-Atlantic rather than a strictly European nation did little to mitigate the massive public opposition to the war in Spain. In his memoirs, Aznar further admits that he alone took the decision to intervene. It was only afterward that the government and the parliament were involved.[41]

Scholarly opinions vary as to Aznar's real motivations. It has been suggested that he truly believed in the "intrinsic goodness" of a hegemonic US foreign policy or that neoconservative thinking constituted the ideological foundation of his foreign policy choices.[42] Others stress that, above all, he wanted Spain to be positioned alongside the big players of international politics.[43] This project was, however, in contrast to the fact that Spain had no offensive military capability that could actually contribute to the invasion of Iraq. Critics therefore pointed to an imbalance between the foreign policy ambitions of Aznar and Spain's true economic and military means.[44] More benevolent interpretations suggest that his rapprochement with Bush was simply part of a wider range of international initiatives to deal effectively with the domestic terror threat.[45] Jorge Dezcallar, who spoke with Aznar on a daily basis, claims that the former Spanish prime minister had a very clear and ambitious vision of where he wanted Spain to be, yet his bad relationship with Chirac was exploited by Tony Blair, who sent him straight into the arms of President Bush. The price for being invited into Washington's inner circles was to show absolute loyalty to the timetables established by the Bush administration for the upcoming military intervention in Iraq. If necessary, he simply had to swallow a war without a resolution. As the war drew closer, Dezcallar claims, Aznar was increasingly isolated and in the Moncloa building he would only surround himself with a group of unconditional loyalists who said what he wanted to

[41]José María Aznar, *Ocho años de gobierno: Una visión personal de España* (Barcelona: Planeta, 2005), 150.

[42]Iglesias-Cavicchioli, "A Period of Turbulent Change," 3–4. For a new study on the impact of neoconservative thinking on Spanish foreign policy, see Manuel Iglesias-Cavicchioli, *Aznar y los 'Neocons'. El impacto del neoconservadurismo en la política exterior de España* (Barcelona: Huygens, 2017).

[43]Rafael García Pérez, "España en un mundo en cambio," 716.

[44]Cf. Iglesias-Cavicchioli, "Spanish-US Relations," 7.

[45]Crespo Palomares, *La alianza americana*, 254.

hear, or perhaps thought exactly the same as he did.[46] However, Dezcallar does not comment on Rumsfeld's later claim that in this period the Spanish intelligence agencies under Dezcallar's command contributed to the US narrative that Saddam Hussein possessed WMD and was even increasing the number of weapons of mass destruction.[47]

Be that as it may, the last Spanish forces left Iraq on 21 May, just five weeks after the Zapatero government had been sworn in. The intervention had cost the lives of thirteen Spaniards (eleven soldiers and two journalists), and in purely economic terms, it had cost a staggering €370 million. Importantly, the Spanish population did not find the war to be worthwhile, as there was a widespread feeling—albeit not backed by any clear evidence—that if Aznar had abstained from military action in Iraq, the terrorist attack in Madrid would never have taken place.[48]

In summer 2004, the PSOE government's decision to pull its forces out of Iraq was challenged by the newfound collaborative spirit in the UN Security Council. In early June, a new formula was actually found in the UN which addressed many of the deficiencies previously denounced by the PSOE. On 8 June 2004, the Security Council agreed on a comprehensive resolution on Iraq, which called for the formation of an interim government and the holding of democratic elections by January 2005, as well as welcoming the end of the occupation by 30 June.[49] Finally, it determined the status of the multinational force and its relationship with the Iraqi government, as well as the role of the United Nations in the political transition. This resolution put the Spanish government in some difficulty as Zapatero was attacked both by the opposition and by international commentators who claimed that Spain's withdrawal from Iraq had been premature and had left it isolated, now that a consensus over Iraq had been reached in the UN. In response, Moratinos underlined that the new resolution failed to provide the UN with sufficient military and political control of the transition. Accordingly, he argued, Spain was right about bringing their soldiers home. Spain still voted in favor of the resolution, despite its shortcomings, in the hope that it might serve the normalization and reconstruction of

[46] Jorge Dezcallar, *El anticuario de Teherán*, 563–564.

[47] Donald Rumsfeld, *Known and Unknown: A Memoir* (London: Allen Lane, 2013), 434.

[48] Carlos Navajas Zubeldia, "Democratization and Professionalis: Security and Defence Policy in Contemporary Spain," in *Contemporary Spanish Foreign Policy*, ed. David García Cantalapiedra and Ramón Pacheco Pardo (Abingdon and New York: Routledge, 2014), 25.

[49] UN Resolution, 1546, June 8, 2004. http://undocs.org/S/RES/1546(2004).

Iraq. The Spanish UN ambassador, Juan Antonio Yañez-Barnuevo, further explained that he had voted in favor of the resolution, although it was not "ideal" as he would have preferred the United Nations to have assumed military control during the transition.[50] Tensions remained in the months to come, though, since Spain—together with Germany, France, Belgium and Greece—refused to send their NATO troops to Iraq to train Iraqi soldiers. The decision not to comply with a NATO decision clearly upset Colin Powell. Michel Barnier, the French foreign minister, evaded the criticism by saying that it was time to look ahead and not dwell on past differences, whereas Moratinos underlined Spain's readiness to "maintain and amplify its presence in Afghanistan."[51]

3.2   The American Way

When Moratinos took office, King Juan Carlos's first words to him were, "Minister, you have to maintain good relations with the United States!"[52] These were not just words. For nearly four decades, the king had played a key role in the US-Spanish relationship, and no one in the government was as well connected to both Democratic and Republican leaders as he was.[53] Given the seriousness of the crisis with Washington and the alarming prospect of having to cope with a hostile Republican Administration for yet another four years, the good services of the king were soon called upon.

In spite of Juan Carlos' early warnings, however, it was symbolically important to the new government that Moratinos' first trip abroad was *not* to the United States, even though the first scheduled trip in his calendar was actually to Washington. For this reason, just before his flight to the US capital the new foreign minister planned an additional stop in Dublin since Ireland was holding the presidency of the European Council. America was important, but Europe even more so. The meeting in Dublin was in stark contrast to the ones which awaited him on the other side of the Atlantic.

---

[50]Cf. the ambassador's remarks in "Security Council Endorses Formation of Sovereign Interim Government in Iraq; Welcomes End of Occupation by 30 June, Democratic Elections by January 2005," Security Council, Press Release, June 8, 2004. https://www.un.org/press/en/2004/sc8117.doc.htm.

[51]Cited in, "EEUU critica a los países de la OTAN que no colaboran en Irak," *El País*, December 10, 2004.

[52]Moratinos Files: Interview, Moratinos.

[53]Heiberg, *US-Spanish Relations After Franco*, 199.

The discussions in the Irish capital were highly constructive and mainly centered on how to deal with the stalemate in the negotiations about the new European constitutional treaty. Afterward tough meetings with Colin Powell, Condoleezza Rice and Joe Biden awaited.

Moratinos had prepared three major points that he wanted to convey to Powell, who despite the tense atmosphere received him cordially. During their interview, the Spanish foreign minister first stated that that new Spanish government was not anti-American. On the contrary, Spain very much wanted to strengthen the bilateral relationship, and—he added—he was not referring only to the level of government. Their ambition was rather that Spanish society as a whole should become much more pro-American. "We have seen anti-US protests, burning of US flags ...," Moratinos said. "We can continue this way – dear Colin – but we do not want to. We want Spanish citizens to be proud of their relationship with the United States. We understand our own society better than you do. And we want our people to understand the importance of a privileged relationship with the United States."[54]

The second point was subtle and aimed at making the Americans understand the correct dimensions of the Spanish decision. To this end, Moratinos made a historical comparison between the situation in 2004 and the situation in 1986–1987, when it had come to an almost complete breakdown in the negotiations between Washington and Madrid because Felipe González wanted to close a number of US airbases and facilities in Spain (eventually put into effect by the 1988 bilateral agreement).[55] Moratinos said that he would like Powell to see all the telegrams that the US diplomats in Madrid had sent to Washington when Felipe González was prime minister. "How did the Americans speak of González? I imagine that you had doubts about him as well," Moratinos said. He then asked Powell to make the following comparison, "What is most important: to take 1,300 Spanish soldiers out of Iraq, from one conflict area and insert them into another [Afghanistan], or close an important military base such as the one in Torrejón? Tell me," Moratinos said while looking Powell straight into the eyes. "Wasn't the closure of Torrejón in 1988 strategically much more important than pulling a few troops out of a military theatre?" Moratinos continued. This was probably also a discrete reminder that Spain was still

[54]Moratinos Files: Interview Moratinos.

[55]Cf. Heiberg, *US-Spanish Relations After Franco*, 173–192.

offering important services to the Americans, who were dependent on the Spanish bases for its war in Iraq.[56] The third point he wanted to convey was that Spain was fully prepared to fulfill its role in NATO and work against the Taliban/Al Qaeda network in Afghanistan who had masterminded 9/11. Above all, according to Moratinos, this fight had the international legitimacy that the war in Iraq lacked. In this way, Spain could increase its participation in the common fight against terrorism but downscale its presence in Iraq. Moratinos was actually stepping out of line with his instructions, at this point, as this offer had not been cleared with Zapatero. True, he had discussed it with the prime minister, but Zapatero told him not to mention this to Powell. Nevertheless, Moratinos saw it as an absolute necessity to put some meat on the negotiating table to mitigate US pressure.

Powell did not immediately react to the three points but asked him instead why his friends called him "Curro." A somewhat surprised Moratinos then gave him a small lecture on how nicknames are formed in Spanish. "From this moment on, Miguel, I'm going to call you 'Curro'," Powell replied. Although for the rest of their conversation Powell was not very concrete in his reactions to Moratinos' three points—the most important one being the Spanish offer to send troops to Afghanistan—the lunch took place in a congenial atmosphere and the offer Moratinos had put on the table had not left Powell untouched. The meeting thus gave the hard-pressed Socialist government new hope. Afterward, Moratinos briefed the Spanish press about the essence of their talk without, however, entering into any details.

Moratinos, accompanied by his vice minister for foreign affairs, Bernardino León, and his chief of staff, Javier Sancho, subsequently went to see Condoleezza Rice, Bush's national security advisor. Moratinos experienced the meeting as "horrible." Rice was "extremely hard" and she used words like "treason" about the sovereign Spanish decision to withdraw its troops. She said that Spain would suffer enormously from this decision and that it would be difficult to rebuild a relationship with an ally who treated the United States like this.[57] She also said that the United States would follow every Spanish move very closely from this moment on.

---

[56]Moratinos Files: Interview Moratinos.

[57]Ibid. This is also corroborated by Rupérez's memoirs, *Memoria de Washington*, 314. According to Rupérez, Rice said the following: "What you have done, taking a very serious decision which gravely endangers our security and that of the other members of the coalition,

Assuredly, these were extremely hard and perhaps also imprudent words to use against an ally who—notwithstanding the decision taken—was still offering crucial base facilities for operations in Iraq. Rice had apparently not thought about what a complete break with Spain might imply, including the impossibility of using Spanish bases and airspace for operations in Iraq and Afghanistan. It apparently never crossed her mind; she simply took it for granted. Had she—like Powell—been better informed of the recent history of US-Spanish relations, she might have thought twice before making such harsh statements.

After the two meetings with Powell and Rice, Moratinos went to see different legislators in the US Congress, among others the influential Democratic senator and future vice president, Joe Biden, who was a friend of the Spanish king. Biden asked Moratinos how things had gone. Moratinos explained that it had gone well with Powell and very badly with Rice to which Biden commented, "Don't have any illusions. You are going to have a tough time because in Washington both the Democratic and the Republican establishment do not understand those kinds of actions." He further said that he did not know Zapatero but he knew the king well, and as a friend of Spain he wanted Moratinos to understand that it was going to be a difficult period. No matter what, Spain would have to suffer from its decision to withdraw.[58]

After his trip to Washington, Moratinos made a written report to Zapatero, in which he accounted for his meetings and also argued in favor of offering a compensatory boost to the Spanish military presence in Afghanistan (something he had already proposed to Powell). He had apparently discussed this idea in private with Yáñez, and he most certainly discussed the matter with Bono, who noted in his diaries what Moratinos had said to him on Monday 3 May, i.e., that the situation with the United States was absolutely unbearable and that there was little alternative to incrementing the number of Spanish troops in Afghanistan: "The reasonable thing to do is to send approximately one thousand two hundred soldiers, but Zapatero has been very interested in sending troops to Haiti since his meeting with Chirac and that is an error because what is important, Pepe, is not

communicating it to us less than 24 hours before the public announcement, is something that you do not do to an ally."

[58] Moratinos Files: Interview, Moratinos.

France, but the United States. Listen to me and don't oppose sending troops to Afghanistan."[59]

Upon his return from Rome on 13 May, Zapatero told Moratinos that he did not like the idea of sending troops to Afghanistan. However, Moratinos was very insistent, something which he attributed to the fact that he felt the US pressure much more than his prime minister did.[60] At the beginning of June, Moratinos called Bono to inform him that Zapatero had told Blair that Spain would only be present in Afghanistan with a humanitarian mission. Meanwhile, the secret services had just passed on a note to Moratinos in which it was anticipated that the United States would soon ask for Spanish soldiers to be sent to a militarily difficult area in Afghanistan, and "even though we could decline," Moratinos told Bono, "I think we should accept the offer."[61] In the end, Moratinos got his will. The decision to opt for Afghanistan was probably influenced by the fact that during 2004 the security scenario in that country gave some cause for optimism, as was also confirmed by the elections later that year when only a few violent incidents were registered.[62]

The report written by Moratinos after his trip to Washington was also used in preparation for the NATO summit in Istanbul, where the final decision to increase the number of Spanish troops in Afghanistan was taken. Prior to the meeting between the heads of state and the governments on Monday 28 June 2004, a preliminary meeting was set up between Rumsfeld, Powell, Bono and Moratinos. Here, it was agreed that Spain could augment its presence of troops in Afghanistan, although the Spanish side reiterated that they still needed to convince Zapatero who was still reluctant about the idea. According to Moratinos, not to accept would seriously damage Spanish interests. The Americans further insisted that Zapatero

---

[59] Bono, *Diario de un ministro*, entry for May 2–5, 2004.

[60] Ibid., entry for May 14, 2004. Zapatero told me—somewhat in contrast to both Bono's memoirs and Moratinos' recollection of events, that he always favored an increased Spanish contribution to the war effort in Afghanistan as a compensatory measure ("Siempre apoyé la intervención"). It was legitimate as the UN had sanctioned it, although the results of the intervention had later turned out to be "debatable" ("discutibles"). Cf. Moratinos Files: Interview, Zapatero.

[61] Bono, *Diario de un Ministro*, entry for June 3, 2004.

[62] UN Security Council, 5955th meeting, statement: "Afghanistan's First Presidential Election Not Perfect, But Sets Stage. Assistant Secretary-General Offers Preliminary Observations, Says Afghans 'Patience, Resilience and Determination' Source of Optimism," October 12, 2004. https://www.un.org/press/en/2004/sc8216.doc.htm.

should personally give the good news to President Bush. In the end, Bush, accompanied by Powell, approached Zapatero with the following suggestion, "Please accept what your ministers do not object to."[63] Zapatero agreed, and while the two leaders shook hands and smiled, Bush said that this was indeed good news. However, their conversation was brief and no love was lost between them.[64]

The Bush administration publicly reiterated its respect for Zapatero's decision to withdraw from Iraq, but in reality the departments outside of the Department of State no longer regarded the Spanish government as a reliable partner.[65] This was, of course, due to the Spanish decision to withdraw, but part of the coldness of the relationship over the next months probably also owed to actions undertaken by Aznar and the former foreign minister, Ana Palacio. On 27 January 2005, Robert Manzanares, chargé d'affaires of the US embassy in Madrid, called Bono to tell him that the PP was meddling with the relationship between the United States and Spain, and that he had already told them to desist since the government of the United States was obliged to have a dialogue with the government which had won the elections. He further added that the goodwill of the Zapatero government was being noted. Importantly, Washington very much appreciated the Spanish decision to augment its military presence in Afghanistan.[66] Again on 22 April 2005, Manzanares insisted, "The PP is acting like this so that my country will never forget our differences with you, but they will not succeed."[67]

It is important to stress, though, that Zapatero also tested the relationship with the United States by suddenly opting for an instant withdrawal after having sent entirely different signals to Powell during their brief encounter in Madrid. Reversely, had Zapatero not acted the way he did, it is not improbable that the withdrawal would have been more complicated, if not impossible. As is often the case in international politics, the solutions available to a government nearly always carry risks, and in this specific case, Zapatero had to choose between not upsetting the Americans or sticking to his electoral promise. In the end, it was not a difficult choice. Nevertheless,

---

[63] Bono, *Diario de un Ministro*, entry for June 28, 2004.

[64] Moratinos Files: Interview, Moratinos.

[65] Cf. also Powell, "A Second Transition," 147.

[66] Bono, *Diario de un Ministro*, entry for January 27 to February 1, 2004.

[67] Ibid., entry for April 19–April 22, 2004.

it is not unlikely that other diplomatic incidents during 2004 could easily have been avoided had Zapatero had more experience in government. One problematic episode happened at the beginning of June when Zapatero visited Tony Blair in Downing Street as part of an intense travel program across Europe during his first six months in office. During this meeting, Zapatero boasted about his young cabinet and his ability to renew Spanish socialism, and he also stated in a clearly uncalled-for and offensive way that Blair had been wrong about Iraq all along, something which explained all the trouble he was in now. This was unnecessary, particularly as Blair had never put any obstacles in the way of Spanish withdrawal. It seemed as though the young, handsome, yet internationally inexperienced Zapatero (resembling the younger Blair known for his innovative interpretation of Socialism in the 1990s) was trying to teach the old dog a trick or two, something that was obviously not well received. His Spanish interlocutors could not fail to notice, moreover, how old Blair had come to look at close range. Clearly, the war in Iraq had worn him down. Another incident occurred in Tunisia in September 2004 when the press asked Zapatero how he felt about the fact that some Central American countries were possibly withdrawing from Iraq. The prime minister answered in a way that could most certainly be interpreted as if he was generally favoring the withdrawal of all nations from Iraq. During the flight back to Torrejón, Moratinos expressed his disapproval with this answer. Zapatero replied with a "¡No te preocupes!" ("Don't worry!"). However, the minute the aircraft landed in Torrejón, Moratinos received a phone call from Powell who demanded an explanation, and Moratinos had to take immediate steps to mitigate the effects of Zapatero's statement.[68]

Seen against this background, it almost goes almost without saying that for the Socialist government the future task of restoring the relationship with Washington would have been enormously helped if the Democratic Senator of Arizona, John Kerry, had won the upcoming presidential elections on 2 November 2004. During election night Rubalcaba, Bono and Moratinos enjoyed a delightful dinner in the Moncloa Building together with Zapatero and members of the prime minister's personal staff. However, the pleasant atmosphere was quickly ruined by the incoming results from the other side of the Atlantic Ocean: four more years with President Bush awaited and the Spanish ministers chose to disrupt the party and go

---

[68] Moratinos Files: Interview, Moratinos.

to bed early that night.[69] At this point, it was deemed necessary to call upon the services of His Majesty King Juan Carlos 1. The king was used to mediating with Washington and he had always offered to help through his own contacts. Thus, he instantly agreed to arrange a private meeting with the Bushes in order to iron out the bilateral differences once and for all.

On 24 November 2004, King Juan Carlos and Queen Sofia visited the Bush family in Crawford, Texas, where both the president and his father, former President George H. W. Bush were present. The latter was an old friend of Juan Carlos. Prior to the meeting, the Spanish king had talked on the phone with Zapatero, who was very hopeful that the meeting might contribute to improving bilateral relations. The meeting went well, but on one point Bush Junior turned out be inflexible. He said he would never meet with Zapatero. During the lunch, Bush Senior excused the president's behavior by saying that not everything that his son did was necessarily correct: "Forget it," he told Juan Carlos, "There is nothing you can do."[70] This attitude was confirmed by another incident registered some days before, from 11 to 13 November 2004, when Bush Senior visited Albacete in Spain for a hunting session together with the Venezuelan billionaire Gustavo Cisneros. Zapatero was very keen on meeting the former president, but Bush Junior had expressly forbidden his father to meet with him.[71]

To ease the pressure, Moratinos also gave a series of press interviews in which he underlined that the relationship with Washington was generally good and that Spain was obtaining tangible and better results than the former government—despite the fact that Zapatero did not enjoy the same status with Bush as Aznar. Emphasis was given to the fact that Moratinos had called Powell to congratulate him on Bush's victory in the presidential elections and that the two would soon meet in Brussels on 18 December to further strengthen the relationship. Moratinos also underlined that both Europe and the United States had to show signs of compromise in order to find common ground. Within the European Union, Spain should be

[69] Ibid.

[70] Moratinos Files: Private information.

[71] Bono, *Diario de un Ministro*, entry for November 11–13, 2004.

seen as one of the leading countries when it came to making new proposals which might strengthen the transatlantic relationship.[72]

It soon became clear, however, that the less hawkish Colin Powell was leaving the Bush administration, and only two weeks after the elections, on 18 November 2004, Moratinos called Condoleezza Rice to congratulate her on her promotion to Secretary of State. This change was certainly not received with enthusiasm in the Santa Cruz Palace due to her rather confrontational behavior in April. Their first telephone conversation was diplomatic, however, and Rice actually seemed much more self-confident and better acquainted with the trade and realities of international diplomacy. Above all, she now expressed herself in far more positive terms with regard to the need for more international cooperation.[73] In Iraq, "mission accomplished" had turned out to be far less accomplished, and the new secretary of state seemed to realize that multilateralism was probably the most important tool in her box when it came to solving the complex problems that Washington was facing. In a speech given in Paris on 8 February 2005, Rice openly admitted to the Europeans that "We have had our disagreements." Yet she also expressed a strong US desire to open a new chapter in the relationship. "After all," she said, "history will surely judge us not by our old disagreements, but by our new achievements."[74] In other words, Washington was willing to turn the page.

The "disagreements" probably referred to the fact that during the run-up to the war in Iraq, Washington had on several occasions highlighted Polish support for the US intervention, in contrast to French and German skepticism about going to war against Saddam Hussein. Rumsfeld, among others, had publicly spoken of a divide between "new" and "old" Europe.[75] Conceivably, 2003 had represented the deepest nadir so far in the history of the bilateral relationship between the United States and Europe. However, all this would change. President Bush had come to realize that the days

---

[72] Miguel A. Moratinos, "La relación de este Gobierno con EEUU dará mejores resultados que los que se dieron con Aznar," *El Mundo*, November 7, 2004. "España es el país que más puede aportar a EEUU en lo internacional," *El País*, November 7, 2004.

[73] Moratinos Files: Interview, Moratinos.

[74] Excerpt of Rice's speech available on YouTube. https://www.youtube.com/watch?v=qfEjQ1ElOag. See also William I. Hitchcock, "The Ghost of Crises Past: The Troubled Alliance in Historical Perspective," in *The End of the West? Crisis and Change in the Atlantic Order*, ed. Jeffrey J. Anderson et al. (Ithaca, NY: Cornell University Press 2008), 78.

[75] See Sect. 5.1

of US unilateralism or ad hoc alliances had reached their limits. In fact, only ten days after Rice's speech, on 22 February, the newly reelected president chose to visit the European Commission and Council in Brussels as his first trip abroad. This was a strong symbolic gesture and showed that there was a real intention on the US side to secure a new collaboration.[76] Essentially, Bush now seemed to believe that he could not deal effectively with the challenges he was facing across the world without collaborating with Brussels and stimulating European unity. The learning curve of the reelected president had indeed been long and steep, and his critics might certainly argue with reference to Iraq that the costs had been tremendous.

This spirit of renewed friendship was much welcomed by the Spanish government, which was now determined to demonstrate that it was, after all, a reliable partner and ally of the United States. Still, it was important for Madrid to clearly indicate that a certain amount of space for differences of opinion had to be allowed for in the bilateral relationship. It soon turned out that the main problem was not the bilateral relations per se, which soon recovered, but almost exclusively President Bush's personal antipathy toward the new Spanish leadership, which was hidden under a facade of very polite behavior, making it sometimes difficult for the new Spanish government to decipher the right signals from the White House.[77]

The reconciliation with Bush was also made difficult by the politically appointed US ambassador to Madrid, George Argyros, a real estate owner with scant knowledge of the diplomatic business. José Bono essentially describes Argyros as deeply untrustworthy, and the words reserved for him by Moratinos are very much in the same vein.[78] The problem with Argyros was allegedly always the same: He would put on a big smile, and say he agreed with the Spanish propositions and then work directly against them. Furthermore, he did not know how to conduct a negotiation, and he never tried to change Bush's negative perception of Zapatero. Zapatero had no faith in Argyros and the king utterly disliked him, too. To compensate for the ambassador's inadequacies, the Spanish government sought to establish a much closer working relationship with the professional diplomatic staff at

---

[76] US Department of State, Archive: "President Meets with EU Leaders," February 22, 2005. http://2001-2009.state.gov/p/eur/rls/rm/42601.htm.

[77] Moratinos Files: Interview, Moratinos; Zapatero.

[78] Moratinos Files: Interview Moratinos. For an overview of some rather bizarre diplomatic cases with Agyros, see Bono, *Diario*, entry for October 14–15, 2004.

the US embassy.[79] It was actually not the first time Madrid had in this way circumvented normal diplomatic procedures due to a hard-to-handle US ambassador. The Santa Cruz Palace still had fervent memories of the US career diplomat Thomas O. Enders, who during the mid-1980s had been a nightmare figure for the Socialist government. For this reason, Madrid had eventually decided to establish a back channel to both the CIA and the vice head of mission at the embassy, thereby hoping to convey a more accurate view of Spanish foreign policies.[80] To the relief of Madrid, Argyros left the embassy on 21 November 2004. This added to Spanish optimism that there was now a real possibility of change. In the midst of all this, the Spanish Foreign Ministry designed a new strategy of rapprochement with the United States. On 10 November, Moratinos wrote a personal letter to Zapatero in which he described a number of important initiatives that could be launched with the prime minister's acceptance.[81]

Crucially, the new Spanish strategy toward the United States was going to be twofold. First, and perhaps most importantly of all, it aimed to avoid too direct dealings with the Americans on matters of dispute. Second, the idea was to continuously find common ground on international issues, which were important to the Bush administration as it entered into its second term. Madrid would also send the message that the two parties should work closely together as this was actually in the US best interests—the main argument being that Spain's different approach to a number of international issues might, paradoxically, be of great advantage to Washington. By collaborating with Spain, Madrid reasoned, the United States would be able to reach out to all those forces in the world, especially in Latin America, who profoundly disagreed with US policies.[82] This strategy was painstakingly followed by Madrid in the years to come, and—as we will see during the course of this book—it also largely explains Madrid's many diplomatic efforts in geographic areas which were perhaps not always of direct material concern to Spain, but which in turn provided an opportunity to work alongside the Americans to the benefit of Spain's overall strategic interests.

[79] Moratinos Files: Interview, Moratinos.

[80] Heiberg, *US-Spanish Relations After Franco*, 152–153.

[81] Moratinos Files: Interview, Moratinos.

[82] Ibid.

In sum, Spain's future political actions, from Latin America to Asia, were to be conducted with a special concern for issues where Spain and the United States might have converging interests. Not only did this approach offer the possibility of assisting the United States, it also implied that on certain issues and in certain regions Spain might even play an important role due to its more efficient contacts. This was especially true of a number of Latin American countries which were truly hostile to what they conceived as US hegemonic policies.

On 22 February 2005, Zapatero traveled to Brussels to attend the meeting between the European Union and NATO. There was no planned meeting with President Bush, but a brief exchange of opinions between the two leaders actually took place in the context of one of the working sessions. Again, no love was lost between them, yet according to Zapatero's official statement the meeting in Brussels had as a whole marked a "new step" in cooperation between the United States and Europe. Very much in line with Moratinos' suggestions, Zapatero presented Bush with a Spanish offer of more cooperation in Iraq and Afghanistan. In Iraq, Spain would offer training to 125 Iraqi soldiers, whereas Spain would take charge of the reconstruction team in the province of Qala-i-Naw, in the Eastern part of Afghanistan. Moratinos was also present in Brussels, where he met with Rice. In line with his own recommendation to Zapatero, he did not touch upon any questions of dispute. In particular, they discussed Iran, the need for an inclusive government in Iraq, and a possible road map for the Middle East process, and they touched upon the Barcelona Process and the Balkans.[83] His brief encounter with Rice actually paved the way for their formal bilateral meeting in April. Meanwhile, on 11 March 2005, exactly one year after the bomb attacks in Madrid, Bush published an open letter to the Spanish people, in which he expressed solidarity and renewed his condolences to the victims of the terrorist attack.[84]

On 12 April, Moratinos traveled to Washington to negotiate directly with Rice. Apart from stating that common ground had been found on several important issues ranging from Afghanistan, North Africa/Western Sahara to Latin America, the meeting was essentially an attempt to publicly send a signal from the Spanish side that bilateral relations had now been

[83] Moratinos Files: Interview, Moratinos.

[84] Peru Egurbide, "Bush envía un mensaje de pésame al pueblo español en el aniversario del 11-M," El País, March 11, 2005. https://elpais.com/diario/2005/03/11/espana/1110495610_850215.html.

normalized. Thus, much was made by the Spanish of the fact that both parties agreed to support the democratic process in Palestine in view of the upcoming elections, and to sustain the efforts of Abbas' government.[85] A leaked US document confirms that by the summer of 2005, the Spanish essentially believed that the lines of communication with Washington were generally good, "particularly after the series of high-level meetings such as Moratinos with Secretary Rice, and Defense Minister Bono with Secretary Rumsfeld." This Spanish sentiment was also shared by the new US ambassador, Eduardo Aguirre, who stressed that President Bush, National Security Advisor Stephen Hadley and Secretary of State Condoleezza Rice were now willing to start a new chapter in the relationship.[86]

To this end, it was of paramount importance that Argyros had finally left Madrid. The new acting ambassador and vice head of mission, Robert Manzanares, made a true effort to get relations back on track. It was thus the new strategy of the US embassy, which was continued after the appointment of Ambassador Aguirre, to strengthen the relationship with Spain in as many different fields as possible, instead of focusing exclusively on the difficult relations between the Moncloa and the White House, which were unlikely to change for the time being. In other words, both the Department of State and the Santa Cruz Palace were working along the same lines. It is within this context that we may understand the many bilateral meetings on different levels held during April and May 2005. A series of private actors were also engaged in this process, among others the Spanish singer Julio Iglesias, who was a good friend of Henry Kissinger's, and the Dominican-American fashion designer Óscar de la Renta, who was on friendly terms with the Bush family. They helped to set up a new meeting between Rumsfeld and Bono in order to settle their differences concerning Spanish arms sales to Venezuela.[87]

[85] Moratinos Files: Interview with Moratinos. The Spanish Minister of the Interior, José Antonio Alonso, met with the US Secretary of Homeland Security, Michael Chertoff, and the newly appointed Attorney General, Alberto Gonzales. Also the Spanish Minister of Justice, Juan Fernando López Aguilar, held similar meetings with Gonzales and other US representatives. Essentially, these meetings were seen as a way of regaining trust to the degree that the two parties could now share more intelligence in the fight against terrorism. These encounters are documented in *Anuario Internacional CIDOB*, multiple entries for 2005.

[86] Aguirre to NSC, June 28, 2005, cable [WikiLeaks]. Reproduced by Spanish newspaper *El País*. http://elpais.com/elpais/2010/12/07/actualidad/1291713422_850215.html.

[87] Cf. Bono, *Diario de un ministro*, entry for April 28–30, 2005.

The overall structural condition that was suddenly favoring the new Spanish strategy was that Washington found it necessary to reconcile with its old allies. However, on one specific point the Santa Cruz Palace clearly underestimated the challenges ahead. Madrid actually believed that it would be possible to establish a formal bilateral encounter between Zapatero and Bush in the near future. Moratinos stated that within a year relations would have improved sufficiently to allow for such a meeting. However, Ambassador Aguirre coolly reminded him that his focus should first of all "be on tangible results in the relationship and [he] would not measure success by high-level visits." This statement was also repeated in the subsequent press briefing.[88] In fact, little happened over the following months and years. Thus, it created some embarrassment when Moratinos again optimistically stated in early 2006 that Bush would receive Zapatero before the celebration of the Virgin of Rocío at the end of May, but as the bank holiday approached, Moratinos had to publicly admit that there was no such meeting in the pipeline.[89] In 2007, when asked about a meeting, Moratinos answered that the failure to meet might be due to mistakes on the US side.[90] The ultimate recognition of the normalization of the diplomatic relationship, a Spanish visit to the White House, would eventually have to wait until Barack Obama assumed the US presidency in 2009.

With hindsight, perhaps, the Spanish government should have played greater attention to the exact words of the new ambassador, quoted above, which were probably a subtle way of saying that Bush would never meet with Zapatero. Before his departure in 2009, Aguirre privately told Moratinos that in concomitance with his appointment as ambassador in 2005, Bush had actually told him that Spain was to be treated as a friend of the United States and as an ally, and that he was more or less free to pursue the established policy objectives set by the United States as he thought best. Nevertheless, the president strongly emphasized that he would never visit Spain while Zapatero was in power.[91] Aguirre's explanation caused several pieces to fall into place: Moratinos had always worked well with Aguirre, in

---

[88] Aguirre to NSC, June 28, 2005, cable [WikiLeaks]. http://elpais.com/elpais/2010/12/07/actualidad/1291713422_850215.html.

[89] "No hay prevista una reunión con Bush, pero lo importante es comportarse como aliados," *La Razón*, May 1, 2006.

[90] "Moratinos insisten en que las relaciones con EEUU son buenas y dice que 'quizás el error' sea de Bush," *Europa Press*, June 19, 2007.

[91] Moratinos Files: Interview, Moratinos.

contrast to his predecessor Argyros, but he had always wondered why the US ambassador had done so little to change Bush's perception of Zapatero. Aguirre had never facilitated reconciliation between them, and only now did Moratinos understand the reason why: Bush would simply not hear of it.

In 2010, WikiLeaks released a series of documents—reproduced by *El País*—which confirmed not only the existence of a troublesome bilateral relationship with Washington but also the somewhat narrow US understanding of Spanish politics. One document in particular gave rise to some debate in Spain, as it suggested that Bernardino León, who had previously worked as Moratinos' Vice Minister for Foreign Affairs and after 2008 as the prime minister's foreign policy advisor was actually the strong man of Spanish foreign policy and that his influence exceeded that of Moratinos and the entire foreign ministry. The release of this document certainly influenced public opinion in Spain and some scholars as well. Yet no one in the Spanish diplomacy that I have spoken to can confirm that this was actually the case and instead they point to the dynamic relationship between the Prime Minister's Office and Santa Cruz Palace. This is also my impression from the cases described throughout this book.[92]

Another critical issue on the bilateral agenda was the question of alleged US rendition flights through Spanish airspace. In November 2005, the Parliamentary Assembly of the Council of Europe (PACE) decided to begin a full-blown investigation into the American use of the illegal detention and transport of terror suspects, named extraordinary renditions. The author of the report, Dick Marty, compared the US prison program to a "spider's web" which could only work through the active collaboration or tacit acceptance of a number of European states—including Spain.[93] At the same time, politicians and NGOs increasingly expressed their concern about the way the US government treated detainees from the war on terror. "Guantánamo," "black sites" and "Abu Ghraib" were words which increasingly dominated the hearts and minds of public opinion and which

---

[92] "Cable secreto en el que Aguirre describe con detalle a Zapatero y los principales ministros," *El País*, December 6, 2010. https://elpais.com/elpais/2010/12/06/actualidad/1291627022_850215.html.

[93] Parliamentary Assembly, Council of Europe, Doc. 10957, June 12, 2006, "Alleged Secret Detentions and Unlawful Inter-State Transfers of Detainees Involving Council of Europe Member States," 59. http://assembly.coe.int/committeedocs/2006/20060606_ejdoc162006partii-final.pdf.

began to haunt the Bush administration. When confronted with the question of extraordinary renditions, Condoleezza Rice always stuck to the same explanation, namely that the United States did not violate the sovereignty of other nations. This statement was, however, deprived of any substance, since a series of laws and conventions, including the important Chicago Convention, were interpreted by the United States differently to the Europeans. This trick allowed the United States to use privately charted aircraft for state purposes, overfly European airspace and also make technical landings without requiring the consent of the hosting nation.[94]

Marty's report was essentially a political condemnation of the United States and the alleged collusion of a number of European states. Yet, as mentioned, it completely ignored important legal aspects which allowed the Americans—in their own interpretation—to do more or less as they saw fit without notifying their allies. Moreover, thorough national investigations into the many allegations have not been able to confirm the conclusions of Marty's report.[95] Still, the question remains as to whether the Americans would have conducted such operations—even though they felt legally free to do so—without some kind of consent from the hosting nation, in order not to stir up unnecessary friction with their allies. Moratinos publicly and truthfully denied that Spain had authorized such flights since there was no evidence of this, yet privately suspected that one high-ranking official in the foreign ministry had previously given a kind of tacit consent, just as long as the arrangement could plausibly be denied by the Spanish authorities.[96] Be that as it may, Moratinos felt obliged to get to the bottom of the problem, also because the whole affair risked becoming the center of a judiciary process after some suspect cases had been denounced to the authorities in Palma de Mallorca. He informed the Department of State of

---

[94]This is one of the conclusions of an independent official Danish inquiry on rendition flight that this author had the priviledge of conducting. Cf. Morten Heiberg, *Et jura at forstå, et andet land at føre: Undersøgelse af en række spørgsmål vedrørende 2008-redegørelsen om påståede hemmelige CIA-flyvninger over og i Grønland samt dansk bistand hertil* (Copenhagen: DIIS, 2012), 59–63.

[95]Cf. Ibid.

[96]Moratinos Files: Interview, Moratinos. See also Ana Carbajosa, "Moratinos asegura que el Gobierno desconocía los vuelos de la CIA," *El País*, September 15, 2006. https://elpais.com/diario/2006/09/15/espana/1158271207_850215.html.

this and asked Agustín Santos Maraver, who was responsible for the minister's liaisons to the Spanish Parliament, to check a wide range of suspicious flights so that the minister could duly report to the parliament.[97]
The bottom line of Santos Maraver's meticulous investigation was that no violations could be proven. In the end, there were only one or two doubtful cases out of sixty-six suspicious flights. Even though the question of rendition flights was high on the public agenda, it was the Spanish position that it should not become a disturbing element in the bilateral relationship with the United States.[98] In September 2006, Moratinos stated before the European Parliament that while no crimes had been committed on Spanish soil, he did not exclude the fact that aircraft which might have committed illegal activities in other countries could have landed in Spain.[99]
Reduced to its essentials, the remaining obstacle between Madrid and Washington from 2004 to 2008 was Bush's personal antipathy toward Zapatero. Toward the end of his presidency, however, Bush softened his attitude to the European leaders who, in his opinion, had let him down in the past. Interestingly, in late 2007 Spain was invited to the important international peace conference on the Middle East in Annapolis. In Madrid, this invitation was perceived not only as recognition of the fact that the Spanish government was an important stakeholder in the peace process, but also that the high-level working relationship with the United States had been normalized.[100] During the G20 meeting in Washington in November 2008, Bush even took the liberty of praising Zapatero's speech on the crisis.[101]
Without doubt, the Spanish decision to withdraw from Iraq in 2004 truly upset the United States, and Spain had to take immediate measures—including an upscaling of its presence in Afghanistan—to mitigate the effects of this decision. Still, if one considers the potential loss of prestige that Spain publicly inflicted upon the United States, i.e., the fact that one of Washington's core allies—present in the Azores—had simply turned

---

[97] Moratinos Files: Interview, Moratinos; Agustín Santos Maraver.

[98] Moratinos Files: Interview, Moratinos; Santos Maraver.

[99] "Moratinos sospecha que la CIA cometió delitos en otros países," *La Vanguardia*, September 15, 2006.

[100] "Rice comunicó a Moratinos el sábado pasado que España estaba invitada a la conferencia internacional sobre Oriente Próximo," *Europa Press*, November 21, 2007.

[101] Moratinos Files: Interview, Zapatero.

its back on President Bush, the US reaction was remarkably tame. To some extent, the consequences of the Spanish decision to withdraw were actually more tangible in Spain's relationship with some of America's closest allies, whether Japan, South Korea or Australia, where a significant share of public opinion strongly contested the intervention. The moderate reaction of the US, given the circumstances, had shown to the world that one could actually get away with quite a lot. There were those, for example, who argued with reference to the Spanish withdrawal of troops that Australia's margin for independent action in Iraq was much bigger than the Australian government gave the public to understand. This created problems for Prime Minister John Howard and accordingly also friction between Spain and Australia. In fact, Spain had to take several diplomatic steps to mend its relationship with the land down under.[102]

Importantly, Spain's overall working relationship with the United States was back on track before the summer of 2005. To understand this development, it is probably important to also bear in mind that the Spanish decision to pull its forces out of Iraq was overwhelmingly legitimized by popular will (some 91% opposed the war), something which limited the US possibility of introducing hard measures against Spain. To further punish a historically skeptical, if not anti-American, nation such as Spain might in the end prove to be counterproductive.[103] Moreover, the Spanish arguments in favor of a withdrawal were sustained by persuasive juridical and political arguments. Interestingly, critical opinions about the invasion—similar to the ones expressed earlier in Spain—actually began to appear in the American political debate as the war in Iraq turned sour. In 2006, the US Congress appointed a panel of ten bipartisan members to analyze the critical situation in Iraq, and over a period of six months the panel, headed by James Baker III, interrogated 170 witnesses, among others President Bush and Prime Minister Tony Blair. In December 2006, they recommended phasing out US troops from Iraq as soon as possible in light of the compromised security situation. It is actually striking how the conclusions drawn by the US committee resembled those made by the PSOE's

---

[102] Moratinos Files: Interview, Salarich.

[103] On the roots of Spanish anti-Americanism see: Daniel Fernández de Miguel, *El enemigo yanqui. Las raíces conservadores del anti-americanismo español* (Zaragoza, Spain: Genueve Ediciones, 2012).

Committee of the Wise during 2003 and 2004.[104] Although Baker's conclusion to withdraw was reached on different grounds, he apparently shared with the PSOE the conviction that it was meaningless to continue military operations in Iraq.

It is not unlikely that the gradual US acknowledgment of having failed in Iraq eventually contributed to bringing US-Spanish as well as US-EU working relations back on track. The Bush administration had come to realize that multilateralism was not such a bad thing after all. In particular, the case of Iraq had shown the world that unilateral foreign policies were perhaps not as efficient in the long run as multilateral solutions. Toward the end of its first term, the Bush administration had gradually reached the conclusion that there was little alternative to increased international collaboration. Seen against this background, the idea of "punishing" Spain for its behavior seemed even less attractive to Washington, also because Madrid was getting increasingly involved in a series of multilateral processes which were beginning to attract the attention of Washington. It so happened that in the end Spain avoided some of the most feared consequences of its decision to withdraw. Admittedly, this scenario could not have been easily foreseen by the Spanish government when Zapatero decided to withdraw immediately from Iraq in April 2004.

---

[104] *The Iraq Study Group Report* (New York: Vintage Books, 2006). The executive summary is also available through *The Wall Street Journal.* https://online.wsj.com/public/resources/documents/WSJ-iraq_study_group.pdf.

CHAPTER 4

A European House of Cards

4.1 Old and New Europe

Moratinos' hand was literally shaking with emotion when he signed the new European constitution in Rome on 29 October 2004. All his EU colleagues were present and so were the highest representatives of the soon-to-be EU member states from Eastern Europe. Even Turkish President Erdogan wanted to take part in this solemn event, which was followed by a formidable Italian dinner reception.[1] The pace at which this important step in European integration was taken was indeed remarkable. The ink used to sign the Treaty of Nice in 2001 had barely dried before it was deemed necessary to revise the text in view of the new EU enlargement rounds. In 2003, the President of the European Convention, Valery Giscard d'Estaing, solemnly presented the draft of a new European constitution. Essentially, the new constitutional treaty was perceived not only as the next natural step in the history of European integration, but also as a necessary response to the fall of the Berlin Wall. Nevertheless, to call the new treaty a "constitution" was to some extent a pleonasm in that the Court of Justice already used the existing treaties as constitutional texts. Still, by stressing the constitutional features in the title and by integrating the Charter of Fundamental Rights into the new text, the European Union very much underlined its

---

[1] Moratinos Files: Interview, Moratinos.

© The Author(s) 2019
M. Heiberg, *Spain and the Wider World since 2000*,
Security, Conflict and Cooperation in the Contemporary World,
https://doi.org/10.1007/978-3-030-27343-9_4

future political ambitions.[2] Europe was growing, and its self-perception as a united and increasingly more important player in international politics was boosted by President Bush's official visit to Brussels in February 2005, the newly reelected president's first official trip abroad. The symbolism was clear: Europe mattered, not only to the Europeans, but also to the world.

Shortly after the promising encounter with President Bush, the European Union was again cast into political turmoil. However, this time it was not the Americans who challenged European unity. On 29 May 2005, first France, and four days later Holland, suddenly ditched the constitutional treaty in a referendum. In case of the French referendum, which was by no means a constitutional requirement, it became a proxy for economic troubles that the people tended to relate to globalization and further integration. Neither did it help that Turkish accession to the EU, which was held to be a real possibility in the near future, was very unpopular in France. In Holland too, the referendum was a welcome opportunity for people to express their discontent with the government and with things that in reality were not connected to the treaty itself.[3]

At this point, a swift rescue operation was needed. European leaders eventually convinced themselves that the enlarged union could not work as intended if the core text of the treaty was not saved in some way. In the process, they dropped much of the explicit constitutional attributes attached to the former treaty proposal, starting with the name. Thus, the idea was to preserve the main text of the constitution, yet also downscale it into a mini-treaty, as Moratinos revealed in a later interview with *Die Zeit*.[4] On 23 July 2007, Zapatero declared that the newfound compromise, which eventually ended as up as the Treaty of Lisbon, was finally "satisfactory."[5] In spite of its downscaling, the new draft also suffered setbacks, this time due to a failed referendum in Ireland. This, however, was successfully repeated in October 2009, thus permitting the treaty to enter

---

[2] Desmond Dinan, *Europe Recast: A History of the European Union*, second edition (Boulder, CO: Lynne Rienner Publishers, 2014), 271–272. The official name of the constitution was the Treaty establishing a Constitution for Europe (TCE).

[3] Dinan, *Europe Recast*, 307.

[4] W. A. Perger, "Die Europa-Rallye," Interview with Moratinos, *Die Zeit*, June 1, 2006. https://www.zeit.de/2006/23/Moratinos; Desmond Dinan, *Europe Recast*, 305.

[5] "Tratado. España está satisfecha con el borrador del nuevo Tratado europea," July 23, 2007.

into force under the Spanish EU presidency in early 2010.[6] Importantly, the Treaty of Lisbon upheld the principle of double majority voting in the Council of the European Union, where the national ministers meet.[7] It was actually this new voting system which had created the deepest divisions among the member states during treaty negotiations since Germany introduced the idea at the beginning of the millennium.

At the turn of the millennium, all member states wanted to contribute to the finalization of unification with Eastern Europe. Yet the increasingly belligerent rhetoric of the Bush administration in 2002 clearly complicated the tasks ahead. Britain and France quarreled over Iraq, and while Blair gave his almost unconditional support to President Bush's invasion plans, Chirac and Schröder fiercely opposed the war, the latter probably also in order to attain domestic consensus in view of the German federal elections in September 2002. This conflict in the heart of the EU reflected an even deeper divide which would soon become visible between the original member states of the West and the soon-to-be member states of the East and would also threaten to endanger recent progress on a variety of security and defense matters.[8] At the same time, however, the dissent over the war also made France and Germany convinced that this was actually the right moment to deepen European integration along the Paris-Berlin axis, thereby transforming the EU into an even more relevant player in the international arena. There was, of course, always the British hesitance about further integration, which however differed a lot from the rest of the challenges facing the European Union. Essentially, the British would opt out from any new treaty proposal containing the word "federalism." But London could be expected to be rather accommodating in many other fields since it had already decided not to participate in some of the most important steps of unification. In this way, these were left in the hands of the other three dominant states of the union: Germany, France and Italy.[9]

A constant element of dispute among the members of the EU was the possible inclusion of Turkey. The UK, as well as Italy, favored entry, whereas France vigorously opposed it, leaving Germany in a very difficult situation

[6]Dinan, *Europe Recast*, 307.

[7]Cf. The Treaty of Lisbon, Article 9C, 4. https://eur-lex.europa.eu/legal-content/EN/TXT/?uri=CELEX:12007L/TXT.

[8]Dinan, *Europe Recast*, 297.

[9]Ibid., 273.

where it could not wholeheartedly pursue Turkish membership. Zapatero lived through these moments with great intensity. He saw Erdogan who comported himself in a climate of harmony and rapprochement and was therefore convinced that Turkey was on the verge of finally embracing Europe. He also saw a Turkey eager to reform itself, but which of course was also still a country with many contradictions. However, the Turks had actually displayed a real understanding of the European vision. Notwithstanding this, the momentum in the negotiations was lost once again. Years later in an interview with *Die Welt am Sonntag* in 2010, Moratinos strongly underlined the fact that Turkey was still part of the European family and his hope was that if Turkey lived up to the Copenhagen criteria, it might receive a real invitation in the near future. The never-ending story of Turkish membership, which began in the 1960s, indeed seemed to be without an end.[10]

For the same reason, the core issue at stake at the European Convention and the subsequent treaty negotiations during 2003–2004 was never Turkey. Neither was it the creation of a series of European symbols aiming to increase European cohesion and foster a stronger sense of European citizenship. The main hurdle was how to increase the capacity to push through effective decisions in the Council through the use of qualified majority decisions and at the same time safeguard the interests of the smaller and medium powers. In other words, decision-making should be efficient, but also have sufficient democratic legitimacy across Europe. Seen from the Spanish perspective, this challenge was certainly the hardest nut to crack.[11]

One main problem was that the equilibrium within the EU over the decades had begun to alter due to the ongoing enlargements. This internal power balance—although this was not formally sanctioned by any treaty— was built on the criteria of "weight."[12] Until the Treaty of Nice entered into force in 2003, Council decisions were based on a voting system, where, without mentioning all members, (West) Germany, France, Italy and Great

[10]Interview, *Welt Am Sontag*, January 24, 2010.

[11] Moratinos Files: Interview, Camilo Villarino.

[12] Ibid.

Britain had ten votes, Spain eight, Holland five, Denmark three and Luxembourg two votes.[13] Clearly, this system was an advantage to Luxembourg, as the difference between Luxembourg and West Germany in GNP
and population was simply not 1–5. On the other hand, this system also
favored integration since small powers felt that they had sufficient capacity
for action, just as the great powers still felt powerful enough despite having
to sacrifice some of their overwhelming weight. However, with the enlargement rounds during the 1970s to the 1990s, the system clearly began to
favor the smaller and medium nations disproportionately, reaching a hypo-
thetical situation where they could obtain a qualified majority in spite of
the fact that the big countries represented 75% of the EU population. This
was seen as politically unacceptable. However, it is important to stress that
although there were rarely any real votes in the Council, to take a decision
one had to ensure sufficient backing, and to block a decision one typically
had to align with one big country and some minor ones.[14]

When negotiations for the Treaty of Nice began, Germany introduced
the principle of double majority for decisions: A majority of states combined with a majority of population. This favored Germany, which had
just absorbed the former GDR. However, the flaw of this proposal was
that it would be too easy to push through a qualified majority decision
without any real negotiation whereby all member states would feel they
were partners in the outcome. France vigorously opposed the German
proposal as it has always been a *sine qua non* for Paris that Germany and
France had the same influence, despite the fact that unified Germany now
clearly outweighed France. In the era of Helmut Kohl, Germany had always
accepted this French imposition, but with Gerhard Schröder as Chancellor
(1998–2005), this was beginning to change. France successfully opposed
Schröder's proposal, and a new solution was found whereby the votes were
cast differently. In the Treaty of Nice, the big four (France, Germany,
Italy and Great Britain) were given twenty-nine votes, whereas the smaller
nations were given only four votes (the ratio being roughly 1–7). Spain, as

[13] *Decision of the Council of the European Communities of 22 January 1972 concerning
the accession of the Kingdom of Denmark, Ireland, the Kingdom of Norway, and the United
Kingdom of Great Britain and Northern Ireland to the European Coal, and Steel Community.*
"Part two: Adjustment to Treaties, chapter 2, article 12, established the new voting system,
which was also observed during the next enlargement rounds." https://eur-lex.europa.eu/
legal-content/EN/TXT/PDF/?uri=OJ:L:1972:073:FULL&from=EN.

[14] Moratinos Files: Interview, Villarino.

well as Poland, obtained no less than twenty-seven votes, thereby increasing its weight considerably. However, even though France upheld formal parity with Germany, the latter gained extra weight through the addition of a demographic criterion.[15] As a matter of fact, the new and somewhat complicated voting system foresaw the inclusion of ten new member states thereby creating a future system where a majority needed 255 of 345 votes (74%) representing 62% of the enlarged EU's total population. In other words, you only needed 91 votes to block a proposal. The understandable criticism against this system was that the threshold for member states' approval was simply too high, creating deadlock for difficult decisions and allowing only for proposals of limited reach to be adopted. Certainly, the twenty-seven votes obtained by Spain was a major success for Aznar's Conservative government, yet the price of this was that the number of Spanish seats in the European Parliament was diminished—a concession that Zapatero was later able to correct with the Treaty of Lisbon.[16]

In late March 2004, just prior to his formal appointment as foreign minister, Moratinos was contacted by a Spanish diplomat who informed him of the different scenarios at stake during the upcoming Intergovernmental Conference, where the EU member states were going to discuss the draft constitution proposed by the Convention. Greatly relieved by the fact that Aznar was no longer an obstacle to the ongoing process of European integration, the diplomat however warned him of the impending danger of suddenly departing from the position of the former government, which was based on a steadfast defense of the voting system of the Treaty of Nice. He also reminded the foreign minister *in spe* that France and Germany, seeing themselves as the inventors of the European project, could block any Spanish initiative if they wanted to. For this reason, it was important, as in the era of Felipe González, to work closely with these two nations without disclosing the real nature of the Spanish position until a much later point in the negotiations. To give in immediately and say that Spain had abandoned the position held by Aznar would no doubt weaken Spanish possibilities at the negotiating table. It was important not to give the impression that Spain was willing to give concessions just because Spain now wanted to join the Franco-German axis. Such automatisms would clearly damage the Spanish negotiating position.

[15] Dinan, *Europe Recast*, 269.
[16] Moratinos Files: Interview, Villarino.

On the other hand, it was also clear that Aznar's hard line was no longer sustainable. As is often the case in politics, Aznar's position had been influenced both by objective, legitimate concerns and by more subjective notions. On 13 June 2003, his foreign minister, Ana Palacio, had declared before the Convention, in line with the Polish government, that Spain had "fundamental reservations" about the constitutional treaty, specifically with the voting system.[17] The Spanish concern was that Giscard d'Estaing had effectively divided the member states by making all sorts of individual concessions until they all agreed to a voting system that was—objectively—not the least beneficial to many medium and smaller member states.[18]

In the summer of 2002, the crisis over Parsley Island took place, where France chose to support Morocco at the expense of Spain. As argued elsewhere in this book, this incident soured a Franco-Spanish relationship already challenged by deadlock over the constitutional treaty.[19] Later, in the run-up to the Iraq war, eight European countries signed a letter clearly opposing the French and German position. In their open letter of 30 January 2003, the leaders wanted to send "a clear, firm and unequivocal message that we would rid the world of the danger posed by Saddam Hussein's weapons of mass destruction."[20] The signatories were among others Aznar, Barroso, Berlusconi, Blair and Havel. This letter was of course very badly received in Paris and Berlin. More importantly, however, a second letter, published a week later, carried the signature of the foreign ministers of practically all the Eastern European countries aspiring to become members of the EU. Although the Vilnius statement was not explicit about the existence of WMD in Iraq and also encouraged the UN to take responsibility, it could however be interpreted—due to the timing of the event—as full support of Colin Powell's presentation in the Security Council of evidence of WMD in Iraq.[21] To make matters worse, in a famous interview of 22 January Rumsfeld had labeled Germany and France as "Old Europe,"

---

[17] Moratinos Files: Private information.

[18] Moratinos Files: Interview, Villarino.

[19] See also Alicia Sorroza Blanco, "Spain and the European Union," in *Contemporary Spanish Foreign Policy*, ed. David García Cantalapiedra and Ramón Pacheco Pardo (Abingdon and New York: Routledge, 2014), 72.

[20] The letter of Eight, "Europe and America Must Stand United," January 30, 2003, reproduced in John Ehrenberg, Patrice McSherry, José Ramón Sánchez, and C. M. Caroleen Sayej, *The Iraq Papers* (New York: Oxford University Press, 2010), 124–125.

[21] "The Vilnius Statement," February 6, 2003, reproduced in ibid., 125–126.

just as he had underlined that the center of European NATO was shifting toward the East because of the ongoing enlargement.[22]

At this point, Spanish negotiators, along with many EU observers, sensed that the French were now fearing that the future enlargement would radically change the equilibrium within the EU since the new member states were all strongly pro-American—a natural reaction, one might add, to the sufferings endured during the era of Soviet hegemony. Accordingly, France preferred a voting system that was more favorable to Germany than to the new group of small and medium powers. Although, geographically the balance of the union was tipping toward the East, France would do its utmost to keep the political counterweight in place. Accordingly, a very effective media campaign was launched to promote the new voting system. As a side effect, this campaign made Aznar's government—together with its Polish counterpart—look very bad and the only obstacle to a proper European solution. By December 2003, however, one Spanish diplomat reckons that even Aznar had come to realize that the current situation was unsustainable.[23]

This interpretation is confirmed by information that was handed over to Moratinos in late March 2004: The Spanish bargaining position had in the preceding months gradually moved toward a compromise on the voting system as well. During the last negotiations on the constitution in Brussels, however, just prior to the elections in 2004, Aznar refused once again to give sufficient concessions and demanded a two-thirds majority to make qualified majority decisions. This was still a very high number. In consequence of this attitude, the Germans and the French decided to leave the negotiating room. The signing of the treaty was blocked and Europe suddenly found itself without the perspective of an adequate juridical frame to meet the challenges imposed by the disintegration of the Warsaw Pact. Aznar then offered some last-minute reductions that could in no way resolve the situation. A sensation of paralysis spread to the European capitals, and when the government of Zapatero took office, the constitutional process was in dire straits. This was the scene behind Moratinos'

[22] U.S. Department of State, Secretary Rumsfeld Briefs at the Foreign Press Center, January 22, 2003. http://archive.defense.gov/Transcripts/Transcript.aspx?TranscriptID=1330.

[23] Moratinos Files: Interview, Villarino.

first official trip to Dublin in April 2004 and also goes to show—from a European perspective—the need for a different Spanish approach.[24]

By March 2004, it was the general Spanish belief that the system itself of double qualified majority mentioned in the draft for the constitutional treaty was unlikely to change. A Europe with ten new member states could simply not function with the system imposed by the Treaty of Nice, yet it was equally clear that it was necessary to improve the current council proposal, whereby a decision could pass if it enjoyed only a 50% majority of the votes representing 60% of the population.[25] It was calculated that Spain might theoretically lose 90% of the votes in the council with the proposed changes. It is also important to bear in mind that due to the Treaty of Nice, Spain had already lost fourteen seats in the European Parliament, something which contributed to making the new proposal even more unpalatable. However, in order to make some concessions to the Spanish side, the Irish presidency considered not only increasing the number of Spanish EU parliamentarians, but also a system of 50–50% majority, in which four states comprising at least one-third of the population of the EU could block the proposal. In addition, if the Council was not acting on a proposal from the Commission or on the initiative of the Union's ministers for foreign affairs, the required qualified majority was to comprise two-thirds of the members of the council, representing at least half of the population of the union. However, four or more members of the council representing at least a third of the population of the union could still block the proposal. Suffice it to say that the question of decision-making was particularly sensitive with regard to foreign and security policies, clearly the ultimate expression of national sovereignty.

At this stage, the Spanish negotiators carefully outlined to Moratinos the positions of the different countries in view of the Intergovernmental Conference, just as they stressed that the major card to play was the shift of government in Spain. Moreover, the Irish presidency did not seem to have a strong interest in striking any particular kind of deal. All this added to the sensation that there was now much greater room for maneuver. However, a major unknown was the French position, as in different circumstances Paris had let it be known that they much preferred a "two-speed Europe" given

[24] Moratinos Files: Interview, Moratinos.

[25] For a further discussion of the concept of qualified majority within the EU, see Camilo Villarino, *Un Mundo en cambio. Perspectivas de la política exterior de la Unión Europea* (Barcelona: Icaria Antrazyt, 2009), 41.

their reluctant attitude toward Eastern enlargement and their disagreement with the previous Italian presidency, who in their view had given too many concessions to the new member states. The German position was rather that those who pay and traditionally lead the European Union must be heard the most—also in the future European constellation. Great Britain had by March 2004 not yet revealed its position but until this stage had carefully resisted all the Franco-German overtures to join a triple directory that could lead the enlargement. Presumably, Britain was eager to protect itself from qualified majority decisions on fiscal issues and the regulation of the financial sector.

On 19 May, Moratinos summed up the state of affairs before the Spanish Parliament. On election day, he said, the Spanish population "had voted Europe" adding that the last eighteen years since joining the EC/EU had been the most prosperous in Spanish history. For the same reason, it was of the utmost importance that Spain now contributed positively to the fifth and ongoing enlargement round, not only because new flourishing markets in Eastern Europe awaited, but also because Spain, after decades of dictatorship, had been able to consolidate its own democracy and market economy thanks to its own entry into the EC. This historical lesson should never be forgotten. Accordingly, Spain was morally obliged to engage constructively in all negotiations, including the question of future financial settlements for each member state which would be affected by the enlargement. Thus, Spain was even willing to pay a price (implicitly to become a net contributor to the European Union), but only if other member states showed the same kind of responsible attitude. Furthermore, it was considered important to move forward with the internal market and in matters of justice as well as in foreign affairs. Finally, Spain should engage further in the new security and defense policies of Europe.[26]

It was, however, of the utmost importance to Spain that the enlargement was preceded by a European constitution which could provide a proper juridical framework. The rationale of the new government was thus—in line with the positions of France and Germany—first to *deepen* European integration and then to *enlarge* the Union with the new Eastern European members. Moratinos expressed high hopes that the new constitution could

---

[26]Cf. Speech of the Foreign Minister in the Parliamentary Committee on Foreign Affairs, May 19, 2004, in *La política exterior de España: balance y debates parlamentarios (2004–2008)* (Madrid: Real Instituto Elcano de Estudios Internacionales y Estratégicos, 2007), 15.

be approved during the next Council meeting in Ireland on 18 July, and even though Spain was strongly in favor of changing the voting system in the Council toward qualified majority decisions, the government was also keen on assuring that Spain's votes would have the right counterweight in case a majority of the member states wanted to push through decisions which severely damaged the interests of Spain. In other words, the fundamental historical compromises regarding European solidarity between bigger and smaller nations, which until this day had been the cornerstone of European integration, should still be upheld.[27]

At an early point in the negotiations, it seemed as though Prime Minister Zapatero was very close to striking an exceptionally good deal for Spain on the question of how to lower the percentage of population needed to block a proposal in the Council. In fact, after one of the council meetings, Zapatero went to speak privately with Schröder and Chirac, but as he was not sufficiently proficient in foreign languages, he brought Moratinos with him as interpreter. During their conversation, Zapatero tried to convince his foreign interlocutors that they had to offer a proper concession to Spain, and thanks to Zapatero's personal status with Chirac and Schröder the latter two were actually ready to meet his request. However, at this crucial point, their conversation attracted the attention of Reinhard Silberberg, the German Vice Minister for European Politics in the *Bundeskanzleramt* and Schröder's man of confidence. Under normal circumstances, Silberberg would never have dared to join a private conversation between three heads of government, but when he saw that Moratinos was present, albeit only as interpreter, he introduced himself into the circle and effectively ditched Zapatero's proposal.

In the end, the Zapatero government followed much of the advice it had received from the senior diplomats involved in the previous negotiations. Importantly, Zapatero did not formally depart from Aznar's position (the demand for a two-thirds majority). Yet, his foreign minister did let it be known to his European colleagues in one of his interventions that Spain was "absolutely" convinced that a compromise could be reached within the Irish presidency. This was an indirect way of saying that Spain would accept a proposal below 66.6%, but the Presidency would have to improve its offer with regard to the possibility of blocking decisions. Moratinos' underlying point was that it would politically unwise ("un 'sinsentido' politico") for

---

[27] Ibid., 15.

the Council to adopt decisions that 160 million Europeans were opposed
to. His main argument was thus built around the principle of the legitimacy of the state and the legitimacy of the people.[28] Spain nevertheless
refused many of the new proposals on the table, and in Moratinos's view,
the Spanish team negotiated hard and long, but always with the objective of
returning to the center of gravity of European politics. After three months
of negotiations, the Council finally gave Spain figures that were very close
to the position held by Aznar. In this way, the Conservative opposition
in Spain could not claim that the new government had sold out Spanish
sovereignty. However, a good argument can be made that the final result
came about because Chirac and Schröder saw Zapatero as a reliable partner.

There are, however, some discrepancies between Moratinos's version
of the negotiations and that of one of the diplomats involved. The diplomat holds that rather than Spanish pressures, it was Poland which deserves
credit for the satisfactory end result. In his view, the Poles were left to fight
alone, yet in the end, they secured a good result also for the Spanish government whose principal merit was to have regained the seats lost in the
European Parliament. Before his official appointment as minister, Moratinos had traveled to Poland to explain the Spanish position, and although
the Spanish delegation was warmly received, according to the diplomat's
version the Poles were nevertheless disappointed by the fact that the new
government was departing from Aznar's position. Moratinos, on the other
hand, stresses that the new Polish government actually agreed with his view
that the previous positions were no longer sustainable and that an accom-
modation with France and Germany had to be found. The Poles, however,
had different opinions on a series of other issues, but not on the need to
reconsider their hitherto intransigent position on the voting system.[29]

Regardless of which of the two versions is closest to the truth, it is
important to bear in mind what was actually at stake for Spain. Formally,
the negotiations were about whether a sense of national sovereignty might
be infringed by future votes in the council. Yet in reality, one should not
overrate the significance of the double majority system. One might argue
that Aznar's previous blockade was to a large extent exaggerated, as decisions in the council are normally made in full agreement in order not to
break with European unity. And on the rare occasion that unity is broken, as

---

[28] Moratinos Files: Interview, Moratinos.

[29] Moratinos Files: Interview with Moratinos; private information given to the author.

was the recent case with the refugee crisis in 2015, the Council's decision is simply not applied. The voting system which is mentioned in the treaties is primarily meant to put pressure on single member states to actively engage in common solutions. The bottom line is probably that some members of the Spanish diplomacy were more sensitive to Aznar's position, which in their view should objectively have been shared by many more medium and small member states. However, Aznar's intransigent attitude—they also admit—had by the end of 2003 become a serious problem for Spain.

In sum, a good argument can be made that the compromise-seeking line of the Zapatero government made sense. Nevertheless, it immediately came under fire over the new EU deal. Zapatero's handling of the negotiations was instantly characterized as "weak and clumsy" by the opposition. Angel Acebes, Vice Secretary-General of the Conservative PP, furthermore claimed to Reuters, "We had the same weight as Germany, France, Italy and the United Kingdom. Now Germany has twice the weight of Spain and the others 50% more than us. Clearly, this is bad for Spain."[30] In contrast, the government underlined that it was unrealistic to maintain only two votes fewer than Germany while having half its population. Zapatero had therefore accepted the constitution principle that most EU laws would pass by a double majority. As a result, they were satisfied with the deal which ensured that 55% of member states representing at least 65% of the EU's population would be required to take most decisions. Zapatero maintained that the deal had augmented Spain's capacity for influence, just as Spain would regain the seats in the European Parliament that Aznar had previously lost.[31] Moratinos added for his part that the deal had actually improved the role and influence of Spain.[32] Vice Prime Minister María Teresa de la Vega followed by saying that Europe's main powers "have acknowledged us and respected our weight and influence. We are satisfied."[33]

[30]"Spanish Government Under Fire Over EU Charter Deal," *Reuters*, June 19, 2004.

[31]"Zapatero: España ha dejado su huella y gana capacidad influencia," *EFE*, June 19, 2004.

[32]"Spanish Government Under Fire Over EU Charter Deal," *Reuters*, June 19, 2004.

[33]"Spanish Opposition Says Government Blundered in Constitutional Talks," *AP*, June 19, 2004. For a useful reflection on Zapatero's European policy during 2004–2007 see Esther Barbé and Laia Mestres, "La España de Zapatero en Europa. El aprendizaje de la negociación en una Unión Europea en crisis," *Quórum. Revista de pensamiento iberoamericano*, no. 19 (2007): 72–79.

In spite of the difficult EU negotiations, the first months of 2005 were also a period filled with illusion and hope, and to give proof of Spain's newfound Europeanism, Zapatero proposed holding the first European referendum on the new treaty on 20 February 2005. The campaign material prepared by the PSOE stressed that the treaty should give new impetus to a new historic project aiming to overcome the long history of wars and inner divisions in Europe. It also stressed the Spanish social and economic backlog with regard to the rest of Europe, and the political isolation and the lack of freedom suffered under General Franco's dictatorship. To vote yes to Europe, the PSOE argued in line with a classical liberal argument in Spain, was to vote for progress, modernity and freedom.[34] With a positive outcome to the vote, the government would have achieved its three stated objectives: to have the constitution completed within the time span of the Irish presidency, to increase Spain's influence and to have Spain seen as a "constructor of Europe, which does not block and which serves as a point of encounter."[35]

Indeed, Europe was integrating and growing, important reforms were being made in multiple fields, and Europe had revealed itself as a foreign player who had been able to put its foot down with regard to the war in Iraq and force the Americans to reconsider their unilateral approach. Furthermore, Europe wanted joint policies, a constitution, a flag and a national anthem. Looking back, it would have been impossible for European leaders to imagine, then, that ten years ahead Europe would be in deep crisis, with Great Britain leaving the union. The PSOE government felt by 2005 that it had played a prominent role in creating a new Europe which ought to culminate with the approval of the new European constitution. Apart from its apparent symbolic value, the constitution should also serve to stimulate joint political actions, especially in foreign affairs.[36]

The referendum was complicated, though, because it was also a test of the legitimacy of the new government, which was accused of being in office thanks only to Al Qaeda. Moratinos even betrayed his own credentials as a fervent supporter of the Spanish football club Atlético Madrid and visited

---

[34]Moratinos Files: PSOE: "Guía de campaña. Referéndum constitución europea," January 2005, 4.

[35]"El Gobierno invitará a la oposición a debatir la mejor fórmula para ratificar la Constitución Europea," *El Mundo*, June 19, 2004. https://www.elmundo.es/elmundo/2004/06/19/internacional/1087652729.html.

[36]Moratinos Files: Interview, Moratinos.

the Bernabeu Stadium of Real Madrid on Sundays to rally support for the vote, which despite low participation was won by a very large margin (77% yes vote).[37] However, the subsequent French and Dutch votes paralyzed the process of European integration. This was probably one of the most significant negative moments in the entire history of the European Union.

After the failed vote in France and the Netherlands, grave political errors occurred one after the other. Above all, the enlargement process was allowed to continue more or less as if nothing had happened. The rationale of the constitutional process had hitherto been "first to deepen, then to enlarge," which meant that the admittance of ten new member states in the midst of a constitutional crisis would prove fatal to the new integration project. Moratinos used the metaphor of a "house" to explain this very point. That in order to welcome family members in exile into your home after forty years apart, you first have to renovate your house: "You cannot have twenty people sitting in a living room that was meant for three people or have daily arguments about who is to sleep in the master bedroom. These things have to be fixed before you invite your new family in."[38] With hindsight, Western European leaders probably also underestimated the lack of democratic tradition in Eastern Europe. True, liberal democracy had been installed there after World War I, but these eastern European democracies rapidly took an authoritarian turn. Political pluralism and the separation of powers are now under attack in both Poland and Hungary.[39]

To cope with the failed referendums in Holland and France, Zapatero summoned Moratinos, Almunia and Solana to the Moncloa. During a meeting in June 2005, they agreed to go ahead with a project for a new treaty, as also proposed by other member states. After the summer crisis and the appointment of Barroso as new President of the Commission, difficult negotiations started between members still favoring a constitution and members foreseeing difficulties with too advanced or strong symbolic

---

[37] José Manuel Romero, "El 'sí' vence por mayoría aplastante en referéndum que registra una abstención del 57%," *El País*, February 21, 2005. https://elpais.com/diario/2005/02/21/espana/1108940401_850215.html.

[38] Moratinos Files: Interview, Moratinos.

[39] Cf. Martin Eiermann, Yascha Mounk, and Limor Gultchin, "Populism: Trends, Threats and Future Prospects," *Report of the Tony Blair Institute for Global Change*, December 2017. https://institute.global/insight/renewing-centre/european-populism-trends-threats-and-future-prospects.

integration. In the end, it was eventually up to the German EU presidency to polish the final text of what later became the Treaty of Lisbon, signed in 2007. Practically everything was settled by the Germans before the Portuguese presidency, and much of what was stated in the failed constitutional treaty was added as an appendix to the new mini-treaty, but the social dimension and not least the strong symbolism of having a European constitution (although it was technically a treaty) was lost in the main text. The elimination of the flag, hymn and the constitution were seen by the Spanish government as damaging in the long run because symbols matter. Momentum was also lost with regard to further integration in matters of security and foreign affairs, just as human rights were no longer considered a core issue.[40]

Looking back, including to the economic crisis which struck Europe in 2008, nearly a decade was lost while Europe was trying to define itself and its institutional corpus. When the Treaty of Lisbon finally came into force in January 2010, European leaders of constitutionalist belief were happy that all the hard work had resulted in a new deal. Yet they soon realized that the world had changed and that this mini-treaty was inadequate for the purpose of European integration and unable to solve the impending European debt crisis.[41]

Importantly, the new enlargement under unclear constitutional circumstances challenged Spain's possibilities of playing a central role in European politics in the years to come. Accordingly, much of the domestic criticism against the Zapatero government was based on a false premise. Zapatero was criticized—also by a part of the intellectual left—for not fighting for the Spanish cause in the European arena in the same dedicated way as Aznar had done, as he always preferred to stay second in line. Moreover, critics argued that his foreign minister was much more interested in Mediterranean questions, the Middle East or Latin America for that matter, leaving the otherwise pro-European Spanish government with no clear objectives or priorities in its European policies.[42] This criticism was objectively wrong. As we have seen throughout this chapter, the Socialist government,

---

[40] Moratinos Files: Interview, Moratinos.

[41] Ibid.

[42] See, for example, the criticism raised by José Ignacio Torreblanca, "La insoportable levedad de la política europea de España (2008–2011)," in *España en crisis. Balance de la segunda legislatura de Rodríguez Zapatero*, ed. César Colino y Ramón Cotarelo (Valencia: Tirant Humanidades, 2012), 455–472.

and Zapatero in particular, ended Spanish isolation in the EU, just as the Spanish prime minister contributed substantially to the new constitutional treaty, not least by submitting it to a very successful referendum. Moreover, Spain worked closely with the German government on the downscaling of the new Treaty of Lisbon. As documented, however, it was not within the reach of the Zapatero government, during either its first or second mandate, to decisively influence those Western European member states which suddenly began to question the value of the European project or, for that matter, alter the profoundly different views held by the Eastern European partners on a wide range of issues. Spain could not undo the structural deficiencies of the new European construction—neither could Germany, as far as that was concerned. As the next chapter reveals, Spain was actually one of the most foremost defenders of a new pan-European settlement which could finally overcome the end of the Cold War and provide Europe with a new political vision for the twenty-first century—a fact that seems to have been largely forgotten or overseen in both the Spanish and international debate.

4.2 Boomerangs

When the PSOE took office in 2004, it coincided with a crucial period of European integration. Whereas the generation of politicians of 1958 had envisioned a Europe with a common market, and the generation of 1990 a Europe with a single currency, the politicians of the new millennium asked themselves the question of how to form an even greater European alliance. This new vision not only included the ten new aspiring EU members of the East; through its European Neighborhood Policies (ENP), it also aimed at further integration with countries further to the east of the EU and to the south of the Mediterranean.[43] One of the greatest challenges in this regard was how to reach a more permanent settlement with the Russian Federation, the former Soviet enemy, which continued to express concerns not only over the ongoing EU enlargement, but also over the eastward expansion of NATO and President Bush's plans for a missile defense system to be stationed in several eastern European countries. The ENP policies were originally also meant to include Russia, yet Moscow had declined this

---

[43] For a contemporary perspective on the ENP in this period, see among many other contributions: Esther Barbé and Elisabeth Johansson-Nogués, "The EU as a Modest 'Force for Good': The European Neighbourhood Policy," *International Affairs*, vol. 84, issue 1 (2008).

idea since relations between the EU and Russia were seen as being of a qualitatively different nature.[44]

Due to its rapprochement with the Franco-German axis, Spain was from the very beginning of Zapatero's premiership allowed a supporting role in the ongoing discussions about a new Euro-Russian arrangement concerning multiple issues which ranged from trade and mobility to security matters. On 18 March 2005, Schröder, Chirac, Putin and Zapatero met in Paris, where they discussed the situation in Syria and Lebanon, in particular, and where Zapatero officially acknowledged the importance of a new agreement with Moscow on collective security. The four leaders further used the summit to promote the French government's yes-campaign in the upcoming referendum on the European constitution. Zapatero's and Moratinos' trips to the Russian capital during the spring of 2005 only confirmed the seriousness of these proposals and that Spain had been included in the inner circles of European politics.[45]

Seen against this background of pan-European optimism, it becomes even harder to understand or perhaps even accept that over the last fifteen years the continent has rapidly moved away from a scenario where the European Union and Russia were collaborating and integrating along the historical axis of European politics, to a situation of mutual mistrust and incessant crises, often followed by Western sanctions and Russian cyberattacks against Western infrastructures. The recent crises in Crimea and Ukraine are but the latest examples of a more general conflict which began to escalate in 2008, first over the question of Kosovo's future as an independent state and a few months later over the Russian-Georgian War. Explaining this breakdown in EU-Russian relations is probably one of the most important and difficult European research questions of our time.

Without doubt, those European governments advocating for more collaboration with Russia were not happy with developments during 2007–2008. Crucially, the Spanish government concluded that much more political capital should be invested in renewing the EU's relationship with Russia. In fact, high-level bilateral encounters with Russia had rapidly decreased in the years following the failed French referendum in 2005. Furthermore, Angela Merkel, who became *Bundeskanzlerin* the same year,

---

[44] Magone, *Contemporary European Politics*, 579. For a useful overview of Europe's different policy initiatives in defense and security matters see: Félix Arteaga Martín, "La política europea de seguridad y defensa," *Cuadernos de estrategia*, no. 145 (2010): 31–67.

[45] *Anuario Internacional CIDOB*, 2005, entries for March 18, May 9 and June 16, 2005.

and Sarkozy, who was elected president in 2007, did not display the same level of enthusiasm for Putin and Medvedev as Schröder and Chirac had previously done. Importantly, in one of the subsequent Franco-German summits with Russia, Merkel decided not to include Zapatero in the ongoing talks with Russia.[46] Thus, the arrival of Merkel, born and raised in East Germany, clearly marked a change in the Euro-Russian relationship, yet to reduce the crisis of confidence simply to her personal lack of trust toward the former Eastern hegemon is clearly not a satisfying answer. Furthermore, Sarkozy actually maintained cordial relations with Russia, as shown by the impressive level of French investments in Russia and also the successful mediation by France during the Russo-Georgian War in August 2008.[47]

In spite of the growing Franco-German skepticism, the Spanish continued to work for the creation of a common Euro-Russian area that could also give a fresh new dimension to the European Union. Spanish optimism was not just fostered by Moratinos' and Zapatero's meetings in August and September 2007 with their respective Russian counterparts, Lavrov and Putin.[48] What particularly contributed to Spanish optimism was the much-awaited takeover by Medvedev as President in 2008. In contrast to Putin's nationalist agenda, Medvedev was clearly more focused on promoting a new sense of Russian citizenship. His political discourse was more centered on civil society and not so much on Mother Russia. Thus, when the new Spanish ambassador, Juan Antonio March, arrived in the Russian capital in February 2008, it was considered the right moment for launching ambitious new ideas and projects that could play along with Medvedev's more progressive political visions.[49]

---

[46] Moratinos Files: Interview, Moratinos.

[47] See below.

[48] Besides stressing the value of increased Russia-EU collaboration, the two leaders also agreed to a Memorandum of Understanding, promoting the Russian-Spanish Civil Society Dialogue Forum. Cf. "España-Rusia. Moratinos apuesta nueva relación Rusia, a la que exige compromisos y actitudes," *EFE*, September 11, 2007; "Moratinos llega a Moscú para preparar la visita de Zapatero," *La Vanguardia*, August 29, 2007. http://www.lavanguardia.com/politica/20070829/53389370404/moratinos-llega-a-moscu-para-preparar-la-visita-de-zapatero.html; "President Vladimir Putin Held Talks with Spanish Prime Minister Jose Luis Rodrigo Zapatero," Website of the President of Russia, September 28, 2007. http://en.kremlin.ru/events/president/news/42705.

[49] Moratinos Files: Interview, Juan Antonio March.

It was within this context of renewed optimism that Spain tried to advance a new European proposal to eliminate visas for Russians visiting the European Union and, vice versa, Europeans visiting the Russian Federation. Intelligence communities in the West would of course have been highly alarmed by such a measure, as they have always feared that uncontrolled Russian access to the West might stimulate further subversive intelligence activities. Yet, March and other diplomats fully believed that such a proposal carried no significant security risks, as the Kremlin had traditionally been able to introduce Russian "illegals," i.e., Russian "sleeper agents" into the West anyway, without arising the suspicion of the Western intelligence services—even in periods of strong Western surveillance. In other words, if the Russians truly wanted to take such subversive action against members of the European Union, they could do so with or without a visa program. The benefits clearly outnumbered the risks and according to this proposal, instead of traveling to places where a visa was not required, such as Turkey or Latin America, Russians would now easily be able to travel to Europe and in this way further mutual integration, tourism and investments.[50]

Critics of this plan pointed to the fact that the Russians were not ready yet to replicate such a drastic proposal from the EU. This may very well have been so, as Moscow's approach to foreigners visiting Russia has always been that after a few days' stay they must report their whereabouts to the police. However, during the Spanish presidency of the EU in the first half of 2010, Spain nevertheless obtained a Russian promise that they would immediately replicate such an opening from the EU. As it turned out, the problem was not so much Russia. Spain was simply not allowed by the other twenty-seven EU member states to even submit their proposal to the Council. France and Italy supported the initiative, though, and the UK was not expected to pose any major obstacles either, as they were not part of the Schengen Treaty in the first place. Above all, it was Germany who decided against it, out of concern for Turkey. Istanbul had waited for decades for a similar arrangement, and there was no way that the Russians could supersede the Turks on this matter.[51]

It is not unthinkable, however, that Moscow would have replicated the Spanish proposal, had been it accepted by the Council, because it perfectly

---

[50] Moratinos Files: Interview, March.

[51] Ibid.

matched the new vision of Medvedev of putting citizens at the center of gravity of Russian politics. On the other hand, one could also question if Russia would seriously have considered a proposal that had the potential to profoundly change the forma mentis of the Russian state. The fact that with this proposal, foreigners would have been able to stay in Russia for 120 days without explaining their whereabouts would have constituted an enormous change of mentality. Regardless of the outcome, the Spanish proposal—had it prospered—would no doubt have given the Europeans a great advantage in future negotiations with Russia, as they would have been able to point to the fact that they were indeed complying with common plans for mutual integration, while Russia was not. Moreover, it would have provided a new vehicle for economic growth in a period of international economic stagnation. Russia would not have felt isolated, and in addition, it would have boosted Medvedev's project of modernizing Russia against the more nationalist groups represented by Putin.

The possibility of freedom of movement from Gibraltar to Magadan did indeed have the potential to convert the Euro-Russian area into a very powerful alliance. Russian politicians, one diplomat told me, often joke about the fact that Russia is very good at turning money into science, but not the other way around. Yet with the Western tradition for small businesses specialized in exactly the opposite kind of knowledge transfer, from science to invoice, the potential of such cooperation would be enormous. Zapatero reckons that the failure of an overall new Euro-Russian arrangement essentially owed to obstacles put forward by the ten new member EU states, whereas March, the ambassador, instead believes that the bottom line was that the Europeans did not feel powerful enough to see such a project through. Germany was truly sensitive to the concerns of its Eastern neighbors, yet probably also felt unsure about how the Americans would react to a de facto Euro-Russian unification on such important topics.[52]

With regard to security matters, a major problem was no doubt the profound skepticism of the Eastern European countries' toward Russia, which collided with Western European ideas for a new European axis running from Paris through Berlin to Moscow. This tension was present in all the meetings in the European Council that Zapatero participated in. Merkel was recognized by her colleagues as a person who would always seek to create balance, and for this reason, she probably appeared to the wider public

[52] Moratinos Files: Interview, March; Zapatero.

to be far less "European" and visionary than she actually was. Merkel would, however, always want to enter into all the concrete details and problems of the questions on the table. Above all, Germany showed special concern for Poland which was again leading the opposition against a deeper alignment with Russia. Essentially, Zapatero experienced the problems with Russia as being closely related to the unwillingness of the Eastern countries to commit to their giant Eastern neighbor. Russia in turn wanted to be seen as an international power to be reckoned with. Not as the old USSR, but still as an important international actor. The fact that Russia did not feel that it was being recognized as such probably contributed to the deterioration of the relationship with the EU. The great structural problem beneath it all, however, was in Zapatero's interpretation the attitude of the ten new EU member states.[53]

To this profound skepticism of Eastern Europe, however, we must add a series of events which rapidly worsened the relationship with Russia. In particular, Moscow did not relish the rapid expansion of NATO to the East, and President Bush's plans for a missile defense system, formally directed at "rogue states," was seen by Moscow as an unnecessary provocation. Moreover, during his second term, the recognition of an independent Kosovo—strongly opposed by Russia—grew into a real obsession for President Bush, who exercised great pressure on Madrid and other skeptical European governments which feared the precedent that such recognition might have for their own countries. Zapatero's constant feeling was that sometimes the great geopolitical power struggles were played in areas of less strategic importance, such as the Balkans at this specific time in history compared to, for example, the Middle East. Importantly, the United States maintained its pressure on the most skeptical European states even after Obama took office. In many ways, the Balkans, like other areas of potential conflict, soon became emblematic of the overall relationship of force between "the big players" in international politics.[54] Therefore, it is probably fair to say that the EU's capacity for diminishing tension in the area was to some degree limited by the traditional major actors of the Cold War: United States, Russia and also China.

A major obstacle to a new European security arrangement was, as it turned out, the future of Kosovo after the end of the Yugoslavian civil war.

[53] Moratinos Files: Interview, Zapatero.
[54] Ibid.

In fact, the Balkans had been a constant cause for friction in the US-Russian relationship since the collapse of the USSR, and with Putin as president between 2000 and 2008, the Kremlin's position hardened even more. To many Russians, the Kremlin's active role in facilitating the capitulation of the Serbs in 1999 was seen as Boris Yeltsin's single greatest foreign policy mistake. Putin was thus determined to block any attempt of the West to simply push through the independence of Kosovo.[55] Kosovo had been under UN control since 1999 and was now seeking independence after the war between militant Kosovo-Albanian separatists and the Yugoslavian army. In contrast to the position of the Serbs and their Russian allies, the independence of Kosovo was high on the US and EU agenda, and negotiations were already at an advanced stage when the PSOE seized power in 2004. This year also witnessed increasingly violent confrontations between Serbs and Kosovars.

The negotiations on Kosovo were led by Martti Ahtisaari, a special envoy of the United Nations who was later awarded the Nobel Peace Prize in 2008 for his capacity to resolve international conflicts. Yet his task was complicated by the fact that Moscow blocked UN decisions on Kosovo, arguing that Ahtisaari failed to take Russian or Serbian concerns seriously.[56] Unable to find a negotiated solution at the UN level, in 2007 Ahtisaari presented the Comprehensive Proposal for the Kosovo Status Settlement (known as the Ahtisaari Plan), which ultimately recommended independence for Kosovo.[57] Moratinos knew Ahtisaari from his own time as a special envoy to the Middle East, and he had the greatest respect for him. However, when the two occasionally met in Vienna to discuss the proposal for a unilateral Kosovan declaration of independence, Moratinos expressed his own doubts and urged new negotiations between the Serbs and the Kosovars. He soon realized, however, that the cards had already been dealt: The United States had de facto guaranteed the independence of Kosovo, something which made the Kosovan delegation completely unwilling to strike any sort of compromise with the Serbs or commit to any serious negotiation.[58]

[55] Angela E. Stent, *The Limits of Partnership. US-Russian Relations in the Twenty-First Century* (Princeton, NJ: Princeton University Press, 2013), 159–160.

[56] Stent, *The Limits of Partnership*, 160.

[57] Rice, *No Higher Honor*, 682.

[58] Moratinos Files: Interview, Moratinos.

After the G8 summit in Heiligendamm on 9 June 2007, President Bush publicly endorsed Kosovan independence at a press conference in Rome. "One more month," President Bush told Condoleezza Rice the following day, "and then we recognize them if we have to do it alone. I've promised them, and we have to carry through."[59] Still, to pay lip service to the attempts of other countries wanting to mediate in the conflict, he agreed to the French proposal of extending negotiations for another 120 days, underlining however that this would be the final delay. After this, there would be full US recognition.[60] This clearly upset the Russians and also the Chinese, who in this particular case followed the Russian line due to concern over what the independence of Kosovo might mean to China's grip on Tibet.

Fully aware of the importance of having Spain on board in order to obtain full European recognition, Kosovan officials began contacting the Spanish Foreign Office. The Kosovars always had doubts about Moratinos, as he had been posted early in his career to the Spanish embassy in Belgrade. In fact, he was widely regarded as pro-Serbian. In the beginning, the Kosovars were nonetheless convinced that Spain would eventually adhere to the almost unanimous common position of the EU countries which supported the US approach. However, Moratinos consulted with Zapatero and the king and behind closed doors also with the leaders of the PP, and they all reached the unanimous conclusion that it was necessary to defend the historical position of Spain, which is to respect the territorial integrity of other recognized countries. This position was of course influenced by Spain's problem in Catalonia and above all the Basque Country, where the local government was defying Madrid over the so-called Ibarretxe Plan and other similar separatist moves. For this exact reason, Spain was afraid that the unilateral declaration of independence of Kosovo would create a dangerous precedent for Spain.[61]

The moment the other Western powers realized that Spain would not fall in with the common position, all kind of pressures started building up, including from inside Spain, where strongly pro-American opinion makers

[59] Rice, *No Higher Honor*, 683.

[60] Ibid., 683.

[61] Moratinos Files: Interview, Moratinos.

began writing newspaper comments to modify the policy of the government. Very strong criticism was also launched personally against Moratinos, who also felt the pressure from within his own ranks, as Javier Solana, who in 1998 had authorized the bombing of Belgrade, was very much in line with the US position. These pressures aiming to weaken the Spanish position were ably exploited by the PP in public, Moratinos admits, even though the opposition party in private actually shared the government's view.[62]

The political process around Kosovo accelerated because Ahtisaari had prepared the plan for independence exceptionally well, with clear milestones and an ultimatum which was clearly unpalatable to the Serbs. Thus, it was only a matter of time before independence would be declared. In front of his European colleagues, Moratinos somewhat sarcastically compared the eagerness with which they implemented Ahtisaari's plan with their unwillingness to employ exactly the same measures in favor of the Palestinians due to their concerns for Israel. The card had been dealt, however, and there were never any real negotiation, in spite of the fact that there was now a different Serbian leadership with a Western-leaning President, Boris Tadić. The Serbs simply had to pay for the horrors of the Milosevic regime, in line with the demand of international public opinion. However, after the declaration of independence was adopted on 17 February 2008, it remained clear that Greece, Rumania, Slovakia, Cyprus and Spain were unwilling to recognize Kosovo out of similar territorial concerns. The entire process naturally upset the Russians as well as the Chinese, who on their side were completely insensitive to the Western claim that the mutual history of Serbs and Kosovars was too bloody to allow for proper negotiations between the two parties.[63]

On 31 January 2008, three weeks prior to the day Kosovan independence was declared, a Spanish diplomatic envoy had a rather unpleasant encounter with a high-rank US official, who acted aggressively and showed no sensitivity toward the Spanish position.[64] The Americans were furious that Spain wanted to delay the European recognition of Kosovo until March, after the upcoming Spanish general elections. In contrast, the Spanish side insisted on the need to create European consensus on Kosovo. In

[62] Ibid.

[63] Moratinos Files: Interview Moratinos; Stent, *The Limits of Partnership*, 161–162.

[64] Moratinos Files: Private information.

fact, Spain's official policy on Kosovo was based on two principles: respect for international law and full agreement among all the members of the EU. For the same reasons, Spain could not accept a unilateral declaration of independence. As it turned out, the United States was completely insensitive to the fact that the upcoming general elections in Spain might be deeply affected by a complacent Spanish attitude toward the Kosovan question. Thus, Spain made it clear that the United States should understand that Spain had already made an enormous sacrifice by accepting an EU policy line which was not one which Spain relished. Spain had already publicly accepted the idea of future de facto independence for Kosovo without formal Spanish recognition as the lesser evil in order to save European unity.

Seemingly, the US administration underestimated, disregarded, or had no knowledge of what the case of Kosovo truly meant to a country like Spain with its long history of tensions and disputes between its center and periphery. However, in discussions with his Greek counterpart Dora Bakoyannis, who was under similar US pressure, Moratinos was encouraged to soften the Spanish position. Moratinos reiterated, however, that Spain could only accept Kosovo as a new state if the declaration of independence was accepted by a resolution in the UN Security Council (impossible to achieve due to the Russian and Chinese positions) or if a negotiated solution with the Serbs was found. A unilateral declaration with no clear foundation in international law was not only a violation of the rights of Serbia, Moratinos reiterated, it also implied great risks for Spain. For tactical reasons, though, Spain often used the case of Gibraltar rather than the Basque Country and Catalonia in its formal arguments.[65]

Spain was, of course, not blind to the fact that the majority of European powers favored a unilateral solution for Kosovo. So a new formula was finally found in the Council by which the EU in its own subtle way recognized Kosovo, yet separate states could express their dissent or reservations in a footnote. Importantly, in international law, the recognition of a new country is the prerogative of the state and not of a supranational organ. For this reason, Spain could maintain that it had not formally recognized Kosovo but accepted that other states did so individually, and that the EU "took note" of the new Kosovan state although juridically it was not the

---

[65] Moratinos Files: Interview, Moratinos.

same thing as formal recognition. On Monday 18 February 2008, follow-ing the unilateral declaration of independence, the EU foreign ministers adopted a common text which according to EU expert comments at the time was a clear concession to Spain which had refused the earlier drafts outright.[66] To its defenders in the Council, Kosovo constituted a *sui generis* case that did not fit the territorial integrity principles of the UN Charter. Spain, Cyprus, Romania and Greece did not object to the final draft but they refused to recognize the new Kosovan state.[67]

Spain continued—as did Russia and China—to call for new negotia-tions between the Serbs and the Kosovars, and there were secret meetings in Paris to find new formulas of recognition. However, these talks were suspended after Anglo-American pressure, and when the Obama adminis-tration won the elections later that year with Hillary Clinton as the new sec-retary of state, the US position remained unaltered. Clinton even decided to circumvent normal diplomatic procedures by speaking directly to Zap-atero in order to persuade him to change the Spanish position on Kosovo. She mistakenly believed that the main obstacle to Spanish recognition was Moratinos' alleged pro-Serbian attitude. This was, however, a deep mis-understanding of what Kosovan independence actually meant for Spain. There was after all a unanimous agreement among the main political forces in Spain that the US position on Kosovo was damaging to Spanish interests. Clinton told Zapatero right out, "I think I have a problem with one of your ministers. Generally, I have a good relationship with Moratinos, but with regard to Kosovo, we are not on the same line. I think it's a personal thing that has to do with his previous posting in Belgrade. Prime Minister, I call upon you to resolve the case so that we can fix the recognition of Kosovo." Afterward, Zapatero told Moratinos that throughout their entire conversa-tion Clinton had complained to him that Moratinos was too inflexible and too hard on the question of Kosovo. The subsequent order from Zapatero to Moratinos was—unsurprisingly—"Keep up the hard line!"[68]

[66]"Main Results of the Council," EU Press release, February 18, 2008. https://www.consilium.europa.eu/ueDocs/cms_Data/docs/pressData/en/gena/98818.pdf; Elitsa Vucheva, "EU Fudges Kosovo Independence Recognition," *Euobserver*, February 18, 2008. https://euobserver.com/foreign/25684.

[67]Vucheva, "EU Fudges Kosovo Independence Recognition."

[68]Moratinos Files: Interview, Moratinos.

In the existing literature, there seems to be a rough agreement as to why the West's relationship with Russia deteriorated over the question of ex-Yugoslavia. Considerable disagreement or uncertainty, however, remains as to precisely what triggered the next East-West crisis over Georgia, a former Soviet republic and now an independent state determined to become a member of the NATO alliance. In fact, no objective account of the short Russian-Georgian War exists.[69] Yet no serious scholar would probably disagree that on the political level, the dramatic events in Georgia in August 2008 were in some way connected to the recent international recognition of Kosovo.

On 7 August, Georgian military forces launched a military operation in the pro-Russian territory of South Ossetia. At this specific time, the attention of the whole world was drawn to the opening ceremony of the Olympic Games in Beijing, which were about to begin the following day. On 8 August, the Russian military entered South Ossetia from North Ossetia, advancing rapidly toward the Georgian capital of Tbilisi. The Russians further occupied the Georgian city of Gori and took control of the port town of Poti after launching new military incursions from Abkhazia, another pro-Russian territory in Georgia. The Russian troops apparently stopped their advance only sixty kilometers from Tbilisi, letting the world understand that they would not advance any further. At the same time, pro-Russian paramilitary units in South Ossetia allegedly beleaguered Georgian minority groups, who started fleeing the area. The following day the UN Security Council assembled, and both the Russian and Georgian emissaries accused each other of having triggered a war that might have set the entire Caucasus on fire. At the following meeting on 10 August, the Security Council was unable to respond clearly to the crisis, as Russia threatened to veto any resolution which did not meet their demands.[70]

The situation might indeed have got out of hand had it not been for the swift mediation of the French EU presidency, which ably negotiated an armistice with both Georgian President Mikhail Saakashvili and later with Medvedev and Putin. Sarkozy apparently managed to make the two parties agree to two different drafts for a cease-fire, first with the Georgians and then with the Russians. Nevertheless, the trick worked as it effectively

[69]Forsberg and Seppo, "The Russo-Georgian War and EU Mediation," 124.

[70]This summary owes to Forsberg and Seppo, "The Russo-Georgian War and EU Mediation," 124–125.

stopped the hostilities. Afterward, Saakashvili—also due to American pressure—accepted the final plan that Sarkozy had developed with Medvedev and Putin. Still, the EU was disappointed that the Russians did not start withdrawing their troops as agreed. Not least, Russia's de facto recognition of the independence of Abkhazia and South Ossetia was a disappointment and was condemned by the EU on 26 August.[71] But how could the EU condemn Russian recognition when it was substantially no different from the one that the West had just conceded to Kosovo?

At the subsequent meeting in the Council, the various EU ministers of foreign affairs spoke one after the other, and they all expressed their anger and condemnation of Russia's violation of Georgia's territorial sovereignty. Moratinos replied to them as one of the last speakers, "I'm delighted, dear colleagues and friends, to hear you say that we should condemn the violation of the territorial integrity of Georgia, because didn't we just violate the territorial integrity of Yugoslavia? Where is the difference?" His colleagues reiterated that Kosovo was a *sui generis* case because of the UN's yearlong administration of the territory. To this Moratinos replied, "No – in international politics, precedents are like boomerangs. They come right back at you. And this is your boomerang!"[72] This assumption was evidently right, as has also been confirmed by the prominent American scholar of US-Russian relations, Angela E. Stent. Her recent research effectively demonstrates how after Kosovo President Putin made the West swallow its own medicine.[73]

Right after Kosovo's declaration of independence in February, the Russian foreign minister, Sergey Lavrov, had proclaimed that the recognition of this new state violated international law and warned of the consequences of this decision for international stability. Putin was even clearer in his condemnation, "This is a harmful and dangerous precedent – the Kosovo precedent is a terrible precedent – you can't observe one set of rules for Kosovo and another for Abkhazia and South Ossetia."[74] So what countermeasures did the Russians take? Right after recognition of Kosovo, the Russian Council of Federation as well as the Russian Duma declared that if Kosovo could declare its independence, then there were no impediments

---

[71] Ibid., 125–127.
[72] Moratinos Files: Interview, Moratinos.
[73] See Stent, *The Limits of Partnership*, chapter 7.
[74] Ibid., 161.

for South Ossetia and Abkhazia to do exactly the same. Of course, this raised concern in the West, which however saw few alternatives to Kosovan independence since in their view, neither the Russians nor the Serbs had forwarded any serious proposal for a solution to the crisis in ex-Yugoslavia. The Western hope was apparently that Russia would eventually understand the "common sense" of Kosovan independence. Later, those who favored this solution could take comfort in the fact that the International Court of Justice in an advisory opinion issued in 2010 actually argued that Kosovo's declaration had not violated the principles of international law.[75] Yet while post ex facto interpretations of international law are one thing, politics are another, and Putin certainly did not hesitate long before he let the West know precisely what the Russian position was.

To fully understand the Russian reaction, however, more elements need to be added to the political context. In April 2008 in Sochi, not far from the Georgian border, at their last formal bilateral encounter as presidents, Bush and Putin made progress on a number of issues, and Bush used the occasion to solemnly declare that the Cold War was over.[76] Still, the conflict in Georgia as well as US plans for a missile defense system hung over the Sochi summit like a dark cloud. As underlined by Angela Stent, a few days before at the NATO summit in Bucharest, US-Russian and US-European tensions had been running high, the most problematic issue being whether Ukraine and Georgia should be offered a Membership Action Plan (MAP), a kind of roadmap which spelled out what the country had to comply with in order to qualify for NATO membership. Suffice it to say that the previous inclusion of the Baltic countries into NATO in 2004 had not been relished by Moscow, and the prospect of both Ukraine and Georgia becoming new members was unpalatable to Russia, which probably feared a kind of encirclement. Importantly, influential figures in the US administration, including Condoleezza Rice and Robert Gates, also had doubts about the wisdom of this step, just as the Europeans were against it, but President Bush pushed all concerns aside, saying that the membership deal was part of his US Freedom Agenda.[77] At a very dramatic NATO summit, Merkel managed to strike a last-minute compromise by which the MAP was abandoned. Instead, a declaration was issued according to which, "We

[75] Ibid., 161–162.
[76] Ibid., 162–163.
[77] Ibid., 164.

agree today that Georgia and Ukraine will become members of NATO."[78] Needless to say, the Russians were very unhappy with the new formulation, which was perceived as sheer provocation although the MAP had actually been axed.

Meanwhile, tension between Georgia and Russia started to build up over the summer of 2008 and, much to the chagrin of the Russians, a US-led military exercise was completed just outside Tbilisi which included soldiers from Georgia, Ukraine, Azerbaijan and Ukraine—all former Soviet satellites. Yet the Russians too were beginning to make military preparations for a crisis, and Moscow soon demanded that Georgia sign a no-use-of-force pledge that could help to abate the crisis. Bush administration officials on the one hand supported Georgia's NATO aspirations, yet also warned against the use of force to persuade the rebellious regions of Abkhazia and South Ossetia. However, there were also members of the administration who apparently sent entirely different signals to President Saakashvili. So, the question pertinently raised by Angela Stent is whether the Georgian president actually understood that the Bush administration would not support him in a war with Russia? And as further argued in the memoirs of Condoleezza Rice, Saakashvili had previously triggered a conflict in another breakaway territory, Adjara, and actually benefitted from it since Georgia—also after international pressure—regained control of this part of the country.[79] So why not repeat the endeavor?

One Spanish diplomatic source told me—on the basis of his own White House contact—that at a formidable reception just prior to the opening of the Olympic Games in Beijing, Putin had actually asked Bush if there was anything happening in the international arena that he should know about, to which Bush allegedly replied, "No!". Shortly afterward, the Georgians started their military operations. Putin apparently got angry, and his temper was especially triggered by the belief that had the Americans truly wanted to stop Saakashvili, they would certainly have been able to. After the crisis died down, the US Ambassador to Russia allegedly put the word around in Moscow that US diplomats had been unable to contain the actions of Saakashvili. However, had Bush called him personally—the Russians reasoned—he would no doubt have stopped his endeavor immediately.[80] In

[78] Ibid., 167.
[79] Ibid., 170; Rice, *No Higher Honor*, 685.
[80] Moratinos Files: Private information.

other words, in the Russian interpretation, the United States had let the Georgian president deliberately go ahead with his war plans. What is probably true, though, is that the Russians were deliberately provoking the hotheaded Saakashvili into carrying out precisely such a "mad dog" act. Seen from this perspective, the overwhelming Russian response may certainly have been premeditated, as noted by Rice and others.[81]

Shortly after the hostilities stopped, Russia recognized Abkhazia and South Ossetia much to the chagrin of the United States and the EU. Without doubt, Eastern European countries were disappointed by the lack of US military support for Saakashvili, claiming further that if the country had received the MAP, Russia would never have dared to perpetrate such an act of aggression. Be that as it may, by invading Georgia Russia had effectively drawn a line as to how far it were going to accept NATO's eastward expansion. Indeed, Russia smartly exploited the basic NATO principle, i.e., that the organization does not accept as new member states those states whose territorial integrity has been compromised. By using disproportionate force in Georgia and—above all—by referring to the precedent of Kosovo as an excuse for recognizing South Ossetia and Abkhazia, Russia effectively stopped NATO's eastward expansion.[82]

In late August 2008, Moratinos' position was abundantly clear. There was no need for stark reactions to Russia's intervention in Georgia.[83] The Georgian conflict should by all means be reduced to a regional incident in order to avoid a more general conflict with Russia. In the Spanish view, it was absolutely essential to preserve a climate of collaboration and thus impede the two sides from drifting apart, as this cooperation had actually contributed to freedom in Eastern Europe and had also eased the tension in many European regions. This was the essential lesson that other, perhaps more hot-blooded, European leaders should not forget. Accordingly, it was seen as crucial to avoid further aggravation with Moscow. Isolating Russia would be a great failure, as it would lead to a less democratic Russia, which would also be far less cooperative in international affairs. In spite of certain Russian provocations, it was also important to try and understand the crisis from a Russian perspective. Russia wanted on the hand to develop Russia socially and economically by binding closer ties

---

[81] Cf. Stent, *The Limits of Partnership*, 171.

[82] Ibid., 176.

[83] Moratinos Files: Interview, Moratinos.

with Europe. However, Russia probably felt at the same time that its security was being threatened by the fast expansion of NATO and the creation of US military facilities in a number of neighboring countries. One must remember that in concomitance with the crisis in Georgia, the United States actually signed agreements to install a missile defense system in both the Czech Republic (10 July) and Poland (20 August), and even though Condoleezza Rice solemnly swears in her memoirs that the two issues were completely detached, she also admits that it is likely that the Russians did not interpret it that way.[84]

Precisely for this reason, the Spanish position was that it was necessary to take steps that could ease the tension and enable Russia to stop the dynamics of confrontation. For all these reasons, a new European settlement was urgently called for. One of Moratinos' closest advisors rightly recalled that most of Russia's foreign trade was with the EU, and the EU represented more than two-thirds of the foreign investments in Russia. Clearly, political collaboration and trade were the way forward. It was also important that the EU was able to act independently of the United States and search for solutions that were also sensitive to Russia's reasons and positions.[85]

It is fair to say that Europe proved itself unequal to the task. Spain's well-reasoned views carried insufficient weight, also because the Americans interpreted the crisis so differently from the Europeans. What is striking about Condoleezza Rice's account of the Georgian crisis is that she actually presents the end result as a kind of US victory, in that "Moscow paid a price for its invasion of Georgia, largely because the Kremlin overreached."[86] One might add to these reflections, however, that Europe—as well as the United States—paid a dear price in that East and West drifted further apart. Surprisingly, nowhere in her memoirs does Rice reflect on the important fact that the intransigent US attitude toward Kosovo may well have influenced Russian actions in Georgia, and more importantly, that Russia—as Angela Stent rightly points out—by its incursion into Georgia successfully blocked NATO's eastward expansion. From a Russian point of view, it was actually NATO which had overreached and Putin effectively drew a red line

[84] Rice, *No Higher Honor*, 576, 685, 692.

[85] Moratinos Files: Private information.

[86] Rice, *No Higher Honor*, 691–692.

which has since that day been respected by the West.[87] Rice simply does not connect the dots.[88]

In the aftermath of the August crisis, the Russians started a new set of negotiations with the EU. Spain was also involved in these discussions as Lavrov presented Moratinos and Zapatero with several proposals for a Treaty on European Security that Putin was also discussing with his French and German counterparts. These draft treaties, which of course were meant to specifically safeguard Russian interests, also contained important concessions to the West, as well as seemingly efficient legal measures which—with hindsight—might have made the later Russian intervention in Ukraine in 2015 more complicated. The underlying point of these drafts—to take one example proposed by President Medvedev in 2008—was to create a reliable and effective system of universal security and guarantees in the Euro-Atlantic zone in order to prevent acts that could undermine the unity of this common security space. This included respect for the sovereignty, territorial integrity and political independence of states, non-interference in internal affairs and the equal rights and self-determination of peoples.[89] With hindsight, had these principles been introduced, it would have made the later actions of the Russian government in eastern Ukraine difficult to sustain.

In one of his first bigger interviews after the Russian invasion of Georgia, Moratinos openly embraced Medvedev's ideas for a pan-European security space, and although he openly acknowledged the fears of an autocratic turn in Russia and criticized the Russian recognition of South Ossetia and Abkhazia, he made it abundantly clear that the new government in Russia

---

[87] Stent, *The Limits of Partnership*, 176.

[88] The crisis with Russia has often been labelled as a "new Cold War," although it clearly lacks the ideological and global dimensions of the original Cold War. The new "Great Game," Gordon Hahn writes, is essentially about Russian efforts to contain the influence of the West, and particularly NATO's eastward expansion, in what Moscow conceives as being its sphere of influence: Eurasia. In turn, Moscow is now challenging Washington by strengthening its ties to Beijing and offering its support to the Chinese in the South China Sea conflict with the United States. Much in the same vein, Russia has given new impetus to its relationship with Iran and Syria, attempting at the same time to weaken the ties of the Eastern Europeans to the West and generally diminish NATO and EU solidarity. See: Gordon M. Hahn, *Ukraine Over the Edge. Russia, the West and the New Cold War* (Jefferson: McFarland & Company, Inc., Publishers, 2018), 299–300.

[89] Moratinos Files: Private information.

was incomparable to that of the Soviet Union or the Yeltsin era.[90] Spain continued to openly support Russia, as was the case on 27 June 2009 at the end of a NATO-Russia Council meeting (NRC), when Moratinos strongly underlined the need to engage constructively with Medvedev's proposals for a common European security space. The problem of Georgia had seemingly been effectively sidelined, and the Council, which had been temporarily suspended, was now seen again as a forum where the two parties might engage in common solutions.[91]

Spanish politicians and diplomats that I have spoken to essentially see Putin and Medvedev as rational players, who under normal circumstances would refrain from hybrid operations which might escalate into a confrontation with NATO or, for that matter, individual EU countries. Even northern European diplomats, who often take a much harder stand on Russia, have openly subscribed to the same view.[92] Nevertheless, the overall Western policy line which has prevailed since 2008 is that it is necessary to stand firm and draw lines.[93] It is further likely that the Russian gas dispute with Ukraine in late 2008 only confirmed the belief that this was the right decision. With direct reference to perceived latent military threats from Russia, Western defense budgets are again on the rise. However, this move is somewhat in contrast to official Russian figures on military spending, which might be seen as objective indicators of Moscow's real military capability. Forty years ago, Soviet military expenditure constituted some 40% of the US military budget. Today Russia, with a GDP rated in between that of Spain and Italy, uses in comparison well under ten percent, and despite increasing investments in military technology, Russian expenditure is comparable to medium-size powers such as France and Saudi Arabia.[94]

In retrospect, the PSOE government's policy toward Russia may certainly be described as both constructive and foresighted, yet the bottom line was that Spain had no way of changing the fact that the big players of

[90]"Debemos evitar que nos coloquen de nuevo en una agenda de guerra fría," *El País*, September 8, 2008.

[91]"España ve 'positivo' el plan ruso de nueva estrategia de seguridad europea," *EFE*, June 27, 2009.

[92]Ole Damkjær, "Danmarks ambassadør i Rusland deler vandene," *Berlingske*, August 21, 2017.

[93]Cf. Rice, *No Higher Honor*, 671–674.

[94]These figures have been reached by comparing various publicly known figures collected by the SIPRI Military Expenditure Database. See: https://www.sipri.org/databases/milex.

international politics had an entirely different perspective. Spain did, however, warn about the boomerang effect of ignoring fundamental Russian security concerns by setting new precedents which challenged the common understanding of international law. It is probably not unfair to say that the world is still struggling today with the negative effects of not having followed at least a part of that advice.

CHAPTER 5

Fidel and Raúl

5.1   Cuba Libre

On 14 February 2009, the Cuban businessman Conrado Hernández was
arrested together with his wife Amalia in the José Martí Airport of Havana.
A local representative of the Basque commerce chamber *Sociedad para la
Promoción y Reconversión Industrial* (SPRI), Hernández, was working as
a liaison between the Cuban authorities and the Basque headquarters in
Vitoria, Spain. To his Cuban friends, Hernández was especially known for
his extravagant barbecue parties in stark contrast to the situation on the rest
of the poverty-stricken island. During the ten years Hernández served the
SPRI, business had thrived and around 2009 more than forty Basque firms
were operating in Cuba, just as Basque exports to the island had increased
significantly over the past decade. Despite being a well-connected businessman, Hernández did not enjoy the full political protection he thought he
did. On 27 February, the Cuban police searched the local offices of the
SPRI and a few days later on 2 March, two of Hernandez's most powerful political contacts, the Vice President of the Cuban government Carlos
Lage and the Cuban Minister of Foreign Affairs Felipe Pérez Roque, both
belonging to Fidel Castro's entourage, were suddenly removed from their
posts. After the purge, the Cuban government officially accused Hernández
of having provided secret intelligence concerning Lage and Pérez Roque to
members of the Spanish intelligence services, the CNI, formally attached
to the Spanish embassy in Havana. In a video that the Cuban authorities

© The Author(s) 2019
M. Heiberg, *Spain and the Wider World since 2000,*
Security, Conflict and Cooperation in the Contemporary World,
https://doi.org/10.1007/978-3-030-27343-9_5

sent to selected members of the local communist party, Hernández publicly confessed that as part of a political conspiracy to remove Raúl Castro he had collaborated with the CNI. Yet according to Spanish media which had access to the video, Hernández appeared remarkably relaxed, especially if one considers the possible sentence that awaited him—anything from twenty years of prison to the death penalty.[1] Had Spain really conspired against the Castro regime? To answer this question, it is necessary to examine the development of Spanish-Cuban relations in their proper historical and political context.

Cuba plausibly represents one of the most interesting cases of decolonization in Latin America since the Caribbean island has vigorously fought to become independent for the last 150 years. During the last three decades of the nineteenth century, this struggle was squeezed between the waning Spanish empire and the rise of the United States. Washington doubtless supported the local insurgents against the Spanish masters on the eastern part of the island, yet it also pursued narrow US economic interests in return. The Spanish-American War which led to the loss of Cuba in 1898 only meant that Cuba changed its political overlord, as the so-called Platt Amendment of the new Cuban constitution—imposed by Washington—gave the United States ample rights to interfere in Cuban affairs. The Cuban Revolution of 1959 put an end to the Batista regime and with that the indirect dominance of the United States over the island. Nevertheless, a constant structural deficiency in Cuba's long and tormented struggle for independence has been its incapacity to diversify its exports and create a significant domestic market. Thus, for decades Cuba depended on the sale of sugar crops to a highly unstable international market. This increased the country's international dependence despite the fierce nationalistic rhetoric of changing regimes and governments. After the Cuban Revolution in 1959, the Castro regime managed to introduce a series of remarkable reforms in the field of health care, social security and education. Internationally, however, the regime got caught up in the dialectics of the Cold War, as it was subjected to US sanctions while becoming even more

---

[1] The spy story has been reconstructed on the basis of Spanish newspaper articles. Cf. José Marí Reviriego and Milagros L. de Guereño, "El espía que 'se perdió' en Cuba," *elcorreo.com*, March 13, 2011. http://www.elcorreo.com/vizcaya/v/20110313/politica/espia-perdio-cuba-20110313.html; Mauricio Vicent, "Conrado y los espías en la isla de Castro," *El País*, July 12, 2009. http://elpais.com/diario/2009/07/12/domingo/1247370755_850215.html.

dependent on Soviet economic aid. For thirteen days during the Missile Crisis of 1962, the fierce anti-American regime in Havana became the center of the world's undivided attention. After the fall of the Berlin Wall and the end of Soviet subsidies, new economic policies and austerity measures were implemented by the Castro brothers with particular impetus from China, which has tried to expand its influence in the region. These reform measures have in great part been introduced by Raúl Castro, who originally was far more Marxist than his older brother Fidel Castro. Yet it is fair to say that in the decades after the Missile Crisis Fidel became more dogmatic, while Raúl eventually turned out to be far more susceptible to reforms.[2]

When the Spanish Socialist government took office in the spring of 2004, relations with Cuba were virtually non-existent. There were no high-level contacts and no plans to break the ice.[3] Cuban obstructionism, combined with Aznar's hard and punitive policies toward the Castro regime, had created deadlock in the bilateral relations.[4] The impasse was only furthered by Aznar's strenuous efforts—as part of his gradual alignment with President Bush—to bring the European Union toward a united critical stance toward Cuba. In 1996, the European Union adopted its "Common Position" in an attempt to bring about peaceful change in Cuba. It was essentially a Spanish proposal which was adopted by the European Union since Spain was practically leading Europe on this question. Importantly, the Common Position was introduced against the advice of the Spanish foreign minister, Matutes, who nevertheless had to follow the line denoted by Aznar. It eventually became the job of another Spanish diplomat, Jorge Dezcallar, to effectively see this policy through, although he openly complained to his colleagues that he was against it since it would bind Spanish-Cuban policies unnecessarily in the years to come. Dezcallar sensed an American hand behind the initiative as it was introduced right after the so-called Helms-Burton Act, which had been approved as a formal US response to the shooting down of two private US aircraft by the Cubans. One might argue that realistically the new US law mainly served to strengthen Bill Clinton's image as being hard on Cuba. Dezcallar claims in his memoirs that there was a direct connection between the approval of the Common Position of

---

[2]This summary of Cuba's recent history owes partly to Clifford L. Staten, *The History of Cuba* (Santa Barbara, CA: Greenwood, 2015).

[3]Moratinos Files: Interview, Moratinos.

[4]Arenal, *Política exterior de España y relaciones con América Latina*, 263.

the EU and the arrival in Madrid on 10 July 1996 of Bill Clinton's special envoy Stuart Eizenstat.[5]

In essence, the Common Position advocated for "a process of transition to pluralist democracy and respect for human rights and fundamental freedoms, as well as a sustainable recovery and improvement in the living standards of the Cuban people." It further stressed that the European Union would not try to bring about change by coercive measures, just as it recognized the tentative economic opening undertaken in Cuba. The European Union also considered that full cooperation with Cuba would depend upon improvements in human rights and political freedom.[6] What upset the Cubans above all was the EU's sudden insistence on a regime change, rather than saying economic reforms, as this had hitherto only been the demand of changing American administrations. The fact that the Europeans under Spanish guidance also insisted on this crucial point definitely worsened the relationship.

In the coming years, Aznar advocated for additional punitive measures to be taken and in this endeavor he was very much helped by the Castro regime itself. During the so-called Black Spring of March 2003, while the eyes of the world were on the US-led invasion of Iraq, the Cuban government arrested and convicted seventy-five dissidents—more than one-third of them independent journalists. They were found guilty of violating the "integrity and sovereignty of the state" and of collaborating with foreign media.[7] Their prison sentences ranged from six to no less than twenty-eight years.[8] This deplorable act led to light, yet symbolically important, diplomatic sanctions and immediate Cuban counter-reactions. On 5 June 2003, the EU decided to limit high-level governmental visits and reduce the member states' participation in cultural events, as well as to invite Cuban dissidents to National Day celebrations. In response, the Cuban government announced on 26 July 2003 their refusal of all direct aid from the European Union and also decided to close the Spanish Cultural Institute

[5] Cf. Dezcallar, *El anticuario de Teherán*, 162–169.

[6] Cf. "Common Position of 2 December 1996 Defined by the Council on the Basis of Article J.2 of the Treaty on European Union, on Cuba (96/697/CFSP)," The Council of the European Union. http://eur-lex.europa.eu/legal-content/EN/TXT/HTML/?uri=CELEX:31996E0697&from=EN.

[7] Cf. "Cuba's Long Black Spring," March 18, 2008, issued by the Committee to Protect Journalists. https://cpj.org/reports/2008/03/cuba-press-crackdown.php.

[8] Staten, *The History of Cuba*, 150.

in Havana, which was accused of hosting events critical of the regime.[9] In sum, in 2004 the conditions for a renewed dialogue with Cuba left a great deal to be desired.

To overcome this deadlock, the new Spanish Socialist government explored the possibility of a new dialogue based on a different approach. The Santa Cruz Palace formulated a policy based on "constructive engagement" with Cuba, hoping that it could inspire reform on the island and also enable Spain to gradually modify the European Union's rather condemnatory attitude toward Cuba. As part of this plan, Moratinos decided to replace Ambassador Jesús Manuel Gracia Aldaz, who had acquired a bad reputation in Cuba. He was no longer welcome in the Cuban Foreign Ministry, where only a very junior officer would only occasionally receive him. To find a more adequate interlocutor, Moratinos appointed Carlos Alonso Zaldívar, a very capable and high-profile Spanish diplomat and former member of the Spanish Communist Party, from which he was expelled in 1981 due to his dissenting views. Moratinos considered him the most suitable man for the job and to Spanish satisfaction Zaldívar was warmly welcomed in Cuba.[10]

Although the new Spanish government wanted to initiate a new relationship with Cuba, it was important to the government that it should not cease to express its concern for the domestic situation in Cuba and the need for political and economic reform. In this way, Cuba fitted into a general policy toward Latin America since the main idea of Zapatero's government was to establish close working relations with all countries in Latin America, regardless of their political ideology. The new Spanish government reckoned that Spain was simply not in a position to abstain from dialogue with Latin America, least of all Cuba. Despite all their political differences, the two countries share a common history and are probably more profoundly linked than is the case with any other Latin American country, with the possible exception of Mexico. During the war in Cuba in the second half of the nineteenth century, thousands of soldiers from the poorest regions of Spain lost their lives on the island, and in the first decades of the twentieth-century hundreds of thousands of Spaniards immigrated to Cuba, Fidel Castro's father being one of them.

[9]Mauricio Vicent, "Cuba cierra el Centro Cultural de España," *El País*, September 11, 2003. https://elpais.com/diario/2003/09/11/cultura/1063231207_850215.html.

[10]The Moratinos Files: Interview, Moratinos.

The decision to restart a dialogue with Cuba was, however, a bitter pillow to swallow for many Spanish Socialists who felt that the Castro regime had previously let them down on too many occasions—the events of "the Black Spring" being just one incident in a long series of transgressions. Felipe González had invested a lot of political capital in improving the relationship with Fidel Castro—largely in vain. In 1994, he had even sent the Minister of Economy Carlos Solchaga to the island to help with a reform plan which basically consisted of eliminating subsidies to state companies, the liberalization of small private businesses and authorizing state cooperatives to work more under normal market conditions. Even though some of these elements have indeed been introduced over the last decades, the Castro regime has—according to its critics—always found a way to avoid profound reforms. Hence vast sectors of the Socialist party distrusted the Castro brothers and considered the regime immune to change. Solchaga later described Cuba as a "lost cause" ("caso perdido").[11] Around 2004, one dominant view in the PSOE found that the Santa Cruz Palace should to some extent, but without declaring it publicly, gradually dissociate itself from Cuba. This was allegedly the view held by influential figures such as Luis Yañez. In contrast, a group of Socialists around Leire Pajín and Moratinos saw dialogue as the principal instrument and collaboration as the most effective means to influence the political process in Cuba.[12]

At the Third Summit between the European Union and Latin America and the Caribbean, celebrated in Guadalajara (Mexico) on 28 May 2004, Moratinos met with his Cuban counterpart, Pérez Roque, while Zapatero had conversations with Vice President Carlos Lage, who represented Fidel Castro. The upshot of these informal discussions was that the two countries reopened their dialogue. There's no doubt that Spain's decision to withdraw from Iraq was warmly welcomed by Havana, and Spanish diplomacy was in this way able to open doors in Latin America that would otherwise have been locked. As a result of the discussions, Spain agreed to try to influence future developments with regard to the Common Position, whereas

[11] Mauricio Vicent, "Solchaga pide a Cuba que liberalice más su economía e impulse la iniciative privada," *El País*, June 24, 1994. http://elpais.com/diario/1994/06/24/espana/772408806_850215.html; "Carlos Solchago afirma que Cuba es un 'caso perdido'," *Europa Press*, March 24, 2011. http://www.europapress.es/nacional/noticia-carlos-solchaga-afirma-cuba-caso-perdido-20110324141047.html.

[12] Moratinos Files: Moratinos, Interview.

Cuba agreed that in order to break its international isolation it was necessary to send some fresh political signals, including the will to improve its
human rights situation.[13]
A concrete result of this bilateral process was the release later that year of
Martha Beatriz Roque and other dissidents.[14] This unequivocal sign sent
by Cuba led to the European Union's crucial decision on 31 January 2005
to temporarily suspend all the measures taken in 2003 in response to the
Cuban Black Spring. The Council stated once again that the EU remained
willing to maintain a constructive dialogue with the Cuban authorities,
aiming at tangible results in the sphere of politics, economics, human rights
and cooperation. Furthermore, it was decided that the EU would develop
more intense relations with the peaceful political opposition and broader
layers of civil society in Cuba, through enhanced and more regular dialogue.
From June onward, the temporary suspension was regularly extended for
a six months' period.[15]
Right after the suspension in January 2005, Manuel Chaves, the President of the Spanish region of Andalucía, went on a formal visit to Cuba as
part of a longer visit to Central America, where he oversaw various projects
that his government was supporting through the *Agencia Andaluza*. As
it was the first official visit of a Spanish leader after the EU had taken
the first step to lift sanctions, its political dimension had increased considerably. As president of the PSOE, Chaves' job was also to prepare the
ground for future high-level bilateral meetings in Cuba. On 5 February,
Chaves and Zaldívar met with Foreign Minister Pérez Roque, his Vice Minister Bruno Rodríguez, various politicians and dissidents (Oswaldo Paya,
Vladimiro Roca, Elizardo Sánchez, Eloy Gutierrez Menoyo and Cuesta
Morúa), thereby complying with the EU dual-track policy. Importantly,
they also met with Fidel Castro in what was probably the *Comandante*'s
last important meeting with a Spanish interlocutor prior to his handing
over of powers.[16]

[13]Ibid.

[14]"Las autoridades de Cuba dejan en libertad a la opositora Martha Beatriz Roque," *El País*,
July 22, 2004. https://elpais.com/internacional/2004/07/22/actualidad/1090447209_
850215.html.

[15]Moratinos Files: Interview, Moratinos. Cf. "2636th Council Meeting, General Affairs
and External Relations, General Affairs," Council of the European Union, Brussels, January
31, 2005. http://europa.eu/rapid/press-release_PRES-05-14_en.htm.

[16]Moratinos Files: Interview, Manuel Chaves. The following is based primarily on his recollection. It also draws upon private information given to the author.

Until the very end of his visit, Chaves was uncertain as to whether the planned meeting with Fidel Castro would actually take place since there had just been a sharp, yet cordial exchange of views between Pérez Roque and Chaves. Pérez Roque had in fact explained his dissatisfaction with the threatening tone of the recent EU Council declaration, complaining that Spain had been conditioned by the Czechs and the Poles into taking a harsh stand against Cuba. He rhetorically asked why there was a Common Position on Cuba and not on Vietnam, China and Saudi Arabia: "No one takes notice of their old colonies? Why should Spain?" Chaves tried to minimize their differences by saying that the two parties were in the midst of a process and that Cuba should continue to cooperate, as there was no need to take a negative view of the process.

The Spanish delegation stressed that the stance taken by the EU—strongly opposed by Washington—was an unequivocal sign that Europe was able to conduct a foreign policy of its own, even though this policy did not please everyone. By this statement, Chaves and Zaldívar doubtless downplayed somewhat the real extent of the friction within the European Union. Approximately one-third of the members did not approve of the more relaxed approach to Cuba, including Sweden, the Netherlands, Germany, and to a large extent, also Great Britain. The Spanish arguments seemingly produced the desired effect as the meeting with Fidel Castro was upheld, on the condition, however, that the Spanish meeting with local dissidents was not held prior to the encounter with the Cuban Head of State.

It is well known that Fidel Castro did not care much for protocol, and this bilateral meeting was no exception. Instead, Castro got carried away by what was on his mind the minute after he had warmly received his guests. Actually, it was the third time Chaves had met with Fidel Castro, the first time being in 1992 in Seville, and the second time in Havana in 1997. Prior to the third meeting, Chaves still held fervent memories of Fidel Castro as a truly impressive and charismatic figure who could spellbind his audience. Even the most critical journalist would forget all the critical and analytical questions on his notepad after only a few minutes in the company of the *Comandante*. Fidel Castro—Chaves told me—was like a snake which mesmerizes a bird just prior to applying its deadly bite. However, by 2005 his fascination had faded. Fidel Castro no longer appeared to be in good shape, and the fact that he had recently broken his arm only contributed to a less formidable image. In fact, Chaves's personal experience of the meeting is of a person who was constantly improvising and speaking without a clear sense of direction. The meeting lasted for nearly two hours and for more than an hour the *Comandante* entertained his guest with stories of the fact that Cuban doctors were working all over the world. He then went on to speak of the purchasing power of one dollar in Cuba compared to the United States. He made a lot of abstract multiplications and divisions and reached the conclusion that with one dollar in Cuba you could buy roughly the same as with 500 dollars in New York. He said that for the price of one movie ticket in the United States you could buy 200 in Cuba. And for the price of one baseball game ticket in the United States you could buy more than 2000 in Cuba!

Fidel Castro repeatedly manifested his appreciation of the new Spanish government, in particular Zapatero and Moratinos. He also stated that Spain's natural anchorage was the European Union, but that the EU with its present composition was more of a burden to Spanish-Cuban relations than any real help. In turn, Chaves also conveyed the government's wish that Fidel Castro would participate in the upcoming Ibero-American summit in Salamanca. However, the *Comandante* would not give any binding promises, saying that it all depended on the development of the EU-Cuba process. Castro also referred ironically to the "divine dissidents" ("celestes disidentes") saying that they had no followers and would not even exist had it not been for the money they received from the United States. He also made it absolutely clear that he would in no way give into pressures regarding political prisoners. He was, however, optimistic with regard to the economy due to new Chinese subsidies. All these statements were confusingly entangled in frequent appraisals of the Venezuelan leader Hugo Chávez. At the press conference at the end of his stay, Chaves briefly touched upon the content of their discussion, highlighting the possibility of a royal visit in 2006. The Royal Court, though, was dissatisfied with the fact that Chaves—as president of Andalucía—publicly interfered with the royal agenda, something which contributed to the non-realization of the visit.

Chaves' mission nevertheless showed that the Cubans were receptive to the Spanish initiative, even though it was clearly an uphill struggle to achieve concrete Cuban signals that could enable Moratinos to work for a change in the Common Position. Admittedly, the new compromise, if indeed there was one, rested on fragile ground. One factor in particular clearly had the capacity to influence future rapprochement in an unforeseeable way. Cuban politics were becoming increasingly paralyzed due to the state of Fidel Castro's health, and various power circles, whether military or civilian was constantly regrouping in view of a possible transition of power. Fidel's brother and minister of defense, Raúl Castro, was expected to triumph, along with Lage and Pérez Roque as the two young reformers and main survivors from Fidel Castro's entourage. Rumors had it that Castro's health was rapidly deteriorating, and by late 2005 many people took it for granted that he was about to die. In a televised speech on 20 October 2004, the *Comandante* had shattered a kneecap and broken an arm, and a few months later it was said that he suffered from Parkinson's disease. Castro told the public in November 2005 that even though he felt he was in excellent shape, he would step down if he ever became too ill to lead Cuba: "I'll call the (Communist) Party and tell them I don't feel I'm in condition ... that please, someone take over the command."[17] In 2006, qualified rumors of his colon cancer spread faster than the speed of light.

The Spanish Foreign Ministry followed these developments closely. Having been provided with a rather dire prognosis of Fidel's health, Spanish authorities had already prepared a communiqué to be issued the moment Fidel died. In order to avoid problems with the opposition in Spain, the text was only to stress Castro's historical significance, without stating anything positive or negative about his policies. The communiqué was also to reiterate Spanish support for future Cuban reforms.[18] While Fidel Castro was undergoing various medical treatment, political power started to slip from his hands. In the evening of 31 July, Fidel's personal assistant announced that his employer had undergone surgery and that interim powers had been transferred to Raúl Castro, who to prevent disturbances in the streets had mobilized more than 200,000 troops. Most people in and outside of Cuba believed that Fidel's death was imminent. Analysts of the CIA were allegedly convinced that Fidel would be dead by 2007. To counter these stories a video of a very fragile Comandante was issued on 28 October 2006.[19]

In Madrid, this was indeed considered a crucial moment. Moratinos exploited all the possibilities he had to talk to the new Cuban leadership in international forums as a means to strengthen the dialogue and secure

[17] "Castro Undergoes Surgery, Relinquishes Power," *Associated Press*, January 8, 2006. http://www.nbcnews.com/id/14126537/ns/world_news-americas/t/castro-undergoes-surgery-relinquishes-power/#.WKWKcxQZfjA.

[18] Moratinos Files: Private information.

[19] Clifford L. Staten, *The History of Cuba*, 150.

a transition that would be beneficial for ending Cuba's hardships. Importantly, Zapatero and King Juan Carlos summoned Moratinos and asked him to go to Cuba to learn more about the ideas of the new leader.[20] What did Raúl want for the future? The conditions for such a trip were far from ideal, as very little reform had been undertaken by the new regime. Yet with this imprecise mandate to be carried out in rather obscure political circumstances, Moratinos was instructed to travel to Cuba on 1 April 2007 as the first Spanish Foreign Minister for more than a decade.

The preparations for the meeting were complicated since the Bush administration had publicly declared that it did not approve of the Spanish overture, and the Conservative opposition in Spain also fiercely opposed the trip, just as the EU criticized it. In the months preceding Moratinos' visit, Spain nevertheless sent high-ranking officials to the island, including the director of the CNI. In separate discussions with Pérez Roque in Madrid on 17 March, the Spanish employed a stick-and-carrot strategy in order to stimulate Cuban action. Spain promised to reopen development aid to Cuba and reduce the regime's bilateral debts in exchange for an improvement in human rights, the release of political prisoners and the reopening of the Spanish Cultural Institute in Havana.[21]

Seemingly, bilateral contacts increased significantly prior to the visit to Cuba. Moratinos had the impression that the Cuban leadership now very much wanted him to come, but that it also had serious doubts as to whether the Spanish foreign minister would eventually show up in Havana. The Spanish side sensed that the Cuban government apparently wanted to use the meeting to send a clear message to the international community, i.e., that Cuba was willing to initiate a dialogue, but that it would also stand firm on the need to maintain the ideals of the Cuban Revolution. What exactly "the ideals of the Cuban Revolution" implied was probably never entirely clear to the Spanish interlocutors. Sometimes the phrase was used in favor of reforms; on other occasions, it was used as a way of defending the status quo.[22]

A challenge for Moratinos was the fact that only two-thirds of EU countries favored a more relaxed policy toward Cuba. The rest were far less willing to abandon the hard-line introduced with the EU sanctions in 2003

---

[20] Moratinos Files: Interview, Moratinos.

[21] Moratinos Files: Private information.

[22] Moratinos Files: Interview, Moratinos.

and only temporarily suspended in 2005. For this reason too, the Cubans wanted the meeting to be a success as they probably saw it as an opportunity to break the unity of the EU even further. Moreover, the visit could be used by Raúl Castro to legitimize his own role as the new undisputed leader, just as it could stimulate bilateral trade and Spanish investments on the island. In turn, the Spanish side needed the meeting in Havana to produce tangible results. It was deemed necessary to reach concrete Cuban progress that was also publicly acceptable. Otherwise the bilateral meeting in Havana could turn into a real boomerang for the Spanish government since the Conservative opposition would welcome any given opportunity to strike back at Zapatero for being soft on communist dictators. However, in contrast to public opinion, the flat-out refusal of the Cuban authorities to allow meetings with the dissidents was eventually seen by Moratinos and his advisors as beneficial to other parts of the agenda: If Spain were to give in on this, it would be possible to apply more pressure and obtain more concrete results in other areas, e.g., an increase in the number of prisoners to be released or a formal and binding format for human right discussions.[23]

In sum, even though a sense of uncertainty prevailed, there was still some room for optimism. What the Spanish side had not considered, however, was that the strange spy story mentioned at the beginning of this chapter soon began to jeopardize the bilateral rapprochement that the Zapatero government had been carefully constructing since 2004. After the arrest of Conrado Hernández, Cuba suddenly threatened to cut off diplomatic relations with Spain.

5.2   He Who Imitates Must Fail

As the *Falcon*, the Spanish state aircraft, approached the José Martí Airport, Moratinos was looking impatiently out of the window at the breathtakingly beautiful Caribbean island. He was a little anxious as he had no idea about what to expect in Havana. The political situation seemed unclear and the signals he had received over the years from Cuba had often been contradictory. However, the new Spanish government had, in its own view, done what it could. From the very beginning, the Santa Cruz Palace had

[23]Ibid.

worked to improve relations with Fidel Castro, who nonetheless continued to openly depict the previous Spanish government of Aznar in the
most denigrating terms and to denounce its "neocolonial" behavior toward
Central and Latin America. This was not helpful, Moratinos reasoned, as
he had to convince the entire Spanish Parliament, including the skeptical
opposition, of the wisdom of his upcoming visit to Cuba.

In Havana, the Spanish foreign minister first met with his counterpart,
Pérez Roque, an intelligent politician and diplomat with great negotiating
skills. There was clearly a good rapport between them. However, Moratinos' ambition was not only to be on good terms with the Cuban foreign
minister, but also to learn more about Raúl Castro's political position,
something which Pérez Roque was not authorized to convey. As is often the
case in authoritarian states, Moratinos' meeting with the new Cuban leader
could not be confirmed in advance. Carrying both a personal message from
Zapatero and from King Juan Carlos, Moratinos hoped nevertheless that
the meeting would eventually be upheld. Importantly, the Cubans had not
issued any guarantees. To the relief of the Spanish, however, the meeting
with Raúl took place, yet it was a close call, as it was postponed to 3 April
2007, only a couple of hours prior to the planned departure of the Spanish
aircraft.[24]

The bilateral meeting was a memorable one. Moratinos found in Raúl
Castro a man of age, but also a very fit and friendly interlocutor. Raúl started
by reading aloud the letter of introduction from King Juan Carlos to Fidel
Castro (still the formal Head of State). The rest of the meeting developed
in a rather unusual way. Moratinos essentially wanted to know what Raúl's
plans for the future of Cuba were. This question triggered a long monologue from Raúl. Apart from lecturing him on the history of Cuba, he told
Moratinos that the regime was prepared for a guerrilla war if the United
States dared to attack Cuba. Raúl then went on to criticize Jimmy Carter,
who during his presidency had allegedly offered Guantánamo to Cuba if
Fidel withdrew his men from Angola. He also talked about the failed US
invasion of the Bay of Pigs. After one and a half hours of such frenzied
monologue, Moratinos was quite desperate. Did he really have to return
to Madrid without having a single clue as to Raúl's plans?

[24] Ibid.

The Cuban leader had simply not answered his basic question even though Moratinos had travelled this far and invested a lot of political capital in the meeting. Furthermore, he feared that Raúl might be leaving the meeting early as his head of protocol was waving his hand and desperately trying to get his attention. At this point, Raúl simply waved off the civil servant who indicated that the aircraft of the delegation was about to leave. Raúl said, "The aircraft will leave, when the President says so!" Then, he suddenly changed his argument, saying that Moratinos' government and the king probably wanted to know what plans the Cubans had for the future: "I will tell you my plans, but first I will tell you an anecdote." Moratinos was clearly getting nervous about this apparently never-ending monologue, but Raúl continued as if he did not care about the time schedule of his foreign guests:

> I was in the Sierra Maestra together with my brother Fidel during the days of the Revolution. One day, Fidel told me, 'Saddle your horse and ride with me to the mountains. Keep me company.' Fidel got on his horse without a saddle, and so did I. We rode up and down the hills of the Sierra Maestra for two and a half hours. Upon our return to the camp I saw my brother get off the horse and saw that he was in a completely good shape. In contrast, my body was aching all over, my legs, my back, you name it. Completely shattered. Then a peasant took my horse, and I asked him, 'How come Fidel is so strong and I am not? After all we are brothers.' The peasant answered, 'He who imitates, must fail' ("el que imita fracasa").[25]

The subtle message Raúl wanted to convey was that he did not wish to imitate his brother politically, as he did not wish to fail. In addition, Moratinos was to bring the message back to Spain that he was ready to begin a process of reform. He also stressed that he would not stay in power for long pointing his hand directly at Lage and Pérez Roque, who was supposed to replace him. Raúl also made it clear that his understanding of reform was radically different from that of the Americans in particular. True reform was not about introducing political parties and Western-style democracy. In Cuba, it was about real people being able to eat and live a dignified life. With regard to human rights, Raúl acknowledged the Spanish approach. However, for the time being he could not release the 130 prisoners Moratinos requested unless the Americans were willing to liberate the five agents

[25] Ibid.

known as the "Cuban Five," who had been arrested in Miami in September 1998 and later convicted of plans to commit espionage and murder on behalf of a foreign government. Raul's statement may be said to mark the beginning of a new role for Moratinos, as the Cuban regime from that day on considered him to be the most reliable informal go-between with the US authorities.[26]

In response, Moratinos insisted that it was important to improve relations with the EU, and that this would only be possible through unilateral Cuban actions such as the liberation of prisoners. Raúl said he understood this but they had to proceed cautiously. Moratinos suggested that the two parties should establish a program for prisoner release and for ending the death penalty. Raúl finally underlined that the death penalty had de facto ceased to exist, as the carrying out of death sentences was now out of the question. It was only a matter of time before this would be officially announced. This goodwill was confirmed by later events. As a matter of fact, the last known effectuated death sentence in Cuba was in 2003.[27]

In sum, Raúl had professed a clear will to reform and to let younger forces take over. This was an extremely positive and useful message to bring back to Spain's European partners, who seemed willing to continue to prolong the suspensions of the 2003 sanctions. As mentioned, however, there were also critics who claimed that Spain had gone too far and even suggested that Madrid had departed from the EU Common Position. Spanish diplomats thus had to work overtime to convince their European colleagues that this was entirely false.[28]

With regard to the future, the Spanish government was willing to accept the renewal of the Common Position, not because Moratinos believed in

---

[26] Ibid. "The Cuban Five" were Gerardo Hernández, Antonio Guerrero, Ramón Labañino, Fernando González and René González and are considered national heroes in Cuba. The whole case is fully described in Wikipedia. The author actually had the opportunity to meet Fernando González in Copenhagen in 2015. Apart from being a very intelligent man, he also gave the impression that as a national hero he outranked all the official Cuban representatives present, including the Cuban ambassador, even though he apparently held no official title.

[27] "On December 28, 2010, Cuba's Supreme Court commuted the death sentence of Cuba's last remaining death row inmate, a Cuban-American convicted of a murder carried out during a 1994 terrorist invasion of the island. No new death sentences are known to have been imposed in 2011, 2012, 2013 or 2014." Quote on Cuba taken from the Cornell Center on the Death Penalty Worldwide (Cornell Law School). http://www.deathpenaltyworldwide. org/country-search-post.cfm?country=Cuba.

[28] Moratinos Files: Interview, Moratinos.

its efficacy, but because it reflected the minimum consensus that could be reached between the European member states. Spain wanted, however, to propose the definitive elimination of the measures of 2003 and not merely continue with a prorogation of its suspension. In the Spanish view, a complete suspension would in fact boost the two-track policy of the EU, as it would create much better terms for a broad dialogue. In fact, over the last months, timid advances had been made: There had been a reduction in the number of political prisoners, just as there had been fewer registered acts of violence against the regime's opponents.

The overriding goal of the Spanish government was now to extend the gradual normalization of Cuba's relations with Spain to the entire European Union. Thus, Moratinos was determined to avoid unnecessary hard language in the future written recommendations of the EU Council of Ministers, the primary goal being the full elimination of the 2003 diplomatic sanctions. In order to maximize pressure on Cuba, he also decided to draw Chile, Mexico, Panama and Brazil into the process. Finally, to ease the tension with Washington over his recent visit to Havana, Moratinos decided to send his vice minister, Bernardino León, to meet with the undersecretary of state for the Western hemisphere, Thomas Shannon, as well as several think tanks and congressmen. A plan was also made as to how to cope with the hostile and influential Cuban-American environment in Miami. However, the problem for Moratinos was not only the hostile environment in Florida: The domestic political scene in Spain required Moratinos' attention as well, as the PP repeatedly accused the government of providing the regime "with fresh air" and "without asking for anything in return."[29] The particular background for this criticism was that the government had decided that the Spanish embassy in Havana should not invite dissidents to its 12 October celebration.[30] The Conservative newspaper *ABC* took this argument even further by denouncing Moratinos as inconsistent, since he on the one hand called for the liberation of the leader of the Birmanian opposition, while at the same time letting down the dissidents on Cuba.[31]

---

[29] "El PP critica la 'bocanada de aire fresco' al régimen de Cuba al reactivar la cooperación 'sin pedir nada en cambio'," *Europa Press*, October 2, 2007.

[30] "La embajada en Cuba no invitará a disidentes el 12 de octubre," *El País*, October 4, 2007.

[31] "Moratinos olvida la disidencia en Cuba, pero exige que se libere a la oposición birmana," *ABC*, October 4, 2007.

With hindsight, the rapprochement with Havana may certainly be considered a success for the Spanish diplomatic service, which was now spearheading new talks between Cuba and the European Union. In June 2008, on Spain's recommendation, the Council decided to finally end the 2003 sanctions in spite of resistance from the Czechs in particular.[32] To this end, it was probably helpful that Spain was able to show that bilateral meetings on human rights issues were now being held on a regular basis and that a group of prisoners had been released a few days after the second round of human rights discussions in February 2008. In total, the number of political prisoners in Cuba had allegedly diminished from well over 300 in January 2006 to 205 in 2008.[33] Around fifty of them belonged to the 2003 group of seventy-five dissidents. The prisoner releases, many of which were due to the fact that their sentences had simply been served, were nevertheless the result of unilateral Cuban decisions and could thus be seen by the EU as a sign of willingness to reform.

By 2009, the Spanish government could optimistically state that winds of change were blowing over the Caribbean island. Yet, suddenly out of the blue, came a series of turbulent political events in February–March which threatened to destroy years of successful diplomatic effort. On Sunday 1 March, Moratinos was supposed to have an interview with Pérez Roque, who had agreed to come to Madrid. At the very last minute, however, the Cuban ambassador in Madrid called Moratinos and told him that the meeting was off. Instead Moratinos spent the following Monday morning together with Zapatero, when the news reached them that Lage and Pérez Roque, the two foremost reformers and members of Fidel Castro's entourage, had been replaced. They quickly learned that a government reshuffle had taken place. "Qué cosa más rara" ("How strange"), was Moratinos' first reaction, as this was in complete contrast to Raúl's personal messages. He immediately called his ambassador and asked him to arrange a conversation with the new foreign minister Bruno Rodríguez, who had previously served as vice minister. Rodríguez got back to him after two days in a rather cold tone. Moratinos was nevertheless told that Cuba

[32]"EU Lifts Sanctions Against Cuba," *BBC News*, June 20, 2008. http://news.bbc.co.uk/2/hi/7463803.stm.

[33]Department of State, Bureau of Democracy, Human Rights and Labor: "2008 Country Reports on Human Rights Practices: Cuba." https://2009-2017.state.gov/j/drl/rls/hrrpt/2008/wha/119155.htm.

would continue the reform process, and they also agreed to meet some-time in the near future. Moratinos was of course worried about the fact that Spain's primary interlocutors in Havana had suddenly been removed from power.[34]

After two months, Rodríguez and Moratinos finally agreed to meet in Brussels on Sunday 10 May in the evening. The venue for the meeting was the Cuban embassy. Moratinos was accompanied by his newly appointed chief of staff, Agustín Santos Maraver. The ambassador received them in a very friendly tone and Moratinos then greeted the new Cuban foreign minister. To the surprise of the Spanish, Rodríguez started out by saying, "I do not know how this meeting will end," and although he was not too explicit in his manner of speaking he indicated that Cuba was on the verge of breaking diplomatic relations with Spain. The reason was that Spain had allegedly participated in a coup aiming to replace Raúl Castro. Moratinos and Santos Maraver were simply at a loss for words.

Rodríguez had apparently been instructed by Raúl Castro personally to clarify the entire role of the Spanish government in this affair. He also said that Spain had already pulled this trick once before during the time of Aznar's government. This was probably a reference to a case from November 1998 when the former foreign minister of Spain, Abel Matutes, had allegedly supported his Cuban counterpart, Roberto Robaina, in an internal Cuban power struggle, something which eventually cost Robaina his post. In Rodríguez's view, the Spanish Socialist government was now trying to repeat the same stunt, only now with Lage and Pérez Roque as their main agents in their attempt to oust Raúl Castro from power. Moratinos and Santos Maraver were so perplexed that Rodríguez actually seemed convinced of their ignorance of this affair, although it is likely that he already knew of their innocence due to the Cuban authorities' month-long investigation and their interrogations of the two ministers and the alleged spy Conrado Hernández.

Moratinos assured him that this had to be a mistake, and that neither he nor Zapatero was involved in this. He demanded forty-eight hours to find out what the truth of these accusations was and promised that he would then get back to Rodríguez. In Madrid, Moratinos immediately talked to Zapatero and they agreed to summon the heads of the CNI, who nonetheless denied being engaged in conspiratorial activities while the Socialist

---

[34] Moratinos Files: Interview, Moratinos.

government was planning a rapprochement with the Cuban regime. The conduct of the Spanish intelligence service in Cuba nevertheless caused Zapatero to lose his temper, as it had given the Cubans the opportunity to stir up a diplomatic crisis at a time when the government was making real progress on behalf of the international community.[35] As reported in the media, Zapatero decided to immediately increase his control of the CNI and ordered the closure of the CNI station in Cuba. Afterward, Moratinos called Bruno Rodríguez to explain the Spanish position. The CNI was immediately withdrawn and not allowed back on the island for another year.[36]

If the Spanish authorities had not been conspiring against the regime, then what was the Conrado Hernández case really all about? Two elements are probably worth considering: first, the chronology and the timing of the Hernández affair; and second, the classical question *Cui bono?* Who benefitted from the sudden government purge that followed the arrests?

In the time between the arrest of Hernández on 14 February and the meeting in Brussels on 10 May, the Spanish government saw no sign of a gathering storm. On 3 March, Moratinos was on the phone with Bruno Rodríguez, who was a protégé of Raul Castro. According to the press release, the new Cuban foreign minister expressed his willingness to maintain all the previous agreements and the established agenda with Spain. He also underlined that the new leadership should be not be seen as a sign of rupture, but as a sign of continuity. Ten days later on 13 March, Santos Maraver had a lengthy discussion with the Cuban ambassador, yet nothing extraordinary came up during their encounter. The only thing that worried the Spanish government in this period was that Basque politicians and representatives of the SPRI began to arrange separate missions to Cuba to find out more about Hernández, who was reported missing. Apparently, the rumors of Hernández's disappearance and his alleged connections with the CNI did not even reach the Spanish government until the second week of April.[37] At this point, Spanish journalists on the island were also becoming increasingly interested in the case.

[35] Moratinos Files: Private information.

[36] Miguel González and J.M. Vicente Perales, "El CNI vuelve a Cuba al año de la expulsión de todos sus agentes," *El País*, May 28, 2010. https://elpais.com/diario/2010/05/28/espana/1274997614_850215.html.

[37] Moratinos Files: Private information.

What is clear is that there was regular diplomatic contact with Havana during this period, but the issues on the table were always the same. Above all, Cuba was highly dissatisfied with Zapatero's new Law on Historical Memory from 2007 which allowed people of Spanish origin to opt for Spanish citizenship, something which had created great expectations among Cubans wanting to flee the island. Apart from this major obstacle, progress was registered in other fields of common interest. In the second week of April, when the spy case was already circulating in the Spanish environment in Havana, the Law on Historical Memory was still the primary object of discussion between Spain and Cuba. In fact, on the whole things seemed to be moving in the right direction: In mid-April, there were actually constructive talks about setting up a meeting between Rodríguez and Moratinos, possibly in Prague, and the timing was considered good since the EU head of mission was on the verge of releasing a report which was clearly more beneficial to the regime than the past reports. This was probably also due to a unilateral proposal from the Cubans concerning the release of yet another twelve prisoners, half of which belonged to the Group of 75. Less than a week before the crucial meeting in Brussels on 10 May when Cuba threatened to break off diplomatic relations with Spain, bilateral discussions with the Cubans still centered on the same issues. There were no signs of a sudden rupture in the relationship in this period.

In sum, two key ministers had been purged and Conrado Hernández had been arrested for his role in an alleged conspiracy, but as the chronology demonstrates it did not become a diplomatic case for another two months—although the three Cubans must have been subjected to intense interrogation day and night. One suspicion is therefore that the meeting in the Cuban embassy on 10 May was carefully planned to take Moratinos and Santos Maraver by surprise. Yet the question remains, to whose benefit?

What is interesting about the Hernández case is that it coincided with a watershed in the internal power relations in Cuba, when the political influence of Fidel Castro was irreversibly curbed as a consequence of the expulsion of his two protégés Lage and Pérez Roque from the government. Thus, a good argument could be made that the spy case was not only designed to take the Spanish government by surprise: The real purpose may well have been to facilitate a government reshuffle in Raúl's favor. In this way, Spain had been cunningly used in an internal power struggle to eliminate the influence of Fidel Castro and his entourage. In fact, since 2007 the Spanish government had regularly received information on Cuban attempts to strip Fidel Castro of his powers. In October 2008, just a few months prior to Hernández's arrest, the Spanish impression was that Fidel Castro was now effectively being sidelined. Furthermore, Raúl Castro made it even clearer in his messages that reforms were needed; however, he did not specify the precise contents of the future measures to be undertaken. An additional problem for Raúl was that whenever he said something on reform, it would almost immediately be contradicted by Fidel in his influential newspaper column in the communist party newspaper *Gramma*.[38] Yet immediately after the purge of Lage and Pérez Roque, it became abundantly clear that not only did Raúl now enjoy an exceptionally free hand in foreign affairs, but that he was also willing to use it constructively in order to break Cuba's international isolation. With or without his brother's explicit support.

Even though this description of events makes perfect sense, we cannot rule out other explanations, including the less intriguing scenario that the Cubans actually believed that a conspiracy had taken place and therefore prudently decided on a series of security precautions, if Lage and Pérez Roque had been compromised. The truth is that we will never know. Regrettably, in this case the historian's interpretation has to rely entirely on contextual information.

5.3   Obama's Back Channel

In spite of the fact that things were beginning to move in the right direction in Cuba politically, the Bush administration was always highly critical of Spain's "constructive engagement" with the Castro regime. The reason for US skepticism was mainly ideological, as President Bush's many speeches remind us. In June 2003, President Bush declared at a rally in Miami, "One thing we believe in America is freedom, for everybody, we love it for the people of Cuba, we love it for the people of Iraq, we love it for the people of Afghanistan."[39] It is probably also in light of such statements that one must understand Fidel Castro's orders to prepare for a guerrilla war against the United States. In fact, the position of President Bush was difficult to comprehend in Havana as the regime had made several rapprochements

---

[38] Cf. Clifford L. Staten, *The History of Cuba*, 153.

[39] Cit. in William M. LeoGrande and Peter Kornbluh, *Back Channel to Cuba: The Hidden History of Negotiations Between Washington and Havana* (Chapel Hill: The University of North Carolina Press, 2014), 345.

with Washington since September 11. It had not only expressed its profound solidarity with the United States after the Al Qaeda attack, it had fully accepted the use of Guantánamo in the war against terror. Moreover, it had signed twelve international protocols against terrorism. It was thus only natural that when President Bush began to include Cuba in his list of "rogue states," Havana sharpened its anti-American rhetoric. During the Cold War, US diplomacy had been essential to defeat the Soviet empire, and in fact, diplomatic relations were never cut off between the two superpowers. Yet as noted by two distinguished American scholars, for Bush to be even talking with the Cuban regime, ("the tropical Gulag" as he later called it), was an option he would not even remotely consider, as it might be read as an implicit diplomatic recognition of the Castro regime.[40]

Bush's attitude was in many ways in sharp contrast to how the rest of the world perceived Cuba, which is widely respected in the international environment, especially in developing countries. Cuba was elected as a member of the initial UN Human Rights Council in 2006, reelected in 2009 and 2014, and again in 2016 with the votes of more than 160 countries. Importantly, in 2006 no less than 183 countries backed the annual motion of Cuba condemning the US embargo at the United Nations General Assembly. In 2017, Cuba performed even better with 191 votes in favor, none against and only two countries—the United States and Israel—abstaining. Crucially, Cuban foreign policy has been remarkably consistent over the last decade with its three main objectives being the diversification of its economic relations, a strengthening of foreign diplomatic support and improved bilateral relations with the United States.[41] It is fair to say that significant advancement has been made in all these fields, yet the road to accomplish this has been long and steep.

In 2003, President Bush appointed a Commission for Assistance to a Free Cuba, the task of which was to "plan for Cuba's transition from Stalinist rule to a free and open society, to identify ways to hasten the arrival of that day." The aim of the commission's first report was further "to bring about an expeditious end to the Castro dictatorship."[42] Such plans were

---

[40]This summary owes to LeoGrande and Kornbluh, *Back Channel to Cuba*, 345–346. See also John M. Kirk, "Historical Introduction to Foreign Policy Under Raúl Castro," in *Cuban Foreign Policy Transformation Under Raúl Castro*, ed. H. Michael Erisman and John M. Kirk (Lanham, Boulder, New York, and London: Rowman & Littlefield, 2018), 4.

[41]John M. Kirk, "Historical Introduction to Foreign Policy Under Raúl Castro," 4–5.

[42]Cit. in LeoGrande and Kornbluh, *Back Channel to Cuba*, 361.

not only a way of pleasing the Conservative Cuban-American community in Florida (the same group that got Bush elected as president in 2000 through a disputed recount). It was also in line with his fundamental view of foreign policy, which according to Condoleezza Rice's memoirs often contained little room for nuances. Rarely did President Bush see grey colors, she writes, he much preferred a black-and-white view of international politics.[43] Concretely, the new measures of the Bush administration particularly aimed to curtail people-to-people exchanges and curb the inflow of US dollars to Cuba. For example, family visits for Cuban-Americans going back to the island were restricted to only one every three years, and the highest amount of money that could be wired to Cuba on an annual basis was $1200.[44] However, the possibility of real action, of actually "doing Cuba" as the bellicose jargon in the White House was sometimes worded, diminished radically as the Bush administration got tangled up in asymmetric wars in the Middle East.[45] In fact, as we have seen in previous chapters, the Bush administration actually learned an important lesson about the value of multilateralism between its first and its second term in office. Without doubt, this affected its appetite for military action against Cuba, although the Bush administration continued to hold a regime change as the main objective of its Cuban policies. It is thus fair to say that when Raúl Castro formally took charge of the government of Cuba in 2006, the normalization of US-Cuban relations was but a distant goal. The 1960 embargo and later punitive legislation such as the 1992 Cuban Democracy Act and the 1996 Cuban Liberty and Democratic Solidary Act (widely known as the Helms-Burton Act) were still in force.[46]

As argued throughout this book, it was the strategy of the Santa Cruz Palace to find new areas where Spain and the United States could work together to gradually rebuild the trust they had lost in one another because of the war in Iraq. One major area turned out to be Latin America and in particular Cuba, where Spain was left with a free hand—essentially because Washington was increasingly focused on its Middle East agenda and to a large extent had also run out of ideas. In addition, Spain knew that despite their increasingly harsh rhetoric toward Bush, the Cubans were

---

[43] Rice, *No Higher Honor*, 20.

[44] John M. Kirk, "Historical Introduction to Foreign Policy Under Raúl Castro," 4.

[45] LeoGrande and Kornbluh, *Back Channel to Cuba*, 345–346.

[46] John M. Kirk, "Historical Introduction to Foreign Policy Under Raúl Castro," 5.

very much interested in informal contacts with the Bush administration, and after Moratinos' visit to Cuba, the Cubans considered the Spanish foreign minister to be the best intermediary in this process. Accordingly, Moratinos was able to discretely forward a confidential note from Felipe Pérez Roque to Condoleezza Rice in the middle of February 2007 about a possible prisoner exchange, also relaying that the Cubans were willing to start informal contacts with Washington in order to explore new ways toward some kind of normalization of relations.[47]

Whether Spain and the United States could actually work together on Cuba was put to the test when Condoleezza Rice visited Madrid on 1 June 2007, a meeting which in many ways confirmed the normalization of relations between the two countries. Yet prior to the meeting Rice had publicly voiced her dissatisfaction about the fact that Moratinos had not held any interviews with Cuban dissidents during his visit to Havana last April. On the contrary, Moratinos stood firm on the need for constructive engagement with the Castro regime. Even though such differences remained, the two ministers were able to issue a joint statement in favor of democracy and liberty in Cuba, something which, however, led Cuba to question Spain's loyalty. Moratinos had the impression, though, that the Cuban protests in this regard were mainly designed for domestic consumption, for which reason it was thought better not to take any further notice of them.[48]

All this led Moratinos to become cautiously optimistic. The probable abolishment of the 2003 EU sanctions was in itself a success. Furthermore, Pérez Roque had expressed himself in positive terms about the European dialogue, and both Cuba and the EU seemed content even though Sweden, and especially the Czech Republic, which was to assume the EU presidency in 2009, were still somewhat problematic. Yet on the whole, the situation seemed far better now. A major cause for concern, however, was the deep split within the Castro regime, between reformers, anti-reformers and those who had not yet decided where to place their bets. For this reason, the negotiations still had to be dealt with in a discrete fashion, and there was always the risk that Cuban affairs would interfere negatively with the upcoming Spanish general elections in March 2008. In addition, Hugo Chávez's involvement in Cuban affairs added to Spanish concern. Spain was

---

[47] Moratinos Files: Interview, Moratinos.

[48] "Rice: U.S., Spain Allies with Differences," *CNN International*, June 1, 2007. http://www.cnn.com/2007/WORLD/europe/06/01/rice.spain/. Moratinos Files: Interview, Moratinos.

actually worried about Cuba's increasing dependence on Venezuela since Chávez was supplying progressively larger quantities of oil on extremely favorable terms. The reason for this collaboration was, of course, to surmount the US economic embargo and from 2003 to 2007 Venezuelan exports of goods to Cuba more than tripled.[49] The Spanish fear was that the Cuban regime might become too susceptible to Chávez's political moods, something which could complicate international negotiations with Cuba and ultimately also make the Americans even more hostile.

Despite the slightly more collaborative tone used by Condoleezza Rice during her visit to Madrid, the Spanish view was that the United States was still conducting a rather unproductive policy in Cuba which constantly tested Castro's will to change. In 2008, further complications were added. Raúl Castro's much awaited election as president of Cuba on 19 February 2008 coincided with a sudden worsening of the Cuban economy due to the beginning of the global recession which simply brought the tourism sector to a halt. In the autumn of 2008, President Hu Jintao of China visited the island and promised to support Raúl's plans for a Chinese economic model for Cuba. Under the nose of the United States, China had quietly become Cuba's second-largest trading partner.[50] Cuba and China struck important agreements concerning port construction and the sale of nickel and sugar, but unlike the Chinese, Raúl Castro still sought to maintain free education, health care and social security for all Cubans. His leadership was also tested by the massive hurricanes which destroyed more than a half a million homes and ruined the already crisis-ridden sugar industry. However, by stating that "in the economic policy that is proposed, socialism is equality of rights and opportunities for the citizen, not egalitarianism," it was no longer in doubt that Raúl had ideologically distanced himself from his brother Fidel.[51]

It was around this time that the Catholic Church entered the scene as an important interlocutor. The Church's influence with the Castro regime

[49] Carlos A. Romero, "Venezuela and Cuba," in *Cuban Foreign Policy Transformation Under Raúl Castro*, ed. H. Michael Erisman and John M. Kirk (Lanham, Boulder, New York, and London: Rowman & Littlefield, 2018), 211, 213.

[50] H. Michael Erisman, "Cuba's International Economic Relations. A Macroperspective on Performance and Challenges," in *Cuban Foreign Policy Transformation Under Raúl Castro*, ed. H. Michael Erisman and John M. Kirk (Lanham, Boulder, New York, and London: Rowman & Littlefield, 2018), 49.

[51] Clifford L. Staten, *The History of Cuba*, 153. Erisman, "Cuba's International Economic Relations," 49.

was—as in the Spanish case—greatly helped by its critical attitude toward the US embargo, which it described as harsh and without cause. Just like Moratinos, Cardinal Bertone, the "foreign minister" of the Vatican, reckoned that Raúl Castro was both pragmatic and reasonable. Bertone had been explicitly asked by the Cuban leader to work toward a formal and definitive lifting of the EU measures. Yet Castro had also repeated his willingness to exchange two hundred Cuban held prisoners for the five detained spies in Miami.[52] Together with Spain, the Vatican worked out a list of more than twenty people, who could be released immediately. What was desperately needed at this point was a concession in the US approach to Cuba which could stimulate further reform in the country. Otherwise there was a risk that the whole process would derail.[53]

Without doubt, the victory of Obama in the presidential elections of November 2008 was seen as perfect timing. It created high expectations in Spain, and the primary objective of the Spanish became using the upcoming Spanish presidency of the EU in 2010 to strike a more personal relationship between Obama and Zapatero. On a political level, the aspiration was that Obama's professed end to unilateralism and preventive wars would permit a new concord between Europe and the United States which could also contribute to the improvement of overall relations with a number of countries, including Cuba. In November, Moratinos had talks with Madeleine Albright, John Kerry (future chairman of the foreign relations committee of the US Senate), John McCain and Condoleezza Rice, and he sensed a true change in their bilateral relationship. The talks were no longer only about troop increases in Afghanistan, but about constructing a viable state. Washington was most interested in learning more about the Spanish position on Latin America, the Maghreb region, the Middle East and the forthcoming Spanish EU presidency. In turn, Moratinos evinced Spain's utmost will to collaborate with the new president in order to close the detention facilities at Guantánamo. In fact, Spain was willing to receive three out of the five proposed "candidates" from a US list of prisoners. To *El Mundo*, Moratinos stated that he would study forthcoming US proposals case by case.[54]

[52] Moratinos Files: Private information.

[53] Moratinos Files: Interview, Moratinos.

[54] "No hay líneas rojas para acoger a presos de Guantánamo, estudiaremos caso por caso," *El Mundo*, June 22, 2009. Moratinos Files: Interview, Moratinos.

Immediately after President Obama's inauguration speech on 20 January 2009, the Spanish diplomacy worked overtime to arrange a telephone conversation between King Juan Carlos and Obama, and to set up a meeting between Hillary Clinton, the new secretary of state, and Moratinos. For the first time, the Zapatero government felt that there was a real possibility of deepening the relationship with the United States. Of course, this also had consequences for the ongoing dialogue with Cuba. Evidently, the new American administration shared some of the same visions as the Spanish government. Indeed, a comment by Obama in 2007, while he was still a US senator, is particularly noteworthy: "The United States is seen as supporting democracy when it produces a desired result. It is vital to reverse that trend." During his election campaign, he further called for a different approach to Cuba and Venezuela stating that "it is time to pursue direct diplomacy, with friend and foe alike, without precondition."[55] This was essentially a replica of the Zapatero government's policy toward Latin America, its aim being to construct a dialogue, in particular with those governments one disagrees with the most. Importantly, Obama had also shown that it was possible to win the state of Florida in the presidential election by appealing to the moderate electorate instead of the most Conservative Cuban-Americans.

The change in Florida's electorate, as well as in the rise of similar views among the two most important foreign actors in Latin America, Spain and the United States, produced a rare conjunction, which in the case of Cuba was adeptly transformed with the help of the Catholic Church into an outstanding diplomatic success. Yet there were still many obstacles to dialogue and even more to come. In December 2009, the Cuban regime suddenly arrested Alan Gross, a US government contractor employed by the United States Agency for International Development (USAID).[56] Gross was convicted of alleged espionage activities in Cuba in March 2011. This of course increased tensions, but it also implied that the Cubans had gained an important asset to bargain with in their attempt to bring home the Cuban Five.

Thanks to two distinguished American scholars, LeoGrande and Kornbluh, the complicated history of the US' back channel diplomacy with

[55] Gregory Weeks, "Soft Power, and the Obama Doctrine in Cuba," *The Latin Americanist*, vol. 60, issue 4 (December 2016): 2.

[56] Aviva Chomsky, *A History of the Cuban Revolution* (New York: Wiley, 2015), 167.

Cuba, which involved numerous informal political actors including President Jimmy Carter and Governor Bill Richardson, has been fully revealed. In this endeavor, the two historians have also been greatly helped by documents of the Department of State which were intercepted and released by WikiLeaks. It is possible, however, with the help of supplementary Spanish sources to enrich our understanding of this process and perhaps also correct some important misunderstandings in LeoGrande and Kornbluh's otherwise impressive historical account. Above all, it is possible to question their notion that despite all the positive efforts made by President Obama, his policies initially shared with previous US administrations the premise that important advances in bilateral relations with Cuba could only be achieved if Cuba began to demolish its political and economic system and install a new democratic state based on a multiparty electoral system and a free market economy.[57] This was not so. It is also not true that Obama only appeared to be willing to take the necessary steps toward a real rapprochement with Cuba in his second term: He did so almost instantly, just as the Cubans became immediately aware of President Obama's new accommodating approach.[58] In fact, the US president should be recognized—and it is my sincere hope that this book will contribute to this—for having done exactly the opposite of what his critics claim. Only a year into his first term, he deliberately abandoned the traditional US stand on Cuba through a bold diplomatic back channel action that has not been unveiled until this day. With this gesture, he paved the way for the process of normalization between the two countries, ably assisted by Spain and later by the Vatican following Moratinos' departure as foreign minister on 21 October 2010. If Obama's astonishing initiative did not produce the immediate effect one might have expected, it was in part due to the Alan Gross case, which clearly complicated the rapprochement.

During 2009, international media increasingly acknowledged that Spain was acting as an unofficial mediator between Cuba and the United States, and that Raúl Castro appeared to be open to new talks with Washington. In fact, the Cuban leader was quoted as saying, "We have sent messages to the US government in private and in public that we are willing to discuss everything, whenever they want," a message that was positively reciprocated by

[57]LeoGrande and Kornbluh, *Back Channel to Cuba*, 400.
[58]Ibid., 397–399.

US Secretary of State Hillary Clinton.[59] The Christian Science Monitor also cited the Spanish ambassador in Washington, Jorge Dezcallar, as saying that the United States "recognize[s] our ability to pass along messages and to mitigate diplomatic incidents, big and small."[60] The article emphasized that according to diplomatic sources in the Santa Cruz Palace, Zapatero and Obama had discussed "US-planned overtures toward Cuba," when the two met in Prague in early April 2009. The article also underlined the fact that Zapatero had met with Vice President Joseph Biden, as well as that high-level officials from both countries met on a regular basis, including Hillary Clinton and Moratinos.[61] Much in the same vein, the Spanish newspaper *El País* was able to report that on 13 October when Zapatero visited the White House, he had been asked by Obama to "tell Raúl that if he does not make steps forward neither can I," a message that Moratinos carried with him on his next trip to Havana on 19 October.[62]

These public as well as anonymous statements clearly indicated that the actors involved in the talks wanted to let the world know that something positive was happening and that Spain was part of the process. In addition, US cables published by WikiLeaks in 2010 give the impression that the United States was truly revising its policies. Spanish Ambassador Cacho stated in his secret conversations with US officials that Spain and the United States "used to differ on both strategy and objectives for Cuba policy, with Spain seeking engagement and gradual liberalization and the USG [US government] seeking confrontation and regime change," whereas now the United States "is engaging with the GOC [government of Cuba] in a low

---

[59] Andrés Cala, "US Reaches Out to Latin America—With Help from Spain," *The Christian Science Monitor*, April 17, 2009. See http://www.csmonitor.com/World/Europe/2009/0417/p07s01-woeu.html.

[60] Ibid.

[61] Ibid.

[62] Mauricio Vicent, "Decidle a Raúl que si él no da pasos tampoco yo podré darlos," *El País*, October 25, 2009. http://elpais.com/diario/2009/10/25/espana/1256421601_850215.html.

key manner on issues where we believe we can make progress …."[63] This was actually a subtle reference to a fundamental change in Obama's policies.

In spite of growing optimism, the Spanish side felt that there were still severe obstacles ahead, including those of a more human nature. In fact, the Santa Cruz Palace was not entirely content with the new US assistant secretary of state for Western hemisphere affairs, Arturo Valenzuela, who was not deemed influential enough and perhaps not entirely dedicated to the diplomatic opening toward Cuba.[64] Thus, Moratinos' version of the informal talks between Valenzuela and the Cuban foreign minister, Rodríguez, is at odds with the more favorable description offered by LeoGrande and Kornbluh, who on the basis of an anonymous US official source blame Rodríguez for sabotaging an important bilateral meeting with the Cubans during the UN Assembly in New York on 23 September 2009. According to Moratinos, it was actually the other way around. Rodríguez suddenly called him during the Assembly to say that the meeting with Valenzuela had been called off because the US officials kept saying that they were not yet prepared for such a meeting. Moratinos immediately approached Hillary Clinton at her seat in the Assembly while Obama was delivering his speech. When Moratinos told her that the meeting had been canceled, she got extremely angry, "Who cancelled it?" "I think Valenzuela did. He doesn't want to meet with them," Moratinos replied. "Who is this guy to cancel?" Clinton said, "Tell the Cubans that Valenzuela is going to meet with them." According to this version, the meeting was on again but of course neither Valenzuela nor the Cubans were now in the mood to commit to anything serious.[65]

In its coverage of Cuban affairs, the Spanish press has probably put far too much emphasis on the significance of the meeting in the White House between Obama and Zapatero in October 2009. This was not the decisive

---

[63] "Spain on Human Rights and Dialogue with Cuba," cable, Havana, December 5, 2009, WikiLeaks. See also from WikiLeaks: Cable, from USINT (Farrar) to State, "GOC Signals 'Readiness to Move Forward'," Havana 592, September 25, 2009; Cable, from USINT (Farrar) to State, "U.S.-Cuba Chill Exaggerated, but Old Ways Threaten Progress," Havana 9, January 6, 2010; Cable, from USINT (Farrar) to State, "Spain on Human Rights and Dialogue with Cuba," Havana 726, December 5, 2009, Cable, from State to USINT, "Secretary Clinton's December 14, 2009 Conversation with Spanish Foreign Minister Miguel Angel," State 129362, December 18, 2009;. Cable from USINT (Farrar) to State, "Spain on Human Rights and Dialogue with Cuba," Havana 726, December 5, 2009.

[64] Moratinos Files: Interview, Moratinos.

[65] Ibid.

encounter with regard to Cuba. Instead, it took place a few months later when King Juan Carlos visited Obama as the first European head of state on 17 February 2010. Hillary Clinton and Moratinos were also present in the White House, as was the US national security advisor, General James Logan Jones. Moratinos noticed during lunch that Juan Carlos was very well-prepared for the meeting, just as he was extraordinarily pleased with the fabulous meal prepared by the White House's famous Spanish chef José Andrés. After forty minutes of pleasant talks, Cuba became the primary topic of discussion. First, the King eloquently explained the Spanish position, then Moratinos renewed an offer to liberate one hundred political prisoners in Cuba for the five spies convicted in Florida. Obama instantly reacted positively to the Spanish request: "A good deal!" he said to the surprise of everybody in the room. Hillary Clinton was far more skeptical and pointed to the fact that the case was complicated, "It is going to be very difficult. We can't change a judiciary process." She then suggested submitting the question to further scrutiny, probably also as a way of killing the Spanish proposal. It was the Spanish impression—right or wrong—that it was actually the first time Obama had ever learned about this proposal, in spite of the fact that Havana had continuously made such offers to Washington. At the end of the meeting, Obama suddenly said,

Your Majesty, if you allow, I would like to give your minister a message: Tell President Raúl Castro *that I do not want a regime change*, and if he makes some gesture, I'm ready to reciprocate. Tell him, I can live with him as President of Cuba. But above all, tell him that *I do not want regime change*. And then you will come back to us through Hillary and her people to tell us his reaction.[66]

This secret message marks nothing less than a watershed in US diplomatic history since Washington had until that day consistently insisted on a regime change in exchange for lifting the sanctions. This is also why it is utterly wrong to claim that Obama's policy shared with previous administrations the premise that progress could only be made if Cuba began dismantling its political and economic system. Obama thought exactly the opposite and acted accordingly from very early on in his presidency. His message to Castro is a rare example of the fact that sometimes the easy solution—to change a policy which no longer makes sense and which is only upheld

[66] Ibid. Emphasis added.

for ideological reasons—is also the most effective solution. In fact, when a couple of months later Moratinos conveyed Obama's message personally to Raúl, the latter was overjoyed ("se puso en otra galaxia"). Raúl asked him again and again if he was serious. Moratinos replied positively. "I think we can work on this basis," was Raúl's instant remark, which Moratinos later reported back to Washington. From this moment on, the back channel diplomacy between Washington and Havana was raised to another level, although the Gross case and the Cuban Five still represented obstacles for future diplomatic normalization between the two countries.[67]

In an important meeting of 19 May 2010, Raúl Castro began reacting to Obama's opening, thinking—and probably being fully convinced for the first time—that a significant Cuban action might actually end Cuba's international isolation. After talking to Cardinal Ortega and other representatives of the Catholic Church, he decided that a major release of prisoners should happen through the Catholic Church and that those prisoners who did not want to stay in Cuba could leave for Spain together with their relatives—an offer that Moratinos had already made to smooth the process. At Castro's request, Ortega called each prisoner personally to convey this possibility.[68] After the first group had been released, Ortega was received in the White House by Obama's national security advisor, who let him know that the gesture—even though it had not been the object of much public notice in the United States—had indeed been noted and was highly appreciated by the president.[69]

As the soccer, World Cup in South Africa was entering its final phase, so were the negotiations on the prisoners' release in Havana. Indeed, three important meetings were held between 6 and 7 July. During the first meeting with Ortega and Moratinos on 6 July, Bruno Rodríguez agreed to liberate prisoners in groups and on condition that they would be able to leave Cuba. During the second meeting, held in the early morning of 7 July, the Spanish side confirmed that Spain would receive those individuals or families who wanted to leave for Spain. Later in the day, they all met in the Presidential Office of Raúl Castro. During this formal gathering, Castro suddenly told Moratinos that he had felt particularly well when he

[67] Ibid.

[68] Jaime Ortega, *Encuentro, diálogo y acuerdo: el papa Francisco, Cuba y Estados Unidos* (Madrid: San Pablo, 2017), 59–60, 67.

[69] Ibid., 74–75.

got up early that morning. He had a good feeling in his stomach and for this reason he had decided to release all one hundred political prisoners (although the Cubans never referred to their prisoners as such). "Today is a lucky day," Castro said. Foreign Minister Rodríguez objected, saying that the real number of prisoners was far lower ("¡No hay para cien presos!"). Nevertheless, Castro decided that the total number of prisoners released should exceed one hundred anyway.[70] Castro asked Ortega to prepare a statement for release, and they all went to his summerhouse to have lunch and to watch the semifinal between Spain and Germany prior to dinner.

After the negotiations, Ortega issued the statement saying that a small number of prisoners were being released, and that five of them were already leaving for Spain with their families. Importantly, the remaining forty-seven of those who had been detained in 2003 was to be released and could leave the country.[71] In the event, 135 prisoners were to be released. Even though Cuba had now made an important gesture, as urged by President Obama, it still did not impress everyone in the US Department of State. The Spanish ambassador told Moratinos that Valenzuela was still reluctant to discuss any vital issues with the Cuban foreign minister. Only Phil Gordon, Assistant Director for European Affairs, had expressed his satisfaction with the recent prisoner release. Importantly, however, Hillary Clinton had written directly to Moratinos showing her personal appreciation.[72]

Thanks to the fundamental change in the US president's attitude toward Cuba and also to Raúl Castro's unilateral gestures, the Vatican was able to facilitate the next rounds of negotiation that ended with a handshake between Castro and Obama at the funeral of Nelson Mandela in 2013, and—not least—with the historic December 2014 declarations by the two presidents which stated that they would now restore diplomatic relations. During this period of negotiation, the Alan Gross case remained a major obstacle, but during a meeting he held with Raúl Castro in Havana on 27 February 2011, when he was no longer foreign minister, Moratinos underlined the fact that Cuba must solve this case in order for Obama to make further gestures toward Cuba.[73] In addition, the appointment of

[70]Moratinos Files: Interview, Moratinos.

[71]"Prensa latina publishes press note from Arch Bishop of Havana," *Gramma International*, July 11, 2010.

[72]Moratinos Files: Interview, Moratinos.

[73]Ibid.

John Kerry as the new secretary of state in 2013 was probably important for the final positive outcome. Unlike Hillary Clinton, he was not thinking about running for president, and accordingly he did not need to be too sensitive to the Conservative Cuban-American community in Florida. Still, US policy toward Cuba continued to send mixed signals. On the one hand, Obama contributed to increase US-Cuban collaborations, staging among other things many high-level encounters between the two countries, and Cuba was removed from the list of countries sponsoring terrorism. There was also a considerable increase in US citizens traveling to the island. Above all, Obama and Castro met on several occasions, most notably when Obama visited Cuba in March 2016, the first presidential visit since 1928. On the other hand, the embargo remained in place due to a still hostile Republican-dominated US Congress, and the United States also continued to sponsor opposition groups in Cuba, something which, of course, contributed to bilateral friction.[74]

From the perspective of the European Union, the road that would lead to the final abolition of the 1996 Common Position was still steep. In a personal letter to Raúl Castro of 23 November 2010, one month after he had been ousted from office, Moratinos lamented that the EU had not yet abandoned the Common Position. His successor as foreign minister, Trinidad Jiménez, had tried but failed to obtain support from all EU countries, and therefore, the official EU stance remained unaltered. Moratinos was, however, able to report that the EU High Representative, Catherine Ashton, had obtained a clear mandate to begin a dialogue with the Cuban authorities in order to abolish the Common Position, just as he personally would remain committed to this objective.[75] The EU had finally abandoned its normative approach to Cuba in favor of a more pragmatic view.[76] As a consequence of the improved international dialogue, the EU was finally able to repeal its Common Position in December 2016 and strike a new positive agreement that the EU High Representative for Foreign Affairs and Security Policy Federica Mogherini rightly describes as "a turning point in the relations between the EU and Cuba." The Political Dialogue and Cooperation Agreement foresaw an enhanced political dialogue, improved

---

[74]John M. Kirk, "Historical Introduction," 7–8.

[75]Moratinos Files: Letter to Raúl Castro, November 23, 2010.

[76]This is also a main point in Susanne Gratius, "Cuba and the European Union," in *Cuban Foreign Policy Transformation Under Raúl Castro*, ed. H. Michael Erisman and John M. Kirk (Lanham, Boulder, New York, and London: Rowman & Littlefield, 2018), 126–140.

bilateral cooperation and the development of joint action in multilateral fora.[77]

The lessons learned—on this occasion, too—were that sanctions and other punitive measures are very easy to introduce, but extremely hard to lift again. Twenty years passed before the EU was able to do the right thing. As mentioned by the Spanish diplomat Jorge Dezcallar, the Common Position in 1996 only hardened Cuban resistance in the years to come, just as it unnecessarily narrowed the options of the EU.[78] The United States initiated their sanctions sixty years ago, and no one knows when the final barrier to the full recovery of US-Cuban relations will eventually fall, even though Cuba does not—in any imaginable way—constitute a threat to the United States.

By its own initiative in 2004, Zapatero's government had decided to spearhead negotiations between the EU and Cuba in order to bring about reform in Cuba and not just to the benefit of narrow Spanish economic interests in the region. Spain skillfully exploited the void in Latin American affairs left by the United States when it was preoccupied with its Middle East agenda, to play a much more influential role in this part of the world. To the surprise of Moratinos, however, the United States never managed during the time he served as minister to develop any clear strategy and policy aims for Latin America, something that he repeatedly complained about in his frequent talks with Condoleezza Rice and, later, Hillary Clinton. In actual fact, Spain's Latin American interlocutors wanted the United States to take a more positive interest in its southern neighbors. On the other hand, this lack of interest left Spain with a greater margin to pursue a different agenda for Latin America, which might not otherwise have been possible. Furthermore, it enabled Spain to work alongside the United States, a core objective of Spanish foreign policy since 2004.

With the arrival of President Obama in January 2009, a rare conjunction occurred in international relations that finally permitted the United States, Spain and the EU to effectively use their most powerful diplomatic tool: their power of attraction as free, prosperous and democratic societies in their appeal for reform on the Caribbean island. Both Raúl Castro and Barack Obama understood that to repeat the policy of their predecessors

---

[77] "EU-Cuba: Council Opens New Chapter in Relations," *Council of the European Union*, December 6, 2016. http://www.consilium.europa.eu/en/press/press-releases/2016/12/06-eu-cuba-relations/.

[78] Dezcallar, *El anticuario de Teherán*, 169.

would only lead to new failure. The peasant of the Sierra Maestra Mountains had been proven right, when after hours of tough horse-riding he had given Raúl Castro the advice not to follow in the footsteps of his brother: "He who imitates must fail."

CHAPTER 6

The Other Comandante

6.1 The Carmona Affair

It was, no doubt, a tired and exhausted foreign minister who on 22 November 2004 participated in the television program "59 Seconds" on Spanish National Television (TVE). Having just returned from a long journey in Latin America, the popular show where the participants are supposed to deliver a consistent argument in only a few seconds was hardly what Moratinos relished the most. Nevertheless, his party insisted upon his participation and also sent a spin doctor to his office to prepare him for the occasion. The interview, which was pre-recorded, had gone well until a certain point when the journalist had asked the foreign minister why his government supported the antidemocratic Venezuelan President Hugo Chávez, who was paying a formal visit to Spain precisely at that time. This question called to mind the pressure on Moratinos from the Conservative opposition, which continued to claim that Zapatero was only in power thanks to Al Qaeda and that Moratinos had changed the foreign policy of Spain in favor of a dubious, purely ideological third world agenda. Moratinos's position was made even more difficult by the fact that another participant in the program, from *Izquierda Unida* (IU) accused him of covering up for the participation of the previous Conservative government in the failed coup d'état by Pedro Carmona against Hugo Chávez in April 2002. To make matters worse, the leftwing IU formed part of PSOE's parliamentary basis and could not be easily ignored. So, in order to strike back at the

© The Author(s) 2019
M. Heiberg, *Spain and the Wider World since 2000*,
Security, Conflict and Cooperation in the Contemporary World,
https://doi.org/10.1007/978-3-030-27343-9_6

Partido Popular and also appease the IU, Moratinos decided to use what was probably the strongest weapon in his arsenal:

> During the former government … the Spanish ambassador [in Caracas] received instructions to support the coup [in Venezuela], something which shall not be repeated in the future. This will not happen again, because we respect the will of the people.[1]

He then went on to say that contrary to what Aznar had done during the recent coup in Venezuela from 12 to 14 April 2002, the new government would respect Hugo Chávez because the Venezuelan president had received massive support in the most recent elections. Accordingly, it was the new government's professed goal to work for the consolidation of democratic institutions in Venezuela and other Latin American countries. Moratinos' outburst immediately made the headlines in all the Spanish media.

Apart from the obviously strong reactions of the opposition, the truth was that the foreign minister's improvised attack was politically risky as he did not have solid information to sustain his claim apart from the usual ministerial hearsay. A major problem was also that, on the previous government's orders, all relevant documents concerning the case were no longer on file in the ministry. Accordingly, Moratinos soon realized that he had probably gone too far in his statement about Venezuela, even though he was convinced that he had essentially stated what he knew to be the truth. He was therefore a little worried, despite the fact that the Moncloa initially viewed his performance positively.[2] His worries were not unfounded since his declaration soon started a fire with the Conservative opposition, which did everything in its power to oust him.

To this day, opinions vary about Spain's possible involvement in the coup d'état and the different interpretations are often cast along ideological lines. Aznar and other exponents of the former PP government reject any wrongdoing, whereas political opinion makers on the left are much

---

[1] "En el anterior Gobierno, cosa inédita en la diplomacia española, el embajador español recibió instrucciones de apoyar el golpe, cosa que no se va a repetir en el futuro. Eso no se va a reproducir, porque nosotros respetamos la voluntad popular." Cit. in "Moratinos acusa a Aznar de haber apoyado el intento de golpe de estado contra Hugo Chávez en 2002," *El Mundo*, November 23, 2004. http://www.elmundo.es/elmundo/2004/11/23/espana/1101172874.html.

[2] Moratinos Files: Interview, Moratinos.

more critical of Spain and also of the United States' actions during the hectic days of the failed coup. It also has to be established precisely what triggered the coup in Venezuela, apart from the fact that many members of the political and military establishment in Venezuela considered Chávez a radical Socialist demagogue. His most recent exchange program with Cuba, including a very generous oil deal in Cuba's favor, was seen as proof of this. Thus, it was hardly surprising that the first public remarks by the coup makers were also about oil. "No more barrels [of petroleum] to Cuba!" ("¡Ni un barril más para Cuba!") was an often-heard outcry during the coup, especially from the headquarters of the Venezuelan oil and natural gas company PDVSA, which according to rumors had colluded in Carmona's plans.[3] This protest statement referred to the fact that President Chávez had previously agreed to supply the Castro regime on extremely favorable terms. The resale of petroleum from Venezuela allowed the Cuban regime to earn crucial foreign exchange, thereby weakening the effect of the US embargo. This deal was, of course, also unpalatable to Washington, and instant rumors—later confirmed by Chávez himself—had it that the Bush administration had been deeply involved in the Carmona coup, something which was denied outright by the Department of State in a special report issued only a few months later in the summer of 2002. The US report above all tried to respond to widespread criticism that Washington had been "too slow to decry Chávez's ouster and too quick to deal with the provisional government."[4]

The background for this report was the following. In a letter of 3 May 2002, the US Senator Christopher J. Dodd asked the Department of State to conduct a review of the US response to the coup d'état in Venezuela during the weekend of 12 to 14 April 2002. He wanted to be informed about US connections to the opposition forces and conspirators in the six-month period leading up to this episode.[5] The report flatly rejected any wrongdoing in Venezuela. In essence, it stated that the US embassy and State Department officials had acted in good faith. It claimed that the State

[3] Ingrid Carvajal Arroyo, ed., *Memorias de un golpe de Estado. Cronología 11, 12, 13 y 14 2002* (Gobierno Bolivariano de Venezuela/Ministerio de Poder Popular para la Comunicación y la Información, 2012), 18. http://minci.gob.ve/wp-content/uploads/downloads/2012/06/abril_memorias_de_un_golpe_de_.pdf.

[4] "A Review of U.S. Policy Toward Venezuela—November 2001–April 2002," OIG Report, No. 02-OIG-003, July 2002, 40.

[5] Ibid., 1.

Department had credible reports suggesting that pro-Chávez supporters had fired on a large crowd of peaceful Chávez opponents, resulting in several casualties.[6] Chávez had, furthermore, tried to stop the media from reporting on these incidents. Finally, the US government was advised that Chávez had sacked his vice president and then voluntarily resigned, so that Carmona's provisional leadership was seen as the most legitimate interlocutor for the United States in that difficult time. The US government thus advised Carmona to call for early elections and to legitimize his own rule by obtaining the endorsement of the National Assembly and the Supreme Court.[7]

The report did, however, acknowledge that US officials had met with opponents of the Chávez government in the six-month period leading up to the coup, a type of behavior which—still according to the same report— was nevertheless completely in line with the Department's policy across the world. It then went on to say that Chávez's opponents had not sought help from the United States "for removing or undermining the Chávez government through undemocratic or unconstitutional means ...." On the contrary, US officials responded to the information from Chavez's opponents regarding their future plans "with statements opposing any effort to remove or undermine the Chávez government through undemocratic and unconstitutional means. These responses were conveyed orally."[8]

The report did, however, find that the National Endowment for Democracy (NED), the Department of Defense (DOD) and other US assistance programs provided training, institution building and other support to individuals and organizations involved in the brief ouster of the Chávez government. Still, the report said it did not find evidence that this support "directly contributed, or was intended to contribute, to that event."[9] This is also the view of Condoleezza Rice, the national security advisor, who in her memoirs claims that the United States had not backed the coup makers, "In fact, we'd warned that the United States would not support extra-constitutional

---

[6] Ibid., 1. This assertion is strongly contested in the 2003 documentary, "The Revolution will not be televised"—made by an Irish film team, who were allowed to follow Hugo Chávez for several months during 2001 and 2002. Available on YouTube.

[7] "A Review of U.S. Policy Toward Venezuela," 1.

[8] Ibid., 2.

[9] Ibid., 3.

efforts against Chávez."[10] Nevertheless, following the argument made by Christopher Clement, it seems fair to say that the Bush administration acted most critically, perhaps even aggressively toward Chavez's legitimate government in this period.[11]

When confronted with new Spanish sources, it remains clear that the reassuring answer from the US government to Senator Dodd was formally correct. Yet one particular phrase in the US report requires our full attention, namely the US claim that it had not supported any extra-constitutional efforts in Venezuela. What does this particular sentence—repeated over and over again by US officials and also Condoleezza Rice—actually mean? New Spanish sources actually point to the fact that the main goal of the coup makers—and of the forces who sustained their plot—was precisely to stage the coup exactly *within* the limits of the Venezuelan constitution. So the fact that the Americans very much underlined the importance of respecting the fundamental laws of Venezuela may say next to nothing about possible US involvement in the plan to throw Chávez. In fact, new evidence which emerged in 2004 convinced the new Spanish government that a number of international actors, as well as Aznar's government, had to a greater or lesser extent sided with Carmona in 2002.

Before examining this new information, we must consider Aznar's own version of the events. In his memoirs, he flatly denies that his government was involved in the coup. He allegedly told Chávez, somewhat presumptuously, "Look Hugo, if I had wanted to make a coup and had I organized it, I can assure you that you would not be here now"[12] (*"Mira, Hugo, si yo hubiera querido dar el golpe y lo hubiera organizado, te aseguro, que tú ahora no estabas aquí"*). He does confirm, however, that right after the coup he received a phone call from Havana, as the Cuban government wanted to organize the extradition of Chávez to Spain, a request that was, however, declined by Aznar. He also admits that he received another phone call from Palacio de Miraflores, the presidential palace in Caracas, and that he was put on the phone with Pedro Carmona who was heading the coup.

[10] Rice, *No Higher Honor*, 255–256.

[11] Christopher I. Clement, "Confronting Hugo Chávez," in *Venezuela: Hugo Chavez and the Decline of an 'Exceptional Democracy'*, ed. Steve Ellner and Miguel Tinker Salas (Lanham, MD: Rowman & Littlefield, 2007), 200.

[12] Aznar, *El compromiso del poder*, 83.

Aznar allegedly ordered Carmona to guarantee Chávez's safety, and as also mentioned in the US report, *to respect the constitution*.[13]

What Aznar does not dwell upon in his diaries—although it is explicitly mentioned in the US 2002 report—is that the Spanish ambassador in Caracas, Manuel Viturro, together with his US counterpart, Charles Shapiro, actually agreed on 13 April 2002 in the midst of the coup to meet with Carmona, the junta leader and provisional head of Venezuela.[14] Through this action, the two governments bestowed some kind of international legitimacy on Carmona's provisional leadership and coup d'état. In fact, Chávez immediately interpreted this gesture—as reported by innumerable international media—as an unequivocal sign that Spain and the United States had played a subversive game in Caracas in order to overthrow his democratically elected government.[15]

What we have stated so far corresponds more or less to what was known about the coup prior to Moratinos' public outburst in 2004. After the foreign minister made his accusation, he had to defend himself. This could only be done by putting more meat on the table. If he could not document his claims, the PSOE government would find itself in difficulties. An important obstacle, however, was that Zapatero would only allow Moratinos to denounce and document the actions of the former Spanish government of Aznar, although the foreign minister was convinced that the Carmona affair was to some extent a concerted international effort. However, after the controversial Spanish withdrawal from Iraq, Zapatero did not want to complicate the relationship with foreign powers over a past issue. This led to some friction between the Santa Cruz Palace and the Moncloa, as the latter censured the original foreign ministry report on the Carmona affair, and only allowed the foreign minister to publicly blame the PP and only for part of their alleged involvement.

In the hectic days following the interview, Moratinos was personally given information from a foreign source on the original plan to oust Chávez.[16] What probably added to the reliability of this new information was the fact that it came from one of the actors in the plot and it exposed his

---

[13] Ibid., 84.

[14] "A Review of U.S. Policy Toward Venezuela," 42–43.

[15] Cf. *Anuario Internacional CIDOB*, entry for 25 November 2004.

[16] This information has not been verified by this author, who in this respect relies on the account of a number of oral sources and a series of contextual information.

own role as well as the extent of cooperation with other foreign actors with vested interests in Venezuelan businesses. Interestingly, the source reported that Fidel Castro had been persuaded into receiving Chávez once he had been ousted. Castro had allegedly been talked into this, as he thought that his friend Chávez was finished and could not save his presidency no matter what. This information also coincides with the above-mentioned passage in Aznar's memoirs. A major player in the plan to bring Chávez to Cuba was a late international businessman, who was extremely well connected to Western governments. However, as Chávez was able to resist all the coup makers' attempts to make him sign his own resignation, the Cuban government—still very sympathetic of Chávez—allegedly changed its view of the situation and backed out. Apparently, one Spanish multinational company and several politicians from across the Spanish political spectrum had participated in the plan. Yet to serve such raw information to parliament or the public in 2004 was not even considered to be remotely possible. Later, Spanish journalists were able to find out that the coup makers had been invited to Spain in early April 2002, where they had allegedly met with government officials and also left a paper trail of bills and invoices. Carmona had purportedly visited a Madrilenian tailor who had made him a military uniform suitable for his future job as head of state.[17]

Moratinos was nevertheless able to come up with a satisfying response to the parliamentary foreign policy committee. After several trips to the basement of the ministry, one of Moratinos' trusted aides was able to reconstruct some of the missing correspondence from the Aznar period which could actually be used to support what the minister had said during the interview on "59 Seconds." On the basis of the findings then, Moratinos' collaborator still believes today that Spain had doubtless taken the lead in the international attempt to help Carmona, whereas the other principle powers mentioned in the plan only reacted, albeit positively, to Spanish propositions.[18]

On Friday, Moratinos took the first draft of his report to the Council of Ministers, where he discussed it after a joint session with Zapatero and his vice prime minister, María Teresa Fernández de la Vega. The latter two agreed that it was necessary to erase all references to foreign governments

---

[17] See, for example, the journalistic inquiries on the personal website of Spanish journalist José Manuel Fernández.

[18] Moratinos Files: Private information.

in the report. After this Moratinos barred himself in the ministry together with his closest aides, and on Sunday they were joined by Rubalcaba and Fernández de la Vega, who helped to polish the text from a political perspective. Despite the effective cleansing of most of the original text, it still offered a strong argument in favor of Moratinos' accusations. The ultimate solution was to convincingly document only the part regarding the meeting of the Spanish ambassador with coup maker Pedro Carmona, thus ignoring Spain's alleged foreign partners in the affair and the existing correspondence between them.

In essence, the final report was based on a number of previously erased telegrams and also an interview that Moratinos had held with the former ambassador in Caracas, Manuel Viturro, who, however, continued to deny any wrongdoing in the affair. Essentially, Moratinos tried to demonstrate two facts: (1) There had indeed been a coup in Venezuela and (2) the Spanish ambassador had received instructions which helped legitimize the coup makers internationally. He also made one important concession to the opposition: He acknowledged that a television show was hardly the right place to make such serious accusations, for which he sincerely apologized.

Crucially, Moratinos argued before the Spanish Parliament that what he meant by the previous government's "support" for the coup was that Aznar during 12–13 April had not condemned the coup; he had instead endorsed it and offered it international legitimacy.[19] To strengthen his case, he cited a number of Conservative politicians who before the coup and after the coup had died out, deliberately labeled the events as a "coup." However, during the coup itself the former government had been extremely careful *not* to use this word. In this period, both in the official joint statement made with the United States and in the statements made by Spain as the holder of the EU presidency, Aznar's government described the situation as only a "void of power."

Interestingly, in the days prior to the coup, for example, on 8 April, the Spanish ambassador had mentioned on several occasions that the opposition forces were likely to exploit the general strike foreseen for 9 April to trigger their plan for ousting Chávez. The following day the ambassador explicitly used the term *"golpe de Estado Militar"* (military coup d'état). The ambassador noted that the demonstrations were likely to trigger a coup

---

[19] *Cortes Generales. Congreso de los diputados, comisiones, VIII Legislatura, Asuntos Exteriores, Sesión núm. 10, 1 December 2004,* 2. The description below is primarily based on this testimony.

aiming to provoke the "unconstitutional ousting of President Chávez."[20] The same language was used on 10 and 11 April. Furthermore, in the morning of 12 April, the ambassador stressed that there had been enough dead to provoke the intervention of the military, "the only force in this country … able to put an end to the government of President Chávez."[21] Viturro also explained that Carmona had persuaded Chávez to resign and called for the Venezuelans to keep calm. During the negotiations, Chávez had allegedly agreed to replace his government and especially his vice president, who was constitutionally supposed to replace him. Only after the signature of this document did Chávez allegedly sign his own resignation.[22]

It is probably fair to say that Viturro did not display a great deal of criticism toward the information he was receiving directly from the coup makers, as the constitution—in order to effect the resignation of a government—must carry not only the signature of the president, but also that of the president and the vice president of the parliament. Such signed documents never surfaced, neither during nor after the coup. Nor were there qualified rumors of their existence. Interestingly, right after the arrest of Chávez, the Spanish and US governments instantly issued a joint declaration in which they said they were following events with "great interest and concern" and that "only the consolidation of a stable democratic framework can offer a future of freedom and progress to the Venezuelan people." Importantly, it urged the Organization of American States to assist Venezuela in consolidating its democratic institutions. They did not in any way condemn Carmona's actions.

However, later the same day Carmona and his Junta issued a decree without consulting with Washington and Madrid, later called the *decretazo*, which designated Carmona as the new provisional president of Venezuela and established a new provisional government, an action which was clearly in conflict with the Venezuelan constitution. Both the United States and Spain now realized that it looked as if they were supporting an unconstitutional government. Therefore, when Viturro visited Carmona in the afternoon of 13 April together with his US counterpart, Charles Shapiro, they both expressed their surprise and dissatisfaction with the new decree. They even went on to say that had they known its wording, they would not have

---

[20] Ibid., 3.
[21] Ibid.
[22] Ibid.

issued their joint statement of the day before, which had clearly been favorable to the rebels by avoiding any mentioning of a "coup" and expressing only their full support and solidarity with the people of Venezuela. Nevertheless, Prime Minister Aznar accepted a telephone call from Carmona on 13 April, thereby bestowing on Carmona's unlawful actions further international legitimacy.[23]

The present study can reveal that the members of the Parliamentary Commission, who listened to Moratinos' explanation, actually received information off the record about the fact that on 12 April 2002, prior to Carmona's unlawful decree, Washington had suddenly decided to limit its favorable statements about Carmona for the time being. The reason for this caution was that the US wanted to avoid a difficult situation in which they might have to determine in public whether the events in Caracas constituted a coup d'état or not.[24] Interestingly, there was nothing secret about the Americans' change of hearts, as these particular worries, which were zealously blurred in the Spanish minister's official account before the parliament, had actually been perfectly spelled out by the US Department of State in its aforementioned report of 2002.[25]

Crucially, the US worries must have been connected to the fact that through the adoption of the Inter-American Democratic Charter on 11 September 2001, the Organization of American States (OAS) had recently made it impossible to recognize a government resulting from a coup d'état. If the coup makers wanted international recognition, they had to argue their case from a juridical perspective by claiming that what was happening in Caracas was nothing more than a legitimate transition of powers following the voluntary resignation of Chávez. Apparently, the flat-out refusal of Chávez to sign his own resignation caught Carmona unprepared and further upset the Americans. In the fog of the unfolding events, Carmona took the false step of decreeing his own interim powers—this was

[23] This had previously been admitted by Aznar before Parliament. Ibid., 6.

[24] Moratinos Files: Private information.

[25] "Both the Department and the embassy worked behind the scenes to persuade the interim government to hold early elections and to legitimize its provisional rule by obtaining the sanction of the National Assembly and the Supreme Court. When, contrary to U.S. advice, the interim government dissolved the assembly and the court and took other undemocratic actions, the Department worked through the Organization of American States (OAS) to condemn those steps and to restore democracy and constitutionality in Venezuela." Cit. in "A Review of U.S. Policy Toward Venezuela," 1.

clearly an unconstitutional act and thereby also impeded his own international recognition. This move was apparently neither foreseen nor relished by the Spanish and the US authorities.

Importantly, on 13 April Spanish Foreign Minister Piqué spoke on the phone with César Gaviria, Secretary-General of the OAS, to delay the extraordinary meeting of the Permanent Council until the Río Group had made a pronouncement on the matter. Furthermore, he wanted to avoid the participation of the permanent Venezuelan representative, Ambassador Jorge Valero, whose presence might provoke a tense situation. Crucially, on 12 April, before the decree was issued, the heads of government of nineteen Latin American countries had already agreed to condemn the events for what they were: a coup d'état. According to Moratinos, the real reason behind the diplomatic visit to Carmona on 13 April was to underline the importance of upholding an apparent constitutional legality.

Precisely for this reason, the report issued by the State Department in the summer of 2002, in which it was repeatedly underlined that the United States had always stressed the necessity of acting within the constitution, says next to nothing about possible foreign involvement in the plan to oust Chávez. Moratinos' entourage interpreted the US behavior as an unequivocal sign that it supported Carmona, yet it had been a precondition for foreign support that his takeover of the government would be staged as a lawful transition. To document that this was also how the Bush administration reasoned at the time would of course require US documents to be made available on the Carmona affair. Nevertheless, this chapter will hopefully help to qualify the future debate on the Carmona affair also from an American perspective.

In sum, the events of Caracas may be summarized as follows: A coup took place in Venezuela from 12 to 14 April 2002, a fact that was made evident by the arrest of Chávez and other members of his cabinet. The coup formally based its legitimacy on article 350 of the constitution, which is a kind of emergency law, and the evolving events which had cost twenty people their lives—murdered by snipers—served as a fig leaf to trigger this article. The Junta further claimed that Chávez had signed his resignation and that the vice president had abandoned his post, without providing any proof of this, however. The Spanish ambassador uncritically accepted the version of the Junta, whereas the US State Department actually remained critical and demanded that the embassy retrieve a signed copy and not just the unsigned document that was circulating in the higher echelons of power in Caracas during 13 April.[26] As all Latin American countries condemned the events, the Spanish Conservative government now had two options: to align itself with them and condemn the coup or take a different position. In the end, the Spanish government decided to support Carmona only as long as he provided sufficient legal cover for the events.[27] Importantly, however, Spain was the last country to condemn the coup. Only after the coup had failed, and also after the Americans on 13 April had adhered to the OAS declaration, did Spain change its official language and accordingly its attitude toward the coup makers.[28] When read today, Moratinos' final report on Venezuela before the parliamentary committee was certainly well-argued. If there was any bias in his reporting, it was that he not only omitted references to possible foreign actors in the coup, but also that he avoided references to Spanish actors outside the PP. A number of pamphlets have since tried to provide the names of some of these actors, without however documenting their claims.[29]

Without doubt, Hugo Chávez had many enemies in the international arena who would have welcomed a new government in Caracas. A part of the reason was probably his Manichean view of foreign affairs. Just like his "favorite adversary," President Bush, he did not have a flair for nuances in international politics. Chávez identified a Bolivarian Axis of nations (Venezuela, Brazil, Argentina, Cuba), whose ostensible goal was to challenge the "US Axis" in Latin America (Colombia, Ecuador, Peru, Bolivia and Chile) and ultimately force a new Latin American unity inspired by the ideas of Simón Bolívar.[30] Moreover, Chávez boldly tried to use Venezuela's energy resources to increase the country's international weight. As is well known, Venezuela holds by far the world's largest oil reserves and has

[26] Ibid., 41.

[27] Ibid.

[28] *Cortes Generales. Congreso de los diputados, comisiones, VIII Legislatura, Asuntos Exteriores, Sesión núm. 10, 1 December 2004*, 25.

[29] See, for example, the journalistic inquiries on the personal website of Spanish journalist José Manuel Fernández.

[30] Fernando Gerbasi, "La política exterior de la Revolución Bolivariana y Colombia," in *Hugo Chávez: Una década en el poder*, ed. Francesca Ramos Pismataro, Carlos A. Romero, and Hugo Eduardo Ramírez Arcos (Colombia and Bogotá: Universidad del Rosario, 2010), 569.

historically been one of the principal suppliers of oil to the United States.[31] It goes without saying that it created unease in Washington, when Chávez suddenly decided to sell fifty-three thousand barrels of petroleum a day to Cuba at fixed artificially low prices thereby revoking—at least to some extent—the effect of the US embargo. The fact that thousands of Cuban workers and intelligence officers were pouring into Venezuela as part of the new exchange program only added to these concerns.[32]

During the run-up to the coup, the United States had definitely revealed a certain anxiety over Venezuela. On 5 February 2002, Secretary of State Colin Powell described Chávez as "a serious irritant in our relationship" before the US Senate Foreign Relations Committee.[33] Powell, among other things, referred to the fact that the US embassy in Caracas, which had had several fallouts with Chávez, on one occasion had even told the Venezuelan leader to "keep his mouth shut on these important issues." On the following day, 6 February, the Director of the CIA George Tenet, described Chávez as a "tough actor for us" who "probably doesn't have the interests of the United States at heart."[34] It is therefore no surprise that shortly after the coup; rumor had it that the United States had actually been the mastermind in the plan to oust Chávez. This version—as strongly underlined in Chávez's later statements—was nurtured by the fact that during the coup the United States had been careful not to condemn the actions of Pedro Carmona immediately. Whether or not it was Chavez's continuous "provocations" which determined the Bush administration's initially positive view of Carmona's actions remains to be documented. On the Spanish side, it was probably not only the fact that Chávez was seen as a menace to Spanish interests in the region that inspired the Spanish to develop contacts with Carmona and his people. Perhaps instead, Aznar was tempted by the fact that Venezuela offered a welcome opportunity to work alongside the Bush administration and perhaps even take the lead

---

[31] Yelitza González Madriz, *Por qué el Estado es débil? El caso de Venezuela* (Granada, Spain: Editorial Comares, 2015), 158.

[32] Carlos A. Romero, "Venezuela and Cuba," in *Cuban Foreign Policy Transformation Under Raúl Castro*, ed. H. Michael Erisman and John M. Kirk (Lanham, Boulder, New York, and London: Rowman & Littlefield, 2018), 212.

[33] Clement, "Confronting Hugo Chávez," 211–212.

[34] Ibid., 193.

on this delicate question. By so doing, Aznar could confirm Spain's new-found position as a European Atlantic state which could act as an important interlocutor between Washington and different Latin American states.

Moratinos' decision to go public about the Carmona affair had dire personal consequences for him. People involved in the affair knew that Moratinos knew that they had been involved, and the Spanish foreign minister soon began experiencing difficulties and bad press coverage. However, Zapatero supported him all the way, and all the parliamentary groups approved Moratinos' text with the exception of the PP, who also refused to accept the apologies offered by the minister. Most importantly, Moratinos had saved his position and even Zapatero seemed somewhat pleased with the outcome: In his Christmas address to his ministerial colleagues, Zapatero's praised Moratinos' explanation of the Venezuelan events.[35] Afterward, orders were given to destroy evidence of the entire affair, including the first uncensored report, and to forget the incident.[36]

6.2   Why Don't You Shut Up?

The Bolivarian Revolution introduced by Chávez in 1999 and continued after his death in 2013 by Nicolás Maduro may appear at first glance to be a very odd phenomenon. On the surface, it represents a kind of political and religious syncretism, where the figure of Simón Bolívar, the Latin American general and liberator, is worshipped like a saint. The Neo-Bolivarian movement began in military quarters in the 1970s and was constituted by officers from the poorer parts of the population that had been deeply affected by the economic crisis. They were appalled by the corruption of the military elite and took the side of soldiers who suffered abuse from their superior officers. This gave birth to their fundamental idea of fighting discrimination and disparity across the whole of Venezuelan society. Educated in the spirit of Bolívar, they were also inherently nationalist. In accordance with these principles, in 1983 the group around Chávez formed a secret organization whose goal was to give new impetus to patriotic values, dignify the military career and, not least, fight corruption. This humble and idealistic origin also largely explains the movement's fascination for vast sectors of the marginalized Venezuelan poor, who saw in Chávez a man who would

---

[35] Bono, *Diario de un ministro*, entry for December 22, 2004.

[36] Moratinos Files: Private information.

redistribute wealth and provide them with a more dignified life. In 1992, Chávez's group organized a coup d'état, which however failed.[37]

Thus, Bolivarianism is essentially a left-wing civic-military alliance, which in spite of fierce political opposition and attempted counter coups has effectively held onto power since 1999. Its powers have been legitimated by both referendums and general elections, although this has also been made possible by the opposition's occasional refusal to partake in the parliamentary process. Bolivarianism represents a new kind of populist left-wing movement in Latin America determined to fight neoliberal capitalism. Yet it is also a very heterogeneous group, and until 2013, its different fractions were kept in constant tension and held together by Chávez's charismatic and authoritarian leadership. During its first decade in power, it was able to initiate a major redistribution of wealth and thus—according to official figures—to lift millions out of poverty.[38]

After the polemics surrounding the Carmona affair, Spain's relationship with the Bolivarian leadership in Venezuela continued to be difficult. The challenges in Venezuela were to some extent similar to the ones experienced in Bolivia and other countries in Latin America, but the problems with Caracas were magnified by Chávez's difficult personality and the special US concerns about this strategically important country. On a more general level, the crisis in Venezuela in 2002 also raised the more complex question of how Spain, as well as the rest of the international community, could most effectively react toward weak states on the South American continent that were considered strategically important but which were also challenged by radical political ideologies. In Bolivia, for example, the Spanish Foreign Ministry knew the former elite well and had developed a series of policies over the years that had suited both Spanish and local hierarchical interests. However, with the revolutionary Evo Morales as new president from January 2006, this policy would clearly no longer be valid. Thus, the ministry had to come up with a new plan that would somehow sustain and recognize the importance of Morales' inclusion policies, whereby multiple

---

[37] This reconstruction owes to Margerita López Maya, "Venezuela: Hugo Chávez y el bolivarianismo," *Revista Venezolana de Economía y Ciencias Sociales*, vol. 14, issue 3 (September–December 2008): 55–57.

[38] Ibid., 56. Cf. the dramatic fall in the percentage of the Venezuelan population living below the poverty line. See for example the *Index Mundi* based among other sources on the CIA Fact Book. https://www.indexmundi.com/g/g.aspx?c=ve&v=69.

ethnic groups, representing two-thirds of the country's inhabitants, had suddenly gained rights as citizens.[39]

A further problem was that Spain had for quite some time been distancing itself politically, if not separating itself from Latin America, despite fast-growing Spanish commercial interests in the region. One of Zapatero's closest collaborators described to me the relations with Latin America in 2004 as being completely destroyed ("*arrasadas*"), underlining, for example, that Spanish firms were suffering enormously in Argentina, where the local authorities did nothing to facilitate Spanish investments. On the contrary, they sabotaged them.[40]

In the Socialists' view, the heart of the problem was that Spain had become increasingly unable to interpret the social and political dynamics of Latin America, which were under radical transformation—Venezuela and Bolivia being only two among several challenging cases. Contrary to the ambitions auspicated by Aznar, at the end of the day there was no real possibility that Spain could sustain a truly privileged relationship with Latin America with Spain playing the role of *primus inter pares.* Aznar's policies had, above all, been ideological in that they reflected the classic Conservative idea of *Hispanidad*, which already in the interwar years had proven itself but a relic of the past. In fact, even General Franco had come to realize that Spain could no longer dominate the Spanish-speaking world.[41] It was therefore no surprise that decades later Fernando Morán, the first Socialist foreign minister of the democracy, simply declared Hispanism dead.

In contrast to Spain's factual decline in direct political influence, Spanish private companies were investing heavily in the region. It so happened that Spanish businesses specializing in the energy sector and in finance were loaded with money after the Spanish privatization policies of the 1990s. This coincided with a growing need for foreign capital and investments in Latin America, where the energy and bank sectors were being privatized due to the neoliberal policies imposed by the Washington consensus. In the period from 1990 to 1996, Spanish investments grew by no less

[39] Moratinos Files: Interview, Moratinos.

[40] Moratinos Files: Interview, María Teresa Fernández de la Vega.

[41] See Pedro Pérez Herrero, "Las relaciones de España con América Latina (1810–2010): discursos, políticas, realidades," in *La política exterior de España. De 1800 hasta hoy*, ed. Juan Carlos Pereira (Barcelona: Ariel, 2010), 423.

than 1182%.[42] Accordingly, Spanish companies were becoming exceedingly powerful in Latin America and controlled vital infrastructure in many countries. For this exact reason, there was also growing popular discontent with the behavior of Spanish businesses among the rising ethnicities and parts of the working or middle-class sectors that were gaining power in a number of countries. There were even stronger signs that new political classes in Latin America wanted to regain control over their natural resources and the strategic and economic sectors held by foreign multinationals. Critics spoke of a second Spanish colonization of Latin America, and many heads of state—also to pay lip service to the populist factions in their home countries—ignored or downplayed their personal participation in the various Ibero-American forums that had been established over the years with Spain as the real instigator.[43] It was against this background that the Zapatero government felt an urgent need to improve relations with the entire continent, as was also stated in the electoral program of the PSOE in 2004.[44]

Moratinos' first trip to Latin America took place on 26 May 2004, when he went to Mexico to attend the Guadalajara Summit between Latin America and the European Union. The summit provided the Spanish government with a crucial first impression of the difficulties of renewing its relationship not only with Mexico and Chile after the fallout over the war in Iraq, but with the entire region. It goes without saying that common cultural heritage is an enormous potential advantage to Spain. Without doubt, these bonds still run deep, but the new government could not help noticing that Latin American societies were beginning to transform at the speed of light, something that alienated them from Spain, even though they continued to regard Madrid as a principal gate to Europe. As foreign minister, Moratinos was also shocked to learn how little the Spanish political system actually knew about Latin America. However, the fact that Spain had now turned its back on the United States in Iraq clearly opened the doors to

[42] Anna Ayuso Pozo, "The Recent History of Spain-Latin American Relations," in *Contemporary Spanish Foreign Policy*, ed. David García Cantalapiedra and Ramón Pacheco Pardo (Abingdon and New York: Routledge, 2014), 118.

[43] Cf. Arenal, *Política exterior de España y relaciones con América Latina*, 145–146; Tomás Pérez Viejo, "El encuentro/desencuentro con la España democrática," in *Historia de la nación y del nacionalismo español*, ed. Antonio Morales Moya, Juan Pablo Fusi Aizpurúa, and Andrés de Blas Guerrero (Barcelona: Galaxia Gutenberg, 2013), 1065–1069.

[44] Cf. PSOE, *Merecemos una España mejor*, 19.

those Latin American governments which were generally skeptical of Bush and Aznar's foreign policy doctrines.[45]

Neither could the new government help noticing the contrast between the current situation and the era of Felipe González, when an excellent job had been done to renew Spain's relationship with Latin America. The former secretary of international relations in the PSOE, Elena Flores, appointed by Felipe González in 1980, had indeed made an enormous effort, assisting both the peace process in El Salvador and overseeing the development of social democracy in the entire region. As vice president of the International Socialist movement, she did a truly important job of tying Europe and Latin America together. Also González's first foreign minister, Fernando Morán, had launched a new ambitious policy in the region.[46] In many ways, what the PSOE had done in Latin America during the 1980s corresponded to what the German SPD offered Spain during the 1970s, namely sustaining democracy and stability in an era of political transition.[47] This process had also forged a very close and personal relationship between important sectors of the new Latin American elites and the PSOE. Much of this, however, had vanished by 2004 after eight years in opposition. Elena Flores had left, and her replacements were not able to match her stature. In this way, the PSOE had become somewhat disconnected from the new realities of Latin American societies. In other words, no one in the new government or the party really knew much about what was going on in this part of the world.[48]

The important message that the Zapatero government wanted to convey was that it would be able to work with all Latin American countries regardless of their political ideologies and state systems. And to this end, the Ibero-American summits were deemed important, particularly the one in Salamanca on 14–15 July 2005, as the PSOE also wanted to renew the formula of these official gatherings. Prior to the meeting in Salamanca, Moratinos underlined in a newspaper article the countries' common cultural heritage as well as the diversity which characterized the member states.

---

[45] Moratinos Files: Interview, Moratinos.

[46] Cf. Heiberg, *US Spanish Relations After Franco*, 148–149. See also Ángel Viñas, *Al servicio de Europa. Innovación y crisis en la Comisión Europea* (Madrid: Editorial Complutense, 2004), 77–78.

[47] Cf. Antonio Muñoz, *El amigo alemán. el SPD y el PSOE de la dictadura a la democracia* (Barcelona: RBA Libros, 2012).

[48] Moratinos Files: Interview, Moratinos.

Above all, he stressed the fact that all Latin American countries had subscribed to the principles of Zapatero's proposed Alliance of Civilizations and that the new summit would be dedicated to finding a common stand on the UN Millennium Goals and the Alliance Against Hunger and Malnutrition, as well as to canceling foreign debt and using the money saved for education and development instead.[49] However, underneath the surface, the organization and the summits were facing structural problems. The problem with the summits was especially reflected in the way the secretariat had hitherto been financed. Spain paid well over 60% of the costs, and it had traditionally been a forum of Spanish rather than of Latin American interest.[50] To change this, Spain proposed a new formula with Spain in a less dominant role so that the other partners would feel a much stronger attachment to the organization. Prior to the summit in Salamanca, Zapatero, Fernández de la Vega and Moratinos travelled to nearly all the main capitals on the continent to renew Spain's relationships on this basis. A relationship of trust was quickly built with Brazil, thanks especially to President Lula's collaborative spirit. The visits to various other capitals gradually began to produce tangible results.[51]

So it was against the drastically changing political landscape in Latin America that the Spanish governments opted for an innovative political approach. No better argument for change existed than Venezuela, where Spain had to safeguard the vital interests of the important Spanish business community and of the more than 150,000 local Spaniards who rightly feared for their properties due to Chávez's expropriation policies. Importantly, the lesson learned from the Carmona coup was that it was clearly not possible to steer the fundamental political direction of Venezuelan politics from the outside. Increased collaboration in as many fields as possible was seen as the only way forward. However, no one truly knew if this strategy would also be effective. There were simply too many unknown factors involved, including Chávez's difficult personality.

On 21 November 2004, Zapatero invited Hugo Chávez to visit Spain, where he solemnly declared that this state visit was his best ever. Clearly, Chávez was seeking a reconciliation. When Moratinos accompanied him

[49] Miguel Angel Moratinos, "Un espacio común iberoamericano," *El Mundo*, February 25, 2005.

[50] Arenal, *Política exterior de España y relaciones con América Latina*, 544; Moratinos Files: Interview, Moratinos.

[51] Moratinos Files: Interview, Moratinos.

in the car from the airport back to Madrid, Chávez suddenly told him that he wanted to pay tribute to the victims of the terror bombing of 11 March 2004. Accordingly, they improvised a visit to the Atocha railway station to commemorate the victims. Through his own channels, however, Chávez had already advised Spanish left-wingers and revolutionaries of his presence in this part of the town. So, the official car was met by hundreds of people outside Atocha screaming "Hugo!, Hugo!" and in front of the crowd, he praised Moratinos as the man who had defended the Venezuelans against Aznar. The crowd responded by shouting their customary anti-US messages: "*¡Chávez, seguro, al Yanqui dale duro!*"[52] This was hardly a comfortable situation for the Spanish foreign minister, who at the same time was trying to restore relations with the United States. During his stay, Chávez met several times with Zapatero, who diplomatically described the talks as "intense and positive."[53] Chávez also visited Toledo, where he was received by the minister of defense, José Bono. The two discussed the sale of Spanish vessels and aircraft to Venezuela, a business transaction which had been deliberately kept from the Spanish Foreign Ministry.[54]

The entire affair of selling Spanish vessels and aircraft to Venezuela had initially been effectuated by Bono behind Moratinos' back, as he rightly feared that the Foreign Ministry would try to block the sales due to concerns over how Washington would react to such a transaction. To Moratinos, in fact, it was of paramount importance not to upset Washington unnecessarily in a moment of bilateral tension. The whole affair was extremely embarrassing for Moratinos as he learned about the sales, not from the Spanish Ministry of Defense, but from the US embassy in Madrid, which was eager to block the transaction. Such lack of communication is by no means unusual. In fact, Spain has had a long history of vital decisions made by the Ministry of Defense and not being communicated to the foreign ministry. During the Franco period in particular, this was by no means a seldom occurrence.[55]

---

[52] "Tumultuoso recibimiento a Chávez en Atocha," *El País*, November 22, 2004. https://elpais.com/diario/2004/11/22/espana/1101078012_850215.html.

[53] *Anuario Internacional CIDOB*, 2004, entry for November 25.

[54] Bono, *Diario de un ministro*, entry for November 23, 2005.

[55] Cf. Heiberg, *US-Spanish Relations After Franco*, 23–24.

On 4 January 2005, Chávez called Bono to tell him that if Zapatero would stop in Caracas on his planned trip to South America, he was willing to sign a letter of intent regarding the purchase of military equipment. According to Bono's diaries, Zapatero instantly accepted to visit Caracas.[56] On 25 January, Bono went to the Venezuelan capital, where he was invited for dinner in the Palace of Miraflores. Prior to this encounter he had flown in Chávez's private helicopter to see La Orchila, the island where the Venezuelan leader had been held prisoner during the April 2002 coup. During dinner, he handed over a letter to Chávez from Zapatero, just as they discussed the protocol for the sale. Bono successfully insisted that the written agreement should not contain any references to "military equipment," as the patrol boats and the aircraft for transportation had no offensive capabilities. The total order amounted to 1.8 billion dollars.[57]

It was only possible to keep the affair from Moratinos because the Spanish ambassador to Venezuela, Raúl Mórodo was a friend of Bono's. In fact, they both belonged to the same political faction of Tierno Galván. Thus, when Moratinos learned about the arms deal, he became very irate, reminding his ambassador that he was working for him and not for the Ministry of Defense. If the ambassador did not duly inform him in the future, the same minister who had nominated him would fire him. The ambassador defended himself by saying that he was told that Bono would personally take the matter up with Moratinos, something he had clearly failed to do.[58] Bono's diaries give the impression, right or wrong, that the freezing out of the Foreign Ministry was made in agreement with Zapatero. Moratinos doubts this was the case, even though Bono convincingly claims so (cf. the fact that Bono allegedly carried a personal letter from Zapatero with him on his first trip to Caracas).

By February 2005, the Spanish sales to Caracas had begun to create international friction, not only with the United States but also with Colombia. Bogotá warned that it was highly concerned about Bono's visit to Caracas and the new agreement to supply Venezuela with defense material.[59] Thus, there was a risk of deteriorating the relationship with Colombia, as well as weakening Spain's standing with the United States, which had

---

[56] Bono, *Diario de un ministro*, entry for January 4, 2005.

[57] Ibid., entry for January 25–26, 2005.

[58] Moratinos Files: Interview Moratinos.

[59] Moratinos Files: Private information.

already labeled Spain as an unreliable partner. This delicate situation was aggravated by the decision of Hugo Chávez to sell petroleum to China and at the same time to cancel agreements previously struck with US oil companies. Against this background, and given the superior weight of Colombia in Latin America, the Spanish government had to consider whether arms sales to Caracas or being on friendly terms with Colombia was best for Spain's overall policies in the region.

Despite US and Colombian pressure, Bono, Moratinos and Zapatero soon agreed to maintain the agreement struck with Venezuela, particularly as the vessels did not have offensive capabilities. However, during a subsequent trip to Caracas in late March 2005, the Venezuelan military informed Bono that the deal, which the Spanish side considered more or less closed, was still only considered to be at a preliminary stage. US pressure was surely beginning to show. However, at a talk the following day in the Palace of Miraflores, Chávez tried to minimize any differences. In fact, the contract was signed immediately and without any modifications.[60] The business deal was profitable to both Spain and Venezuela and also inspired hopes that the two countries could work together in other areas where they had hitherto held conflicting positions.

After this relatively good start, the bilateral relationship started to take a negative turn, and one of the most talked about diplomatic crises with Venezuela actually involved the Spanish king. In November 2007, at the plenary session of the Ibero-American Summit in Santiago de Chile, Juan Carlos suddenly told Chávez to "shut up." To make things worse, the fallout was broadcast on live television. Importantly, the bilateral crisis was actually much more complicated than it was described in the press at the time. It is revealing of some of the fundamental ideological differences which characterized the political scene in Latin America at that time and which the Zapatero government had to cope with.

Over the last year, there had been a growing political misunderstanding between Chávez and Zapatero, who increasingly used Moratinos as his intermediate to avoid direct dealings with the Venezuelan leader. Among other things, the relationship was made difficult by Chávez's outspoken anti-Americanism, which tended to poison every political discussion. In the days preceding the summit, Chávez had also publicly repeated his denouncement of Aznar's involvement in the coup in 2002, and Zapatero

---

[60]Bono, *Diario de un ministro*, entry for March 27 and 30, 2005.

therefore asked Moratinos to speak to Chávez's foreign minister, Nicolás Maduro, to put an end to all these accusations once and for all so that they would not repeat themselves during the summit. Chávez should at least try to show some public respect for the former government of Spain. When Moratinos approached Maduro on this matter, the latter showed some understanding of the Spanish position, but he also gave Moratinos to understand that he did not have any margin for independent action or influence on Chávez.

The meeting in Santiago de Chile initially went ahead as planned. First, there was the traditional open session when all the ministers were present. In the evening, there was the so-called retreat where the heads of state and the prime ministers saw each other alone. During the retreat, there was a heated debate on social development in Latin America, and Zapatero had arguments with President Daniel Ortega of Nicaragua and also with Chávez, who both kept blaming American imperialism for all the problems that Latin America was suffering. Zapatero said that to keep singing this old song would be to lie to oneself, and he lectured them about the fact that they had to take matters into their own hands and introduce structural changes starting with their fiscal and financial systems. In Spain's view, the two Latin American leaders were caught in an old political discourse, and while Chávez and Ortega became more and more agitated, the remaining Latin American leaders actually supported Zapatero. Thus, it was the political thesis put forward by Zapatero that won the debate during the retreat.[61]

The plenary session of the following day saw the intervention of Ortega, who kept attacking Bush, Aznar, Zapatero, etc. In order to stop the incessant attacks, Zapatero said that he could not accept such criticism directed at a former Spanish prime minister. The Spanish king was becoming even more agitated and to calm him down, Zapatero asked to be allowed to answer. However, during his reply to Ortega, Chávez suddenly intervened without the microphone switched on, talking very loudly and defending Ortega's criticism of Aznar. At this point, the king interfered with his famous outburst "*¿Por qué no te callas?*" ("Why don't you shut up?"). He then got up

[61]Moratinos Files: Interview, Moratinos.

from his chair and left the room. The situation was actually poorly managed by the panel moderator, the Chilean president, Michelle Bachelet,
who should have stopped the discussion much before.[62]

Afterward, Zapatero received a surprise call from Aznar, who was thank-
ful for the fact that Zapatero had defended him from Ortega's criticism.[63]
The king received a lot of credit because in the eyes of the international
press this was the first time that someone had spoken the truth to the
Venezuelan leader.[64] Zapatero also gained recognition at home for having
defended his Conservative predecessor. Nevertheless, this left the difficult
task of cleaning up the diplomatic mess in the hands of Moratinos, who
had to somehow reestablish contact between the king and Chávez. On the
plane back home, the king admitted that he had complicated things for his
foreign minister. The crisis was profound, no doubt, and intense diplomatic
activities were needed to overcome these difficulties, particularly because
Spain wanted to close some major business deals with Venezuela. Chávez
was deeply offended and demanded an apology from the king. He further
threatened to nationalize Spanish firms and banks if Spain did not deliver.[65]

To iron out the differences, Moratinos tried to establish a more or
less formal encounter between Don Felipe, the Spanish crown prince, and
Chávez, while the foreign ministry sent a letter to Chávez congratulating
him on the most recent successful referendum in the name of the king.
Moratinos also called the Venezuelan ambassador and proposed that the
two parties could use an upcoming event in Argentina in December to
formally reconcile, namely the unusual transfer of power from President
Néstor Kirchner to the new president-elect, his wife Cristina Fernández de
Kirchner.[66] It was agreed that Chávez should use the occasion to approach
the crown prince, who was representing Spain at this event, and in remem-
brance of the normally good relations between the two countries, they
would shake hands with each other. However, two days prior to the summit

[62]The incident can be seen on YouTube. See https://www.youtube.com/watch?v=
Q8LjERqsXhM.

[63]"Rajoy culpa a Zapatero pese a la llamada de Aznar," El País, November 12, 2007.

[64]"La imagen del Rey ha salido reforzado," El País, November 12, 2007.

[65]Juan Ignacio Irigary, "El controvertido cara a cara del Príncipe Felipe y Hugo Chávez
en Argentina," El Mundo, December 10, 2012. http://www.elmundo.es/elmundo/2007/
12/09/internacional/1197214097.html.

[66]Cf. "Moratinos persigue un encuentro de Don Felipe con Chávez al margen de Zarzuela,"
ABC, December 6, 2007.

the future king told the press that he had no intention of shaking hands with Chávez. The Venezuelans got nervous and immediately called Moratinos. At this point, the Venezuelans were about to issue a fierce communiqué as to why they had no wish to meet with the Prince and they reiterated a number of threats. To control the damage, Moratinos immediately contacted the Spanish royal court, and they had in his own words a "very tough" exchange of opinions. Don Felipe and Chávez eventually shook hands in Buenos Aires, albeit not in a formal setting, and Chávez, who was still upset with Don Felipe's attitude, now demanded a full excuse from the king and other concessions.[67]

In spring 2008, a solution was finally found, and—as expected—it involved the Spanish king personally. Chávez was going to Moscow, and it was agreed that he could make a stop in Spain on 25 July 2008. The idea was to invite Chávez to the Palace of Marivent, the king's residence in Mallorca. When the day of the visit finally arrived, the king was very nervous about the fact that Chávez was late and he took it as a personal offense, but Moratinos was able to calm him down during their telephone conversation. In the event, Chávez arrived 45 minutes late on what turned out to be a splendid summer day. Chávez also seemed to be nervous when Moratinos accompanied him in the car from the airport to the Palace of Marivent: "*Esto va a salir bien, ¿no?*" ("This will work out fine, right?"). "Of course Mr. President," Moratinos replied. Chávez then continued, "I come here with the best intentions, but what about his Majesty?" "Everything will be fine," Moratinos said, and in that exact moment, while Chávez was expressing his nervousness about the king's intentions, the equally nervous Spanish king called Moratinos and said, "This will work out fine, right?"

The talks in Mallorca proceeded well, and an oil deal which involved the Spanish multinational Repsol was put back on track. Juan Carlos and Chávez embraced each other, and before leaving, the king gave him a T-shirt with "*¿Por qué no te callas?*" ("Why don't you shut up") written all over it. Chávez liked it a lot. He said that the two of them should wear the T-shirt in front of the press, to which the king replied, "Only on one condition. You do not tell them who gave me the T-shirt." "Who?" said Chávez. "President Bush of course," Juan Carlos replied, and they both laughed. The king thus played a large part in reestablishing the relationship. Indeed,

[67] "Chávez niega reunión con Don Felipe e insiste en una disculpa del Rey," *Diario Exterior*, December 12, 2007. https://www.eldiarioexterior.com/chavez-niega-reunion-con-don-17828.htm.

Juan Carlos had a unique way of using informal settings or situations to make his interlocutor feel comfortable. On one occasion, around the year 2000 when the king had met Chávez as president for the first time, he gave Chávez a slight push in the back, to which Chávez replied, "Why did you do that?" The king replied in Spanish, "I've been told that you like pushes," probably referring to Chávez's participation in the 1992 coup.[68]

In September 2009, Chávez went back to Spain, and the meetings held in the Spanish capital with the king and Zapatero were largely positive. Chávez announced that the Venezuelan state-owned oil company PDVSA had, in a joint venture with Repsol and the Italian ENI, discovered huge natural gas reservoirs, making Venezuela the holder of the fifth largest reserves in the world. Furthermore, contracts were signed in the field of wind energy and housing as well.[69] Chávez also used the occasion to go to the Gran Vía to buy books under immense police protection. Among the big crowd, Chávez told Antonio Brufau, CEO of Repsol, to accompany him to Torrejón Airport, and during the ride, they discussed different business proposals which were soon effectuated. On his subsequent visit to Caracas in July 2009, Moratinos was able to assist in the closing of three important contracts for Repsol, Iberdrola and Elector, worth billions of euros and also thousands of jobs for the Venezuelans. Among other companies participating in this mission were representatives from Banco Santander, who settled the question of compensation for the nationalization of the Banco de Venezuela, owned by the Spanish bank, at $1050 million. This transaction—negotiated by Moratinos personally—was actually a much better deal than a previous offer to buy the bank from a private Venezuelan investor group, which Banco Santander had seriously considered.[70]

Much more difficult were the negotiations concerning the expropriations of minor Spanish companies and especially farms in Venezuela, which had begun in 2005 under Chávez's new program for nationalization.

[68] Moratinos Files: Interview, Moratinos.

[69] Kiraz Janicke, "Venezuela's Chavez Talks Gas Cooperation, Climate Change During Visit to Spain," *Venezuelaanalysis.com*, September 11, 2009. https://venezuelanalysis.com/news/4790.

[70] "Otro viaje polémico de Moratinos: visita Venezuela para mejorar las relaciones económicas con Chávez," *El Confidencial*, July 27, 2007. http://www.elconfidencial.com/espana/2009-07-27/otro-viaje-polemico-de-moratinos-visita-venezuela-para-mejorar-las-relaciones-economicas-con-chavez_483194/; "Chávez: 'Llévales un abrazo al Rey y Zapatero. Estamos esperando que nos visiten'," *El Mundo*, July 30, 2009. http://www.elmundo.es/elmundo/2009/07/29/espana/1248894574.html.

According to the local government, these properties had been confiscated due to their unproductivity. On 20 June 2007, Moratinos denounced seventy such cases of Spanish–Venezuelans who had been affected by expropriations or occupations of land, something which the PP used to attack the minister for being too soft on Chávez, calling the PSOE policy "embarrassing" (*"vergonzosa"*).[71] In early February 2008, the Spanish Foreign Ministry had become truly fed up with Venezuela's lack of collaboration and eternal provocation. In fact, a considerable increase in home invasions, robberies and the intimidation of Spanish–Venezuelan citizens were occurring in the state of Yaracuy, just as images of King Juan Carlos and Aznar had been burned in front of the embassy. Moreover, Madrid felt that the Venezuelans were deliberately sabotaging diplomatic relations. For the first time, the ministry was thus considering corresponding in equal fashion by freezing relations with the Venezuelan ambassador for the time being.[72] However, in the end the Santa Cruz Palace reacted more cautiously and was able to overcome many of the obstacles, and also solve many of the cases of harassment by procuring satisfactory economic compensation. Admittedly, some unresolved cases still left a great deal to be desired.

In many ways, the difficulties experienced in Venezuela were comparable to the problems that Spain was facing in Bolivia, and the strategy employed in both countries was for this reason quite similar. Bolivia was a huge challenge because the local government wanted to nationalize sectors and resources that Spanish companies had previously been allowed to purchase legally. Bolivia has the second greatest gas reserves in Latin America, and Spanish Repsol was by 2006 the single greatest foreign investor in Bolivia, controlling one-third of the gas reserves of the country.[73]

During his first official visit to Spain in early January 2006, the Bolivian president-elect Evo Morales wore his famous revolutionary jersey—a strong signal of the radical political changes his new government was going to carry out. Moratinos received him in his office, and he could not fail to notice that the Bolivian leader was actually very timid, although at the same time he also displayed great political strength. His shyness may well have been linked to his limited formal education which in part made him

[71] "Moratinos dice que quedan 70 hispano-venezulanos afectados por las expropiaciones y defiende a Morodo," *Europa Press*, June 20, 2007.

[72] Moratinos Files: Private information.

[73] *Anuario Internacional CIDOB*, entry for January 4, 2006.

feel inferior. They talked about Spanish investments in Bolivia, specifically the case of Repsol-YPF. Afterward, they went to see the king, and then Zapatero. Morales asked a lot of questions, and he always carried with him a small paper notepad in which he—with some difficulty—took notes of all the advice that Moratinos gave him. The foreign minister also gave him a book to read.

However, Morales soon increased in confidence, and during its entire mandate, Zapatero's government had a politically tense relationship with Bolivia, also because Morales' vice president, Álvaro Marcelo García Linera, was in many ways Chávez's opposite. Educated, and of Western origin, yet also very ideological and very left-wing, García Linera did not view his Spanish interlocutors for who they were, but for what they represented: a foreign nation which controlled everything in Bolivia from airports, insurance companies and banks, and carbides. To the vice president, it made little difference that Zapatero had just announced that Spain was willing to cancel a significant part of Bolivia's bilateral debts in exchange for education plans for the broader Bolivian population. However, Morales turned out to be much more susceptible to the Spanish overtures.

One particular conflict may illustrate some of the difficulties that the Spanish government had to surmount. On 9 March 2006, Moratinos was contacted by García Linera who told him that the Bolivian authorities had occupied the oil platforms of Repsol and that the police had also searched the offices of the same Spanish company. The background was formally that Bolivian authorities suspected that Repsol was involved in the contraband of crude oil to Chile and Argentina. However, there was much speculation in the press as to whether the entire operation had been mounted by either the opposition or by forces wanting to obstruct the good personal working relationship between Antonio Brufau, CEO of Repsol, and Evo Morales.[74] Moratinos immediately talked to Foreign Minister David Choquehuanca Céspedes, while both he and Fernández de la Vega talked to Morales personally.[75]

Fernández de la Vega took on the role as the "bad cop" in these negotiations. After some difficulties, she managed to locate Morales, who was somewhere on the Pampas. Apparently, Morales knew of the operation,

---

[74]Mabel Azcui, "La Fiscalía de Bolivia registra la sede de Repsol para detener a dos directivos," *El País*, March 10, 2010. https://elpais.com/diario/2006/03/10/economia/1141945203_850215.html.

[75]Moratinos Files: Interview, Moratinos.

although he claimed that he did not. Clearly, he had not orchestrated it. Nevertheless, the Spanish vice president spoke in no uncertain terms when she warned him, "You are going to be alone because you don't have any support as president in Latin America. You will be all by yourself. You know that." She then led him to understand, on the other hand, that Spain was a friend and would be helpful in his struggle against the opposition forces, but he had to call off the entire operation now.[76] Moratinos took a different approach. On the following day, while attending an informal meeting with the foreign ministers of the European Union, he said that he "respected," but that he did not "approve of" the Bolivian decision.[77] He further instructed Bernardino León to speak with Morales during the investiture ceremony in Chile of President Michelle Bachelet.

In the event, development aid and the canceling of Bolivian bilateral debts were used by the Spanish Foreign Ministry as a carrot to moderate such actions from Morales' government. This was, however, only possible because Zapatero's government had introduced structural changes in the Spanish foreign policy programs by increasing development aid, one example being the *Fondo de Agua*, an €800 million project to improve water supplies to benefit the Latin American poor. Other initiatives to reduce poverty and illiteracy in Latin America were taken by the Zapatero government in much the same way. Nevertheless, it was difficult terrain because there was still widespread animosity in Latin America toward Spain, just as many local governments would seek different domestic agendas which did not always coincide with Spanish ideas. However, Moratinos' vice minister for development, Leire Pajín, did an excellent job in promoting Spanish development policies, especially during her first years of service. Coming from the same sector she understood perfectly how NGOs work, and she knew how to collaborate with them for the benefit of the local population. She was very well received in all circles, especially in the countries where the biggest changes were happening such as Bolivia.[78]

Thus, a wide range of measures were employed to defend vital Spanish interests in Latin America. In the Bolivian case which involved Repsol, the Spanish government managed to block the initiative of the Morales government and sent a delegation to Bolivia to sort out the more technical

[76] Moratinos Files: Private information.
[77] "Moratinos dice caso Repsol no favorece a Gobierno boliviano," *EFE*, March 10, 2006.
[78] Moratinos Files: Interview, Moratinos.

questions. In this way, Repsol's Bolivian interests were safeguarded, and a new long-term drilling contract was eventually signed. The Spanish government was not involved in subsequent transactions between Repsol and the Bolivian government, but as Fernández de la Vega told me, the PSOE government surely "opened the political doors which made the agreement possible."[79]

In another case, Morales had asked for five hundred ambulances, even though in Bolivia there were hardly enough clinics or viable roads to serve this amount of specialized vehicles, something which of course limited their use considerably. A study group examined the question and eventually designed a more realistic aid plan. Additionally, in foreign affairs, Moratinos helped Choquehuanca understand the functioning of multilateral organs like the UN. So instead of condemning Morales' regime, the PSOE government tried to show them another way, much in the same way as the German SPD had done to the PSOE itself during the 1970s by stimulating moderation and vision as a vehicle for real political change. And most importantly, doing so without paternalism.

According to Antonio Brufau, the positive outcome of these yearlong negotiations with Bolivia was essentially due to the personal abilities of Moratinos. Apart from acting as a tough negotiator, the foreign minister took the utmost care not to pass judgements on anyone. He never lectured his interlocutors, but always showed that he respected them. It was this personal quality, also largely present in the other PSOE ministers involved in Latin American affairs but to a much lesser degree, which made the difference in the difficult moments when Repsol experienced trouble in Latin America.[80] With regard to Venezuela, Brufau also told me, the policy course of the Zapatero government was evidently right, but again he stresses Moratinos' personal qualities without which this policy could never have been effectuated. Through his conscious and sensible approach, Moratinos had been able to create a relationship of trust with Hugo Chávez, a relationship which was not one between a president and a foreign minister, but rather one between two equals who respected one another. Brufau was of course fully aware that Moratinos' "accommodating" approach gave rise to a lot of domestic criticism and accusations against him for being a

[79] Moratinos Files: Interview, Fernández de la Vega.

[80] Moratinos Files: Interview, Brufau.

Bolivarian revolutionary and so forth. This was in his view, however, more telling of the ignorance of his critics.

Brufau, like other stakeholders I have spoken to, essentially sees Evo Morales and the late Hugo Chávez as pragmatic politicians. The criticism against them was in part due to a complete lack of understanding of the historical, political and cultural development in Latin America, where the indigenous population and new classes are beginning to dominate at the expense of the former dominating white elite. Chávez was of indigenous origin, and so is Morales and other Latin American mandatories. Moratinos, who had no previous knowledge of the region, understood that he should not try to give them lessons in democracy, but instead try to establish a relationship of trust which could be used to promote Spanish interests, and in the long run perhaps also contribute to political stabilization in the region.[81] Seen from this perspective, Moratinos was probably not without cause, when he reminded the critical opposition at home about what was at stake in Latin America: Many countries were struggling to overcome a situation where the vast majority of the inhabitants had been completely marginalized. Indeed, many ethnic groups had hitherto not been considered citizens in the political sense. They had no rights. He further reminded them that in Bolivia, Spain had actually achieved a deal for Repsol that no other foreign company had been able to match, while a large number of cases regarding the confiscation of land and small businesses in Venezuela had been solved, too.[82]

The pragmatism of Chávez and Morales was further displayed by their understanding of *nationalization*, the alpha and the omega of the Bolivarian revolution. However, in Western public opinion this economic and political concept is often subject to simplistic interpretations. In Venezuela, for example, the PDVSA, the Venezuelan state-owned oil company, wanted the majority of the shares of a joint venture company, which was until then in Repsol's hands. In turn, Venezuela compensated the Spanish multinational by abandoning its previous policy of letting the state fix the price of crude oil, which could now be sold—to the great benefit of the Spanish company—at market prices. By all measures, it was a very fair bargain. In Bolivia, Morales' government sometimes made "spectacular" police

[81] Ibid.

[82] "Moratinos asegura que la política del Gobierno ha permitido proteger intereses españoles en Venezuela, Ecuador y Bolivia," *Europa Press*, December 19, 2007.

searches of Repsol offices or drilling platforms, or even sent some of Brufau's trusted men to jail. At the end of the day, what was essential to the
Bolivian government was to seize control of the Bolivian soil under drilling,
which was formally owned by Repsol. The Spanish company accepted this
term, which also implied that the company could no longer include the soil
as a company asset. Still, it was a transaction which in no way affected Repsol's ability to work, drill or earn money in the country. And the settlement
was thus a fair give and take, where—as already mentioned—Repsol was
enabled to renew its contracts with Bolivia for an extended period. The situation in Bolivia and Venezuela was thus incomparable to Argentina, where
Repsol—in its own understanding—was subject to sheer robbery when
the Kirchner government decided to simply take over company shares.
Argentina is in many critics' view probably the country which offers the
worst legal protection in Latin America, if not the world. It says a lot about
the pragmatism of Bolivia and Venezuela that both governments were completely silent when Kirchner embarked upon her populist nationalizations.
One might have expected the two Bolivarian leaders to applaud, but they
silently distanced themselves from Kirchner's undertakings.[83]

A fundamental challenge was, of course, that the inequalities of the
Bolivian and Venezuelan societies are so immense as to inspire radical solutions rather than well-pondered moderate transformation processes. In the
Bolivian case, the problem is that Morales' party base is very demanding
and very populist when it comes to reform, whereas Morales has gradually
become more of a professional administrator. Morales has come to appreciate the importance of an efficient administration, the balancing of the
books and of having a severe minister of finance with a clear mandate to
intervene in the economy when necessary. In fact, the Bolivian economy
is performing quite well, despite being by far the poorest country in the
region. One only has to take a look at the macroeconomic figures and read
international evaluations to understand that the former *guerrilleros* have
actually learned an important economic lesson or two.[84] On the negative

---

[83] Moratinos Files: Interview, Brufau.

[84] "During the 2004–2014 decade, the Bolivian economy grew at an average annual rate
of 4.9 percent due to the high commodities prices, the expansion of natural gas exports
to Argentina and a prudent macroeconomic policy. Consequently, moderate poverty was
reduced from 59 percent to 39 percent and the Gini coefficient of inequality fell from 0.60
to 0.47." Quotation taken from the World Bank's analysis. See http://www.worldbank.org/
en/country/bolivia/overview.

side, however, it should be mentioned that there have been attempts from the Bolivian government to institutionalize its own revolution beyond the boundaries of the constitution, a move which has, however, been rejected by popular vote.[85]

Likewise, Hugo Chávez actually complied with many Spanish requests, essentially because he trusted the new Spanish government. This was also true with regard to the remaining ETA members still present in Venezuela. It so happened that Zapatero's government had initiated a new dialogue with ETA in order to bring an end to the violence of the Basque terrorist organization. The presence of ETA members in Venezuela was due to the fact that during the 1980s it had been impossible for Spain to obtain extraditions of prisoners from France to Spain. However, a compromise was struck with Paris, whereby ETA members could be deported to third countries like Panamá or Cabo Verde and then on to Venezuela and Cuba. Both Venezuela and Cuba helped the Zapatero government by sending the clear message to ETA that their unlawful activities would have to cease, otherwise they would lose their position in the country. In the event, Chávez sent the same message to ETA as he had sent to FARC (Fuerzas Armadas Revolucionarias de Colombia) in Colombia, i.e., that the era of armed revolution was over, and that the revolution would now have to pass through democratic elections.

In turn, Zapatero offered his help with solving Venezuela's problems with Colombia, which in 2009 was outraged by Chávez's support to the FARC. The fact that FARC was allegedly operating from Venezuelan soil was unacceptable to Colombia, who sent a major dossier on the matter to the Spanish government. Following a Colombian petition, new plans were drawn up by the Santa Cruz Palace on how to improve the relationship between Colombia and Venezuela. This difficult process also had links to Spain, as Spanish prosecutor Eloy Velasco was building a case concerning the alleged connivance of the Venezuelan government with the illegal collaboration between the FARC and ETA members in Venezuela. However, through a number of talks with Chávez and Maduro, Spain succeeded in making Venezuela condemn terrorism, and the first talks showed that Chávez personally had no knowledge of the special obligations regarding ETA that the Venezuelan government had committed itself to in the 1980s. During his last months in office, Moratinos highlighted the need for the

---

[85] Javier Lafuente, "Bolivia le dice no a la intención de Evo Morales de buscar otra reelección," *El País*, February 24, 2016.

extradition of ETA members and increased police collaboration between the two countries, just as he stressed the possibility of sending observers to the upcoming Venezuelan elections.[86]

Today, the political dialogue in Venezuela, now under the Presidency of Nicolás Maduro, has collapsed, in part because the international community seems to have lost faith in the process. In addition, inflation is skyrocketing, while hunger is becoming more widespread in a country that ought to be rich enough to ensure all its citizens a decent, if not prosperous life. Sadly, the abandonment of political dialogue, only sustained this far by a small group of former foreign leaders, among others Zapatero, and representatives of the Catholic Church, has led to a difficult and extremely dangerous situation, where a civil war cannot entirely be ruled out.[87] If anything, this chapter has tried to demonstrate that in the case of Venezuela and Bolivia, there is little alternative to sustained political dialogue, even though it is tempting at times to respond in a harder fashion.

By applying the basic principle of dialogue, from 2004 to 2011 Spain avoided major nationalizations in Latin America, whereas the Conservative PP government after 2012 suffered the burdensome nationalization of Repsol's assets in Argentina. On 16 April 2012, the president of Argentina announced an upcoming law which foresaw the expropriation of 51% of the holding company of Repsol, notwithstanding the fact that Repsol-YPF had paid billions of US dollars in taxes and invested huge sums in exploration and exploitation facilities.[88] To my knowledge, during the Zapatero period no whole Spanish-controlled sector was nationalized, but those individual companies that were affected by nationalizations were compensated. Importantly, Spanish companies were allowed to continue to work unhindered in Bolivia, in spite of the fact that Morales' party was ideologically hostile to their presence. This fact probably shows the strength of dialogue in a situation where the two parties defended two completely different

---

[86] Moratinos Files: Interview, Moratinos. Cf. José Yoldi, "El Gobierno venezolano colaboró con ETA y las FARC, según el juez Velazco," *El País*, March 2, 2010. http://elpais.com/diario/2010/03/02/espana/1267484407_850215.html.

[87] On the origins of the weak and divided Venezuelan state see González Madriz, *¿Por qué el Estado es débil?*

[88] On Repsol's protests see: Francisco Peregil, "Argentina expropria a Repsol su filial YPF," *El País*, April 17, 2012. https://elpais.com/economia/2012/04/16/actualidad/1334590509_507539.html.

agendas, i.e., nationalization versus the maintenance of foreign control over vital infrastructures.

In sum, the first rule of the renewed Spanish diplomatic effort in Latin America had been to show respect and acceptance of the altered political situation in order to safeguard Spanish interests. Zapatero would, however, always tell Morales and Chávez that their political projects were probably more left-wing, and definitely more revolutionary, whereas his own project was much more moderate, but with greater chances of being executed. Two models of socialism and progressivism were thus continuously being confronted: one anti-imperialistic, anti-American and collectivist, the other progressive and social democratic. This tension was always present in the bilateral relations, but it was a tension between leaders who did their utmost to respect one another, something which facilitated an otherwise difficult dialogue.[89]

[89] Moratinos Files: Interview, Moratinos.

CHAPTER 7

Stupid Little Island

7.1   THE PSOE's SECRET CHANNEL

On 11 July 2002, Moroccan gendarmes suddenly occupied Parsley Island, an islet 150 meters off the Moroccan coast, which few Spaniards had heard of until then. The Spanish government of Aznar considered the occupation a hostile act, a sheer violation of Spanish sovereign territory. Indeed, the existence of Spanish enclaves on the Northwest African coast has been a constant cause for friction between the two Mediterranean neighbors, and it is unsurprising that Spain's official defense doctrine traditionally considers the Maghreb area in North Africa the most likely security threat.[1] Yet this occupation, which caught the Spanish government by complete surprise, led to the worst diplomatic crisis in decades. In fact, the preceding democratic governments in Spain had all done much to improve the relationship. Above all, Spain had seriously reconsidered its relationship with Rabat, which under the Franco regime was based on classical geostrategic considerations. Hence, the idea of the Socialist governments of the 1980s was to create multiple economic interdependencies between

[1] Cf. Jordi Vaquer I Fanes, "Spain in the Mediterranean and the Middle East: The Quest for Security and Status," in *Contemporary Spanish Foreign Policy*, ed. David García Cantalapiedra and Ramón Pacheco Pardo (Abingdon and New York: Routledge, 2014), 131.

© The Author(s) 2019   185
M. Heiberg, *Spain and the Wider World since 2000*,
Security, Conflict and Cooperation in the Contemporary World,
https://doi.org/10.1007/978-3-030-27343-9_7

the two neighbors which could mitigate the effects of a potential political or military crisis.[2] By 2002, these "cushions of interest" apparently no longer worked. Importantly, the new dispute was not only about territorial matters. It was preceded and probably also fueled by the stalemate over a new fisheries agreement, quarrels over migration issues and a profound Moroccan dissatisfaction with Aznar's position on Western Sahara.

Much to the chagrin of the Spanish Conservative government, Zapatero decided in the midst of this bilateral crisis to visit Morocco together with Trinidad Jiménez, a member of the executive committee of the PSOE. Crucially, this controversial meeting took place only a couple of months after Morocco had withdrawn its ambassador from Madrid in October 2001. The PP interpreted the visit as an act of complete disloyalty, as well as indirect criticism of the Spanish policy line toward Morocco. Allegedly, the new Moroccan king, Mohammed VI, told Zapatero that Morocco's outspoken claims for Ceuta and Melilla were not truly on the political agenda since Rabat now had other priorities. In turn, Zapatero sent signals of détente and argued in favor of a Spanish rapprochement with Morocco on several crucial points.[3] What has probably been missing so far in the political analyses of this reunion is that it was not an isolated incident. It was actually followed by numerous secret contacts between the PSOE and Rabat. In this way, the Socialist government hoped to establish a back channel which could improve relations with Rabat in view of a possible change of government in Spain in 2004. Only a couple of months prior to the general elections, Moratinos held secret talks with Taieb Fassi Fihri, the Vice Minister of Foreign Affairs and a close confident of King Mohammed VI. The meeting took place in the residence of the Moroccan ambassador in Madrid, right under the nose of the Spanish Conservative government.[4]

One of the issues which had truly worsened the relationship with Rabat after 2000 was the strong personal ties that Aznar had forged with the Algerian leader Abdelaziz Bouteflika, who in turn was engaged in innumerable disputes with the Moroccan king. Above all, Bouteflika was pushing for an international settlement for Western Sahara which in Rabat's view rode

---

[2] Irene Fernández-Molina, *Moroccan Foreign Policy Under Mohammed VI, 1999–2014* (London and New York: Routledge, 2016), 171. See also Dezcallar, *El anticuario de Teherán*, 180–181.

[3] Ignacio Cembrero, *Vecinos alejados: Los secretos de la crisis entre España y Marruecos* (Barcelona: Galaxia Gutenberg, 2006), 115.

[4] Moratinos Files: Interview, Moratinos.

roughshod over Moroccan interests. Madrid was now supporting Algiers by going against the internationally accepted Baker Plan I, which foresaw the integration of Western Sahara into Morocco. This clearly poisoned relations with Rabat. In addition, bilateral tension was heightened by the sudden arrival on Spanish shores of hundreds of *pateras*, small boats with migrants from Morocco, since this increased public pressure on the Spanish government to confront Morocco about its alleged non-collaboration in the fight against human trafficking. With regard to the fisheries agreements, Aznar blamed the French government outright for putting obstacles in the way of ongoing Spanish-Moroccan conversations, since it was the Spanish understanding that Chirac had advised Morocco not to conclude any new agreement with Spain.[5] Regardless of what might or might not have been said by the French government in this context, little doubt remains that the fisheries negotiations with the EU were extremely difficult as the Moroccans were highly unsatisfied with the previous 1995 agreement and took an unusually firm stand. Jorge Dezcallar, at that time the Spanish ambassador to Rabat, was clearly under the impression "that the Moroccans don't want a deal with the European Union."[6] Rabat's claims appeared particularly inflexible because the Moroccans knew perfectly well that their requests were unacceptable to Spain with regard to the length of the agreement, the volume of fishing allowed and the technical conditions, since Spain as an EU member also exemplified overall EU positions. After the European Commission threatened to abort negotiations, the Moroccan negotiators offered a partial agreement which allowed for temporary fishing in Moroccan waters of small-scale ships. However, this offer was dismissed by the Commission at Madrid's request because Aznar was determined to defend a united and indivisible Spanish fishing industry. Aznar immediately put the entire blame for the failure of the negotiations on Morocco and warned of the "consequences" that this failure would have for Spanish-Moroccan and EU-Moroccan relations. This was interpreted as nothing but a threat by Rabat.[7]

Another possibility, which has not received much attention in the existing literature, is that the failure to reach a compromise in 2001 may also have been due to cultural misunderstandings. Mohammed VI had been in

---

[5] Cembrero, *Vecinos alejados*, 50; Fernández-Molina, *Moroccan Foreign Policy*, 164.
[6] Dezcallar, *El anticuario de Teherán*, 192.
[7] This summary owes to Fernández-Molina, *Moroccan Foreign Policy*, 171.

Madrid to settle the fisheries agreement with Aznar, yet to the surprise of the Moroccan king, Aznar had refused to make the traditional counteroffer to the king's "final offer," and thus completely misinterpreted the culture of the Moroccans, who take pride in a long and tiresome give-and-take.[8] Be that as it may, the directions of the different agreements over the years have indeed been moving toward more rights for Morocco, although Spanish boats have been fishing in those waters for centuries as well. This is perhaps a natural development, as Morocco is a relatively new state which is now vigorously fighting for its fundamental rights. It is immensely focused on its role as "territorial champion" due to its submission in the past to French and Spanish colonial interests in particular.[9]

Thus, the fisheries negotiations merely reflected a logical historical development whereby the Spanish Foreign Ministry had traditionally been susceptible to Moroccan arguments because it was more concerned with Spain's overall strategic interests in the region. In contrast, the Spanish Ministry of Agriculture and Fisheries has always tried to promote the views of the powerful Spanish fishing industry in an attempt to protect the volumes of fishing allowed and the special interests of the Spanish calamari fishers. Earlier in his diplomatic career, as General Director for North Africa in the Foreign Ministry, Moratinos had struck several compromises with Morocco. They normally included secret agreements which aimed to compensate formal Moroccan concessions to the EU in one area, with Spanish/EU subsidies to Morocco in other areas. Typically, the Moroccans would try to obtain concessions until the very last minute.

At the final round of negotiations with Aznar, Mohammed VI allegedly agreed to a new agreement in principle, but in line with Moroccan cultural and political traditions he wanted something more, and made a new proposal which Aznar flatly declined instead of making the expected concession. This move took the Moroccans by surprise and provoked a rupture in the relationship. In response, a hard communiqué was issued from the Moncloa and also from the Santa Cruz Palace. Shortly afterward, the crisis of Perejil began and clandestine African immigrants from south of the Sahara began to reach the Spanish coastline in large numbers. Although Morocco did not directly used the topic of migration to pressure Spain into giving in on fishing rights, the indirect message was probably that if

[8] Moratinos Files: Interview, Moratinos.
[9] Cf. Fernández-Molina, *Moroccan Foreign Policy*, chapter 2.

Spain was unable to establish a normal working relationship of trust with its southern neighbor, it would have to expect to deal with its problems by itself.[10]

Outwardly, the Moroccan authorities let it be known that they only wanted to use Perejil to fight illegal migration, drug smuggling and terrorism in the strait area.[11] In turn, in its telephone conversations with Rabat the Spanish Conservative government demanded an immediate withdrawal from the islet, and Aznar also contacted the other EU partners and the United States to line up support for the Spanish position.[12] On 16 July, Madrid suddenly recalled its ambassador from Rabat, although according to official Moroccan sources, a political compromise was actually in the making. This Moroccan notion is also confirmed by Spanish sources. In fact, on 16 July, Ramón Gil-Casares, foreign policy advisor of the Moncloa, called Moratinos in New York and told him to be prepared to travel to Rabat to find a diplomatic solution. Moratinos, who had numerous friends in high places in Morocco, immediately agreed to help. Yet, during the night of 17 July, he suddenly received a call from Foreign Minister Ana Palacio saying that his services were not needed after all, as Spain had dispatched a special forces unit of the Spanish army to the islet.[13] In the Moroccan view, this act constituted a sheer violation of the bilateral Treaty of Friendship, which advocates for the diplomatic settlement of disputes. Furthermore, the move was politically and diplomatically risky as Spanish sovereignty of the islet could easily be disputed. For the same reason, a note issued by the Spanish Foreign Ministry did not vindicate Spanish sovereignty, but instead demanded a return to the situation before the occupation.[14]

Morocco perceived the Spanish action as an attempt to deliberately humiliate its southern neighbor, especially because Aznar had apparently sent signals through his Spanish ambassador which contradicted an armed intervention. Ana Palacio, the Spanish foreign minister, had done the same in a public statement. Importantly, Zapatero gave his full support to the Aznar government in this moment of grave crisis, yet he also complained

[10] Moratinos Files: Interview, Moratinos.

[11] As Fassi Fihri later underlined: "…the fight against all kinds of criminal traffic is the only explanation to the Moroccan presence on the islet." Cit. in Cembrero, *Vecinos alejados*, 47.

[12] Aznar, *El compromiso del poder*, 67.

[13] Moratinos Files: Interview, Moratinos.

[14] Cf. Cembrero, *Vecinos alejados*, 31–34.

that he had not been informed of the military action before it was put into effect.[15] The Moroccan response was obviously an acrimonious one. According to the communiqué issued by the Moroccan Foreign Ministry on 17 July, "This is a use of force contrary to the rules of international law and unjustifiable in a time when discussions were being held since Morocco and Spain had agreed to resolve the crisis through diplomatic channels, as is evident from the Spanish official statements yesterday."[16] This version is to some extent also borne out by Spanish sources, which confirmed that Morocco had actually agreed to a withdrawal during the day of 17 July. Seemingly, the Spanish side feared that it was a delay tactic because the islet would be filled with journalists the next day, thereby making it impossible to launch military action. The attack was therefore launched right after the ultimatum ran out at four in the morning.[17] Be that as it may, the Moroccan reaction was one of complete incomprehension. Mohammed VI later claimed in a well-known interview with Ignacio Cembrero of *El País* that Morocco felt "slapped in the face."[18]

In the end, the US Secretary of State Colin Powell had to personally mediate between his two Mediterranean allies to solve the crisis. He skillfully negotiated a solution to rewind the situation back to when there were no military or security forces on the islet and no outspoken territorial claims. Powell cleverly diminished the importance at stake for the two parties by referring to Perejil as "this stupid little island."[19] He clearly succeeded in his endeavor, yet Moroccan political rhetoric remained filled with references to the disputed Spanish enclaves Ceuta and Melilla in the months to come. By January 2003, however, bilateral negotiations had been resumed on topics such as migration, Western Sahara, maritime boundaries, economic relations, mutual perceptions and civil society, so that the following month the ambassadors returned to Rabat and Madrid. In December, a financial aid package to Morocco worth 390 million Euros helped to ease relations

[15] Ibid., 36, 112–113.

[16] Cited in Fernández-Molina, *Moroccan Foreign Policy*, 178.

[17] Cembrero, *Vecinos alejados*, 38–41.

[18] Interview with Mohammed VI in *El País*, 16 January 2005, cited in Fernández-Molina, *Moroccan Foreign Policy*, 178.

[19] Cembrero, *Vecinos alejados*, 45. See also Richard Gillespie, "'This Stupid Island': A Neighbourhood Confrontation in the Western Mediterranean," *International Politics*, vol. 43, issue 1 (2006): 110–132, and the interview with Colin Powell in *GQ Magazine*, October 30, 2006. https://www.gq.com/story/colin-powell-bush-administration.

even further, while at the same time different Spanish and Moroccan organizations helped to push in the right direction, knowing full well that at the end of the day the Moroccan government was keen on further Spanish investments.[20]

A somewhat unexpected opportunity to mitigate the discord with Morocco presented itself in July 2003, when the so-called Baker Plan II for Western Sahara was formally presented to the UN. The plan was flatly rejected by Rabat precisely at a time when Spain was holding the rotating presidency the UN Security Council. Spain cleverly used the occasion to accommodate Morocco and ease the friction. It avoided a French veto by persuading the US representative, Negroponte, to alter the first version of Resolution 1495 to the degree that there were no strong political commitments left in the plan, a clear concession to the Moroccans.[21] As stated previously, this new Spanish behavior was very much in contrast to the one displayed in June 2001 when Madrid had firmly blocked James Baker's first proposal for Western Sahara, thus aligning itself explicitly with the position of Algeria and the Polisario against the views of Rabat, Washington, London and Paris.[22] Seemingly, after the Perejil incident, Aznar was beginning to rectify his Moroccan policies.

In sum, Spanish concessions during 2003 definitely helped to improve the relationship with Rabat. Nevertheless, the confrontation over Perejil had disclosed a disturbing truth to Aznar, namely that in case of Spanish friction with Morocco, Paris would not hesitate to mobilize its undivided sympathy and active support for Rabat, to the detriment of good relations with Madrid. According to Aznar's own account, he was told by Chirac on 15 July—in the midst of the Perejil crisis—that Spain ought to return all the disputed isles and Ceuta and Melilla to Morocco. He also suggests that Chirac might have been the real instigator of the Perejil incident.[23] According to former French ambassador to Morocco Michel de Bonnecorse, Aznar's version is simply a reconstruction *a posteriori*, as the Spanish prime minister had always been of the opinion that the Moroccans

---

[20] Fernández-Molina, *Moroccan Foreign Policy*, 179.

[21] Cembrero, *Vecinos alejados*, 96.

[22] In fact, in 2001 Moroccan newspapers spread the oficial view that "United States and Europe favors the deal, while Algeria and Spain, as usual, are against." Cit. in Cembrero, *Vecinos alejados*, 91.

[23] Aznar, *El compromiso del poder*, 59, 65–70.

were incapable of making independent decisions.[24] What is probably true is that Aznar's rapprochement to Algeria was seen by Rabat as a threat to its fundamental interests. Morocco simply felt constricted by this new partnership and naturally used its good relationship with Paris to apply more pressure on Madrid. In fact, French pressure was not confined to Spain alone, but to the whole of the EU. It is indeed noteworthy that in the midst of the crisis, the Danish EU presidency urged Morocco to withdraw from Perejil, an utterance that was immediately criticized by the French ambassador to Rabat. Within a short time, also the EU distanced itself from this stand in its official statements, which now referred to a "bilateral problem" between Morocco and Spain.[25]

The Spanish friction with France over Morocco and Perejil, together with the previously described collapse of the European treaty negotiations, probably explains why Aznar was becoming increasingly dissatisfied with Chirac and the "European Europe" he represented. During a lunch at the Élysée Palace, Aznar exposed his new views on the need for a more Atlantic-oriented Europe, but Chirac allegedly reiterated that the EU was based on the Franco-German axis and if Aznar had a problem with this construction, Spain would do well to place itself outside the Union. This was perceived by Aznar as a clear threat. Thus, Spain's gradual alignment with Washington may well also be related in part to Aznar's frictions with Chirac over Morocco. His talks in Paris revealed to him the limits of Spanish influence in a Europe dominated by France and Germany.[26]

Still, if Aznar truly thought that Washington would treat Spain differently from France with regard to Morocco, he would soon be disappointed. As will be argued in the next chapter, the United States had over the years given abundant proof of the fact that in the case of conflict between Spain and Morocco, it would either seek a reconciliation of its two allies, wash its hands of the conflict or ultimately support Morocco.[27] As could be expected, Colin Powell worked primarily toward a reconciliation of the parties. The geostrategic reality in the Western Mediterranean is probably that, regardless of whom Spain aligns itself with in its foreign policy,

[24] Cembrero, *Vecinos alejados*, 50–53.

[25] Ibid., 54–55.

[26] Aznar, *El compromiso del poder*, 34.

[27] See also Angel Viñas, "Negotiating the US-Spanish Agreement, 1953–1988: A Spanish Perspective," Jean Monnet/Robert Schuman Paper Series, vol. 3, issue 7 (September 2003), 16.

it has little or no alternative to keeping up good relations with Morocco. At least, this was the lesson learned by the new PSOE leadership when it seized power in 2004, and also the real reason behind the secret mission of Moratinos to the residence of the Moroccan ambassador in Madrid early the same year.

Aznar claims in his memoirs that the relationship with Morocco had actually normalized by December 2003, when he led a major Spanish delegation to the bilateral summit in Marrakech.[28] However, this is at odds with Moratinos' version of the events and, for that matter, also with that of one of the Moratinos' closest political advisors.[29] When Moratinos became foreign minister, he found the relationship with Morocco to be in such dire straits as never before.[30] This clash of opinion naturally calls for clarification. As shown, Aznar had indeed made concessions to Morocco during 2003, and as the Moroccans were under the impression that Rajoy would easily win the general elections, they also started sending signals of détente to Madrid during February–March 2004. To be precise, the Moroccan rapprochement with the Spanish Conservative government in Spain can probably be dated back to 13 December 2002, when Mohammed VI extended an offer to sixty-four Spanish fishing boats to fish in Moroccan waters due to the severe leak caused by the oil spill from the tanker Prestige off the Galician coast. Twenty-five of the boats accepted. Three weeks later, joint Spanish-Moroccan working groups were set up to resolve questions regarding migration, pending political issues, territorial issues related to fishing rights and so forth. And in January 2003, the two foreign ministers, Benaissa and Palacio, were able to pronounce the return of their respective ambassadors. In addition, the tragic terrorist attack against the *Casa de España* in Casablanca on 16 May 2003, which left thirty-three people dead, helped to increase the collaboration between the authorities.[31]

Nevertheless, Moratinos and Zapatero soon realized during their first trips to Rabat in 2004 that despite the existence of a modest working relationship, Aznar had made a very bad impression not only upon the Moroccan king and government, but also on Moroccan society as a whole.

---

[28] "Se produjo una normalización plena." Cit. in Aznar, *El compromiso del poder*, 72. See also Cembrero, *Vecinos alejados*, 82.

[29] Moratinos Files: Interview, Moratinos; Santos Maraver.

[30] Moratinos Files: Interview, Moratinos.

[31] Cembrero, *Vecinos alejados*, 75–76.

In spite of Aznar's political and economic concessions, mutual trust was gone—there had simply been too many crises. This is also corroborated by the most recent scholarly research. As argued by Fernández-Molina, the hostility toward Aznar in Morocco had actually been so intense that the victory of Zapatero was acclaimed almost unanimously by Rabat, and in early 2005, before the upcoming Spanish state visit, Mohammed VI made no bones about his enthusiasm for the new Spanish leadership: "I will summarize it in one word: trust. [. ..] Now, between us, mutual respect has been restored."[32] On a lower diplomatic level, it was agreed to open several communication channels in order to avoid situations like the Perejil incident. Thus, Spanish officials frequently held meetings and private dinners with their Moroccan counterparts in order to reduce tension and potential misunderstandings.[33]

All this meant that the road was finally clear to pursue one of the Spain's most ambitious foreign policy goals, namely that of bringing peace and stability to Western Sahara. As it turned out, without good working relations with both Rabat and Algiers, this was but a distant dream.

7.2   Even If I Do Not Agree with You, I Love You

Zapatero paid his first official visit to Morocco on 24 April 2004. According to tradition, the first trip abroad for any new Spanish prime minister is always to Morocco, and even though Western Sahara was not formally at the top of the agenda, which was dominated by the bomb attacks of 11 March, Zapatero knew that this important issue would be raised during the meeting. Rabat had, in fact, high hopes that the new Spanish government would take a more accommodating view of Moroccan claims. This hope was not without grounds. Moratinos, who accompanied the Spanish prime minister, knew from his previous diplomatic experience with Morocco that an involuntary solution for Western Sahara which went directly against the interests of Rabat would never succeed. He feared that it would only destabilize the entire region with negative repercussions for southern Europe as well. Importantly, the new position of the Spanish government was not unknown to Algiers, who still remembered how the PSOE as part of its rapid transformation into a catch-all middle-class party in the late 1970s

[32] Fernández-Molina, *Moroccan Foreign Policy*, 180.
[33] Moratinos Files: Interview, Santos Maraver.

had gradually abandoned its previous undivided support for the Polisario Front, Algiers' sworn allies in Western Sahara.[34]

During the 1970s, the United States upheld a neutral position with regard to the future of Western Sahara still under Spanish administration—known as Spanish Sahara. Behind the scenes, though, Washington feared that an independent Sahrawi state might forge an alliance with Mauritania, Algeria and eventually the Soviet Union. Accordingly, the US government worked secretly to ensure that Spanish Sahara effectively came under Moroccan dominion.[35] This Cold War rationale coincided to some extent with the position of Spain and France, which also preferred the Moroccan annexation of Western Sahara to a new state, which might increase instability in the region.[36] Unlike Spain, however, the US government did not find it necessary to insist on Algerian participation in these talks, but was satisfied that France would take the lead in the political discussions about the future of the region.[37]

In 1975, Hassan II effectively exploited these fears as well as the political uncertainty in Spain caused by General Franco's foreseeable death to impose his own solution for Western Sahara. On 16 October 1975, the International Court of Justice in the Hague issued a pronouncement which overruled Morocco's and Mauritania's claim to the territories. The Moroccan king ignored the ruling and instead authorized the so-called Green March into Spanish Sahara, later taking effective control of it. By so doing, the king completely ignored the essential claim of the international community, namely that people of Western Sahara, the Sahrawis, had a right to self-determination. As part of the Madrid Agreements, Spain formally handed over administration to Morocco and Mauritania on 14 November, and three months later Spain officially abandoned Western Sahara, letting the world know that it was no longer responsible for the administration

---

[34] Moratinos Files: Interview, Moratinos.

[35] José Luis Rodríguez Jiménez, *Agonía, traición, huida. El final del Sahara Español* (Barcelona, Spain: Critica, 2015), 424. Jacob Mundy, "Neutrality or Complicity? The United States and the 1975 Moroccan Takeover of the Spanish Sahara," *The Journal of North African Studies*, vol. 11, issue 3 (2006): 275–306. https://doi.org/10.1080/13629380600803001.

[36] Lemus, *Estados Unidos y la Transición Española. Enre la Revolución de los Claveles y la Marcha Verde* (Madrid: Silex, 2011), 310. Cf. Heiberg, *US-Spanish Relations After Franco*, 49–50.

[37] Department of State, Archive: Secretary of State to U.S. Delegation Secretary, cable, May 22, 1975. http://aad.archives.gov/aad/createpdf?rid=232165&dt=2476&dl=1345.

of the disputed territory.[38] After the Spanish withdrawal, Morocco immediately seized control of Saguia el-Hamra, whereas Mauritania absorbed the area of Río de Oro. In response, the Polisario Front proclaimed the Sahrawi Arab Democratic Republic (SADR) on 27 February 1976 and started a guerrilla war against the new occupiers. With regard to Spain, the main problem with its adhesion to the principles of the Madrid Agreements was that it ignored the Hague ruling and thus complicated Spain's future diplomatic actions with regard to the Maghreb region.[39]

A truce wasn't obtained until 1991, when the United Nations established its Mission for the Referendum in Western Sahara (MINURSO). The UN mission was not only to monitor a cease-fire, but as the name indicates, also to organize a referendum on self-determination in the territory in case the parties agreed to an eventual solution. The settlement plan approved by the Security Council allowed for a transitional period for the preparation of the referendum. Specifically, according to the settlement plan, the Sahrawis would eventually have to choose between independence and integration with Morocco. The disputed territories have roughly the size of Great Britain, yet they are largely uninhabited.[40]

This historical background was, of course, in the back of the minds of the Spanish delegation which accompanied Zapatero to the meeting in Morocco. During the reunion, which lasted nearly six hours, the Moroccans sent clear signals of rapprochement. Seemingly, PSOE's back channel, which had been established prior to the general elections, had paid off. There was an informal and relaxed atmosphere during lunch in the king's residence in Casablanca, and no interpreters were used. The old territorial disputes were simply cast aside as a nonissue, the main challenge on the agenda being how to ensure a better application of the bilateral treaty of 1991. The Moroccans expressed their skepticism toward future negotiations with Algeria and the possibility of further integration in the Maghreb Union due to the eternal border disputes between the two countries. Above all, they were pleased with Spain's sincere and forthright commitment to

---

[38] "The Madrid Agreements" is the name commonly used to describe the settlement. In reality, it was a Declaration of Principles. Cf. José Cuenca, *De Suárez a Gorbachov. Testimonios y confidencias de un embajador* (Madrid: Plaza y Valdés Editores, 2014), 69.

[39] See Francisco Villar, *La Transición exterior de España. Del aislamiento a la influencia (1976–1996)* (Madrid: Marcial Pons, 2016), 32–33; Heiberg, *US-Spanish Relations After Franco*, 49–50.

[40] On the MINURSO, see the official UN website. https://minurso.unmissions.org.

providing Morocco with a special relationship with the EU, a long-term ambition of the government of Rabat. With regard to Western Sahara, the tone was markedly different, though. The Moroccan side expressed its deep dissatisfaction with the forthcoming report of James Baker to the UN Security Council, which blamed Rabat for the collapse in the negotiations. This stand was of course unacceptable to Rabat.[41]

After the meeting in Rabat, it was clear to Moratinos that any new Spanish proposal for a solution to Western Sahara would have to respect the principle of "self-determination" for the Sahrawis, as expressed in the UN resolution. On the other hand, the PSOE government knew full well that the Moroccans would never accept the Baker Plan in its present form, no matter what. Accordingly, the only sensible thing to do was to keep the term "self-determination" sufficiently vague as to make it palatable to Rabat. To achieve this, Moratinos would have to start a new dialogue with Algiers, which like the Polisario Front took an entirely different view of the situation. A new possibility for resetting discussions over Western Sahara occurred when James Baker suddenly resigned on 11 June 2004.

Since his appointment as Personal Envoy of the UN Secretary-General in 1997, Baker had essentially proposed two plans (known as Baker I and II). As mentioned in the previous chapter, the first Baker Plan of 2001 was very favorable to Morocco, as it foresaw the integration of Western Sahara with a degree of autonomy within Morocco. Negotiations came to an impasse during 2002, however, but in May 2003 Baker presented a new plan which envisaged the self-determination of the people of Western Sahara after a period of three years of provisional administration by a governing body elected by the local population in the territory. Three days prior to Zapatero's visit to Rabat, Morocco had once more rejected the plan, and it was probably against this background that James Baker threw in the towel.[42] When Zapatero visited Algiers for the second time in July 2004, he too distanced himself from the second Baker Plan.[43] Meanwhile,

[41] Moratinos Files: Interview, Moratinos. For further details and a more colorful description of this meeting, see: Javier Valenzuela, *Viajando con ZP* (Barcelona: Debate, 2007), 26–28.

[42] Cf. the chronology of events according to the official MINURSO website under the UN. https://minurso.unmissions.org/chronology-events.

[43] Cembrero, *Vecinos alejados*, 100.

Moratinos received the new UN envoy, Álvaro de Soto, with the purpose of finding a new formula for future discussions over Western Sahara.[44]

As stated in the previous chapter, Aznar's policy line toward Western Sahara had been somewhat unpredictable. During his first term in office, he had roughly followed the traditional Spanish line with regard to Western Sahara, which clearly favored the Moroccan stance. Then, after 2001, he had suddenly aligned himself with Algiers and the Polisario against Morocco and the rest of the international community, only to rectify this policy after 2003. The new Socialist leadership probably learned two things from this past experience: Above all, it was necessary to conduct a comprehensive policy for the entire Maghreb region, since to align itself with one of the parties would clearly lead to failure. Having said that, and as the meetings analyzed below will reveal, the Zapatero government would always be more susceptible to Moroccan than to Algerian claims at the end of the day, simply because Morocco was considered more vital to Spain's overall interests.[45] In other words, Spain was to conduct a comprehensive policy which was sensitive to all the parties in the region, but it should also be clear that Spain considered solutions that went directly against the Moroccans as non-viable, an interpretation that was increasingly shared by the different UN envoys sent to the region after Baker resigned. Algiers was, of course, very much aware of this new Spanish position and was accordingly suspicious of the PSOE's continuous overtures toward Rabat. Nevertheless, the PSOE's historic sensibility toward the Moroccans never prevented the party from doing its utmost to uphold cordial relations with the Algerians, too. It cannot have escaped Bouteflika's notice and that of the rest of the Algerian leadership that Zapatero was ready to make important concessions to Algiers.

As was to be expected, the Algerian proposal for a second gas pipeline between Oran and Almería in Spain was going to be the real litmus test of future Spanish goodwill. The proposal raised complex questions, as on the one hand the Spanish gas and oil industry had important interests in Algeria, yet on the other it also found itself in fierce competition with its southeastern neighbor, and to have more Algerian gas directly entering

[44] "Primer encuentro entre Moratinos y el Nuevo enviado de la ONU para el Sáhara occidental," *Europa Press*, July 15, 2004.

[45] See also Vaquer I Fanes, "Spain in the Mediterranean," 133; H. M. de Larramendi, "The Mediterranean Policy of Spain," *Mediterranean Policies from Above and Below*, ed. I. Schäfer and O. Henry (Baden-Baden: Nomos Publishers, 2009), 38–62.

into Spain was not relished by many of the Spanish stakeholders in the negotiations. This dual nature of the issue no doubt created friction inside the Madrid government and also in bilateral relations with Algiers. In fact, when Zapatero went to Algiers on 3 May 2004, there was a fierce discussion onboard the aircraft regarding the construction of the second gas pipeline from Algeria. The problem was that the pipeline was the result of a proposal which came directly from the Algerian government but which, however, went very much against the interests of Spanish multinationals such as Gas Natural, Repsol and a series of Catalan companies, which all wished to maintain undisputed control of the Spanish market through their liquid gas deposits in Catalonia. They had no interest in creating a dominant alternative Algerian supplier.[46]

Onboard the aircraft, the Minister for Industry, Tourism and Commerce José Montilla Aguilera, who was also a leading Catalan Socialist, essentially put forward the case of the gas lobby to Zapatero, while Moratinos strongly defended the foreign policy angle by calling for more collaboration with Algiers. In the end, Moratinos won the debate by underlining the strategic advantage of such a pipeline for Spain's overall policies. Accordingly, Zapatero told a pleased Bouteflika that Spain would accept the deal, something which made Montilla suffer even more in his relationship with the powerful gas lobby. Despite his wish for rapprochement with Morocco, Moratinos arranged nearly as many visits to Algiers as to Rabat during his first mandate as foreign minister (seven to eleven). This sent a clear signal to the parties in the Maghreb region, and the first visit to Algiers was by all measures a bilateral success, as Spain had publicly shown its sensitivity to Algerian demands in disregard of the Spanish gas lobby. Further concessions were made in the years to come, for example, when Zapatero decided to receive the Polisario leader in 2005. Furthermore, the Vice Minister for Foreign Affairs, Bernardino León, and Leire Pajín travelled to the Sahrawi camps in Tindouf, Algeria, thereby showing Spain's sensitivity toward the fate of the Sahrawi people.[47]

Thus, things seemed to be slowly moving in the right direction, which is why it was considered all the more important to make progress on the

[46] Moratinos Files: Interview, Moratinos.

[47] Ibid.; Cembrero, *Vecinos alejados*, 104; and Peru Egurbide, "El secretario de Estado de Exteriores se entrevista por primera vez en Tinduf con la dirección del Polisario," *El País*, June 3, 2004. See https://elpais.com/diario/2004/06/03/espana/1086213607_850215.html.

Sahrawi question as well. In actual fact, when Moratinos visited Bouteflika again on 12 July, he went there to present an ambitious roadmap for Western Sahara based on three specific criteria. He asked Bouteflika in fluent French, "Mr. President, I'll ask you a series of questions and you'll tell me whether you agree or not. 1) Do you want – as stated in the UN resolution – that there is a just and equal solution mutually acceptable for the two parties, Morocco and the Polisario Front?" Bouteflika said "yes." This did not cost Moratinos anything because if Morocco did not agree, there would not be a deal anyway. Moratinos then asked, "2) Do you agree that eventually you would have to accept a Sahrawi entity [*entité saharaui*]?" Bouteflika said "yes," before Moratinos asked him his final question, "3) And, finally, do you agree that this entity can have self-determination from the moment that the parties accept a common plan?" Bouteflika said "yes." Moratinos thanked him, adding that "I can assure you that with these three affirmations I can convince the Moroccans to work towards a final common solution." He then spoke to the Moroccans who seemed to think that this new basis might work.[48]

On 12 October 2004, Moratinos travelled to Morocco to speak more thoroughly with King Mohammed VI. The meeting was also supposed to pave the way for the upcoming visit of King Juan Carlos in January 2005. Importantly, Mohammed VI promised him full collaboration in the fight against terrorism, clandestine immigration and crime. This was important news to Moratinos, as Zapatero was about to bear witness in the Parliamentary Commission on the Madrid terrorist attack, where he wanted to be able to reassure the public of the goodwill and intentions of Rabat. The Moroccan king explained that with regard to the Madrid attack his country had given all the information it had, including names. Moratinos also used the meeting to reiterate Spain's commitment to improving Morocco's status with the EU.

Moratinos then explained to his Moroccan interlocutor the new Spanish take on Western Sahara. He reassured Rabat that his government would never consider proposals that were unpalatable to Rabat. They would never go beyond what was acceptable to Rabat. Compared to Aznar's occasional pro-Algerian line, this was indeed a remarkable change in Spanish foreign policy. Moratinos further reiterated that the conflict could only be resolved through a process of integration and modernization of the entire Maghreb

[48] Moratinos Files: Interview, Moratinos.

region. Crucially, he suggested creating an "entente" with France and the
United States that might overcome the historical barriers for a settlement
in Western Sahara, an idea that Moratinos would insist upon right until he
was dismissed as foreign minister in 2010. If these three powers could make
a concerted diplomatic effort—went the Spanish reasoning—the problem
of Western Sahara could actually be solved—perhaps not in six months, as
Zapatero had somewhat optimistically stated during his first trip to Paris
in 2004—but in the fullness of time. Moreover, it would increase Spain's
importance and status as an international broker to be reckoned with.[49]
Unsurprisingly, the Moroccan leadership deemed the Baker Plan II to be
dead.[50]

In the same period, Moratinos managed to hold a series of meetings,
often in the context of multilateral forums, with the French Foreign Minister Michel Barnier and his Moroccan counterpart Mohammed Benaissa.
These encounters were often reported in the press. When he returned to
Algiers on 23 November, he was therefore surprised to be received by an
irate Bouteflika, who accused him of playing an underhand game: "You have
betrayed us, you have been negotiating with the French and the Moroccans. You have lied to us. We have reports. Everything that I told you some
months ago is no longer valid. We do not trust you."[51]

On the basis of the sources that I have talked to, it is difficult to establish
the exact reasons why the Spanish diplomatic service failed in its attempt to
maintain Bouteflika's support. For sure, Bouteflika must have had his reasons for feeling betrayed. Today, it is still Moratinos' strong belief that the
Algerian intelligence services somehow manipulated his plan, which had
every chance of prospering, because it gave the parties what they formally
expressed to be their minimum requirements for a future agreement.[52] Of
course, how to interpret the term "self-determination" for the Sahrawis
was still the major nut to crack, yet things had truly begun to move in
the right direction. Whatever the real reason, the Algerians continued to
be outraged, and even more so when Zapatero soon returned to Morocco
for the second time to celebrate the fifty-year anniversary of the Moroccan state. On this occasion, Zapatero was very explicit about the fact that

[49]On Zapatero's statement, see Cembrero, *Vecinos alejados*, 100.
[50]Moratinos Files: Interview, Moratinos.
[51]Ibid.
[52]Ibid.

he welcomed new Moroccan proposals for Western Sahara. The Algerians and the Polisario Front rightly suspected that Moratinos was behind this increased strategic rapprochement with Morocco.

It goes without saying that Bouteflika's outrage also meant that the Polisario Front would be hostile to Moratinos as well. In fact, the Polisario Front leader, Mohamed Abdelaziz, immediately wanted to see Zapatero, who, however, declined in order not to upset Rabat. Moratinos was nevertheless able to convince Zapatero to receive Abdelaziz informally in the PSOE's headquarters in Calle Ferraz.[53] Moratinos saw at the time two types of Sahrawis: the dignified people who were by no means hostile to Spain, and the political apparatus under the strong influence of Algeria and its intelligence services. In his view, Mohamed Abdelaziz clearly belonged to the latter category.[54]

A factor which complicated the situation in the coming years was the behavior of the Conservative Spanish opposition. As is the normal parliamentary practice, the Socialist government shared both information and views with the opposition on important Spanish foreign policy initiatives. Importantly, the PP did not seem to disagree with the new Spanish proposals. Moratinos was therefore surprised when he was suddenly attacked in the Senate by the former Conservative foreign minister, Josep Piqué, for his view of the Polisario Front. Moratinos found it odd because Piqué had been perfectly briefed on all the secret arrangement and channels to the different parties, and he did not seem to fundamentally disagree, also because in Spain it has predominantly been the political left which has defended the rights of the Sahrawi people. Not this time, however. The Conservative party fiercely accused him of riding roughshod over the rights of the Sahrawis. Moratinos argues that the Conservative party started an anti-Moroccan campaign in alliance with the Polisario Front and Algeria mainly to stir up trouble within the PSOE, where a part of its left wing was still very sensitive to the cause of the people of Western Sahara. The Polisario Front even invited the former prime minister, Aznar, to the Sahrawi camps in Western Sahara, a trip that was only cancelled hours prior to his planned visit. Moratinos claims that he has elements to suggest that Bouteflika, his secret services and perhaps the oil industry were responsible for

---

[53] Ibid.

[54] Ibid. See also Marta Suárez, "El Polisario pide a Zapatero que se implique más con el Sáhara," *La voz de Galicia*, November 26, 2004. https://media.lavozdegalicia.es/noticia/espana/2004/11/26/polisario-pide-zapatero-implique-sahara/0003_3243034.htm.

this escalation. Be that as it may, pro-Polisario demonstrations in Spain suddenly emerged within the strangest contexts—for example, on the occasion of Moratinos' historic meeting in Gibraltar with British Foreign Minister Miliband and the Gibraltarian leader, Caruana, on 21 July 2009. When he approached the frontier, he saw a group of protesters and thought they were hardcore *Españolistas*, who were there to protest against the first visit of a Spanish foreign minister to Gibraltar. It was, however, nothing of the kind. They were there to demonstrate in favor of the Sahrawis.[55]

After James Baker resigned in 2004, his functions were temporarily assumed by Alvaro de Soto, then head of the MINURSO, until May 2005. In this period, De Soto visited Madrid, where he unofficially presented a plan, which in contrast to the Baker Plan II was very accommodating to the Moroccans. The information somehow reached Algiers, and this meant that his time as envoy was over within eleven months.[56] After a short period without any envoy, Ambassador Peter van Walsum, a former Permanent Representative of the Netherlands to the UN, was appointed as the new Personal Envoy of the UN Secretary-General for Western Sahara. He occupied the position until the arrival of Christopher Ross on 7 January 2009.[57]

To cut a long and agonizing story short, the main problem was always the parties' unwillingness to treat the Sahrawi question for what it was: an international question which needed binding international commitments. Instead, the stakeholders nearly always used the conflict in Western Sahara for domestic purposes. In fact, since the 1970s, the parties had never spontaneously contacted each other to find a solution or new models of negotiation. By 2006, Algeria was in a much stronger position due to its newfound relationship with the United States in the fight against terror, their control of the Sahel Strip and, not least, the increasing oil prices. Still, Moratinos and his advisors all found international suggestions to include Algeria in the negotiations over the Sahrawi question to be catastrophic, as Algiers would always have to consider public opinion at home when entering into such discussions. In other words, it would deprive Algerians of the possibility to use the Sahrawis, who were deeply dependent on them, to take

[55] Moratinos Files: Interview, Moratinos.

[56] Moratinos Files: Private information.

[57] Cf. the chronology of events according to the official MINURSO website under the UN. https://minurso.unmissions.org/chronology-events.

a different and perhaps more collaborative stand toward Morocco. To the relief of the Spanish, Algiers totally agreed on the need for a free hand. Fully aware of the Moroccan position, Spain also rejected new proposals for a referendum if independence from Morocco was to be a possible outcome of such a democratic exercise. Spain's pragmatic suggestion, which was also conveyed to the Americans, was above all to work for a basic improvement in the bilateral relations between Algeria and Morocco, and to work simultaneously to ease the sufferings of the people living in the Sahrawi camps. This had to be obtained through increased external pressure, and the Spanish government considered that both Spain and the United States could deliver on this specific point. Nevertheless, it was important that direct negotiations were mainly kept between Morocco and the Polisario Front.

By June 2009, the Moroccans had clearly let it be understood that the federal solution was unviable. Instead, Morocco proposed an autonomy plan for its "southern provinces" as they still called Western Sahara. This was apparently the highest concession Rabat was willing to give. Rabat's offer thus went directly against the proposal of Ross and others working toward a federal associated state. To Morocco, the case of Western Sahara was clearly a question of national territorial integrity. To reinforce this point, over the years Morocco had effectively encouraged native Moroccans to move to the "southern provinces" to the degree that the original Sahrawi population was becoming a minority.[58] Accordingly, Morocco's starting point for any new negotiation would be that the incorporation of Western Sahara had de facto taken place.

At this point, the idea of conceding Western Sahara with the status of a federal state entered the international negotiations again. In the Spanish view, to concede this status would roughly correspond to international recognition, something that the Moroccans would never commit to. A federal solution might, furthermore, inspire other regions in Morocco troubled by separatism and regionalism to pursue the same objective. This was simply unpalatable to the Moroccans. For this exact reason, Moratinos reasoned, "autonomy" was probably as far as the regime would go in any future negotiations with the Polisario Front. It is also against this background that one must understand the many Spanish attempts over the years to stimulate and influence new Moroccan proposals for an autonomy model that might

[58] Cembrero, *Vecinos alejados*, 89.

effectively integrate a "Sahrawi entity" into the Moroccan state system. As long as the French blindly supported Morocco, it was deemed impossible to make Rabat even consider a federal model.[59]

In August 2010, Madrid's relationship with Rabat entered into a minor crisis. It is difficult to say whether the crisis was somehow related to the ongoing negotiations on Western Sahara, where Ross, according to the Moroccans, was inclining too much toward the Algerian position. The bottom line was that Spanish authorities repeatedly complained that Rabat did little or nothing to stop migrants from trying to reach the Spanish enclave Melilla by sea from Morocco.[60] In turn, Mohammed VI was furious that a Spanish helicopter had apparently flown right over his personal yacht.[61] Another incident—directly related to Western Sahara—was that a group of thirteen Spanish demonstrators had entered Western Sahara to support the Polisario Front. They had apparently been badly beaten by what they thought were the Moroccan police authorities, a fact that was, however, denied by the Moroccan government. Moratinos thus had little choice but to send a high-level diplomat to Rabat, who spent most of 6–7 September 2010 trying to ease the tension.[62]

Although this was certainly a time of turmoil, there was still movement in the right direction. In the same period, Moratinos was working to obtain explicit US and French support in order to push through a solution for Western Sahara which the Algerians could objectively live with and which was also highly sensitive to the fundamental Moroccan claim that independence was out of the question. For Moratinos, the challenge all along had been that the United States did not have a precise strategic priority for the Maghreb, but above all sought stability for the region without specifying how this could be reached. In Moratinos' recollection, Condoleezza Rice had displayed a complete lack of interest in the Sahrawis during her time

---

[59]Cf. Various Spanish proposals mentioned in the US cables released by WikiLeaks. Cf. Ignacio Cembrero, "España apoyó en el Sáhara una solución favorable a Marruecos," *El País*, December 13, 2010. https://elpais.com/elpais/2010/12/13/actualidad/1292231842_850215.html. The relevant documents can be accessed from the same website.

[60]Mayka Navarro and Pilar Santos, "La crisis con Marruecos dispara la inmigración irregular en Melilla," *El periódico*, September 21, 2010. http://www.elperiodico.com/es/politica/20100921/la-crisis-con-marruecos-dispara-la-inmigracion-irregular-en-melilla-489682.

[61]Miguel González, "Mohamed VI se quejó a Rubalcaba de que un helicóptero sobrevoló su yate," *El País*, September 2, 2010. https://elpais.com/diario/2010/09/02/espana/1283378408_850215.html.

[62]Moratinos Files: Interview, Moratinos.

in office. In fact, her 800-page memoir hardly mentions this strategically important region.[63] The reason was apparently that after Baker's resignation in 2004, Washington simply lost interest in the issue. From 2009, Hillary Clinton showed a greater willingness to invest political capital in a solution. The renewed US interest was probably due to concerns with the spreading of Islamism in the region. Obama, like Clinton, perfectly understood that the United States had to acknowledge the Moroccan position and at the same time favor economic and political integration across the entire Maghreb area if a solution to the Western Sahara problem was ever to be found.

Despite the recent and very successful collaboration between Spain and the United States with regard to Cuba, Moratinos' new idea of a creating "triple entente" which could ultimately solve the question of Western Sahara initially encountered some resistance in the US capital. Clinton had actually agreed to the idea in a telephone conversation on 14 September, but apparently her Assistant Secretary for European and Eurasian Affairs, Philip Gordon, was not aware of this or disagreed with the idea, and thus continued to show considerable resistance in the matter. However, the Spanish exercised effective pressure by signalizing that only a decisive action on the part of Spain, the United States and France could change the situation in Western Sahara for the better.[64]

A few days later, Moratinos saw the French foreign minister, Bernard Kouchner, and Hillary Clinton in New York for the General Assembly of the UN, where he reiterated that the three of them should visit the region together to get the process started. He also used the occasion to have an informal encounter with the Moroccan foreign minister, a fact that was deliberately circulated to the press. By acting as one united block—for the first time in history—the most important Western stakeholders in the process were able to send a strong and unequivocal signal that none of the parties in the region would be in a position to use the *divide et impera* tactics of the past to ditch solutions which didn't suit their interests. The three foreign ministers finally decided to visit the region together by the end of the year. A potential success, comparable to that of Cuba, was in the making. Then, events out of their control suddenly altered the basic

---

[63] Apart from one sentence about increased development aid to a series of countries including Morocco. See Rice, *No Higher Honor*, 428.

[64] Moratinos Files: Interview, Moratinos.

conditions for the work of the entente. Moratinos was dismissed in October, as was Kouchner in November. With two of the three most dedicated actors leaving the arena, the entente simply fell apart.

In November 2010, right after Moratinos' dismissal, WikiLeaks published a series of US cables on Morocco from the preceding years.[65] These papers might suggest—especially if read out of context—that Spain was playing a crooked game with the other stakeholders: Outwardly, Spain formally followed the UN path, while behind closed doors it tried to enforce a solution that was beneficial only to Moroccan interests. As shown, the reality was more complex. True, Algeria and the Polisario Front had publicly complained about Zapatero's lukewarm support for the Baker Plan II as well as his reluctance to use the word "self-determination" in relation to the Sahrawis. Yet, Algeria also knew that Spain was fully determined to work for the construction of a political "Sahrawi entity" and also to build a relationship of trust and interdependence with Algiers, as displayed by the important bilateral energy deal that the two countries closed in 2004. Spain's official support for the UN resolution, filled as it was with deliberate linguistic ambiguities, did not clash in any way with Spain's idea, or for that matter that of the majority of the international community, that a solution that went fundamentally against Moroccan interests was simply not viable. The only way forward was a plan that was open to Moroccan claims while maintaining the idea of a Sahrawi entity. Yet such a plan would also have to be coupled with much stronger efforts to increase political and economic integration in the Maghreb region, and to put a stop to the eternal border conflicts between Morocco and Algeria.

After his dismissal, Moratinos could not help thinking about how close he and his French and American colleagues had come to offering a viable roadmap for Western Sahara. Even Bouteflika had, in his own peculiar way, softened his resistance over the past years. When Moratinos saw Bouteflika for the last time on 7 January 2010, the two were traveling alone in a car from Madrid airport, Barajas, to the Moncloa building. The aging president suddenly confided to him, "Je vous aime, vous faites partie de ma vie. Même si je ne suis pas d'accord avec vous, je vous aime." ("*I love you. You are part of my life. Even if I do not agree with you, I love you.*") The days when he

---

[65] Cf. Ignacio Cembrero, "España apoyó en el Sáhara una solución favorable a Marruecos," *El País*, December 13, 2010. See https://elpais.com/elpais/2010/12/13/actualidad/1292231842_850215.html.

had perceived Moratinos simply as a traitor were apparently long gone.[66] Yet, Bouteflika's commitment to actually finding a solution that could end the suffering for the Sahrawis still left a great deal to be desired.

[66] Moratinos Files: Interview, Moratinos.

CHAPTER 8

Alliance or Clash of Civilizations?

8.1 The Child on the Beach

Over the preceding three decades, the bilateral relationship with Morocco had become deeply interwoven, and of the many novel aspects of the relationship emerging after 2004, several deserve to be highlighted. On the positive side, one might stress the unique decision in 2004 to deploy under the UN a joint Spanish–Moroccan military police unit in Haiti. On the negative side, one could emphasize the friction created by the Haidar case, concerning a Sahrawi activist on hunger strike in a Spanish airport in 2009, or the diplomatic crisis provoked by the visit of King Juan Carlos and Queen Sofia to Ceuta and Melilla on 5–6 November 2007, which coincided—much to the chagrin of the Moroccan authorities—with the anniversary of the Green March. Objectively, Morocco and Spain's joint migration management and border control is probably the most interesting case, in view of the renewed efforts of the EU in 2017 to effectively curtail irregular migration from Africa after a long period of disenchantment.[1] From early on, it was the ambition of both the Zapatero government and the government of Rabat to Europeanize the migration problem and to demand more

---

[1] Cf. Alissa J. Rubin and Jason Horowitz, "European Leaders Look to Africa to Stem Migration," *New York Times*, August 28, 2017. https://www.nytimes.com/2017/08/28/world/europe/africa-migrants-europe.html.

© The Author(s) 2019   209
M. Heiberg, *Spain and the Wider World since 2000*,
Security, Conflict and Cooperation in the Contemporary World,
https://doi.org/10.1007/978-3-030-27343-9_8

economic, political and logistic assistance.[2] The support of the EU was initially lukewarm, but Brussels was gradually talked into providing further economic and legal assistance to Spain. In spite of the initially half-hearted European support, Morocco and Spain embarked on a collaboration which showed remarkable results.

This new collaboration arose from the difficulty in dealing effectively with the collective assaults by migrants on the border fences at Ceuta and Melilla in the autumn of 2005. The migrants were mainly from sub-Saharan countries, and widespread criticism and condemnation emerged over the ill-treatment by Moroccan security forces of the migrants seeking to cross the barriers. In particular, one incident in which a dozen illegal migrants died caught international attention. As did the detention of 4000 migrants in only three weeks, who in some cases were deported back to the Algerian border and the Sahara. In contrast to international opinion, which blamed the Moroccans for their undignified treatment of migrants, Rabat tried to present itself as "the first African victim of this phenomenon," as it did not have the necessary resources to stop the enormous flow of irregular migrants who were willing to risk their lives to enter Spain and the EU. Spain, as one of the largest economies in the world and together with the rest of the EU, possessed such a strong pull factor that no African government could counter it. In this way—Fernández-Molina argues—Morocco skillfully placed the burden of the migrant problem on the shoulders of the EU.[3] Several international NGOs protested fiercely against the Moroccans, who however pointed out that the incidents were a logical consequence of the European request to Morocco to defend the borders of the EU more effectively, and—moreover—to protect the two cities of Ceuta and Melilla, which according to traditional Moroccan claims should actually be under Moroccan rule.[4]

If the situation was tense in the two enclaves, it was probably nothing compared to the Canary Islands, where tourists were now becoming regular witnesses to the arrival on the local beaches of small boats (*pateras*) with hundreds of migrants. The migrants' failure to enter Melilla and Ceuta had, in fact, increased the pressure on the Canary Islands. From 2005 to 2006, the registered number of irregular migrants reaching Spanish shores

---

[2]Fernández-Molina, *Moroccan Foreign Policy Under Mohammed VI*, 181.

[3]Ibid., 123.

[4]Moratinos Files: Interview, Moratinos.

suddenly rose from 11,781 to 39,180.[5] In February 1992, a bilateral agreement had been struck which allowed Spain to send back illegal migrants, whether they were Moroccans or people originating from third countries. This accord, however, had never been applied.[6] An explanation for this may have been that in a not-so-distant past the migrants had mainly been Moroccans hoping to find a better future on the European continent. This had created tension because the Spanish side suspected that the Moroccan authorities secretly encouraged the traffic, or at least did not block it, as it helped ease domestic social pressure, just as the money sent home from migrants abroad accounted for an increasingly larger part of the Moroccan economy.[7] By the new millennium, the situation had radically changed, however, as the migrants were now mainly from other African countries, mostly to the south of the Sahara, but also from as far away as Bangladesh and Pakistan. In the latter case, people would cross the entire Sahel region to enter Spain. This meant that a new political solution would have to include not only Morocco, but essentially Africa as whole.[8]

To handle the new emergency, Spain had daily contacts and bilateral negotiations with Morocco on many levels, and the vice president of the government, María Teresa Fernández de la Vega, received direct orders from Zapatero to take extraordinary measures to solve the crisis. The government was under great pressure from the press and the media. There were also strong, yet legitimate demands from the Canary Islands, whose local government had to reconcile their status as a popular holiday resort with being an important arrival point for thousands of migrants, among them hundreds of unaccompanied children, who after a long a dangerous journey were literally washed onto a Spanish beach. To deal with this difficult situation, a cross-ministerial committee was set up under the direct leadership and supervision of Fernández de la Vega.[9]

To obtain concessions from the EU, she conducted tough negotiations with José Manuel Barroso, chairman of the EU Commission, and Franco

---

[5] 31,681 migrants arrived in the Canary Islands alone. Cf. "Inmigración irregular. Balance 2015 Lucha contra la inmigración regular," Spanish Ministry of the Interior, 2015. http://www.interior.gob.es/documents/10180/3066430/Balance+2015+de+la+lucha+contra+la+inmigraci%C3%B3n+irregular.pdf/d67e7d4b-1cb9-4b1d-94a0-9a9ca1028f3d.

[6] Cembrero, *Vecinos alejados*, 164.

[7] Ibid., 159.

[8] Moratinos Files: Interview, Moratinos.

[9] Ibid.

Frattini, EU Commissioner for Justice, Freedom and Security. These negotiations were even more difficult because of existing tensions regarding other matters related to the Spanish industry, specifically the Spanish company E.ON. During a meeting in the summer of 2006, Fernández de la Vega insisted that the migration problem had to be discussed as the first point on the agenda of the upcoming meeting of the Council, as the Spanish government found the situation at Europe's southern frontier to be unsustainable. These were problems that Spain could neither resolve alone nor tolerate. However, Barroso took a completely different view of the situation by saying that it was tiresome that the Spaniards had come to ask for more money again. Fernández de la Vega then rose from her seat and defied Barroso: "Mr. President! We have not come to ask for more, but to demand it. First of all, you know perfectly well that this is not Spain's problem. Second, you are here because you are paid by me. You are here because you are paid by the Spanish state, as well. And you are here to serve the European project. We have not come to ask." In turn, Barroso lamented not only the incessant Spanish requests during the recent discussions over E.ON, but also the fact that Madrid had leaked the content of their previous conversations to the press. In response, Fernández de la Vega replied, "Do you want me to repeat what your Vice President, Frattini, who is sitting next to you, has just leaked to the press?"

Heated discussions continued for the next half an hour, and the other members of the Spanish delegation were increasingly worried that Fernández de la Vega was damaging Spain's external relations with the EU on a permanent basis. She complained that Frontex was not working, and she demanded a new program, including money and more protection for the southern frontier, as well as better conditions for five hundred unaccompanied children in the Canary Islands, who could neither be distributed nor given education. "I will bring them to your house, if you don't come up with a solution!" she said. Eventually, the hard approach paid off and the two parties came up with a plan, according to which Spain would also contact the Finnish presidency in order to include migration on the upcoming agenda, which had actually already been concluded. In the end, Frontex was given further resources and the EU Commissioner for Development became instrumental to Spain's effort to send migrants back to their country of origin.[10] It is fair to say that a European plan of action was conceived,

---

[10]Moratinos Files: Private information given to the author.

but the effectuation of that plan was entirely up to the individual member states, and Spain in particular. If Spain had not been vigilant and had not been present in the areas from which the migration originated, the whole plan would have crumbled because the EU had no people on the ground to actually execute its policies.

To cope with these deficiencies, the interministerial committee under Fernández de la Vega's leadership took on a very practical approach. The committee met every Friday, just before the meeting in the Council of Ministers. Each participating ministry held specific areas of competences and was held directly responsible for finding adequate solutions in each and every case. Fernández de la Vega was insistent, and according to people present in the meetings, she did not favor long speeches but demanded concrete results instead. This may well also have been the case in other countries trying to mitigate the pressure of migration, yet the main difference between the Spanish approach and the solutions offered by the rest of the European Union and Italy was probably the strong emphasis given by Madrid to the foreign policy dimension of the migration crisis.[11] In most countries, as had also been the case in Spain prior to the new emergency, irregular migration had been under the control of the Ministry of the Interior, which traditionally oversees border controls, ship inspections, registration of migrants, the running of refugee camps, repatriation and so forth. However, with the setting up of this interministerial steering group it was possible to rethink the entire migration endeavor.

To exemplify some of the creativity shown by the interministerial commission, Spain had found out that all the shoddy boats used for human trafficking were equipped with Japanese motors, and in one of its Friday sessions, the steering group decided to contact the motor company. Eventually, a deal was struck which obliged the Japanese company not to sell spare parts in specific locations in North West Africa. Instead, Spain would buy the same quantity of spare parts usually sold by the company in this area to compensate for the company's economic loss.[12] On Fridays, Fernández de la Vega and her group would analyze every single boat that had arrived during the week: Where did it come from? From which port?

---

[11] Moratinos Files: Interview, Moratinos.

[12] This story was also recently leaked to the press. Cf. "El CNI pagó a propietarios de cayucos para que dejaran de transportar inmigrantes a Canarias en 2006," *El Diario*, July 14, 2018. https://www.eldiario.es/canariasahora/politica/CNI-cayucos-transportar-inmigrantes-Canarias_0_792670825.html.

She demanded precise answers from the intelligence services, the foreign ministry and other government agencies in order to take the necessary measures to close down this or that route of human trafficking. And it certainly worked. Over the next years, the migrant flow to the Canary Islands was reduced by 97.2%.[13] When I asked Fernández de la Vega what the secret behind this apparent success was, she simply answered, "It's work!"[14]

Moratinos contributed to this joint effort by creating a General Directorate for Africa in his ministry, while also using the migration crisis as a pretext to generally promote Africa as a new focus area. The Santa Cruz Palace essentially argued that more funding was needed for cooperation and development. Moratinos was deeply unsatisfied with the existing models of communication and cooperation with Africa. He thus proposed strengthening relations in multiple fields and ensuring a stronger diplomatic and consular presence on the African continent. He also wished to considerably increase economic development aid to these countries. His recent visits to Ghana, Angola, Mozambique, Nigeria, Niger and Mali had fully convinced him of the need to create a new Action Plan for Africa.[15] He further called for a renewed political dialogue based on "effective multilateralism" which could contribute to the political, social and economic development of the region and foster democracy, peace and security, all of which he saw as the real key to stopping the migration flows in the long term. Many migrants came from Mali and Niger, two of the world's poorest nations, where famine, fragile institutions and health problems were the real push factors.[16]

His next round trip to Africa in June 2006 was due to increasing problems with the existing readmission programs set up by the Ministry of the Interior and signed by Aznar, to effectuate repatriations by forcing immigrants onboard aircraft back to their native African country. Over the years, there had indeed been some very undignified cases of maltreatment and drugging of migrants before sending them back to Ghana and elsewhere. This had led to severe protests from Human Rights organizations,

[13]Cf. "Inmigración irregular. Balance 2015."

[14]Moratinos Files: Interview, Fernández de la Vega.

[15]Miguel Angel Moratinos, "An Ethical and Political Commitment to Africa," article published by the Real Instituto El Cano, December 2005. http://www.realinstitutoelcano.org/wps/wcm/connect/0970a9804f0187debe02fe3170baead1/Moratinos874.pdf?MOD=AJPERES&CACHEID=0970a9804f0187debe02fe3170baead1.

[16]Moratinos Files: Interview, Moratinos.

who rightly denounced the fact that the personal dignity of these people had been deeply violated. Another problem was that the African countries involved were unsure whether the deported nationals from Spain were actually their citizens. There was thus an increasing unwillingness from a number of African countries to accept these forced repatriation flights.

By contrast, during his visits to Africa, Moratinos had found a surprisingly receptive attitude toward his new suggestion, i.e., to essentially adopt a global approach where plans to stop the migration flows were coupled with increased efforts to improve living conditions and sustain local development. To his surprise, he found a fertile terrain for such initiatives, as he could successfully propose cooperation and Spanish investments and at the same time work separately for securing effective agreements between source, transit and destination countries to mitigate the migratory flows.[17] In fact, Ghana, Mali and Nigeria were willing to establish such cooperation and re-admittance mechanisms for immigrants, just as a number of sub-Saharan African countries agreed to partake in the forthcoming Euro-African conference on migration and development in Rabat, sponsored by Morocco and Spain. This conference was supposed to lead to the establishment of new channels of understanding between African and European countries in dealing with migration flows.

To further the cultural understanding, the foreign ministry also took the initiative to build a new consortium named *Casa África*, which aimed to promote cultural exchange and educational programs between the Canary Islands and Africa. Above all, the government wanted its African interlocutors to understand that Spain's commitment was not only based on the sudden need to "close a hole," but was the result of a sincere ethical vocation.[18] In a speech given at the Casa África in front of politicians from the CEDEAO (West African Economic Union), Moratinos strongly underlined the fact that Europe should cease to perceive Africa only as a threat and instead sustain the moment of hope that these increasingly democratic countries were actually experiencing. He further stressed the importance of the fact that Spain had augmented its yearly development aid to the sub-Saharan region.[19] In contrast, critics saw these agreements as

---

[17] "¿Bienvenido Mr Moratinos?," *La Vanguardia*, October 15, 2006. Moratinos Files: Interview, Moratinos.

[18] Moratinos, "An Ethical and Political Commitment to Africa."

[19] "Moratinos anuncia una nueva etapa histórica relaciones España y África Occidental," *EFE*, September 21, 2007.

a kind of *do ut des* arrangement, whereby Spain, to take one example from the press, cynically repatriated 156 unregistered migrants to Guinea at the price of €32,000 each.[20] However, this may be a fundamental misunderstanding. The new foreign policy worked precisely because development aid to Africa, which grew from €200 million in 2003 to €1 billion in 2010, and increased diplomatic engagement with a number of African countries were completely detached from ongoing discussions on the readmission programs.[21]

During 25–30 January 2008, Moratinos effectuated a new round of visits to Mali, Guinea-Bissau, Democratic Republic of Congo and Ethiopia. This time he committed Spain to providing the countries from which migrants to Spain originated, with a further €55 million, while a number of joint ventures were undertaken, especially with Mali.[22] Yet Moratinos also stressed that there was no link between immigration policies and the development aid given.[23] He struck a deal with sufficient legal guarantees which allowed 134 unaccompanied children to return to their families in Senegal from the Canary Islands.[24]

All these efforts were made to prevent migrants from arriving in Morocco and from there crossing the border fences to Ceuta and Melilla or traveling by boat to the Canary Islands from Western Sahara. However, to close this hole completely, an effective agreement with Rabat had to be reached on how to deal with those migrants who had nevertheless made it to Morocco. Accordingly, Moratinos proposed from early on setting up migration camps in Morocco instead of Spain, as this would further discourage illegal migration. With this purpose in mind, he travelled to Rabat on 10 October 2005 together with his Vice Minister for Development, Leire Pajín, who was known to be very pro-Sahrawi, to discuss the case with

[20]"Moratinos reparte millones en África para repatriar a los 'sin papeles'," *La Razón*, October 10, 2006.

[21]The figures of the Spanish Official Development Aid (ODA) are reproduced in Cristina Barrios Fernández, "Spain and Sub-Saharan Africa. Toward a Strategic Approach," in *Contemporary Spanish Foreign Policy*, ed. David García Cantalapiedra and Ramón Pacheco Pardo (Abingdon and New York: Routledge, 2014), 153.

[22]"España donará 55 millones a los países de África emisores de emigrantes," *El País*, January 27, 2008.

[23]"Moratinos inicia su gira con el estreno de la Embajada en Mali," *El Mundo*, January 27, 2008.

[24]"España y Senegal dan los primeros pasos para repatriar a 134 menores inmigrantes acogidos en Canarias," *Canarias*, February 14, 2008.

Benaissa and Fassi Fihri.[25] Moratinos and Pajín boarded the aircraft, convinced that they would easily obtain such an agreement. To their surprise, however, they were received with the utmost coldness, although they were invited to dine privately with the foreign minister. When they arrived at the minister's residence, they found their hosts were all dressed in their national dress, the *djellaba*, a long white garment, and a red cap, the *bernousse*. It was—in Moratinos' opinion—a way of displaying Moroccan sovereignty and independence toward their Spanish neighbors. They soon realized that the Moroccans had no intention of accepting "Spanish" refugee camps on Moroccan soil and under the proposed conditions. Morocco would not continue as Spain's paid gendarmes, and Madrid would simply have to change its neocolonialist attitude. It was a very tense and tough meeting which lasted for several hours. As a last resort, during an unofficial talk after dinner, Moratinos tried to appeal to his Moroccan hosts by saying that he could not return to Madrid empty-handed. It would be a disaster for his Socialist government. "You have to offer me something," Moratinos said. Shortly afterward Fassi Fihri talked to the king on the phone and then returned with a new proposal, namely to make Morocco and Spain true partners in the resolution of the migrant crisis.[26]

What did this proposal imply? As mentioned above, the idea was to hold a joint international conference in Rabat on migration. This may not sound much, but this event actually marks the beginning of the Euro-African Dialogue on Migration and Development, which still today exists as a forum for intergovernmental dialogue on migration, bringing together some sixty countries from Europe, and North, West and Central Africa as well as the European Union and the Commission of the Economic Community of West African States. In the final political declaration, the meeting was described as a "partnership between the countries of origin, transit and destination" of migration. The meeting also resulted in an action plan with many new measures, including police and judicial cooperation. This conference on migration was followed by new conferences in Paris (2008) and Dakar (2011) and became widely known as the Rabat Process.[27]

---

[25] "Moratinos viaja a Marruecos para abordar con el Gobierno las últimas avalanchas de inmigrantes," *El País*, October 10, 2010. See https://elpais.com/elpais/2005/10/10/actualidad/1128932220_850215.html.

[26] Moratinos Files: Interview, Moratinos.

[27] Cf. Fernández-Molina, *Moroccan Foreign Policy*, 124.

The Spanish side found that the first conference in Rabat indeed went well, although to some extent it had been sabotaged by the attitude of Algeria and also the African Union, both of which did not want to take part due to their eternal quarrels with Morocco. A new alternative conference was thus held in Tripoli less than a year later, in which Moratinos also participated together with Rubalcaba, the Spanish Minister of the Interior. In these new forums, Spain and Morocco gradually began to work toward common goals.[28] Above all, Rabat now displayed a willingness to finally implement the 1992 bilateral readmission agreement, also in relation to third country citizens. Morocco also accepted better control mechanisms on both sides of the border and agreed, in general, to a high level of cooperation. In the era of Aznar, Rabat had insisted that immigrants should return to their home country and not to the country of transit (Morocco). The new agreement ensured that if it could be proven that the immigrants had passed through Morocco, Rabat would accept them, and at the same time, agreements were made with their home countries saying that they would receive them if they were duly identified. Of course, it could be difficult for the Spanish authorities to prove that a migrant had effectively passed through Morocco, unless he or she willingly admitted to this, but the direction indicated in the agreement was indeed a major leap forward.

The newfound understanding between Morocco and Spain, in combination with a new action plan for Africa and all the other interministerial initiatives, effectively blocked migration to Spain. New political and legal agreements between Madrid and Rabat were made, and joint actions were taken to monitor the migration flow toward the Canary Islands. As shown, the figures published by the Spanish Ministry of the Interior on irregular migration flows to Spain over the last decade document beyond doubt the efficacy of all these combined measures. Along the way, the Spanish intelligence services were also able to dismantle some of the mafias related to the human trafficking toward Spain. An interesting side effect of the new African engagement was that it also generated innumerable informal contacts that later became extremely important for resolving all the sad cases of hostage taking in Africa which Spain and other European countries alike were subjected to.[29] It would, of course, have been much better if all the new control mechanisms had been embedded in the EU partnership with

[28] Moratinos Files: Interview, Moratinos.
[29] Ibid.

Morocco in actual fact and not just on paper. Instead, Spain had to largely cope by itself by striking all sorts of deals with Morocco and a variety of African stakeholders in order to keep the migration flow at bay—immigration which, at the end of the day, affects all Europeans.

Assuredly, the actions of the Zapatero government in the field of migration, especially its deportation of migrants, can be subjected to criticism. Above all, this regards the fact that Spain contributed greatly to the construction of "Fortress Europe" in this period and that this policy of "plugging the holes" has led to poor migrants being increasingly framed as potential national security threats, rather than as fellow human beings in search of a better life.[30] A valid counterargument is that the PSOE government did its utmost to apply a global approach in which increased development aid to Africa played a crucial part. It is fair to say that the Spanish policy worked because it was based on ethical principles.

The lesson to be learned from the migration crisis is obvious. Seemingly, the traditional European "domestic" approach to migration does not get to the core of the problem, which is often a combination of demography, poverty, hunger, climate change and underdevelopment. Wars are a further push factor at the origin of the problem. To ignore these basic facts can only lead to further trouble. One should consider that Africa has approximately 1.2 billion inhabitants; in 2050, it will have twice as many.[31] Millions of Africans will probably leave their place of origin; no sea is deep enough and no wall high enough to keep them out of Europe. Large-scale investments are needed. As soon as migrants enter Europe, they immediately become a domestic issue to be dealt with by local authorities and by humanitarian organizations. Without a comprehensive foreign policy, the root of the migrant crisis cannot be tackled. If the ambition is to have less, safer and more regulated, migration toward Europe, an African foreign policy is needed.

While this book was being completed, there was a sudden surge in the number of migrants arriving on Spanish shores. No one knows if it is a temporary increase or the beginning of a more permanent migrant flow. Although more research needs to be done on the subject, one plausible cause is that Spain, due to the economic crisis, cut much of its funds to

---

[30]David Mofette, *Governing Irregular Migration. Bordering Culture, Labour, and Security in Spain* (Vancouver and Toronto: UBC Press, 2018), 5–7, 109–110.

[31]Ruth Gursch-Adam and Lívia Benková, "The Impact of Demographic Developments in Africa and Europe," *European View*, vol. 15, issue 2 (December 2016). https://link.springer.com/article/10.1007/s12290-016-0425-3.

development and cooperation, the cornerstone of Spain's successful African policies over the past decade. Another obvious reason is that the migration route through Libya to Italy is now less viable. In fact, part of the original Spanish success in combatting illegal migration also owed to the fact that the new Spanish measures forced migrants to seek alternative routes. After 2006, an unknown number of those migrants who would previously have tried to reach Spain through either Senegal, Mauritania or Morocco began traveling to Italy through Libya. Today, this trend has apparently been reversed. Still, the new Socialist government under Pedro Sánchez, installed in 2018, seems to have responded swiftly to the new crisis by successfully demanding more funds for Morocco, one of the key elements in his government's attempt to mitigate the flow of migrants toward the Spanish peninsula.[32] No one knows if these new measures will actually work, but it is fair to say that the PSOE has all the knowledge necessary to succeed again.

With regard to Libya, it has often been claimed in the international media that the lack of a state apparatus in Libya has impeded any effort to deal with the migrant problem properly.[33] Yet, much the same could be said about several of the regions in Western Africa which were a source or a transit area for migration to Spain, including Western Sahara. In the Spanish view, there has been too much passivity on the part of the EU when it comes to establishing an African policy, and to actually traveling to the most problematic areas and making foreign policy work there. The Italians have rightly been eager to Europeanize the refugee crisis, and Spain has supported their claim, yet it is equally true that the Italians have until recently done too little too late to turn the affair from a domestic Italian problem into a foreign policy challenge that can be effectively addressed. Italy, in collaboration with the EU, has now begun to really work on the ground in Libya. The view of the Zapatero government was always that where there is no state, there are always other interlocutors who can be approached. It is a question of will. Europe needs to have effective interlocutors on both a formal level and informal level who can conduct negotiations all

---

[32]"Sánchez y Merkel pactan ayuda prioritaria para Marruecos," *El Periódico*, August 12, 2018. See https://www.elperiodico.com/es/politica/20180811/sanchez-merkel-inmigracion-marruecos-6985229.

[33]Cf. Lisa Watanabe, "Challenges in Libya Complicate EU Measures to Stem Migration," *IPI Global Observatory*, October 20, 2017. https://theglobalobservatory.org/2017/10/challenges-libya-complicate-eu-measures-migration/.

over Africa.[34] The setting up of Frontex, the European Border and Coast Guard Agency, in Warsaw, which is much closer to the Baltic Sea than to the Mediterranean Sea, is to its critics somehow symbolic of the inadequacy of the EU measures taken so far.

8.2 Carpe Diem

On 14 February 2005 at 12:55, unknown perpetrators detonated hundreds of kilos of explosives on Rue Minet El Hosn in Beirut in the precise moment that the motorcade of Rafic Hariri, the former prime minister of Lebanon, was passing by. The explosives were cleverly concealed in a Mitsubishi Canter van. The result was that Hariri and several of his bodyguards, as well as the former Minister of the Economy, Bassel Fleihan, were killed instantly. Shortly after the explosion, the Al Jazeera news network in Beirut published a video in which a man named Ahmad Abu Adass untruthfully claimed to be the suicide bomber on behalf of a fundamentalist group called "Victory and Jihad in Greater Syria."[35] Over the years, the killing has been subjected to several international investigations, resulting in different conclusions. In fact, there have always been serious doubts as to the alleged responsibility of the Syrian President Bashar al-Assad, although his direct or indirect accountability for the murder was for many years held to be a public truth.

The popular notion of Assad's complicity probably owed to an interview with the former vice president of Syria, Abdul Halim Khaddam, in which he claimed that Assad had threatened Hariri in the period leading up to the bomb attack.[36] However, it is important to remember that right up to the time of Hariri's assassination, Moratinos was actually mediating between Hariri and Assad as part of Spain's desire to break the isolation of Syria and draw Assad closer to Spain's strategic interests. The latter strongly disputed that Hariri should be allowed to become prime minister in Lebanon again, and seemingly Assad had little to gain from killing someone he was

---

[34] Moratinos Files: Interview, Moratinos.

[35] Cf. "The Prosecutor v. Salim Jamil Ayyash, Hassan Habib Merhi, Hussein Hassan Oneissi & Assad Hassan Sabra, 12 July 2016." The consolidated amended indictment can be downloaded from https://www.stl-tsl.org/en/the-cases/stl-11-01/main/indictments-6/5321-f2640.

[36] "Hariri Threatened by Syria Head," *BBC News*, December 30, 2005. http://news.bbc.co.uk/1/hi/world/middle_east/4570652.stm.

actually interested in dealing with, regardless of how tough these negotiations were. In turn, Hariri had turned to Moratinos for help to obtain more independence from Syrian influence for his future government. To advance a new proposal by Hariri, Moratinos went to Damascus on Sunday 13 February, the day before Hariri was killed. When he met Assad the following morning, the latter was absolutely furious and accused Hariri of being Jacques Chirac's marionette: "He had to resign. He did not defend the interests of the Lebanese people. Only French interests. Go tell him that his resignation still stands and that he may return to power within a few years."[37]

After the meeting with Assad, Moratinos had lunch with the Syrian foreign minister Farouk al-Sharaa and the Spanish ambassadors to the Middle East, who were in Damascus for their yearly gathering—a further sign of the new Spanish rapprochement with Syria. During lunch, al-Sharaa received a note on a possible bomb explosion in Beirut. Fifteen minutes later, news had it that it was a convoy in which Hariri was present, and that he was apparently wounded. Half an hour later, a new note confirmed the death of Hariri. The Syrian foreign minister was detached, whereas Vice Minister for Foreign Affairs Walid Muallem, who at that time was in charge of Lebanon affairs, was in despair: "This is a disaster, this is the end for us."[38] al-Sharaa simply suggested that he and Moratinos should make a joint declaration, but Moratinos declined. Instead, he instantly flew to Beirut to present his condolences to Hariri's family.

It has been widely believed over the years that Bashar al-Assad and Syria was behind the attack. However, this was unlikely to have been the case. Moratinos personally discussed the case with the head of a Middle East intelligence service, and after having analyzed the different elements of the case, they both agreed that the murder was likely to have been conducted without the knowledge of Assad, who had no interest in killing Hariri. In their view, the perpetrators were likely to be the Iranian secret services who seemed to have mounted the entire operation.[39] Nevertheless, Assad's personal responsibility was for years a widely held truth, something which only increased with the escalation of the civil war and the atrocities he committed in Syria. Importantly, in July 2016, the Special Tribunal for

[37] Moratinos Files: Interview, Moratinos.
[38] Ibid.
[39] Ibid.

Lebanon indicted in absentia four Hezbollah-related individuals for the attack.[40] Hezbollah and Iran are known to be inextricably linked. Seemingly, Moratinos' intuition was correct. Yet, for years few people in Lebanon would accept Moratinos' interpretation, as he was considered by many to be on Assad's side, although he was actually a close friend of Hariri. This perception has no doubt harmed his position as an impartial negotiator with the other stakeholders in Lebanon.[41] Another way of looking at Moratinos' actions is to say that he simply followed a traditional line of Spanish foreign policy which hails close relations with Syria as a priority, a policy line that has also been strictly observed by previous Spanish governments, regardless of the shifting positions of the French and the Americans over the last twenty years with regard to the Syrian regime. As shown, the existence of close bonds with Syria never prevented Moratinos from arguing Hariri's case to Assad. But why did Moratinos even want to engage in such discussions? Apart from his deep personal and professional commitment to the peace process, one must also consider the fact that Spanish diplomacy has traditionally considered the Middle East to be an important region in which to improve Spain's international prestige.[42]

Spain's role as mediator between two such important actors as Hariri and Assad is also telling of the PSOE's understanding of the Middle East and the Arab world. The tragic event of 11 March 2004 did in fact inspire the new Spanish leadership to reconsider its collaboration with the Arab countries and invest more diplomatic efforts in finding an enduring solution for the Middle East. However, the timing was hardly the best for this kind of renewed diplomatic efforts. In fact, when Moratinos returned to Madrid in 2003—after many years dedicated to the Middle East peace process—his feeling was that the prospect of a settlement for the region had vanished, although peace had actually come close on a couple of occasions during his seven-year-long EU mission.[43] With the arrival of Sharon as prime minister of Israel in March 2001, the situation had ended in complete deadlock, and for this reason, Moratinos asked to be relieved of his position. He sent a letter of farewell which was published in both Israeli

[40] "The Prosecutor v. Salim Jamil Ayyash."

[41] Moratinos Files: Interview, Moratinos.

[42] Cf. Vaquer I Fanes, "Spain in the Mediterranean," 140.

[43] I here refer to a forthcoming French book of interviews with Moratinos.

and Palestinian newspapers. In his farewell comment, he outlined possible future conditions for a comprehensive peace deal.[44]

In 2006, however, the unexpected happened in Israeli politics: Sharon had a stroke and went into a coma, just after having formed his new centrist party, the Kadima. Sharon may well be remembered today by many in Israel as a pragmatic politician, but in the Spanish view he was nothing of the kind, although he did loosen Israel's grip on the Gaza Strip. In contrast, when Ehud Olmert, also of the Kadima, took over as prime minister, he immediately understood that the prognosis for peace was changing for the better. So a real possibility for peace existed after 2006, and in the Council of the European Union Moratinos naturally took the lead on this initiative as the foremost expert on the region.[45]

Right from the start of his career as a minister, Moratinos had been confronted with rumors which he still today believes to be without any real foundation, namely that powerful Jewish lobbies and especially the Mossad—the Israeli intelligence service—viewed him in a negative light. It is more likely that the rumors were triggered by forces in Spain who used Moratinos' well-known views on the Palestinians to stir up trouble with Israel.[46] If this is true, their efforts may be said to have been largely in vain. It should be remembered that Moratinos actually passed a lot of legislation in the Spanish Parliament which was favorable to Israeli interests—whether changing laws to prevent Israeli officials from being extradited from Spain to meet international charges for war crimes in Gaza, establishing new cultural exchange programs with Israel, or promoting commemorations of the Holocaust. Of course, Moratinos' personal mission to find a durable solution for the Palestinians through a dual-state solution was well known to the Israelis, yet his position coincided completely with the official view of the European Union and other important international stakeholders in the peace process. The United States also favored a two-state solution and backed Moratinos' efforts to alleviate the humanitarian situation in Gaza, as a personal letter from Hillary Clinton to Moratinos of 5 March 2009 reveals.[47] The rumors were also at odds with the fact that Moratinos had always encountered excellent treatment from Israeli politicians and

---

[44] Moratinos Files: Interview, Moratinos.

[45] Ibid.

[46] Ibid.

[47] Ibid.

officials. It can be documented that the Israeli side shared peace proposals with him as late as December 2009, on condition that only he and his British counterpart, Miliband, could know of their precise content. The information was not to be shared with the other European partners.[48]

Critics also maintained that the Zapatero government was biased in its approach to the Israeli–Palestinian conflict. This view is somewhat at odds with the role Moratinos played in important Israeli initiatives such as the negotiations to free the Israeli soldier Gilad Shalit, who had been captured on 25 June 2006 and held prisoner in the Gaza Strip. Moratinos was, in fact, part of the year-long negotiation process that didn't end until Tuesday 18 October 2011, when Hamas agreed to a prisoner exchange in which Israel released the first 477 out of 1027 prisoners in exchange for Shalit.[49] The truth is, however, that on 12 August 2006, Moratinos was already actively working toward a prisoner exchange between Hamas and Israel, a solution which involved the exchange of hundreds of Palestinians for the one Israeli soldier. Moratinos had been authorized by none other than the socialist Israeli minister of defense, Amir Peretz, to mediate indirectly with Hamas. Accordingly, Moratinos had sent two liaison officers to speak to people connected to the Hamas leadership. In the end, the Israelis decided to give the Shalit case to the Germans who eventually dealt with Hamas.[50] This is yet another example of the fact that Spain was involved in nearly all the important Middle East cases; whether finding a political solution for Lebanon, forging a peace deal between Israelis and Palestinians or aiding the Israelis to bring their soldiers back home.

The bottom line is that since the 1990s, the Israelis as well as the Syrians and their opponents in Lebanon had considered Moratinos a capable broker. This may well be related to Moratinos' well-known approach to such negotiations: As a mediator one should never criticize the different actors, but always try to understand their visions and try to help them from their perspective. "This may very well be true in theory," I critically told Moratinos in one of our interviews, "but does Israel truly want peace? Many in my own generation have come to doubt this." "Yes," he answered

---

[48] Moratinos Files: Private information given to the author.

[49] "Hamas and Israel Exchange Prisoners," *Al-Jazeera.com*, October 18, 2011. http://www.aljazeera.com/news/middleeast/2011/10/20111017221258366393.html.

[50] Moratinos Files: Interview, Moratinos.

without hesitation. "But the Israelis do not want peace at all costs. They dispassionately evaluate the situation and what suits their interest in any given situation. This approach of course makes it more difficult to act as a broker, and the Israelis would do well to reconsider it."[51] To illustrate his point, Moratinos told his version of an imminent peace deal in the Middle East, which is confirmed by recently published US and Israeli sources.

In September 2008, Ehud Olmert made a significant peace offer to the Palestinian Authority President Mahmoud Abbas, also known as Abu Mazen. It was no doubt one of the best peace proposals ever made to the Palestinians in history. Moratinos thus partly confirms a story that hit Israeli newspapers in 2013, but which was flatly denied by Olmert's former foreign minister, Tzipi Livni. On 16 September 2008, Olmert presented Abu Mazen with the details of an unprecedented plan. In it, he allegedly agreed to forgo Israeli sovereignty of the Temple Mount in Jerusalem, and he also drew a map of the borders of the future Palestinian state which was clearly predisposed to meeting Mazen's demands.[52] According to this plan, Condoleezza Rice confirms in her memoirs, Israel would only annex somewhere between 5.8 and 6.3% of the West Bank.[53] Mazen was, however, not allowed to take the map with him unless he agreed to sign the plan instantly. Instead, he drew a copy out of his memory and presented the proposal to the rest of the Palestinian leadership. It so happened that in 2013 the *Sof Hashavua* magazine, published by *The Jerusalem Post* Group, was able to obtain a copy of Mazen's sketch when it conducted a journalistic inquiry into the secret negotiations between Olmert and Mazen.[54] The two leaders—as also confirmed by Moratinos—discussed a draft agreement that was clearly advantageous to the Palestinians. Olmert's far-reaching offer probably had to do with the fact that he had decided not to run for the 2009 elections due to the heavy corruption charges hanging over his head, and he may well have felt that a lasting peace agreement should be his political legacy. Perhaps he also thought that with time such a far-reaching initiative might alleviate the judiciary pressure on him.

---

[51] Ibid.

[52] Cf. Avi Isacharoff, "Revealed: Olmert's 2008 Peace Offer to the Palestinians," *The Jerusalem Post*, May 24, 2013. https://www.jpost.com/Diplomacy-and-Politics/Details-of-Olmerts-peace-offer-to-Palestinians-exposed-314261.

[53] Rice, *No Higher Honor*, 723. Moratinos agrees with Rice's version, but cannot confirm *Jerusalem Post*'s version with regard to the Temple of the Mount.

[54] Isacharoff, "Revealed: Olmert's 2008 Peace Offer to the Palestinians."

When asked by the magazine why Mazen never returned to the negotiating table, Olmert answered speculatively that the Palestinians knew that the Bush administration was failing toward the end, and that they might have hoped to gain more from the possible victory of Barack Obama. Olmert also attributes importance to the fact that he was at the end of his political career. Interestingly, and here he coincides with Moratinos' account, he specifically blamed the meltdown on his foreign minister Tzipi Livni. Olmert cites in his defense Condoleezza Rice's book *No Higher Honor* in which the former Secretary of State indeed mentions that Livni had told her as well as Mazen not to "enshrine" Olmert's peace proposal.[55] Olmert also claimed that Defense Minister Barak, a real hardliner, had sent representatives to Mazen to persuade them to kill Olmert's proposal. In contrast, Mazen simply told the *Sof Hashavua* in 2013 that he thought that Olmert's plan was in great part unacceptable. Mazen's claim is, however, at odds with Olmert's version, and also clashes with both Rice's memoir and Moratinos' recollection of his conversations with both sides during this period.[56] Rice does not go into detail, but clearly places the responsibility on Mazen, who ignored US appeals to reconsider his no to the peace proposal.[57] Importantly, Moratinos' inside account confirms Olmert's and the magazine's fundamental claim, with some minor modifications, however, as he divides the responsibility for the failure equally between Tzipi Livni and the Palestinian leadership. According to Moratinos, a high-ranking member of Kadima in collusion with Tzipi Livni actually warned the Palestinians not to accept the new peace proposal, as Olmert was considered a "lame duck" due to the corruption charges hanging over his head. This was also the message that Livni had sent to Condoleezza Rice.[58] Livni was allegedly convinced that she was going to be the new prime minister after the upcoming elections, and she argued that it would be much better for the Palestinians to wait until she had effectively assumed power. She apparently told the Palestinians that they would be offered an even better peace deal. In turn, Kadima and Livni would take all the credit on the Israeli side.

[55] Cf. Rice, *No Higher Honor*, 723.

[56] Avi Isacharoff, "Revealed: Olmert's 2008 Peace Offer to the Palestinians," *The Jerusalem Post*, May 24, 2013. See http://www.jpost.com/Diplomacy-and-Politics/Details-of-Olmerts-peace-offer-to-Palestinians-exposed-314261.

[57] Rice, *No Higher Honor*, 724.

[58] "He Has No Standing in Israel," she told Rice. Cf. Rice, *No Higher Honor*, 723.

According to this version, Mazen made the fatal error of trusting Livni and not immediately accepting Olmert's proposal.

Olmert received Moratinos on 12 January 2009 in the midst of the government crisis which eventually ended with Netanyahu's takeover. During their meeting, Olmert showed him what had been offered to the Palestinians. He then urged Moratinos to persuade Abu Mazen once more that this was the right moment to embrace peace. Moratinos obeyed, but on this occasion Abu Mazen yet again left his interlocutor waiting for a positive reply, deceived as he probably was by Livni's promise of an even better deal. In the middle of February, Livni optimistically told Moratinos that she would establish a new government as soon as possible. It was in her words going to be a government which sincerely aspired to live in peace and security with its neighbors. As is well known, this government did not materialize, and on 31 March the more hawkish Netanyahu assumed power, and much to the despair of the Palestinians the deal was off.[59]

If there is any lesson to be learned from these failed peace talks, it is probably that in Middle East politics, as in international politics in general, only seldom do we witness a situation in which events and conditions perfectly combine to reach a settlement. Yet to be able to exploit that precise moment requires the parties to be willing to invest the political capital needed and, not least, cast some of their personal ambitions aside.

8.3   THE SEED OF EVIL

The strenuous efforts of Moratinos to make peace in the Middle East were perfectly in tune with the basic principles outlined in the 2004 electoral program of the PSOE. The Socialist government had always believed that to end the hardship of the Palestinians was by far the easiest way to defuse the global terror threat, as the Palestinian problem was effectively serving to legitimize Al Qaeda's actions across the Muslim world.[60] However, the PSOE also expressed awareness that their commitment to the Palestinians could not stand alone. Other measures more broadly directed at Spain's Arab neighbors were clearly needed. It was against this background that the Spanish government launched the idea of an international Alliance of

---

[59] Moratinos Files: Interview, Moratinos.

[60] PSOE, "Merecemos una España mejor," 21–24.

Civilizations in 2004.[61] To its critics, the Alliance was just further proof of the PSOE government's preference for soft diplomatic measures aiming to ensure "better understanding" and "dialogue" with the Arab world, the effect of which they considered to be doubtful. This was essentially the cornerstone in the criticism raised by the Spanish Conservative opposition and also by some officials within the foreign ministry, who in their private conversations in the corridors of the Ministry allegedly depicted the new doctrine on effective multilateralism as "gay diplomacy" ("*diplomacia maricona*").[62]

This criticism probably misses one important point. It suffices to read the different yearbooks on Spanish foreign policy from 2004 and 2005 to learn that the Zapatero government actually made many important steps in the field of *hard* security and anti-terrorism measures.[63] The problem was, however, that in order to be effective these measures needed to be shrouded in a great deal of secrecy. In actual fact, in his first speech to his employees in the Santa Cruz Palace, Moratinos had underlined that Spain should be at the forefront of the fight against terror.[64] These were not just words. A special anti-terrorism and security unit was soon set up in the Foreign Ministry with Vice Minister for Foreign Affairs Angel Losada in charge.[65] In coordination with other ministries, this new office launched innumerable security agreements and arrangements with foreign powers over the following years, especially with the United States. Yet the government's other and "softer" initiatives were clearly the most progressive ones and also those which caught the widest media attention. Thus, the

[61] Moratinos Files: Interview, Moratinos.

[62] Moratinos Files: Private information.

[63] *Anuario Internacional CIDOB*, multiple entries for 2004 and 2005.

[64] As stated by the minister: "Y por último, yo creo, la novedad y, sobre todo, la exigencia participativa delos ciudadanos españoles hoy de ocuparse y preocuparse de la política exterior viene dada porque tenemos enfrente de nosotros en este comenzar del siglo XXI retos que no podemos renunciar a resolverlos. Y principalmente, el prioritario de todos ellos, es esa lucha internacional contra el terrorismo. Sean, por lo tanto, mis palabras y mi reconocimiento a la hora de abordar este compromiso de lucha del terrorismo internacional con todas aquellas víctimas, nacionales y no nacionales, que sufrieron el brutal atentado del 11 de marzo." Cit. in "Palabras en su toma de posesión, Palacio de Santa Cruz," 19 de abril de 2004, in *Discursos y declaraciones del ministro de Asuntos Exteriores y de cooperación D. Miguel Ángel Moratinos Cuyaubé* (Madrid: Ministerio de Asuntos Exteriores y de Cooperación, Oficina de Informacion Diplomatica, 2005).

[65] Moratinos Files: Interview, Moratinos.

media probably missed the important point that these new soft policies could not be separated from the other hard security measures which were being implemented at the same time.

Importantly, both hard and soft measures were born out of the same rationale which inspired PSOE's overall policy vision, namely that it should be possible to adopt a kind of "smart power" strategy which included a whole range of initiatives, whether in the field of security, economy, trade, culture and so forth. In 2003, Harvard Professor Joseph Nye developed this influential term to describe one of the major challenges of the new millennium.[66] His point was that the use of "hard" and realistic methods in Afghanistan was necessary after the terrorist attacks on 11 September 2001. Yet he also underlined that the same methods would be directly harmful to the Muslim world as a whole, where "soft" or idealistic actions should be implemented to a much higher degree in order to create dialogue and promote mutual understanding. In the new foreign policy for the twenty-first century—Nye explains, with explicit reference to the United States—those nations which manage to use soft and hard power in exactly the right combination, in a kind of "smart power," will be able to meet the challenges of globalization.[67] In many ways, Nye effectively summarizes what the Spanish vision of security was all about.

On 15 July 2004, Moratinos was invited to speak at the traditional summer university courses held at San Lorenzo de El Escorial. Here, as underlined by the press at the time, he not only spoke about the difficult situation in Western Sahara, where he linked the success of a negotiated solution for the Moroccan-occupied territory to the success of preventing future terrorist attacks on Spain. "This government," Moratinos told the journalists present at El Escorial, "may commit many errors, but not to engage politically [in the solution of the conflict in Western Sahara] is not one of them," as such negligence might lead to terror threats against Spain.[68] He then outlined the government's broader visions, and among the written recommendations that Angel Losada had introduced in the minister's speech,

---

[66]Cf. Joseph Nye, "Get Smart. Combining Hard and Soft Power," *Foreign Affairs*, July–August 2009. https://www.foreignaffairs.com/articles/2009-07-01/get-smart.

[67]Ibid.

[68]"Moratinos dice que si no se resuelve el conflicto del Sahara viviremos 'situaciones como el 11-M'," *Libertad Digital*, July 15, 2004. http://www.libertaddigital.com/mundo/moratinos-dice-que-si-no-se-resuelve-el-conflicto-del-sahara-viviremos-situaciones-como-el-11-m-1276227945/.

was the idea of forging an alliance between Spain and the Arab world to fight terrorism. In Moratinos' own recollection, he added the adjective "strategic" to Losada's concept of an "alliance."[69] The press echoed the speech positively, and since Moratinos was growing even fonder of the concept "strategic alliance," he immediately tried to sell the expression to the Moncloa in view of Zapatero's upcoming speech to the General Assembly of the United Nations. In early September, he underlined in a press statement that it was of the utmost importance to eliminate the sources which breed the most fanatic terror groups, yet he also emphasized the need for a more general international plan for collaboration with the Arab and Muslim world, which was equally threatened by terrorism. The new plan should emphasize political, social and cultural solutions without which the work of the intelligence services would be in vain, as it would be impossible to stop the recruitment of Al Qaeda.

Zapatero was very much aware of the importance of his upcoming talk in the UN, as it would give him the perfect platform to explain Spain's withdrawal from Iraq. As usual the preparation for Zapatero's speech began weeks before in the foreign ministry, and the text was then sent back and forth between the Santa Cruz Palace and the Moncloa, where Zapatero's foreign policy advisor continuously altered the text. When Moratinos and Zapatero finally boarded the aircraft for New York on 21 September, the latter expressed his dissatisfaction with the drafted speech. It needed something out of the ordinary, Zapatero reckoned, and he asked Moratinos to read the latest version prepared by his advisor. Moratinos immediately commented that the section on the "strategic alliance" with the Arab world had been erased. The prime minister then asked for the original text produced by the foreign ministry, and although he very much liked the concept developed by Moratinos and Losada, he was unhappy with the name. Inspired, in the opposite sense, by Samuel Huntington's dystopian vision of a clash of civilizations, Zapatero immediately proposed the name "Alliance of Civilizations." Moratinos could not but acknowledge that this was a far better and politically more persuasive term. They immediately agreed that the Alliance of Civilizations should not be an exclusively Spanish initiative, but rather a UN initiative with Spain as one of the driving forces.[70]

---

[69] Moratinos Files: Interview, Moratinos.
[70] Ibid.

In a moving speech on 21 September—possibly one of his best ever—
Zapatero expressed his hopes and fears for this world, as well as launching
the idea of an Alliance of Civilizations. What is also clear from the speech—
but largely forgotten in today's debate about the fate of the alliance—is
that the Alliance was predominantly born out of security considerations.
In a twenty-one-minute seductive appeal to ethics, emotions and logic,
Zapatero used the recent terrorist attack to express his sympathy with the
American people, yet he also warned, without mentioning the United States
directly, against the consequences of the US war on terror in its present
form:

> … From thirty years of terrorism we have learned that the risk of a terrorist
> victory rises sharply when, in order to fight terror, democracy betrays its fun-
> damental nature, governments curtail civil liberties, put judicial guaranties
> at risk, or carry out pre-emptive military operations. This is what our peo-
> ple have learned: that it is legality, democracy and political means and ways
> what[71] makes us stronger and them weaker. We will resist terrorism. Our
> history endorses our resolve. We will pursue our fight against terrorism. But
> we will always do so within the framework of both domestic and international
> legality.[72]

He then went on to say that terrorism was irrational, like the Black Death.
Nevertheless, it was possible to uncover the roots of terrorism rationally.
In his view, there would always be fanatics ready to kill and ready "to dis-
seminate the seed of evil." Still, this seed could not take root if it were to
fall onto the rock of justice, well-being, freedom and hope. Conversely, it
could easily take root if it landed "on the soil of injustice, poverty, humil-
iation and despair. The more people there are who enjoy dignified conditions around the world, the safer we will all be."[73] During the remains
of his speech, he justified Spain's decision to pull out its troops from Iraq
and further coined the Middle East conflict as the "the primary tumor for
many sources of instability." He then arrived at his final point, namely to
propose an Alliance of Civilizations between the Western and the Arab and

---

[71] Ought to be "which."

[72] "Statement by the President of the Government of Spain. HE Mr. José Luis Rodríguez
Zapatero," United Nations General Assembly, New York, September 21, 2004. http://www.
un.org/webcast/ga/59/statements/spaeng040921.pdf.

[73] Ibid.

Muslim worlds.[74] Finally, he linked this initiative to the need for increased development aid, stating that Spain endorsed the UN Millennium objectives regarding development, poverty eradication and the preservation of the environment and committed Spain to substantially increasing its official development aid, in order to reach the threshold of 0.7% of GDP.[75]

It so happened that Zapatero, almost without consulting his manuscript, had given a formidable speech which was strongly applauded by the UN Assembly, something which was also certainly due to the increasing unpopularity of the Bush administration. After his speech, Zapatero authorized the Spanish-UN Ambassador, Juan Antonio Yañez-Barnuevo to speak to Kofi Annan, who immediately embraced the initiative and nominated his chief of staff, Iqbal Riza, as his liaison with the new alliance. With the support of the UN, it was decided to create a High-Level Group of Friends.

To give real impetus to the new alliance, the Spanish government appointed the capable and respected diplomat Máximo Cajal to lead the new initiative from the Spanish side. Cajal had previously shown his worth as a distinguished and intellectually compelling diplomat. In the 1980s, he had been crucial to Felipe González's policy of revising the US base policies in Spain, and prior to the elections in 2004, Cajal had taken part in the PSOE's special foreign policy advisor group. He had, however, taken the false step of publishing a book just prior to the elections, in which he stated that it might be better to cede the two Spanish enclaves on the African Coast, Ceuta and Melilla to Morocco, a statement which triggered a fierce debate in the press and also put the PSOE in some difficulty.[76] Therefore, no one in the Zapatero camp felt that they owed Cajal any particular job, also because he had formally retired from service, but due to his long history of loyal collaboration with the party it was finally decided to give him the task of forging the new alliance. As was to be expected, Cajal performed well and also managed to place the former Director General of Unesco, Federico Mayor Zaragoza, as head of the High-Level Group of Friends.[77]

---

[74] Ibid.

[75] Ibid.

[76] Máximo Cajal, *Ceuta, Melilla, Olivenza y Gibraltar: ¿dónde acaba España?* (Madrid: Siglo XXI de España, 2003).

[77] Moratinos Files: Interview, Moratinos.

After Zapatero's speech to the UN, Moratinos presented a more polished proposal for the alliance before the Arab League, and very soon a joint working group including representatives from several countries was set up. However, to make the alliance truly prosper it was imperative to find a partner country, preferably in the Arab or Muslim world, who could officially co-sponsor the Spanish initiative. Several countries were under consideration. Egypt was proposed, but was deemed to be too undemocratic. Morocco was geographically too close to Spain, just as the eternal rivalry with Algeria might increase tensions even further in the Maghreb region. Even Israel was considered, but too many Middle East countries were in conflict with Israel, just as Saud Arabia was deemed far too conservative. This made the choice of Turkey almost self-explanatory. In 2004, Turkey was regarded as having sufficient democratic credentials, as well as having the required European backing. Turkey defended Islam, but also seemed willing to meet the Copenhagen criteria. In this way, an unusual political tandem between Erdogan and Zapatero was forged. Ankara embraced the idea of an Alliance of Civilizations, and not just because it allowed Turkey to play a prominent international role. The idea also prospered because Erdogan noticed that there was a sincere will in Madrid to truly overcome those forces who were trying to stir up conflict between civilizations. The Spanish initiative was also well received in the Maghreb countries, which could not fail to notice that despite the fact that nearly all the perpetrators in the Madrid attack had come from that region, no repressive means had been introduced in Spain toward the Maghrebis living in Spain.

In the Spanish government's understanding, the new initiative differed in essential ways from the Geneva-based Foundation for Dialogue Among Civilizations, in which Iran played an important part. In Moratinos' view, dialogue is a good thing, but dialogue alone is insufficient. Dialogue consists of one person talking and the other listening, and the other way around, but when the discussions are over, one tends to return to one's old habits and vices. Semantically, an alliance is much more binding: One works together and designs the future together with the purpose of diminishing the atmosphere of pressure and confrontation. An alliance implies that the different members are under pressure to implement their joint decisions.[78]

Máximo Cajal's ambitions went even further. He conceived the Alliance within the broader context of an evolving multi-polarity and pluralism in

[78] Ibid.

the international environment which would inevitably change the global relationship of force to the detriment of the US hegemony. In essence, Cajal saw the Alliance as an expression of a rising new world order, as an attempt to create new concerted mechanisms which would ultimately govern relations between peoples. These laws were to be unanimously and freely accepted, and inspired by a few ethical principles that would make it possible for all countries in the world to coexist, cooperate and compete peacefully in an increasingly interdependent world. He saw multilateralism as a way to guarantee peace in a context of potential instability caused by the multipolar nature of international relations. The Alliance was thus to be a global framework in which all nations, large and small, ultimately play by the same rules. It was a first move away from the "the West" to "the rest," that is, a system where the major powers would eventually have to accept the necessity of cooperation to preserve their fundamental interests.[79] It is fair to say that his idea of converting the alliance into a kind of United Nations 2.0 never prospered.

Kofi Annan formally launched the Alliance with Spain and Turkey as sponsors on 14 July 2005. He asked the High-Level Group to produce a report explaining the fundaments and the political means of the Alliance. It was finally presented to him in November 2006.[80] Subsequently, Kofi Annan appointed the former Portuguese President Jorge Sampaio as the alliance's first high representative. On 10 November 2010, the United Nation General Assembly gave its formal support to the initiative through a new resolution and Sampaio held the position as high representative until 2013. He gave great impetus to the building of the new organization, but far less political energy has been invested in the Alliance over the last years, thereby raising fundamental questions as to its efficiency and legitimacy. The first—and according to press cuttings at the time—very successful forum of the alliance was held in Madrid in 2008, followed by Istanbul (2009), Río de Janeiro (2010), Doha (2011), Vienna (2013), Bali (2014) and Baku (2016). Conceptually, the forum has gradually moved away from its original security-oriented focus in the relations between the West and the Islamic world to also focus on other civilizations such as China and

---

[79] Máximo Cajal, *La Alianza de Civilizaciones de las Naciones Unidas: una mirada al futuro* (Madrid: Biblioteca Nueva, 2011), 49, 55.

[80] Cf. "Alianza de Civilizaciones," the official Spanish presentation of the initiative on *exteriores.gob.es*. http://www.exteriores.gob.es/Portal/es/PoliticaExteriorCooperacion/NacionesUnidas/Paginas/AlianzaCivilizaciones.aspx.

India. Moreover, questions regarding the indigenous populations in Latin America have been formally raised in the forum. In other words, it has been necessary to broaden the theme of the alliance, as it now includes more than 130 countries. Fervent intellectual debates on what constitutes a civilization or not have certainly taken place over the years, but for the Spanish government, the end goal of the alliance was much narrower and essentially security-oriented. However, the alliance did bestow Spain with the international prestige that comes from sponsoring a global UN initiative.[81]

Even though the political efficacy of the organization can certainly be debated today, it did actually prove its potential value almost immediately. The first opportunity arose in 2005, when the so-called cartoon crisis hit Denmark and other European states. On 30 September 2005, the Danish newspaper *Jyllandsposten* printed twelve satirical cartoons of the Prophet Mohammed, who according to the Sunni interpretation of Islam may not be depicted in any way. This led to local protests by the Muslim community in Denmark and demands for both an apology and the withdrawal of the cartoons. The Danish newspaper declined to do either. Two weeks later, eleven ambassadors from Muslim countries were denied a meeting with the Danish Prime Minister Anders Fogh Rasmussen and the conflict soon escalated, in part because a delegation of Danish Muslims traveled to the Middle East in November to stir up public and official condemnation. Libya soon closed its embassy in Denmark, and on 29 January 2006, Scandinavians were requested to leave the Gaza Strip within seventy-two hours. Three days later, *Charlie Hebdo* reproduced the satirical drawings, and on 5 February, the Danish embassy in Lebanon was burned to the ground. Attacks were also made against the Danish embassy in Tehran. On 18 February, fifteen people were killed in demonstrations against the cartoons in Nigeria. On 1 May 2010, to take one of many international ramifications of the cartoon crisis, a man tried to detonate a car bomb in Times Square in New York, as he was angry with the satirical American cartoon series *South Park*, which ridiculed the fact that it was no longer possible to show pictures of the Prophet publicly.[82] The terrorist attack on Charlie Hebdo in 2015 is one of the latest and most cruel acts. In other

---

[81] Moratinos Files: Interview, Moratinos.

[82] A timeline of the crisis can be found in the Danish newspaper *Berlingske*, January 7, 2015. https://www.b.dk/globalt/tidslinje-saadan-forloeb-muhammed-krisen.

words, the publication of the cartoons—completely in line with Danish and Western publicist traditions—produced the worst Danish diplomatic crisis since World War II and also deepened the cultural divide between the West and the Muslim world in the years to come. Without doubt, the cartoon crisis showed a deeply disturbing side effect of globalization.

Moratinos claims that the Alliance of Civilizations—although it was only in the making when the cartoon crisis got out of control in early 2006—certainly played a role in mitigating the pressure on the Danish government. This is also confirmed by Moratinos' conservative counterpart, the former Danish Foreign Minister Per Stig Møller, who already knew Moratinos from the second semester of 2002 when Denmark was holding the EU presidency and Moratinos was still the EU's special envoy to the Middle East.[83] Møller reckons that the Alliance was extremely helpful when it came to reaching out to those forces in the Middle East that were most hostile to Denmark.[84] When things started to take a negative turn in January and February, Møller called Moratinos for help. Moratinos contacted the Islamic Conference on his behalf in order to explain the Danish position on freedom of speech and respect for religious feelings, something which together with a series of other initiatives helped to ease the pressure. In addition, Condoleezza Rice—probably as a favor to her close Danish ally—called Moratinos while he was in Montevideo to raise the question of the cartoon crisis—now including Charlie Hebdo and also serious riots in the Middle East. She strongly encouraged him to act, something to which, nonetheless, he was already committed.[85] In a joint article with Sergey Lavrov, the Russian Foreign Minister, Moratinos stressed respect for the liberty of speech within the limits of the constitution on the one hand and on the other the responsibility that one must take for one's actions when it comes to hurting other people's feelings. He used the occasion to reiterate that the Alliance of Civilizations had been established exactly for this purpose, to build bridges and promote dialogue across the Islamic, Arab and Western civilizations.[86] Moratinos later called Møller and asked Denmark to join the Alliance in order to build better bridges to the Arab

---

[83] Moratinos Files: Interview, Per Stig Møller.

[84] Ibid.

[85] "El ministro y Rice coinciden en apoyar al grupo 'Súmate', de oposición al régimen de Chávez," *ABC*, February 16, 2006.

[86] Miguel Ángel Moratinos and Sergey Lavrov, "Más allá de la caricatura," published among other newspapers in *El Mundo*, February 10, 2010.

world. The Danish government instantly did so and in addition donated funds to the Spanish-UN initiative. In return, Moratinos paid a visit to Copenhagen in early April 2006. Møller also remembers that during one of the first meetings of the Alliance, Moratinos made a special effort to reconcile Denmark with the Muslim world: The Spanish foreign minister helped drafting a resolution that could work as a compromise between the two parties.[87] The Alliance had indeed showed its worth.

In mid-January 2008, the first international forum of the Alliance took place in Madrid under the leadership of Jorge Sampaio. UN Secretary-General Ban Ki-moon opened the session that was attended by nearly 400 government ministers and many nongovernmental organizations. It was agreed that the Alliance would concentrate on areas of youth, education, the media and migration. In view of the cartoon crisis, a decision was taken to establish a "Rapid Response Media Mechanism," which was essentially a list of major international experts that journalists could draw upon if there was a cultural crisis. Among the twelve projects which received funding was the production and distribution of films focusing on "normalizing images of stereotyped communities and minorities."[88]

The need for an alliance dedicated entirely to preventing a clash of civilizations was underlined in nearly all the interventions at the first meeting, but the fact that the initiative was ignored by some of the major powers naturally posed a problem. Nevertheless, Moratinos chose to take a positive approach when he stressed that this was not a summit of heads of governments, but rather a forum for reflection, although it was still important that the meeting should end with concrete tangible results.[89] Whereas Denmark, which had been deeply affected by the cartoon crisis, instantly joined the Alliance of Civilizations, US support for the Spanish initiative was always lukewarm or ambiguous. Initially, the United States viewed the Alliance with extreme caution, not least because it implicitly criticized Bush's war on terror. Furthermore, Zapatero was considered *persona non grata* in the White House during the Bush years. But above all, US hesitation probably owed to concerns for Israel. In actual fact, the High-Level

---

[87] Moratinos Files: Interview, Per Stig Møller. See also Per Stig Møller, *Udenrigsminister i krig og fred* (Copenhagen: Gyldendal, 2006), 371–372.

[88] "Alliance of Civilizations Forum Ends with Agreements to Bridge Differences Between Cultures," *AP*, January 16, 2008.

[89] "Moratinos dice que el Gobierno está 'muy satisfecho' con la participación y los resultados del Foro," *AP*, January 16, 2008.

Group had proposed a document on the Palestinian problem in which they appealed for a definitive solution and urged Israel to increase its commitment. For the same reason Israel—always suspicious of binding initiatives—viewed the Alliance with skepticism. Even though Moratinos had always maintained excellent working relations with the Israelis, they were nevertheless suspicious of Zapatero, whom they considered an anti-Zionist due to his critique of the Israeli shelling of Gaza in 2006. This Israeli skepticism clearly influenced the US position on the Alliance of Civilizations.[90]

Only toward the end of the Bush presidency did Condoleezza Rice take a more positive view of the Alliance, a line that was followed by Hillary Clinton upon her nomination as Secretary of State in January 2009. Accordingly, the United States now backed the UN initiative, yet still abstained from any active participation. On 14 August 2009, Hillary Clinton stated in a personal letter to Moratinos—in response to his request for further US participation in the Alliance—that the United States fundamentally supported the idea of improving understanding and cooperative relations among nations and peoples across cultures and religion. However, the United Stated was for the moment unwilling to do more than explore the possibility of joining the Group of Friends. In contrast, Moratinos highlights the genuine interest of Tony Blair, who donated a considerable amount of money to the initiative. France formally supported the Alliance, but did not engage in it, whereas the Germans apparently considered it too "soft" to be interesting.[91]

It is probably fair to say that a lot of fruitful activities have occurred within the Alliance at the NGO level and in designated areas such as education, youth and emigration, whereas other fields still leave a great deal to be desired. Still, one must never underestimate the fact that the initiative has obtained worldwide support, and that governments across civilizations wanting to eradicate the root of conflict have embraced the idea. Curiously enough, the Alliance was heavily criticized by the Conservative Spanish opposition which found it useless and ridiculed its efforts. However, when the party returned to power in December 2011, it had to publicly recognize the importance of the Alliance. It was after all the *only* Spanish initiative of such proportions in the history of the United Nations which had ever been executed. The Group of Friends of the Alliance meet in New York in

[90] Ibid.
[91] Moratinos Files: Interview, Moratinos.

concomitance with the General Assembly of the UN, and these meetings are always presided over by the ministers of Turkey and Spain. No Spanish foreign minister—regardless of ideology—would ever deprive himself or herself of such an opportunity to promote one's country. This probably explains why the PP government kept in place a commitment it had previously and continuously criticized.

CHAPTER 9

Capitalism Has Died

9.1   The Meltdown of Wall Street

The crisis provoked by the fall of Lehman Brothers on 15 September 2008 was met by the international community with surprise, bordering on disbelief. World leaders clearly underestimated the possible longer-term effects of the meltdown of Wall Street, namely that the American subprime mortgage crisis, which had started the year before, would lead to an international financial crisis where the ability of European states to pay their sovereign debts would eventually be put to the test. Only occasionally were such warnings articulated, as was the case in late September 2008, when Moratinos held a special dinner for the Spanish community in New York. Among the many influential people on the guest list were Ban Ki-moon, Zapatero and Enrique V. Iglesias, head of the Ibero-American General Secretariat. During dinner, the talk was naturally about Lehman Brothers and the effect of its fall on the world economy. To the surprise of everybody, Iglesias argued in a very assured fashion, "This is a very serious crisis which will last for ten years at least." Moratinos and Zapatero, as well as the other prominent guests, all thought that Iglesias was exaggerating. Certainly, they argued, it was a severe crisis, but also one that could be overcome within a reasonable time span through a joint international effort. No one in the Spanish

© The Author(s) 2019
M. Heiberg, *Spain and the Wider World since 2000*,
Security, Conflict and Cooperation in the Contemporary World,
https://Doi.org/10.1007/978-3-030-27343-9_9

government anticipated that the crisis would lead to a political meltdown in Spain as well.[1]

What was obvious to the Spanish government, though, was that a new multilateral global governance structure was needed to deal with such crises in the future. Clearly, no single nation had the ability to effectively address transnational challenges of this magnitude, and the Santa Cruz Palace correctly believed that the Group of Twenty was going to be the forum designated for this purpose in the future. In fact, in 2007 the foreign ministry had prepared a series of notes for the government which argued that Spain, as the eighth biggest economy in the world, should make a bid for G20 membership in the near future rather than for G8 membership, as the latter was seen to some extent as an expression of the old world order.[2]

What was interesting about the G20 was that it included the world's rising powers and as such it fitted much better into Spain's overall understanding of effective multilateralism. The G20 comprised nineteen countries worldwide plus the European Union and was originally born out of the meeting of G7 finance ministers and central bank governors who in 1999 had formulated a need for a broader economic forum which could also represent a wider spectrum of the fast-growing economies in Asia, Africa and Latin America.[3] At that time, the G20 did not exist in its present form as there were only occasional meetings at the level of the minister of the economy. However, together with other countries with economies of a similar size, such as South Korea, Australia, Pakistan and Argentina, the Zapatero government supported the idea of creating a new economic organization around the G20. Brazil was not part of this working group, though, as its main preoccupation after the turn of the millennium was to be accepted as a permanent member of the United Nation Security Council and thereby also be recognized as a major international player.

The Spanish government interpreted the global financial crisis in 2008 as a real game changer, as it expected that the future summits of the G20 would be attended by heads of states and governments wanting to steer the economic course of the world.[4] It was actually President Obama, in

---

[1] Moratinos Files: Interview, Moratinos.

[2] Ibid.

[3] "About the G20," the official G20 Web site. See: https://www.g20.org/en/g20/what-is-the-g20.

[4] Moratinos Files: Interview, Moratinos.

Pittsburg on 25 September 2009, who officially labeled it as the organ authorized to deal with the global economic situation.[5] This led to a gradual institutionalization of the G20, and during the years of severe crisis, Zapatero participated in no less than six such summits. In its most active period, coinciding with the first phase of the economic crisis, it looked as though the G20 had the potential to become a type of world government.

According to my Spanish sources, the importance of this economic consensus-building forum also owed to President Bush's previous difficulty in providing a global response to the crisis in 2008. In the days following the fall of Lehman Brothers, Henry Paulson, the treasury secretary, and Ben Bernanke, head of the Federal Reserve Board, were primarily working to unblock the frozen credit markets. To this end, Paulson urged President Bush to spend billions of public dollars to help firms clean up toxic loans which were jeopardizing their existence. In fact, the US challenges were enormous. On 4 September 2008, Paulson had to ask for $100 billions of capital support for both Fannie Mae and Freddie Mac, two of America's housing finance giants, while later in the autumn he had to launch the Temporary Liquidity Guarantee Program, among many other important rescue initiatives.[6] The fact that Washington was primarily focused on this domestic challenge, which was actually addressed quite effectively, apparently left an unusually large political space in which the other important world economies could now act. This assertion is, however, contradicted by Henry M. Paulson, who underlines that Sarkozy tried to persuade President Bush to just accept a G8 summit on the financial crisis, whereas it was President Bush who insisted on a much more inclusive approach, namely the G20.[7]

Be that as it may, when Zapatero participated in the G20 in Washington in November 2008, both he and the other heads of government engaged decisively in the decision-making process. The Chinese President gave an important, yet also very formal and cold speech, whereas Sarkozy, as always very dramatic, repeated his argument that financial capitalism had died.[8] During 2008, he argued in several official statements, in fact, that the state

[5] José Luis Rodríguez Zapatero, *El dilema. 600 días de vértigo* (Barcelona: Planeta, 2013), 269.

[6] Henry M. Paulson, Jr., *On the Brink: Inside the Race to Stop the Collapse of the Global Financial System* (New York and Boston: Business Plus, 2010), 1, 363.

[7] Paulson, *On the Brink*, 375.

[8] Moratinos Files: Interview, Zapatero.

now had to impose itself upon the savagery of the market.[9] In Washington, Zapatero was also invited to a working dinner with a reduced number of heads of states and heads of government. To his great surprise, President Bush actually cited Zapatero's talk on the world economy as a very positive contribution to resolving the economic challenges ahead. So, in their last interaction together in 2008 the political tension finally eased between the two leaders, while Bush—on the verge of leaving office—seemed relieved and more than happy to let others countries take the lead.[10]

Despite its fast-growing economy, Spain had never been able to formally enter the G20. Still, in 2007, the Zapatero government judged that the right moment was approaching, and it was determined to use its year-long rapprochement with France to finally obtain the membership it felt entitled to. This operation had to be conducted in difficult terrain, however. It coincided not only with the unfolding economic crisis, but also with the end of the Chirac government and the still uncertain electoral contest between the two new presidential candidates, Ségolène Royal of the French Socialist party, and Nicolas Sarkozy of the UMP. During the last years of the Chirac government, there had been some tension with France and especially with Sarkozy, who at that time was minister of the interior. On repeated occasions, Sarkozy had heavily criticized the Spanish and Italian decision to naturalize hundreds of thousands of immigrants, as this—he argued—attracted even more migrants to Europe.[11] In contrast, in an interview with the Austrian daily newspaper *Kurier,* Moratinos said that the real enemies were the human trafficking mafias, while the legalization of the 600,000 illegal immigrants in Spain was merely recognition of their important contribution to Spanish economic growth. In another interview at a later date, he called for a joint European migration policy in order to avoid similar tension in the future.[12]

[9]Cf. "Sarkozy Stresses Global Financial Overhaul," *The New York Times,* September 25, 2008. www.nytimes.com/2008/09/26/business/worldbusiness/26france.html.

[10]Moratinos Files: Interview, Zapatero.

[11]"Zapatero y Sarkozy cierran la polémica por su cruce de declaraciones sobre inmigración," *El Mundo,* October 1, 2006. http://www.elmundo.es/elmundo/2006/09/30/espana/1159608605.html.

[12]"Einwanderern wurden Recht gegeben," *Kurier,* November 27, 2006; "Moratinos defiende que regularización de inmigrantes fue un 'éxito' y un 'modelo' frente a los recelos de Francia," *Europa Press,* August 27, 2007. http://www.europapress.es/sociedad/noticia-moratinos-defiende-regularizacion-inmigrantes-exito-modelo-frente-recelos-francia-20070827133402.html.

Before she officially announced her candidature, Ségolène Royal visited the Spanish Socialist party conference in September 2006, and as could be expected, the press photo of her shaking hands with Zapatero was fiercely criticized by the French right. Nevertheless, it soon turned out that the UMP was just as eager to gain access to Zapatero with more or less the same purpose. At an international meeting on migration in Madrid, Sarkozy was extremely polite to Moratinos calling him an *"afrancesado,"* a Francophile, due to his French wife Dominique. The real aim of this flattery, however, was to set up a meeting with the Spanish prime minister. Knowing full well that Zapatero was not too keen on such an encounter, Moratinos tried to find excuses to decline the French proposal—that Zapatero was extremely busy and so forth. Nonetheless, the French pressure continued. In the end, Moratinos recommended to Zapatero that he should receive Sarkozy after all, as the UMP had a good chance of winning the presidential elections. It goes without saying that it was vital for the Socialist government to maintain good relations with France, regardless of who was in power. The two met on 27 February 2007, yet it was agreed that there should be no official photos—a deal that was, however, not respected by the French.[13] It also created some irritation in the Spanish government when Sarkozy tried to derail the so-called Barcelona process during the presidential campaign by replacing it with a France-dominated intergovernmental Mediterranean Union.[14] In the end, Sarkozy turned out to be very helpful to Spain thanks to his extraordinary political energy and efficiency. His contribution to dismantling ETA, both as minister of the interior and later as president, cannot be overestimated. His dedication to defeating Basque terrorism was impressive by all standards, and among other things, he allowed armed officers of the Spanish *Guardia Civil* to enter French territory when necessary.

People I have consulted during the preparation for this book agree that it was actually Sarkozy who took the most important initiative to save the international financial system, just as he also masterminded the European public spending strategy after 2008, for which Zapatero was later heavily criticized. In Washington, in November 2008, Sarkozy effectively persuaded the other members of the G20 to act. Compared to his successor, François Hollande, Sarkozy possessed the rare talent of a problem-solving

[13]Moratinos Files: Interview, Moratinos; "Nicolas Sarkozy y Rubalcaba acuerdan seguir colaborando contra ETA," *El Mundo*, February 27, 2007. http://www.elmundo.es/elmundo/2007/02/27/espana/1172572892.html.

[14]Vaquer i Fanes, "Spain in the Mediterranean," 147.

international statesman, but he had a darker personal side. He was considered unreliable by many because he tended to easily forget his friends. An incident in the spring of 2012 is very revealing of this. Only a couple of months after Sarkozy had received the *Collar de Toison d'or*, a prestigious Spanish order, he indirectly attacked Zapatero, now the former prime minister but also the very person who had worked to provide him with the official Spanish order.[15] Despite this, Sarkozy's commitment in 2008 to helping Spain (and the rest of the world) during a period of economic crisis should not be erased from the history books.

During the meeting of the European Council on 16 October 2008, Spain gave its support to the French presidency and the President of the European Commission, Barroso, to call for an international summit on the economic crisis. With American support, the forum eventually designated for the purpose was the G20, and soon afterward, Washington sent out invitations to all the G20 members. Meanwhile, Zapatero instructed Bernardino León, who was now working directly for the prime minister, to fight for Spanish representation at the meeting in Washington, and this was eventually achieved with the help of President Sarkozy. As France held both its own chair and that of the EU in its capacity as President of the Council, Sarkozy agreed to cede one chair to Spain with the tacit agreement of the United States. Spain also managed to take part in the second summit of the G20 in London, but the next summit in Pittsburg was more difficult, as the United States thought that too many countries had been allowed to join the G20 meetings. However, with the help of Berlusconi's Italy, Spain was invited to the G8 meeting in Aquila in Italy from 8–10 July 2009, where Spain managed to convince Obama's delegation of the need for Spain to be present in Pittsburg. A week later, Spain received a formal invitation. The summit in Pittsburg was important as Obama was now set on the idea of institutionalizing the G20. However, China and the United States were still concerned that too many countries would join this new institution and thus make it inefficient.[16]

Zapatero accounts in his memoirs for the countries across the world which gradually changed their attitude in Spain's favor and eventually

---

[15] Moratinos Files: Interview, Moratinos; "El PP dice que las críticas de Sarkozy se referían a las políticas del PSOE," *La Razón*, April 6, 2012. See: https://www.larazon.es/historico/512-el-pp-dice-que-las-criticas-de-sarkozy-se-referian-a-las-politicas-del-psoe-NLLA_RAZON_448249.

[16] Zapatero, *El dilema*, 273–277.

allowed Spain to enter the G20 organization on a permanent basis in 2009, albeit with a special status. Among other countries, Zapatero mentions the UK, Brazil, Mexico, China, Korea, Japan and Australia. With respect to Australia, he regards their acceptance as a "surprise," because the land down under had been extremely critical of his government since the Spanish withdrawal of forces from Iraq.[17] In the end, Spain was allowed to enter the G20 as a "permanent guest," yet with full rights to take part in the decisions of the forum. The considerable size of the Spanish economy, the eighth largest prior to the crisis, more than justified Spain joining the economic forum.

As Zapatero rightly stresses, the opportunity to enter the G20 arose as a result of the financial crisis and was first of all made possible by the good relationship with France which the Spanish government had cultivated over the years. Zapatero's account is accurate, just as he is right in underlining the merits of his foreign policy advisor Bernardino León. What is perhaps not fully reflected in Zapatero's version is the active role played by the Spanish Foreign Ministry on various fronts, without which Spanish participation would simply never have been possible. With hindsight, it is fair to say that the government's strategy of effective multilateralism, by which it had gained influence in multiple regions, was what essentially awarded Spain a seat in the G20. Noteworthy is not only the change of attitude of the United States, but also of that of China and of three of America's closest allies: South Korea, Japan and Australia. If Spain had not established a foreign policy with global reach over the years, if it had not struck agreements in other areas with Russia and China and if it had not given a great impulse to the European project under Chirac and built a relationship of trust with Germany and France, as well as with Great Britain on Gibraltar, it would simply not have been able to pull off the negotiations prior to the Pittsburg summit. Spain entered the G20 because it had demonstrated that it was a global actor to be reckoned with.

To emphasize this important point, one may take a brief look at Spain's renewed efforts in the East, which for many years had been virtually unknown territory to the Spanish diplomacy and business community. In 2000, the Aznar government had developed a two-year action plan for Asia—eventually extended to four years—yet it was mainly concerned with India and East Asia. It was only with the arrival of the Zapatero government

[17]Ibid., 276.

that a much broader and nuanced approach to Asia was conceived.[18] In the Santa Cruz Palace, a new plan for Asia was designed in 2004 and it identified four clusters of countries in this area which Spain should cultivate.[19] However, a major problem was that there were only two small offices in the foreign ministry to take care of such a vast part of the world, where nations of the size of continents exist alongside other nations, typically islands, which are hardly visible on the map. In addition, the area comprised some of the greatest poles of wealth and some of the greatest poles of poverty. There were nations with thousands of years of history of advanced civilization, yet at the same time, several of them had only recently been reconstituted as nation-states after the era of decolonization had begun. In its plan, the foreign ministry highlighted that 60% of the world's population was currently living in Asia and that with more than two decades of sustained economic growth Asia was also the most dynamic region on the planet. In 2004, Asia numbered two of the ten largest economies in the world and more than two-thirds of the world's total currency reserves. Accordingly, Asia played a central role in the financial markets and in setting interest rates on a global scale.[20] However, the huge traveling distances in Asia were a major impediment to the execution of the ambitious new ministerial plan, as the ministry rightly deemed that to be effective Spanish diplomacy had to be much more present in the area. Therefore, José Eugenio Salarich, general director in the Santa Cruz Palace and responsible for Asia and the Pacific area, was more or less permanently confined to life on an airplane during the six years he served in this position from 2004 to 2010.[21]

Given the Spanish withdrawal from Iraq, a major challenge was how to bond with three of the United States' most important allies in this part of the world: Japan, Australia and South Korea, all of whom came to play a role in Spain's later accession to the G20. These countries had reacted very strongly against the Spanish withdrawal, with Australia being the most outspoken of the three. The problem with the Spanish withdrawal was that Australia had to deal with considerable domestic opposition to its

---

[18] Ramón Pacheco Pardo, "Spain and Asia. Towards a Closer Relationship," in *Contemporary Spanish Foreign Policy*, ed. David García Cantalapiedra and Ramón Pacheco Pardo (Abingdon and New York: Routledge, 2014), 172.

[19] Cf. "España hacia Asia y el Pacífico. Plan de acción 2005–2008," *MAEC*, 2005, 45–80. Available on https://www.casaasia.es/documentos/plan_accion_asia2005.pdf.

[20] "España hacia Asia y el Pacífico," 13.

[21] Moratinos Files: Interview, Salarich.

participation in the war in Iraq. Spain had in fact shown to the public that one could leave Iraq without major consequences, something which of course increased the domestic pressure on the Australian government. Canberra frequently blamed Spain for its decision to pull its forces out. As a matter of fact, Prime Minister John Howard timed one of his most critical statements for Monday 19 April 2004, right after the Zapatero government had been sworn in. Howard's harsh claim was that "Spain's decision will give heart to those people who are trying to delay the emergence of a free and democratic Iraq. Every time a country appears to be retreating from a difficult situation, encouragement is given to those people who have created the difficulty."[22] This statement probably represents a nadir in the Spanish relationship with Australia. Yet the crisis of confidence between the two countries was from then on slowly overcome by multiple Spanish diplomatic measures. In one of his first visits to Canberra, Salarich had to sit and wait very patiently before the Australian undersecretary for foreign affairs eventually decided to receive him. However, as a sign of Spanish goodwill, he proposed official state visits hoping that Canberra would be susceptible to such a gesture. Perhaps more importantly, he also proposed new joint collaborations in Latin America, especially in Chile, Colombia and Mexico, all countries where Spain had considerable weight. Spain also offered its vote in the UN to help Australia become a member of different organs.

This is not to say that difficulties were immediately overcome, but both parties gradually managed to keep their differences out of the spotlight of the media. As a sign of the renewed friendship, Australia offered important industrial contracts in return, as in 2007 when Navantia won two contracts for the design and construction of five warships worth 1300 million Euros.[23] It is also worth mentioning that just as Zapatero was starting negotiations in Washington at the G20 in November 2008, Moratinos signed a mutual defense agreement with Australia.[24] Seen in this broader

[22] Cited after "Spain's Iraq Decision Angers Canberra," *ABC*, April 19, 2004. http://www.abc.net.au/pm/content/2004/s1090514.htm.

[23] *Anuario Internacional CIDOB*, entry for June 20, 2007. https://www.cidob.org/publicaciones/documentacion/cronologias/australia_empresa_espanola_construira_buques_para_la_armada_australiana_20_junio_2007/(language)/esl-ES.

[24] Ibid., entry for November 24, 2008. https://www.cidob.org/publicaciones/documentacion/cronologias/australia_firma_de_un_memorando_de_entendimiento_en_materia_de_defensa_24_noviembre_2008/(language)/esl-ES.

diplomatic context, it was hardly a surprise that a year later, Australia eventually decided in favor of Spanish accession to the G20. Similar policies were applied by Madrid toward Tokyo and Seoul, the latter also being a contender for a place at the table of the G20, although the real competitor due to its geographic vicinity to Spain was actually Holland. It was probably the swiftness of Spanish aid after the tsunami hit the Pacific in December 2004 which made an impact on countries like Sri Lanka, Indonesia and Thailand. Indonesia in particular became an ally that voted with Spain on practically all international questions.[25]

This policy of collaboration with South Korea, Japan and Australia had the added bonus that the United States took good notice of it, something which indirectly contributed to improving the relationship between Washington and Madrid. It also created new possibilities in view of the G20, where the Americans—skeptical of the enlargement—could easily have ousted the Spanish had they wanted to. Instead, they did not object to the French proposal in 2008 to cede one chair to Madrid, just as the United States accepted the Spanish arguments when the two delegations met in Aquila in 2009 to discuss Spain joining the G20. Overall, the Asian alliance was crucial in order to obtain full consensus around Spain's entry into the economic forum.[26]

Besides the United States, China was the other big player which could easily have blocked Spanish participation, as it too was skeptical about expanding the circle of the G20. In this case, as rightly underlined by Zapatero, the actions of the foreign service were also crucial for obtaining Beijing's support.[27] And, one might add, this went above and beyond the frequent contact that Moratinos had with his Chinese counterpart during the most intense period of negotiations. Over the years, the Santa Cruz Palace had actually organized numerous official visits and arranged cultural and commercial promotions such as the "*año de China en España*." It had opened no less than three consulates and two Cervantes institutes in Beijing and Shanghai, as well as organizing one of the most expensive pavilions at the EXPO in Shanghai. It was not without reason that

---

[25] Moratinos Files: Interview, Salarich.

[26] Moratinos Files: Interview Moratinos. See also Zapatero, *El dilema*, 274–277.

[27] Zapatero, *El dilema*, 274.

Prime Minister Wen Jiabao had reiterated over the years—also out of courtesy, of course—that Spain was China's closest friend within the EU.[28]

This friendship was to a large extent based on the premise that no one in the Spanish government received the Dalai Lama officially or questioned that Tibet was an integral part of China. Although the EU had introduced the topic of human rights in its formal bilateral discussions with China, Spain never truly waved this flag. To put it simply, Spain's strategy was instead based on the idea of seeking political and cultural affinity with China, in the hope of gaining economic preferential treatment in return. This led foreign critics to describe Spain as an "accommodating mercantilist."[29] Spain's somewhat softer approach also had to do with the fact that in Northern Europe governments were far more pressured by civil rights group. On the positive side, however, one might argue that Spain did not use the human rights card as cynically as some northern European states did. In fact, Spanish diplomats often complained about how other European countries effectively offered to hold back the pressure on civil right issues in return for economic concessions.[30] Unable to play this card, Spanish exports nevertheless grew considerably, increasing nearly eight times between 2000 and 2014, while Spanish annual investments in China grew from €42 million during the 2000–2005 period to €464 million between 2006 and 2012. Nonetheless, Spain has not been able to fix its current trade deficit with China. In 2004, the Spanish Foreign Ministry estimated that there were well over one hundred Spanish companies operating in China. In 2010, there were nearly one thousand. It was still a very small number, as there were probably more than 200,000 EU companies working in China, all in all. Needless to say, France, Italy and Great Britain were miles ahead in their Asian policies.[31]

If Spain did not exercise much pressure on China with regard to human rights, it most certainly did toward the Philippines, its former colony. Madrid actually convinced them, quite spectacularly, to end the death

[28] "Hu Jintao considera 'todo un éxito' la visita de Zapatero a China," *La Razón*, April 14, 2011. https://www.larazon.es/historico/8660-hu-jintao-considera-todo-un-exito-la-visita-de-zapatero-a-china-NLLA_RAZON_370377.

[29] Mario Esteban, "Spain's Relations with China: Friends but Not Partners," *Chinese Political Science Review*, vol. 1, issue 2 (June 2016): 373–386. https://link.springer.com/article/10.1007/s41111-016-0019-x.

[30] Moratinos Files: Interview, Salarich.

[31] Ibid.

penalty in their country. The background for this important decision was a case where a young man of Spanish and Philippine descent had been sentenced to death for having hijacked, raped and killed two sisters in the City of Cebu in 1997, together with five other men. The young man's family continued to claim his innocence, however, and there were also presumed irregularities in the judiciary process. First, he had been sentenced to twenty years, and then he had appealed, only to be confronted with the capital sentence. He therefore changed his nationality to Spanish. Afterward, there was a media campaign in Spain and elsewhere to defend his rights and also to protest his innocence. The Spanish government soon found out that it was impossible to defend him legally, so a political solution was considered the only way to save him from the death penalty. The Spanish Parliament stated that if the Philippines did not comply, Spain would cut off political relations.[32]

To solve the case, Salarich was sent on a discrete mission to speak to the secretary for foreign affairs, Alberto Rómulo, asking him more or less straight out what it would take to stop the execution of the young man. The mission was complicated, however, as the Spanish diplomat went there every day for a whole week without being received. He returned again on another occasion and was finally received. His trick was as old as diplomacy itself, namely to be polite beyond reason: the rationale being that the more they "torture" you, the politer you have to act and the more you must offer. Spain offered state visits and increased budgets for cooperation and development, and it worked. The Philippines abolished the death penalty—first as a temporary measure and then by decree. Moreover, the measures strengthened the political as well as the economic bonds between the two countries.[33]

However, a peculiar episode occurred on 21 November 2005, when the Spanish Minister of Defense José Bono, apparently claimed during an official visit to the Philippines to have personally ended the death penalty in their country, although it was actually the Spanish Foreign Ministry which had conducted the negotiations to this end during the preceding months. Much to the chagrin of the Santa Cruz Palace, Bono called the family of the prisoner in front of the media, so as to give the impression that he

[32] Moratinos Files: Interview, Salarich; Jorge A. Rodríguez, "Bono se atribuye un éxito diplomático con Filipinas que Moratinos logró en septiembre," *El País*, November 22, 2005. https://elpais.com/diario/2005/11/22/espana/1132614018_850215.html.

[33] Moratinos Files: Interview, Salarich.

brought them vital new information concerning their son. The following day, *El País* published the story that Bono was trying to take the honors for a diplomatic success obtained by Moratinos two months earlier. The article carefully reconstructed the details of the entire negotiation process, something which gives rise to the suspicion that information for the article was leaked by the foreign ministry.[34]

Importantly, the Philippines became the first Asian country to actually abolish the death sentence. In 2006, President Gloria Macapagal Arroyo formally issued the decree to end the death penalty on 30 June, the date on which the Philippines celebrate the end of the famous church siege in 1898 which led to independence from Spain. This is also the official date which commemorates Spanish–Philippine relations. Moreover, the date chosen for signing the decree was 24 June, the day of Saint John, which the Spanish side interpreted as a tribute to the Spanish king, Juan Carlos.[35] The symbolism was clear: The abolition of the death penalty was done as a gesture to Spain. In Madrid, a new bilateral treaty on the exchange of prisoners was signed, as a result of which one could ask for a prison transfer either way after a certain period of imprisonment. The entire case was of course also highly valuable for Spanish diplomacy, with the event used internationally to promote Spain as a champion of human rights.

In sum, Spain's new foreign policy toward Asia and the Pacific area contributed to forging closer relations with a series of strategically important countries, including China and a number of key US allies. It paved the way for better trade relations, as well as contributing indirectly to the improvement of overall relations with the United States. Importantly, the Eastern policies designed by the Santa Cruz Palace helped to remove the final obstacles to Spain's accession to the G20 international forum, something which remains one of the Zapatero government's most important achievements in the international arena.

9.2   The Perfect Storm

Initially, the PSOE government was comfortable with the first international response to the financial crisis in 2008 because it was perfectly in line with

---

[34] Rodríguez, "Bono se atribuye un éxito diplomático."

[35] "La presidenta de Filipinas firma la ley que suprime la pena de muerte," *El Mundo*, June 24, 2006. http://www.elmundo.es/elmundo/2006/06/24/internacional/1151122990. html.

traditional social democratic and Keynesian economic thinking. This did not mean, however, that the Spanish government was not aware of the potential pitfalls of the Spanish economy and the fact that increased public spending could not go on forever. Spanish overdependence on the construction sector and the high indebtedness of families and companies had, in fact, already been highlighted in the party's electoral program in 2004. Actually, the Spanish National Bank had been warning about the dangers of such excessive debts since 2003. Moreover, 2007 had seen the Spanish current account deficit reach above ten per cent of GDP—the second largest in the world after the United States and a revealing indication of the importance of external funding for the continuing growth of the Spanish economy.[36] A current account deficit of this magnitude was clearly unsustainable in the long run.[37] Significantly, the private debt of Spanish families had gone from 60 to 140% of GNP in the ten years from 1997 to 2007, whereas the debt of the whole private sector had gone up from 200 to 350% of GNP in the same period.[38] In 2005, the PSOE's party delegation in Brussels had encouraged the government to suppress the fiscal rebate for first house purchases in order to contain the rise in real estate prices and thus reduce private debt. The report was delivered firsthand to José Blanco, who—like the rest of the PSOE—did not react to this specific recommendation.[39]

It is tempting to criticize Zapatero for not having used the word "crisis" about the increasingly critical situation that Spain was facing during the

[36] Paul Kennedy, *Nemesis: Economic Policy Under the PSOE and the Road to Defeat* (Manchester, UK: Manchester University Press, 2013), 194.

[37] In actual fact, the IMF provides its member countries with short-term loans to fund current account deficits and authorizes changes in its exchange rates in case they suffer a so-called *fundamental balance of payment disequilibrium*, which tacitly corresponds to 3% in the *basic balance deficit*. Most economists perceive these fundamental disequilibria as long-term, structural disequilibria, which cannot be corrected by means of demand management policies within a reasonable span of time without producing harmful unemployment and excessive inflation. I owe this and other pieces of information used in this chapter to Manuel Sanchis i Marco, Associate Professor of Applied Economics at the University of Valencia and a former employee of the European Commission.

[38] Document of the Ministry of the Economy, dated January 8, 2009, cit. in Pedro Solbes, *Recuerdos: 40 años de servicio público* (Barcelona: Ediciones Deusto, 2013), 404.

[39] "Balance del primer año de Gobierno socialista," *Foro Europeo de Progreso*, Brussels, 2005, 51. I'm indebted to Manuel Sanchis i Marco, who provided me with a copy of this report.

first half of 2008, and the prime minister openly regrets this in his memoirs.[40] Yet the truth is also that very few people inside and outside Spain expected a major economic crisis, although there were certainly economists who correctly warned of an upcoming recession due to the recent entry into the Eurozone.[41] Pedro Solbes, minister of the economy and one of Zapatero's most outspoken critics, admits that in the first half of 2008, he could only see a "conventional recession" on the horizon. The fact that the economic problems seemed to be of a more temporary kind was in Solbes' view confirmed by the Central European Bank, which actually raised the interest rates in July, only to lower them shortly after.[42] It was apparently the firm belief of the Spanish government in 2008, and a view shared by many Western governments, that the crisis they were dealing with was essentially a systemic deficiency of the international monetary system which could be repaired by the system itself, provided it received assistance from national governments. Critics rightly point to the fact that to many European leaders, this was also the most convenient interpretation since it comfortably ignored the fundamental flaws of the Eurozone construction and the objective need for structural reforms in several European countries, including Spain.

When the PSOE won the general elections in March 2008, obtaining for the first time more than eleven million votes, unemployment was still at a sustainable level, and against this background, the government promised to create no less than two million more jobs before 2012. Furthermore, the objective of the party, as expressed in point 36 of its electoral program, was to modernize the Spanish economy by improving productivity—something which they saw as a guarantee of sustainable growth—and to strengthen the purchasing power of wages.[43] An additional reason for optimism was that the Spanish per capita income in 2007 had just overtaken that of Italy.

---

[40] Zapatero, *El dilema*, 316.

[41] Manuel Sanchis i Marco, "¿Minirecesión en primavera?," *El País*, November 12, 2007. https://elpais.com/diario/2007/11/12/economia/1194822008_850215.html; ibid., "Negacionismo económico 'versus' credibilidad," *El País*, July 25, 2008. https://elpais.com/diario/2008/07/25/opinion/1216936805_850215.html. See also ibid., *El fracaso de las élites. Cómo reparar los daños de la Gran Recesión* (Barcelona: Pasado & Presente, 2014), 170.

[42] Solbes, *Recuerdos*, 372.

[43] "100 Motivos," Summary of the PSOE's Electoral Program, 2008. http://web.psoe.es/source-media/000000119500/000000119694.pdf.

The famous *sorpasso* of the Italian economy and the surpluses in public accounts made Zapatero confident that Spain would be robust enough to keep any crisis at bay. In addition, Zapatero's personal grip on power and political legitimacy was validated not only by the election result, but also by the fact that no less than 98% of the party delegates at this year's congress openly endorsed his leadership. In spite of occasionally fierce attacks from the press, his powers—at least on the surface—appeared to be as strong as those of Felipe González during the 1980s.[44]

Although there were certainly dark clouds on the horizon, as he partially admitted in an interview with *El País* on 29 June, Zapatero was able to plausibly argue that Spanish public accounts were formally in order and that the government could therefore easily trigger a stimulus package for the economy if it looked to be going into recession during the second half of 2008.[45] In the aftermath of this interview, however, unemployment started hitting Spain exceptionally hard, growing to 14% within a few months. During the boom years, Spain had employed nearly as many workers in construction as in the industrial sector (2.7 million), yet when investments in bricks and mortar suddenly came to a halt in 2008, unemployment skyrocketed, with negative repercussions for private consumption into the bargain. Scared about the future people suddenly increased their precautionary savings. New infrastructure projects and loans to small businesses, as well as significant increases in social welfare benefits, were among the swift responses from the Zapatero government.[46]

As the crisis deteriorated, the fundamental difference between Zapatero's Keynesian view of the economy and Solbes' (to use his own expression) more "conservative" understanding of the need for fiscal discipline became visible in the press. Solbes was frustrated by the fact that his views carried less weight with the prime minister, who was increasingly susceptible to the opinions of other ministers calling for increased public spending. Essentially, Zapatero believed that growth would only recover through increased public stimulus packages, leading eventually to a rebalancing of the public finances. In contrast, Solbes found it vital to keep public spending under control and to introduce further labor reforms in order to regain

---

[44] Kennedy, *Nemesis*, 191.

[45] "Es un tema opinable si hay crisis o no hay crisis," *El País*, June 29, 2008. See: https://elpais.com/diario/2008/06/29/domingo/1214711556_850215.html.

[46] Kennedy, *Nemesis*, 194–195.

the confidence of the investors, something which was crucial to the Spanish economy in light of its great demand for external funding.[47]

The fiscal stimulus packages, which were eventually adopted by Zapatero, must however be understood in their proper context. It was actually part of a concerted international effort by the Group of Twenty. During the hectic days of the economic summit in Washington, from 14–15 November 2008, a general settlement was reached on how to deal with the economy and stimulate further economic growth. Only ten days later this agreement was translated by the EU into a European Economic Recovery Plan, which was meant to ensure a major injection of purchasing power into the economy, thereby stimulating private consumption and generating trust in the economy. This total budgetary stimulus amounted to approximately €200 billion. This implied that the public deficit of the member states could now go above the 3% deficit level established by the EU. The other, and less ambitious, part of the deal—largely ignored by the Zapatero government—was to divert future investment into new sectors, especially clean technologies, and to call for further structural labor market reform. When criticizing the Spanish and other European governments for their "laissez-faire" attitude prior to the explosion of the sovereign debt crisis in early 2010, one must also consider that these Keynesian-inspired national solutions were actually the result of the implementation of international economic agreements.[48]

The director of the *Banco de España*, Luis María Linde, recognized in an article in *El País* in February 2017 that his bank, as well as other European central banks, had made "grave errors of prevision" during the period of 2008 to 2012 and essentially failed to supervise the financial sector.[49] Less than half a year later in June 2017, the same bank published a report containing the main macroeconomic figures of the financial crisis,

[47] Solbes, *Recuerdos*, 369–370.

[48] "A European Economic Recovery Plan," *Communication from the Commission to the European Council*, Brussels, November 26, 2008. http://ec.europa.eu/economy_finance/publications/pages/publication13504_en.pdf

[49] Iñigo de Barrón, "El Banco de España quiere aclarar su papel en la crisis financiera," *El País*, February 10, 2017. https://elpais.com/economia/2017/02/09/actualidad/1486670064_845752.html

yet the report was careful not to respond directly to the growing criticism that it had acted too late and done too little.[50]

Interestingly, between 2008 and 2010, the Spanish financial system was—at least on the surface—still one of those least affected by the European crisis. As stated by Sebastian Royo, not a single Spanish bank was among the forty financial institutions that had received help from Brussels by June 2010, and in December 2010, Moody listed the Spanish banking system as the strongest in Europe, only superseded by Finland and France. It had actually introduced regulatory and supervisory mechanisms which helped protect the financial system from the direct effects of the global financial crisis. For example, the Bank of Spain had effectively discouraged lenders from adopting risky accounting methods and from acquiring toxic assets.[51] However, when the crisis deepened, the collapse of the real estate market led to a traditional bank crisis fueled by record unemployment, increasing government debt (albeit from an extremely low level) and difficulties in obtaining credit in wholesale markets. Spain was simply not prepared for this. In particular, the *Cajas de Ahorros*, saving banks under the political control of the regional governments, turned out to be vulnerable to the drop in real estate. The sector's overreliance on wholesale funding, and deficiencies in the policy and regulatory frameworks did the rest. By September 2012, the problem with real estate toxic assets led to the nationalization of eight financial institutions, with *Bankia* as the most important.[52] The new Conservative government under Mariano Rajoy's leadership thus chose to recapitalize the banking sector from 2012 by means of EU financial assistance. The European Stability Mechanism (ESM) lent a total of €41.5 billion, corresponding to roughly 4% of Spanish GDP, to the Spanish government, which left the program after a year because it rightfully deemed that there was no need to request further assistance from the ESM. The increase in public debt due to these operations amounted

---

[50]Cf. "Informe sobre la Crisis financiera y bancaria en España, 2008–2014," *Banco de España*, Madrid, May 2017. https://www.bde.es/f/webbde/Secciones/Publicaciones/OtrasPublicaciones/Fich/InformeCrisis_Completo_web.pdf; Iñigo de Barrón, "El Banco de España elude la autocrítica en su explicación sobre la crisis financiera," *El País*, June 16, 2017. https://elpais.com/economia/2017/06/15/actualidad/1497563172_277916.html.

[51]Sebastian Royo, *Lessons from the Economic Crisis in Spain* (New York: Palgrave Macmillan, 2013), 187.

[52]Ibid., 177, 188.

to no less than €54 billion.[53] With hindsight, it is probably correct to say that the starting point of the crisis was the entry into the Eurozone, which brought about extremely loose credit conditions. These in turn fueled the housing market, causing domestic expenditure to grow faster than domestic output. All this led to a widening current account deficit and higher prices.[54]

To return to the first economic measures taken by the Zapatero government after 2008, there are at least two ways that one can examine them consistently. The most frequently used method is to point to the government's actions at different stages during the crisis and to consider whether these initiatives were efficient and congruent with what was objectively needed or what was known by the main state actors of the time to be the main economic and structural challenges. Rivers of ink have already been used to do this, and the memoirs of Solbes and Zapatero both follow this trend, although their conclusions differ.

The starting point of all these analyses is roughly the same, namely that when the PSOE assumed power in 2004, Spanish growth rates had been outpacing those of other EU countries for a decade. From 2004 to 2008, Spain continued to perform extraordinarily well with a constant budget surplus and one of the lowest public sector debts in the European Union. This development was surely fueled by extremely low or even negative interest rates. Spanish per capita income was surpassing that of Italy, and Zapatero publicly announced that France was realistically the next great European nation to be overtaken by Spain. However, as stated previously, some signs of stagnation—also caused by the structural deficiencies of the Spanish economy—were beginning to show toward the end of Zapatero's first term, yet the prime minister apparently remained convinced that the surpluses in the public accounts would contain whatever crisis might be waiting around the corner.[55] Still, it must be taken into account that although the surplus was 2.2% of GDP, it was nevertheless negative when cyclically adjusted.

---

[53] Francisco Martí and Javier J. Pérez, "Spanish Public Finances Through the Financial Crisis," *Documentos de Trabajo* (Banco de España), no. 1620 (2016): 14. Working Paper of the Spanish national bank, which however stresses that the paper does not necessarily express the view of the bank. See: https://www.bde.es/f/webbde/SES/Secciones/Publicaciones/PublicacionesSeriadas/DocumentosTrabajo/16/Fich/dt1620e.pdf.

[54] I'm grateful to Manuel Sanchis i Marco, who provided me with his views on this issue.

[55] Kennedy, *Nemesis*, 191.

Therefore, in reality, there was little or no room for further spending to contain the incoming crisis.[56]

During the rest of 2009, after the first fiscal stimulus packages had been launched, differences within the Spanish government regarding the state of the economy grew stronger. While Zapatero publicly stated that the worst part of the crisis was over, Pedro Solbes warned against continuing the expansionist economic policies and called for more fiscal discipline. Yet he only did so during the very last weeks and months of his time in office, when he should probably have waved the red flag much earlier. However, Zapatero somewhat downplays these personal and political differences in his memoirs, in particular stating that the ousting of Solbes, which was probably decided in January 2009, was actually in line with an agreement the two ministers had struck after the elections in 2008. Solbes had emphasized to the prime minister that he did not want to complete a full term in office.[57] Solbes admits that he was determined not to continue in office for too long after his reappointment, yet his memoirs also recall his growing dissent and the many times he warned against the increase in Spanish debt during the first quarter of 2009. He draws particular attention to a document from 8 January 2009, in which he called for structural reforms to increase Spanish competitiveness, combined with a reduction of the level of debt and of the current account deficit. Eventually, the Stability Program sent to Brussels on 16 January only included Solbes' proposals concerning microeconomic reforms: There was no mention of a reform of the pension system and the labor market or a plan as to how to reduce labor costs. Allegedly, Zapatero reacted to Solbes' wide-ranging proposal by saying, "Pedro, this document is unacceptable. What you are suggesting implies two general strikes."[58] Another cabinet member recalls Solbes' oral warnings in this period as far less dramatic and outspoken, more in line with the kind of recommendations that one would always expect to hear from the minister of the economy. This might suggest an element of *ex post facto* interpretation in Solbes' explanation, influenced by the financial crisis which eventually broke out in early 2010. Solbes was eventually relieved of his post on 7 April 2009.[59]

[56] I'm grateful to Manuel Sanchis i Marco, who provided me with his views on this issue.

[57] Zapatero, *El dilema*, 185.

[58] Solbes, *Recuerdos*, 404–406, 408.

[59] Moratinos Files: Interview, Moratinos.

However, what has been entirely absent from these *ex post facto* reflections over the handling of the Spanish economy is a debate as to why a European financial emergency eventually transformed itself into a domestic, political and economic crisis from which the PSOE has not recovered until this very day. Was enough done politically in the international arena to prevent the European imposition of severe austerity measures in 2010? And did the PSOE government itself actually believe in the necessity of these new measures? To answer these questions, it is certainly worthwhile to examine what has rightfully been described by Zapatero himself as the darkest moment of his premiership, namely the days from 7 to 12 May 2010 when the prime minister complied with a decision of the EU's Economic and Financial Affairs Council (ECOFIN) to introduce draconian cuts to the Spanish state budgets.[60] According to its critics, this decision implied the end of the progressive social democratic foundations that Zapatero's policies were built upon. Importantly, it also marked the beginning of the end of his political leadership. After this U-turn in the PSOE's economic policies, an important segment of Socialist voters abandoned the party in favor of either apathy or new political parties on the left or center right.

Key episodes from the dark days in May are still very much shrouded in uncertainty, also because they are strikingly absent from Zapatero's own account of the crisis, where he shows a remarkable loyalty to other party figures, who—according to my research—were set on ousting him from the Moncloa building. Raised within the PSOE, with its different political families and regular settling of accounts, Zapatero apparently accepted such behavior as part of the game.[61]

The background for the May crisis was the following. In 2009, the financial markets began expressing concerns about the Spanish public sector deficit, something which led to increased costs and interest rates on the Spanish public debt, which had grown from below 40% in 2008 to around 60% of GNP in 2010, thereby challenging the government's already limited possibilities for discretionary spending. Spain actually received a warning from the EU as early as February 2009 because of its public sector deficit, which had reached 11% of GDP. To its critics, Zapatero's next economic response, the Sustainable Economy Bill of November 2009, was completely inadequate as it did not provide the structural reforms hoped for in areas

[60] See Zapatero, *El dilema*, chapter 1.

[61] Moratinos Files: Private information given to the author.

such as pensions, the labor market and education or address the country's complex energy model.[62] A few months later, international pressure on Spain gradually increased, leading to the draconian budget cuts finally announced by Zapatero in parliament on 12 May 2010. On this day, he announced that in line with the agreements adopted by the political leaders of the Eurozone as part of the deal to salvage Greece, Spain had to adopt hard economic measures. Objectively, the background for this decision was that the so-called Spanish-German bond spread, which during April had oscillated between 80 and 100 points, suddenly rose in three days from 3 to 6 May, from 94 points to 149, thus maximizing pressure on European leaders meeting in Brussels the next day to act. In other words, the Eurozone was under attack from the markets. However, pressure suddenly eased as the spread fell to 99 on 12 May, when it was clear that Spain had given in and agreed to a budget cut of no less than 1.5% of GNP.[63] This meant that the deficit had to be reduced by €15,000 million—a considerable amount if one takes into account that the vast majority of the expenditure in the state budget is more or less reserved for the payment of wages, leaving areas such as education and social benefits extremely vulnerable to severe government cuts.[64]

In his own account, Zapatero's major concern during the May days was the "ordinary people." He thought about what the draconian cuts in social welfare would mean to unprivileged men and women, yet at the same time, he took comfort in the fact that he had sworn an oath to his country not to let it down and in the current situation he saw no viable alternative to introducing the drastic measures required by the other European governments.[65] From a purely economic perspective, there is no doubt that the adjustment was needed. Still, it is debatable whether it was necessary to impose it with such rigor and haste. A longer period of implementation combined with smoother measures might very well have led to the same result, yet with less suffering inflicted on the Spanish population. Be that as it may, at the end of the day the Germans simply imposed their view. In a later interview given to *El País*, Zapatero justifies the fact that the PSOE had to introduce an economic austerity program, regardless of the

[62] Kennedy, *Nemesis*, 196–197.
[63] Zapatero, *El dilema*, 17–18.
[64] Ibid., 15, 31–32.
[65] Ibid., 23.

fact that it led to a public sector strike in June 2010 and to an instant crisis of confidence with the Socialist electorate. His explanation was that had he not reacted the way he did, "the following day market instability and doubts about sovereign debt, including our own, would have placed us in a difficult situation ... the markets were capable of placing our solvency in question."[66] What is strikingly absent in Zapatero's otherwise candid account is the possible correlation between the unfolding economic crisis and the personal and political battles which were beginning to wear down the PSOE. To take one example, in Zapatero's memoirs—in line with the general attitude of the Spanish press at the time—he praises the handling of the May crisis in Brussels by Solbes' successor as responsible for the economy, Elena Salgado. Nevertheless, it is not difficult to find people in the PSOE who take a much more critical view of the actions of the ministry under her command.

This criticism is rooted in an interpretation of the actions of the Ministry of Economy over the preceding months. As mentioned, during the first months of 2009, the macroeconomic indicators of Spain were beginning to show some concerning signs, and Salgado regularly briefed the government on the signs of international pressure she was receiving from abroad. As Spain was chairing the European Council, Salgado was automatically heading the ECOFIN, and she was also able to report on the concerns from this international forum. During the same period, from March to April, there were debates within the PSOE, where Salgado underlined the seriousness of the crisis. Moratinos backed Salgado by confirming that his sources, especially the German ones, showed equal signs of concern, and he thus supported Salgado's idea that certain measures had to be taken. However, even though unemployment was on the rise and other indicators were clearly going in the wrong direction, there were far from serious concerns over the economy as a whole. Neither Moratinos nor Zapatero perceived the situation as being anything near an economic meltdown.[67] Also the Spanish press seems to have shared this view. From a series of newspaper articles from the spring of 2010, it is clear that the undivided attention of

---

[66] Cited after Kennedy, *Nemesis*, 197.

[67] Moratinos Files: Interview, Moratinos.

the press was being given to the European measures taken with regard to the evolving Greek crisis.[68]

However, it is important to bear in mind that at this point, a certain breach in the PSOE was beginning to show. People close to Zapatero were under the impression that the Ministry of Economy was not sharing vital economic data with them.[69] Meanwhile, an out-and-out storm was gathering. In the run-up to the May crisis, the Ministry of Economy presented a plan for severe budget cuts which took everybody by surprise, apparently including Zapatero. The ministry argued that the situation was now unsustainable, that the budget deficit had to be reduced, and for this reason, public salaries and social benefits needed to be subjected to extreme cuts. The plan comprised reducing spending by nearly 1.5%. Zapatero's wing of the party argued that one could certainly make serious cuts, but the present proposal was politically inadmissible. Their point was that it was unacceptable that speculating markets could dictate Spain's economic course and impose such drastic welfare cuts. The psychology of the markets was such that to give even the slightest concession to them would mean that they would end up deciding everything. Spain ought to fight this with international support, in line with what Sarkozy had also publicly stated: The beast had to be tamed since it was permanently insatiable. They further argued that what was at stake was the survival of the progressive welfare ideals of social democracy and that the markets were not only speculating against the euro, but specifically against a country, Spain, which had been held up as a model for Europe. This was not an economic issue, but an ideological battle about how society should be organized. Unsurprisingly, the opinion of the investors was profoundly different. In their view, financial markets were merely trying not to lose money. They demanded adequate returns for the risks assumed when lending money to a government which, in their view, had failed to address fundamental structural problems of the Spanish economy. Importantly, the other wing of the PSOE very much favored the austerity plan. What was clear at this point was that a rift in the PSOE had occurred.

After prolonged and heated discussions in the party, Zapatero's trustees seemed to share the impression that the prime minister would continue

---

[68]See, for example, "Alemania habla sin tapujos y'no descarta' que el FMI salga en ayuda de Grecia," *ABC*, March 20, 2010; "Bruselas presiona a Merkel para sacar adelante el rescate griego esta semana," *El País*, March 23, 2010.

[69]Moratinos Files: Interview, Moratinos.

to support their view. However, this notion was premature. The real truth was that Zapatero was increasingly isolated. On Sunday 9 May, which was actually Europe Day, there was an extraordinary meeting of ECOFIN in Brussels, presided over by Salgado, followed by a meeting on Monday of the Council of Foreign Ministers, presided over by Catherine Ashton, and on Tuesday by a meeting of the European Council (heads of state and governments). On Sunday evening, while he was dining with his closest collaborators, Moratinos was contacted on the phone to prepare the meeting for the next day. The call came from the Spanish ambassador to the EU, who said that the ECOFIN meeting had been a disaster since Spain had been forced to accept a demand for a 2.5% budget cut. Spain had been seriously put in the corner, he said. The ambassador then cried out, "Call the Prime Minister, call Kouchner, call Steinmeier! Tell them to give us a better deal."[70] Moratinos and several diplomats kept calling all night, speaking to all the most relevant European interlocutors. The compromise was eventually 1.5%, the original figure proposed by the Spanish Ministry of Economy and still a very dramatic cut.[71]

Meanwhile, the Santa Cruz Palace was taken aback by the fact that the press actually lauded the Spanish handing of the ECOFIN meeting in Brussels. In their view, the minister of economy had not used her position as chairman to defend the line of her government as vigorously as one could have hoped for. In Salgado's defense, however, it should be mentioned that ECOFIN had objectively pointed to the need for serious reform in Spain and that the minister of the economy, and the PSOE members who supported her had, in their own understanding, only tried to correct the hitherto mistaken economic policies of the Zapatero government.

If all this was known to Zapatero, then why did he not fight the austerity plan more vigorously than he did during the spring of 2010? After all, his leadership and his public image were at stake. In my view, we cannot rule out the fact that Zapatero was to some extent playing along with the plans of the Ministry of the economy because he knew it would be hopeless to fight a European consensus based on the fear of the markets and, accordingly, also on the need to intervene in the economies of the most vulnerable European countries. In fact, during the preparation of the 2010

[70]Ibid.

[71]During this hectic week, Moratinos enjoyed the full support of his chief of staff, Agustín Santos Maraver, who encouraged the foreign minister to stand firm because he too saw the speculating markets as insatiable; Cf. Moratinos Files: Interview, Santos Maraver.

Spanish EU presidency, the prime minister had suddenly, and quite unusually, meddled with ministerial planning by adding "the strengthening of the Euro" to the objectives which had already been established, something which caught the Santa Cruz Palace completely by surprise. This move was probably due to the fact that Zapatero knew from other sources that sufficient protective mechanisms had not been included in the construction of the Eurozone. When Zapatero and Moratinos left a pizzeria in Brussels on 11 May after the dice had been thrown, Zapatero simply said, "the powerful have prevailed." The prime minister was clearly no longer capable of withstanding the pressure.[72]

In the eyes of the critics of the austerity plan, the so-called markets had won a stinging victory. Madrid, as well as the other European governments, found out too late that behind the markets are institutions and real people who can be identified and whose actions can be regulated and accounted for. Sarkozy had stated this over and over again, but had been unable to act, probably due to demands from the British (as always, uninterested in hard regulation of the bond market) and also pressure from the Germans (eager to improve fiscal discipline across Europe). The progressive socialism of Zapatero had become a success story and a moral and ideological reference for other countries, and the believers in his project strongly felt that the "dark forces" of the markets had wanted to defeat them, as they had publicly hailed the need for both more national and international regulation. In contrast, economists would probably claim that the failure to address the well-known structural deficiencies of the Spanish economy was the real reason for failure, just as they would point to the fact that institutional investors are already heavily regulated.

Regardless of the validity of such speculation, the political cost of the crisis for the Spanish Socialist party was extremely significant. The party lost the confidence of its voters, its bond with civil society was broken and with that it also lost its freshness, its ideas and its capacity for mass mobilization. Accordingly, the ECOFIN meeting on 9 May could well be described as a Waterloo for the Socialist party, as from this day on the party simply lost the trust the voters had placed in it. Subsequently, Zapatero took on the role of crisis manager, whereas he should probably have called for general elections. His position as leader was also undermined by the fact that qualified rumors had it that he would not run for office again. He had apparently already promised Rubalcaba that he should succeed him as

---

[72]Moratinos Files: Interview, Moratinos.

leader of the party. The political error was perhaps to make such concessions before they were absolutely necessary.

Rubalcaba's pressure on Zapatero had been building up for years, more precisely since the successful general elections in March 2008. Apparently, Zapatero's landslide victory had created concerns among those forces in the PSOE, who hadn't actually considered Zapatero to be more than a transitory figure within the party. After the elections, this wing of the party started to make more demands, as was also reflected in Zapatero's difficulties to appoint his new government. The main challenge was that Rubalcaba wanted Zapatero to name him deputy prime minister, yet the prime minister did not want to sacrifice Fernández de la Vega or for that matter, Solbes, his second deputy prime minister.[73]

Rubalcaba was clearly anxious to increase his own powers, and the only reason he could put forward such claims was that he was also a very able politician, the kind of problem-solver every government needs. From early on, Rubalcaba confided to other ministers that he was fed up with the Ministry of the Interior, and he soon planned his move toward the Moncloa. One obstacle, however, was Pedro Solbes, who continued to hold the position of second deputy prime minister. During the election campaign in February 2008, Solbes had actually won an important debate with the rising star of the PP, Manuel Pizarro, something which strengthened his claim to continue in the post, which he in fact did until he was ousted in 2009.[74] In April 2009, politicians close to the prime minister started noting that Zapatero was giving into the continuous pressure from Rubalcaba's wing of the party. A clear sign was the sacrifice of Magdalena Álvarez and the appointment of José Blanco as Minister for Public Works and Transports (*Fomento*).[75] During 2010, it became increasingly clear that Zapatero was not going to run for a third period, a fact he eventually chose to be open about in 2011, while Rubalcaba adroitly positioned himself as a likely candidate for the leadership of the party prior to the next elections.

Without doubt, the economic crisis led to a rupture in the relationship between the PSOE and its voters. The U-turn in its economic policies, which happened within the very short period of time from November 2008 to May 2010, was never explained to, nor understood by, large sectors of

---

[73]Moratinos Files: Private information given to the author.

[74]Cf. Solbes, *Recuerdos*, 363–364.

[75]Moratinos Files: Private information given to the author.

PSOE voters. Ordinary people could not help noticing that first the crisis was denied, only to be succeeded by an infinite series of budget cuts and layoffs, especially in the construction sector, followed by the so-called *desahucios*, whereby people unable to pay their mortgages were thrown out of their properties by banks which were eventually saved with public money.[76] In addition, the 2011 reform of article 135 of the Spanish Constitution, which now prevented the government from increasing public expenditure above the limit established by the European Union, was not convincingly explained either. It is also important to remember the background against which all this was taking place. Until well into 2008, Spain had been living through moments of sheer economic euphoria, to the benefit of most Spaniards, and the sudden austerity measures introduced after 2010 clearly hit like the country like a tsunami. Prior to the crisis, Spain had enjoyed fiscal surpluses (albeit not "cyclically adjusted") and low levels of public debt (nearly half of the euro area recommendation). Yet within months, it became clear that there was not enough fiscal leeway to implement further countercyclical policies. An increasing number of economists agree that this was due to the structural fiscal imbalances created before the crisis. These deficiencies, combined with the euro area sovereign debt crisis of 2010, put Spain in a very difficult position. To deal with these fiscal imbalances, many new taxes combined with draconian cuts in public spending saw light between 2010 and 2014.[77]

No one inside or outside the government was mentally or politically prepared for this marked shift in the economy. Like many politicians before him, Zapatero was reluctant to face the trade unions at the beginning of the crisis and to call for wage increases that were in line with productivity growth. By 2010, however, the pressure on the Spanish government to intervene in the economy had become intolerable. Eventually, Zapatero sacrificed himself in the process of economic reconstruction, while four million voters fled the PSOE in search of new parties or movements which provided easily understandable solutions to end their hardships. From the end of 2010, growing youth mobilization, mainly from the very middle-class sectors that the PSOE had always wanted to appeal to, developed into a diverse anti-party movement, which from 15 May to 15 October 2011 occupied central squares in major Spanish cities. They were from the

[76]Cf. Anna Bosco, "The Long Adios," 28.
[77]Martí and Pérez, "Spanish Public Finances Through the Financial Crisis," 7.

jobless *Ni-Ni* (neither–nor) generation of 18–29-year-olds, who later came
to form the basis of Podemos' electoral platform. Painfully for the PSOE,
it was exactly this segment of the population who, by protesting against
the doubtful actions of the Aznar government, had brought the party to
power in 2004.[78]

A decade has passed since Europe was first cast into recession, and as
pointed out by Sebastian Royo, two tales of the economic crisis continue to
prevail. The first argument roughly stresses that, historically, the south has
not been able to balance the books of its public finances, for which reason it
was a grave mistake to allow Spain, Portugal, Greece and Italy—all known
for their historic economic mismanagement—to enter a monetary union
which requires a high degree of fiscal discipline. Besides taking advantage
of low interest rates on a type of loan which eventually led to bubbles, the
south repeatedly ignored the apparent need for structural reform, especially of the labor market, which is essential to make the Economic Monetary Union (EMU) work as intended. Moreover, when the crisis hit them
in 2008, they continued to apply for low interest loans from abroad to
uphold their welfare systems, and instead of addressing the fundamental
flaws at home, they increasingly demanded a European fiscal union and
a reform of the EMU in order to continue their "unjustified" living standards, including some very generous retirement policies which were simply
unheard of in northern Europe.

In contrast, the southern version of the crisis points to the fact that
the EMU is a flawed construction based on rigid fiscal rules imposed by
France and Germany, who were also the first to break these rules scot-free.
In the years prior to 2008, northern European banks—eager to increase
profits—chose to invest heavily in the European periphery, as their own
domestic markets were stalling. Importantly, it soon turned out that due to
bubbles—mainly in the building sector—these investments in the periphery
were practically lost, yet in order to keep northern banks afloat, the EMU
governments embarked on a bailing program by lending money to the
peripheral debtor countries, which would otherwise have been unable to
pay back their loans, in particular to German, French and Dutch banks.
However, after 2010, when the markets began speculating heavily against
the most vulnerable EMU countries, these new loans were granted on

[78] See Carmelo Adagio, "Youth Protests and the End of the Zapatero Government," in
Politics and Society in Contemporary Spain: From Rajoy to Zapatero, ed. Bonnie N. Field and
Alfonso Botti (New York: Palgrave Macmillan, 2013), 143–160.

radically different terms which essentially implied much higher interest rates combined with draconian cuts in state budgets, something which eventually led to a severe loss of economic sovereignty and an increase in social distress and people at risk of poverty in the periphery.[79]

Regardless of which version is closest to the truth, the European crisis magnified the fundamental differences over the economy within the PSOE, which again weakened the possibility of the Spanish government to eventually withstand international pressure. With hindsight, those Spanish cabinet members who vigorously fought the austerity plan in 2010 can today take some comfort in the fact that their analysis of the crisis actually coincided with that of one of the most important financial actors of the United States. As Ben Bernanke, head of the Federal Reserve Board between 2006 and 2014, writes in his memoirs:

> … faulty macroeconomic analysis also led to Europe's problems. As Tim Geithner and I had warned, Germany and its allies within the eurozone pushed too hard and too soon for fiscal austerity in countries (including Germany) that did not have near-term fiscal problems, while at the same time resisting unconventional monetary actions (like quantitative easing). The European Central Bank, under Mario Draghi's leadership, finally did implement a large quantitative easing program, but it did not begin until early 2015, almost six years after similar programs were initiated in the United States and the United Kingdom.[80]

The result was, as Bernanke objectively underlines, that while unemployment grew in the Eurozone, it declined in the United States. Importantly, as was also very much the case in Spain, European unemployment has been concentrated among the youngest segment of the workforce. This means that young people have been barred from developing their skills through new job experiences, and with a less qualified labor, force Europe's evident growth problems might continue even longer than anticipated.[81]

---

[79]This summary of the northern and southern perceptions of the crisis owes to Royo, *Lessons from the Economic Crisis in Spain*, 1–2.

[80]Ben S. Bernanke, *The Courage to Act: A Memoir of a Crisis and Its Aftermath* (New York and London: W. W. Norton & Company, 2015), 569.

[81]Ibid., 569.

In spite of the introduction of these debatable austerity measures, the Santa Cruz Palace was lucky to avoid the drastic budget cuts that other ministries were subjected to. Only funds to development aid were significantly affected. The original goal of the Zapatero government had been to spend 0.7% of GNP on development aid, but this goal was immediately lowered to 0.5 when the economic crisis kicked in, eventually decreasing to 0.46 in 2009. This may sound to be a major setback compared to the original goal, yet the final result was actually an almost threefold rise in percentage points since the year 2000.[82] To meet the new budgetary demands, the government had also planned a reduction in the number of employees in the Santa Cruz Palace and in their salaries. As part of this plan, Moratinos was asked to reduce the number of vice ministers, and he planned to use this opportunity to reorganize and reform the ministry. He was especially keen on eliminating the vice minister position for the EU, which he deemed superfluous because EU policies were already integrated into different ministries which were all represented in Brussels. There were also good arguments for sacrificing the vice minister position for Latin America. Moratinos took this new and very detailed project to the Moncloa, where it was approved with some minor modifications. However, he was asked to keep Trinidad Jiménez as vice minister for Latin America and just before the plan reached the Council of Ministers, Zapatero called to inform him that the cuts were off. Apparently, people around Rubalcaba were also fighting to keep Diego López Garrido in place as vice minister for the EU.[83] In the end, the reform came to nothing, yet the entire process shows that it had become complicated for the foreign ministry to proceed with some of its policies since Zapatero was subjected to strong pressure from the other wing of the party.

2010 also saw the difficult task of fully deploying and operating the new system of European presidencies under the Treaty of Lisbon. Critics immediately pointed to the fact that Spain, which from January presided over the Council of the European Union, lacked credibility as a driver of change due to the grave situation of the Spanish economy.[84] Furthermore, Zapatero

---

[82] "Spain Needs to Fulfil Its Commitment to Reverse Decline in Development Aid," OECD Recommendation, March 4, 2016. http://www.oecd.org/newsroom/spain-needs-to-fulfil-its-commitment-to-reverse-decline-in-development-aid.htm.

[83] Moratinos Files: Interview, Moratinos.

[84] Paul M. Heywood, "Spain's EU Presidency: Ambitions Beyond Capacity?," *Journal of Common Market Studies*, vol. 49 (2011): 77–79.

came under immediate attack from the German press, which accused him of "presenting a spectacular firework of ideas that won't achieve anything apart from securing him a moment of glory."[85]

The main priorities of the Spanish presidency were to achieve the full implementation of the Treaty of Lisbon, coordinate economic policies, strengthen the foreign policy action of the EU and, finally, highlight the social rights of citizens of the European Union, which were sorely missing in the treaty. Spain had indeed listed a series of ambitious reforms which could potentially provide better protection for the Eurozone and give impetus to a new European economic model. In reality, as Salgado's infamous ECOFIN meeting in May also goes to show, Spain had to defer such complex questions to the French and especially the German government, which however ignored them. Only later, when the EU again came under increased financial pressure, would the European governments reconsider proposals for the economy of a more federalizing nature. Nevertheless, the Spanish presidency was able to pass important initiatives such as the 2020 Strategy at the European Council of June. Above all, the closing of the EU trade agreement with Mercosur stands out as the single greatest Spanish achievement.

Importantly, the negative international atmosphere during the spring of 2010 contributed to the non-realization of three out of six planned international summits. The Spanish presidency was also challenged by the fact that it was the first time that a presidency had to co-exist with the presence of the newly appointed President of the European Council, Herman Van Rompuy, and the High Representative for Foreign and Security Policy, Catherine Ashton. This naturally meant that the Spanish government—in contrast to the preceding holders of the presidency—had to give the floor to these new supranational leaders. It is not unlikely that uncertainty about who was actually leading the EU in this period of organizational transition contributed to the non-realization of the EU summit with Obama. In actual fact, the Treaty of Lisbon deprived the presidency of its historic role of representing the EU abroad.[86]

---

[85] Cited in ibid., 83.

[86] This summary of the challenges of the Spanish presidency owes to A. Fernández Pasarín and F. Morata, "Spain at the Helm: The Spanish Presidencies of the Council of the European Union," *International Journal of Iberian Studies*, vol. 28, issues 2 & 3 (2015): 163–164, 170; Ignacio Molina, "The 2010 Spanish EU Presidency: Trying to Innovate Europe in Troubled Times," *Swedish Institute for European Policy Studies*, 1op (2010): 7, 30, 46; Laia

Despite such difficulties, Moratinos took an optimistic view of the future, also because at the end of the day, his ministry had performed remarkably well since the second Zapatero government was installed in 2008. Whereas other ministries were feeling the pressure from the economic crisis, in 2008 the foreign ministry was just beginning to harvest the fruits of many years hard work of global outreach. Indeed, 2009 saw Spain's accession to the G20, and by 2010, Spain had established diplomatic relations with nearly all the member states of the United Nations. Furthermore, the Alliance of Civilizations was fully functioning, and Cuba represented a major diplomatic triumph with the release of more than a hundred prisoners in July, while August saw the successful liberation of Spanish hostages in Mauritania. Spain's relationship with the Obama administration was also fruitful, as evinced by the recent invitation to the White House and its increasing role as a diplomatic mediator between Washington and Cuba. In addition, Spain was working well with a number of important Latin American countries. Much in the same vein, Asia was offering increasingly more political and economic opportunities due to new collaborations and the significant upsurge in Spanish exports, and—as mentioned—the Treaty of Lisbon had just entered into force under the Spanish presidency of the Council of the European Union. Moreover, Moratinos was still judged very positively in various opinion polls and regularly viewed as one of the most popular ministers.[87] And, perhaps most importantly, he was still enjoying his job. A few months earlier, in fact, he had declined an offer to become the EU High Representative of the European Union for Foreign Affairs and Security Policy, and in September, unfounded rumors had it that he was likely to run for mayor in Cordoba. Moratinos stated to a local newspaper that he would remain minister as long as "he enjoyed the trust and the respect of Zapatero."[88] Given his uncomplicated working relationship with the prime minister, the future certainly looked bright.

Mestres, "Bilateralism in the Spanish Presidencies of the European Union: Alliances for the Development of European Foreign Policy," *International Journal of Iberian Studies*, vol. 28, issues 2 & 3 (2015): 184; Heywood, "Spain's EU Presidency: Ambitions Beyond Capacity?", 82, 85. See also Pol Morillas i Bassedas, Carlos Carnicero Urabayen, "Europa y EE UU: hacia una relación pragmática," *Política exterior*, vol. 25, issue 139 (Extra) (2011): 84–94.

[87] "Rajoy se queda a sólo 0,35 puntos de Zapatero," *El País*, January 2, 2010.

[88] Cf. "Moratinos rechaza liderar la lista del PSOE a las elecciones municipales," *El Día de Córdoba*. September 4, 2010.

Still, life in general, and perhaps politics in particular, is full of surprises. Had Moratinos known what the future had in store for him, he would probably have thought twice before declining the EU post, which was eventually assigned to Catherine Ashton. In fact, Moratinos' ousting from the Santa Cruz Palace happened at a time when he least expected it. The six and half years he had spent in office had passed by rapidly, and there had certainly been moments of great difficulty and tension. There had also been several calls over the years from Zapatero in which the prime minister announced a future remodeling of the executive, something which of course upset Moratinos as he did not know if he was going to be affected by it—but the prime minister always assured him immediately of his continued presence in the government. When Zapatero finally decided to remove him, however, there was no such call.

When Moratinos accompanied Zapatero on his trip to Japan on 28 August 2010, the two had a long and fruitful conversation about the future organization of the foreign ministry, and the prime minister gave his blessing to a number of new appointments. Everything pointed to a productive and serene last year in the Santa Cruz Palace before the next general elections, which were to be held in the spring of 2012 at the very latest. Still, there was one unknown factor which Moratinos clearly underestimated and which certainly had the capacity to shake up the government. As mentioned, the PSOE was plagued by internal friction and influential people in the party were beginning to seek new challenges because they were uncertain about what the future had in store for the party due to the negative impact of the economic crisis. Trinidad Jiménez, who belonged to Zapatero's fraction of the party, had just lost the primaries to become the party's candidate for the presidency of the Autonomous Region of Madrid and was now desperately looking for another post, more specifically Moratinos' position. In addition to this, there was added uncertainty produced by the qualified, yet unconfirmed rumors that Zapatero did not wish repeat his candidacy for the upcoming elections. This meant that people in the party were discretely looking for his replacement. This complex political context was of course well-known to Moratinos, who, however, decided to ignore it. Being more of a diplomat than a politician, he much preferred to occupy himself with Spain's foreign obligations than to become engaged in internal party struggles.[89]

---

[89] Moratinos Files: Interview, Moratinos.

What was objectively known to the cabinet members during the summer and autumn of 2010 was that the minister of employment, Celestino Corbacho, was going to be replaced, as he had decided to return to Catalan politics. Yet there were no clear signs that Zapatero was going to carry out a more profound reshuffle of his cabinet. Under these circumstances, Moratinos travelled to Marrakesh to take part in the World Policy Conference on 15 October, where he dined with Fassi Fihri and his secretary of state Youssef Amrani, who only had minor complaints about Spanish mafias and drug trafficking. Bilateral relations were under control, and the meeting had taken place in a convivial atmosphere. All this was conveyed by telephone to Zapatero on the Sunday evening of 17 October. Everything seemed fine, although Moratinos did notice that Zapatero was not in the best of moods. However, he did not pay much attention to this, as it was hardly the first time that the prime minister had been under pressure.

Three days later, on Wednesday 20 October, events started to unfold rapidly. Prior to a routine control session in parliament, in which Moratinos participated although he was not feeling well, he greeted Zapatero and Fernández de la Vega before he sat down in his seat. To his surprise, he saw both of them looked devastated, and Zapatero merely asked him if he had planned any trips that week. Moratinos indicated that he had none, to which Zapatero answered, "Better so." The prime minister wanted him to stay in Madrid. Shortly afterward, Zapatero summoned him to his office in the parliament. Moratinos did not pay particular attention to this, yet when he finally arrived at the prime minister's office, he found Zapatero to be very serious. The prime minister began asking all sorts of questions about the general situation with the United States, China, Cuba and about his last trip to Morocco. Moratinos immediately intuited that Zapatero was being evasive because he did not know how to say what was on his mind. Zapatero finally got to the point: "I have thought about reshuffling the government." At this point, Moratinos understood that he was going to be affected by the decision. In his own recollection, Moratinos' reaction was one of calmness. He told Zapatero not to worry and that for him it had been an honor to serve. He thanked Zapatero for his friendship and the confidence he had placed in him. The two embraced each other for a long time, and afterward, Moratinos called his wife. The press caught a glimpse of Moratinos shedding a tear as he left parliament. He was formally replaced by Trinidad Jiménez the next day. However, it is fair to say that during the next year, until the elections in December 2011, Spain did little to promote ambitious new international initiatives. What was left was simply a caretaker government, also in the field of foreign affairs.

Moratinos concluded his last hours in office with a meeting with the prime minister of Bhutan, and in his last exchange of notes with his Majesty Juan Carlos, he was able to convey the fact that Spain had now achieved diplomatic relations with all the members of the international community. This had indeed been the priority of his Majesty since his famous speech in parliament on the day of his coronation in 1975. Bhutan was the only country that had been missing, and Moratinos was able to deliver on this during his final hour as foreign minister of Spain. At noon on 21 October 2010, he wrote his last personal note as foreign minister while packing his belongings. In it, he expressed no regret, only gratitude toward the prime minister who had just ousted him.[90]

After the reshuffle, which also affected Fernández de la Vega, Rubalcaba became the new first deputy prime minister and evidently also the strong man of the executive. Little legislation could pass without his blessing. This development was enhanced by the fact that the voters' faith in Zapatero had been falling dramatically and proportionally with the austerity measures he was undertaking, dropping from 66.5% in July 2008 to 35.2% in July 2011.[91] On 2 April 2011, the prime minister finally announced his decision not to seek a third term. His hope was probably that this decision would have a positive effect on the regional and municipal elections in May. Nevertheless, the party experienced a stinging electoral defeat, and soon the long rivalry between the two dominant factions in the party came out into the open. Each of the two wings promoted their own candidate for the post-Zapatero era. Carme Chacón, who later died at the age of 45 due to a fatal heart condition, represented Zapatero's wing of the party, whereas Rubalcaba enjoyed the support of the older guard of *Felipistas*.

To cut a long and rather agonizing story short, the *Felipistas* effectively blocked the other wing's attempt to call for primaries to decide the name of the new candidate for prime minister. This was achieved by a surprisingly simple move. The general secretary of the Socialist party in the Basque Country, Patxi López, who was known for his friendship with Rubalcaba, suddenly asked to bring forward the date of the party convention, implicitly to elect the new leader of the PSOE while Zapatero was actually still in

---

[90]Moratinos Files: Biographical, personal note, October 21, 2010.

[91]Anna Bosco, "The Long Adios," 28.

power. If pulled off, this would have led to an unprecedented disavowal of Zapatero's leadership. The outcome of this surprise move was just as the *Felipistas* expected: The Zapatero camp ceded to the pressure, and on May 28, the party's federal committee jointly proposed Rubalcaba as the party's new candidate for the premiership. The relatively positive performance of Rubalcaba in the opinion polls later convinced Zapatero and the rest of the leadership to call for early elections on 20 November 2011. However, the result only confirmed the worst predictions. The PSOE lost to the PP by nearly 17% (29.9 to 46.6%).[92] The Zapatero era was now over.

[92] This summary owes to ibid., 30–37.

CHAPTER 10

Conclusions

When Zapatero seized power in 2004, he undeniably altered Spain's foreign and security policies. As promised during the election campaign, he immediately withdrew Spanish military forces from Iraq, thereby questioning the wisdom of Aznar's decision to follow the military and political doctrine of the Bush administration. Yet if viewed in a longer historical perspective, it is indeed questionable whether Zapatero's new course constituted a rupture with the traditional Spanish foreign policy and security model, as critics at the time tended to argue. Without doubt, if we compare Zapatero's actions to those of Aznar, they most certainly represented a break. However, if we compare them to the undertakings of the preceding Spanish governments of the democratic era from 1975 to 1996, or even to the first four years of Aznar's premiership until 2000, the question becomes more complex. Seen in this perspective, the real break in Spanish foreign policy was not produced by either of the two Zapatero governments, but rather by Aznar's second government, which started questioning the worth of Spain's traditional alignment with the Franco-German axis of European politics.

During the 1970s and 1980s, it had been the ambition of Spain's first democratic governments (whether left or center-right) to rebalance the uneven relationship with the United States, which since the 1950s had

© The Author(s) 2019
M. Heiberg, *Spain and the Wider World since 2000,*
Security, Conflict and Cooperation in the Contemporary World,
https://Doi.org/10.1007/978-3-030-27343-9_10

effectively converted Spain into a US satellite.[1] Specifically, Spain's most ostensible goal became to alter the base agreements with the United States, all of which infringed the Spanish sense of sovereignty. Only in 1988, and after years of intense negotiation, did Prime Minister Felipe González manage to strike a new base deal that was palatable to Spain. Importantly, Spain entered NATO in 1982 and the EC in 1986, whereby Spain became fully integrated into the European and Western state system. In the following years, Spain contributed positively to the process of European integration, and almost miraculously, if one considers the country's tormented history, Spain became everything it had ever hoped for: a democratic, prosperous and modern European nation. Thus, the first democratic government's principal merit was to have finally reached a better balance with the United States, and above all to have situated Spain "in its rightful place" in Europe—to paraphrase the title of an influential book written by the former Spanish Foreign Minister Fernando Morán in 1990.[2]

Seen against this historical, cultural and political heritage, Zapatero's decision to Europeanize Spain's foreign policy was hardly surprising. His physical embracement of Chirac and Schröder on the day of the mass funeral in Madrid merely symbolized a return to the professed European values of previous Spanish governments. Zapatero's commitment to finding a solution to the question of the double majority voting system in the European Council and his decision to subject the constitutional treaty to a referendum in Spain, as the first country in Europe, were both perfectly in line with this traditional stance. In the Spanish liberal tradition, European integration is seen as the most obvious solution to the nation's more profound structural problems.

However, the rebalancing of Spain's basic priorities was not only constrained to the EU and the United States. It also included another fundamental pillar of Spanish foreign policy, namely Latin America. In 2004, the Zapatero government found relations with Latin America to be severely compromised. This had in many ways to do with the Iraqi war, which was strongly opposed across the continent. Above all, Aznar's attempt to drag both Mexico and Chile onto the side of the United States didn't go down

---

[1] Cf. the main thesis in Heiberg, *US-Spanish Relations After Franco,* prologue.

[2] Fernando Morán, *España en su sitio* (Barcelona: Plaza & Janes, Cambio, 1990).

well in many Latin American capitals, and the ability of the Aznar government to acknowledge and react to the radical political and social transformation that was taking place across the continent was called into question. The unclear US-Spanish position during the coup to overthrow Chávez in 2002 only added to the suspicion that Aznar's government would only side with traditional power structures in Latin America. When the Zapatero government abandoned the idea of Spain trying to steer events in Latin America from the outside, it was not only a way of creating a bond with the new political classes in Latin America. It was also a return to a long-held position in the Spanish foreign policy of the democratic era, which regards Hispanidad—the idea that Spain can truly lead the Spanish-speaking world—as but a relic of the Francoist past. Without doubt, Spain can exercise influence, even considerable influence, in Latin America, but it cannot pretend to be the leader of this community.

With regard to the last fundamental pillar of its foreign policy, North Africa, the picture is very much the same. As has been shown, Aznar had complicated Spain's relationship with Morocco by opting for even closer cooperation with Algiers, and by supporting Algerian claims against those of Rabat with regard to Western Sahara. Migration problems and failed fisheries agreements also contributed to the deterioration of relations, as did Aznar's handling of the Perejil crisis in 2002. Zapatero's subsequent rapprochement with Morocco, coupled with his government's comprehensive policy for the entire Maghreb region, was also very much in line with a policy notion developed in the 1980s and further sustained during the 1990s. According to this view, Spain had few, if any, alternatives to building strong relations with Morocco in as many fields as possible in order to "cushion" the country against existing tensions in other areas. Furthermore, developing good relations with Morocco also had the obvious advantage of contributing to the strengthening of Spain's overall relations with France, which could be expected to take the side of Morocco in case of conflict in North Africa.

In sum, Zapatero's foreign policy was built from the outset on a classical conception, gradually developed during the democratic age, of how Spain should act in the face of the four fundamental challenges in its foreign policy represented by Europe, the United States, Latin America and the Maghreb area. This is hardly surprising, as this had been clearly expressed in public speeches and in the policy papers developed by the party prior to the elections in 2004. By all criteria, Aznar—not Zapatero—represents the real rupture in Spanish foreign policy. All other governments of the democratic era—with different accentuations, shifting ideologies, varying ambitions, competence and, not least, luck—have followed roughly the same coordinates.

It is equally important to stress, however, that the Zapatero government also innovated Spain's foreign policy in important ways, something which in large part owed to new ideas stemming from its dynamic relationship with civil society. If it is reasonable to say that the first Socialist governments of the 1980s restored Spain to its rightful place in Europe, as argued by Morán, it is equally fair to argue that the Zapatero government provided Spain with a global agenda. Probably more than any previous government, it effectively underlined how globalizing trends were affecting Spain, the tragedy of 11 March 2004 being just one example of this trend. As they saw it, the political margin left to pursue one's own narrow national interest was dwindling. Thus, the doctrine of effective multilateralism added interesting new dimensions to the four classical features of Spanish foreign policy, as it aimed to increase Spanish influence in multiple ways.

Before broaching this question more thoroughly, it is important to stress—once and for all—that the first Zapatero government (2004–2008) was fully legitimate when it took office, although the new leadership felt that it constantly had to argue that this was actually the case. It was *not* Al Qaeda who won the general elections for the PSOE in 2004, as argued by several observers at the time. The PP knew that they were likely to lose, and serious academic analyses of the changes in the intentions of voters during 2000–2004 confirm this beyond any reasonable doubt. However, the PP's actions after 11 March and their poor handling of all the information which pointed away from ETA as being responsible for the terrorist attack on 11 March 2004 surely played in the PSOE's favor, although these actions did not decisively influence the election result.

This book further documents that the PSOE already knew in the afternoon or evening of 11 March that Al Qaeda was behind the attack and handed this important information to the government's intelligence agencies, which, however, failed to act upon it. Apparently, it did not fit the prevailing political narrative. There is no way that the PP could plausibly argue from 11 to 14 March that they had doubts about the authorship of the attack. Noteworthy is the unfortunate role played by the Spanish secret intelligence services, which were apparently kept in the dark about the results of the police investigation by their own government. Yet, the *Centro Nacional de Inteligencia* (CNI) could easily have paid more attention to the information it received from the PSOE.

In spite of the questions raised as to its formal legitimacy, the new government maintained its main electoral promise to withdraw Spanish forces in Iraq. This led to a dramatic political crisis with Washington, and the crucial bilateral meetings with Condoleezza Rice and Colin Powell in the immediate aftermath of this decision were probably not among the most pleasant encounters that Foreign Minister Miguel Ángel Moratinos experienced in his diplomatic career. Importantly, it was his proposal to increase the Spanish military contribution in Afghanistan—as a kind of compensatory measure—which eventually contributed to the normalization of the relationship with the United States. Nevertheless, President Bush personally never forgave Zapatero for his decision to withdraw from Iraq and therefore refused to invite him to the White House. Yet, as documented, the overall working relationship was soon back on track and Spain tried in the coming years to exploit every opportunity, whether in Asia, Latin America or Africa, to work alongside the Americans or their closest allies in the hope of attracting positive attention from Washington. This strategy was, in spite of the difficult circumstances, largely successful. The immediate withdrawal from Iraq was politically risky, and Moratinos had originally argued in favor of a negotiated withdrawal. Still, Zapatero sensed that it was important not to give Washington sufficient time to apply pressure. Significantly, the Spanish withdrawal also sent a signal to the international community that it was actually possible to challenge Washington's policies on Iraq, a point that was immediately heeded by the anti-war movements in many countries. This naturally upset several US allies, and Spanish diplomacy had to work overtime to mitigate the effects of this crucial decision, as the case of Australia shows.

Plausibly, the single greatest disappointment during the nearly eight years of Zapatero's government, one that Spain shared with all its European neighbors, was the failure in 2005 to see through a new European constitutional treaty which could have effectively answered the challenges caused by the Eastern enlargement process. Spain did all that was within its reach, however. As promised by the PSOE, the new government struck a compromise on the double majority voting system in the European Council, a question which had previously led to a real rift between Aznar and Chirac, just as the constitutional treaty was successfully submitted to referendum in Spain in early 2005. Yet the subsequent failure of the French and Dutch referendums sent the European project into dire straits, and the new Treaty of Lisbon, which came into force under Spain's Presidency of the Council of the European Union (EU) in 2010, did not provide sufficient answers to the inherent problems of the European construction that was so cruelly exposed by the financial crisis. Much in the same vein, the PSOE government played an important, albeit supporting role in the ongoing discussions on how to organize a new European security space built along the Paris-Berlin-Moscow axis.

Another important question which clearly divided the Europeans was whether to support Kosovo's unilateral declaration of independence in 2008. Spain advised against it due to the dangerous precedent it represented for a Spain which was still struggling with separatist movements in both Catalonia and the Basque Country. Furthermore, Spain feared for future complications with Russia. Madrid found it to be an uphill struggle, however, as Washington had a priori guaranteed Kosovo's future as an independent state. The Western recognition of Kosovo, combined with the eastward expansion of NATO, raised deep concerns in Moscow, which did not hesitate to use the Kosovan precedent—exactly as foreseen by the Spanish leadership—as a pretext for recognizing the de facto independence of Abkhazia and South Ossetia in the aftermath of the Russo-Georgian war. With this move, Putin cunningly blocked NATO's eastward expansion. It is fair to say that the East-West relationship has never truly recovered from this conflict, although new attempts to create a European security space have been launched, also with active Spanish participation. Spain saw the political isolation of Russia as one of the potentially gravest failures that the international community could commit.

Overall, Spain's commitment to European integration, internally in the EU, and externally toward the EU's other European neighbors, was no doubt profound. However, Spain could not overcome the structural deficiencies of the European construction by itself, or for that matter effectively influence the big players of international politics who were trying to determine a new relationship of force between East and West. Importantly, Spain did what was within its reach to promote European integration at all levels. It promoted solutions and ideas that were—objectively—in the broad European interest. To say that the Zapatero government was not ambitious or did not prioritize its European policies is probably one of the deepest misunderstandings which I have come across during the research for this book.

By contrast, one of the real triumphs of Spanish diplomacy was, without doubt, its efforts to end European sanctions against Cuba and ultimately work for a rapprochement between Cuba and the United States. This was a diplomatic masterpiece, which was, admittedly, favored by a rare conjunction in international politics: Without Fidel Castro's retirement from politics and the arrival of President Obama roughly at the same time, the chances for success would have been radically diminished. Raúl Castro defended the need for reforms, just as Obama called for a radically different approach to Cuba during his election campaign in 2007. These were not just words. Both leaders acted upon them and Spain actively passed on messages between the parties, the real game changer being President Obama's message through Moratinos that the United States would not demand a regime change in Cuba. He could live with Raúl Castro as president. This new American approach was essentially a replica of the Zapatero government's policy toward Latin America, namely to construct a dialogue with those Latin American governments he disagreed with the most.

Importantly, this "Moratinian philosophy"—to use an expression invented by *The Wall Street Journal*—implied that one could not have any prejudice in the choosing or handling of international interlocutors. Furthermore, effective diplomatic mediation must always try to help the different parties from precisely their perspective. This is actually the key to understanding the historic diplomatic rapprochement between Cuba and the United States, in which Spain played a crucial role. On its own initiative, the Spanish government decided to try and make a difference with regard to Cuba, inspiring both political reform and important prisoner releases on the Caribbean island. In this way, Spain was able to spearhead the EU negotiations, draw in multiple Latin American actors and eventually work alongside the United States. Undoubtedly, the success of this initiative magnified Madrid's standing as a reliable international broker, thereby increasing Spain's diplomatic influence. This probably explains why Moratinos was able to convince his French and American counterparts to start new negotiations over Western Sahara. By 2010, Spain had shown that it could deliver on important and complex international questions, and the main international actors took positive notice of this merit.

Much in the same vein, the Socialist government effectively dealt with the challenges represented by new controversial leaders in Latin America, such as Evo Morales and Hugo Chávez. As a major foreign investor, Spain had to overcome some difficult periods during which Bolivia and Venezuela imposed new and very drastic nationalization measures. At this point, the Zapatero government had the option of trying to align with traditional forces in Latin America—as the previous government had done— or of trying to establish a working relationship built on trust with the new

Bolivarian-inspired leaderships in the region. As argued in this book, Spain's dialogue-based approach did much to contain the potential economic and political damage to Spain.

Spain under Zapatero abandoned the idea that it would pay to align with the more traditional forces in Latin America against the new forces. The PSOE government knew that they were dealing with a political development that was in many ways unstoppable, not only in Latin America but all over the world, with more rights being given to increasingly more people who had previously been marginalized or who were not even considered citizens of the state. The Zapatero government reacted cautiously to such globalizing trends, and not only out of ideological and political conviction. Importantly, the government had to take the potential harm to Spanish investments to heart. This behavior represents a stark contrast to the conduct offered by the United States and Spain during the coup in Venezuela in 2002, where they apparently sided with Carmona as long as he could stage his undertakings as happening within the formal boundaries of the Venezuelan constitution.

As a consequence of the new political approach, no entire sector was nationalized in Latin America during the years of the Zapatero government, and those specific companies which were affected by such measures were compensated. Madrid gradually understood that what it had to offer to its Latin American counterparts was reasonable concessions that could most certainly be given under the right circumstances. Bolivia wanted to take back ownership of Bolivian soil, yet this move did not affect Repsol's possibilities to drill and earn money in any way. In turn, Repsol was eventually offered a new long-term contract. In Venezuela, the Venezuelan state-owned oil company demanded the majority of the shares of a joint venture company controlled by Repsol. To compensate for this loss, Venezuela was ready to abandon its previous policy of letting the state fix the price of crude oil, which could now be sold at market prices. Under the circumstances, it was a very fair bargain.

No doubt, the success of the Zapatero government went beyond the cases of Bolivia and Venezuela. It is actually fair to say that Spain contributed to laying the groundwork for what later became the EU-LAC Foundation, created in 2010 by the heads of state and governments of the EU and the Community of Latin American and Caribbean States (CELAC) member states. Under Zapatero's leadership, Spain very much favored a process of regional integration in Latin America that mirrored the EU.

With hindsight, however, one might claim that more could have been done to promote Spanish relations with the countries of Latin America and to make them feel as if they were real stakeholders in the Ibero-American Summit, which is still seen across the continent—and rightly so—as a predominantly Spanish institution serving predominantly Spanish interests. Admittedly, the process of separation between Spain and its former colonies has to some extent continued, in spite of the efforts made to renew their common cultural and linguistic heritage. This negative development has to do not only with the rapid transformation of Latin American societies, but probably also with the economic crisis which hit Spain hard in 2010. Although Spain still exercises considerable influence, it is questionable whether Spain today is still the privileged interlocutor between Latin America and Europe that it used to be. This became evident during the last summit between the EU and Latin America, where Angela Merkel—according to Spanish diplomats that I have spoken to—played the role formerly attributed to Felipe González, Zapatero and Aznar. However, the decline had already begun during the last phase of Zapatero's premiership, when the Spanish prime minister chose not to attend the XX Ibero-American Summit in Mar del Plata in 2010.[3]

Perhaps Spain should, in the years to come, learn more from Portugal, which seems to have accepted its fate—that is, that the vast territory it once dominated in Latin America, Brazil, is now the big brother in international relations. In world affairs, apart from enjoying the benefits of the EU and NATO, Portugal has thus positioned itself comfortably in the slipstream of Brazil. Spain must never underestimate what it means for a medium European power to have an entire continent, Latin America, as its potential ally. This is a hugely potent instrument in international politics, but to achieve this Spain must probably further rethink its position, and on certain issues lean more on these countries rather than trying to actually influence them, just as Great Britain has done in relation to its former colony, the United States. This may well be the fate of Europe as a whole if Europe does not integrate further—that is, that the territories we once dominated will now take the lead. It may not be a bad thing, but Europe certainly needs to adapt to these new circumstances.

---

[3] Cf. Ayuso Pozo, "The Recent History of Spain-Latin America Relations," 126.

A novelty in Spanish foreign policy was no doubt the government's increased focus on Asia and the Pacific area. The new plans for Asia contributed to forging much closer relations with a series of strategically important countries, not least China. It paved the way for better trade relations and a real surge in Spanish exports, just as it contributed indirectly to the improvement of overall relations with the United States through intense collaboration with some of Washington's closest allies in the world: South Korea, Japan and Australia. Importantly, the Eastern policies designed by the Santa Cruz Palace helped to pave the way for Spanish accession to the G20 international forum. It was also through its increased presence in this part of the world that Spain quite spectacularly managed to convince the Philippines to end the death penalty in their country.

If we turn to North Africa, it is today largely forgotten that the first collective foreign policy of the European Communities was actually aimed at the Maghreb region. Tunis, Algeria and Morocco are indeed mentioned in the first treaties as important suppliers of agricultural products and gas, in particular to France and Italy. In other words, the first joint European foreign policy was essentially a trade policy. However, with Spain's entry into the EC in 1986, followed by the establishment of full Spanish diplomatic recognition of Israel, the Mediterranean policies of the European communities gradually gained weight. The Barcelona declaration of 1995, which was soon followed by other similar initiatives, solemnly stated that the ambition of the EU was now to turn "the Mediterranean basin into an area of dialogue, exchange and cooperation guaranteeing peace, stability and prosperity."[4]

Seen against this historical and political heritage, the Zapatero government was left alone by the EU to a surprising degree to tackle problems stemming from this region—problems, which affect all Europeans at the end of the day. Nevertheless, with only feeble European support, Spain found new and creative ways to fight illegal migration. As mentioned, no African port or fishing boat was too small to avoid instant scrutiny by the Spanish authorities, and all potential channels of influence were used to curb the migration flows. More importantly, Spain was determined to treat the migration problem for what it actually was, namely a foreign policy challenge. This Spanish approach, which combined development aid

---

[4]Martí Grau I Segú, "Voluntarismo o legado? El proceso de Barcelona y las alusiones históricas en la justificación de la política mediterránea de España (1995–2011)," *Studia Histórica Contemporánea*, vol. 34 (2016): 88.

to a number of Central African countries, separate bilateral repatriation programs and a series of innovative border initiatives taken together with Morocco, almost eliminated the problem. Later it became a model for the EU, which after years of disenchantment is now set on finding similar solutions for the Mediterranean region as a whole. The reason is, of course, that the migration problem is today one of the issues which causes the deepest concern among the European population. The handling of the migration crisis fully displays the fundamental belief of the Zapatero government, namely that in an era of globalization the key to tackling many domestic challenges starts with conducting an efficient multilateral foreign policy.

Spain's formula of aligning with other powers to bring peace and stability to crisis-ridden areas was also put to the test elsewhere in Northwest Africa, as Spain hoped to reach a settlement that could bring an end to the sufferings of the Sahrawis in Western Sahara—a conflict which threatens to destabilize the entire region with additional severe consequences for Spanish security. To solve this Gordian knot would indeed have constituted a historical triumph for Spanish diplomacy. Significantly, in 2010 the United States, France and Spain had finally brought about a roadmap for the area that might actually have succeeded, had it not been for the sudden government reshuffles in both Spain and France. After the Socialist government left office in late 2011, the Spanish Conservative government under Mariano Rajoy continued—in contrast to the government under his predecessor Aznar—to hail good relations with Morocco as an absolute imperative, yet it is fair to say that it did next to nothing to solve the crisis in Western Sahara. Seemingly, real momentum was lost in 2010.

In addition, Spain contributed to the peace process in the Middle East. It is of course debatable whether a country like Spain can actually make a difference on such a complex issue. Still, by aligning with the United States and other European powers, Spain was actually able to contribute with new ideas and political solutions, just it worked overtime to improve the Israeli-Palestinian relationship. As argued in this book, there was a real possibility for peace in 2009, but a number of unfortunate circumstances, including the political opportunism displayed by one Israeli minister and the severe miscalculation made by the Palestinian leadership, spoiled a historic opportunity which is unlikely to repeat itself in the foreseeable future. Importantly, Spain was regarded as an effective go-between in the peace process.

It is also within this context of political upheaval in the Middle East that the Spanish-UN initiative "Alliance of Civilizations" must be understood.

In the Spanish view, the new Alliance offered a welcome opportunity to decrease tension with the Muslim world in the aftermath of the Madrid attacks. In other words, the Alliance was predominantly seen as a complementary security measure aiming to diminish the terror threat against Spain. Over the years, however, the Alliance expanded its scope and now deals with a variety of issues which potentially threaten the peaceful coexistence between civilizations. Initially, the Alliance of Civilizations was not only well-received by Turkey, which immediately agreed to co-sponsor the initiative, but more importantly, the Maghreb countries also warmly welcomed it. They saw the Alliance promoted by Spain as being consistent with the fact that no repressive means had been introduced toward the many Maghrebis living in Spain in the aftermath of the 2004 terrorist attack.

One the one hand, it is probably fair to say that a lot of fruitful activities have been happening within the Alliance, including a series of important cultural and educational initiatives. Not least, its assistance to Denmark during the so-called cartoon crisis contributed to a very promising start. On the other hand, it is probably also fair to say that much more could have been done in designated areas during the relatively short lifetime of this global initiative. Still, one must never underestimate the fact that the Alliance has nevertheless obtained worldwide support, and that governments across civilizations wanting to eradicate the root of conflict have embraced this fundamental idea. As such, one can say that the Alliance constitutes by far the most important, if not the only successful Spanish-UN initiative in the history of Spanish diplomacy.

As seen throughout this book, the Zapatero government was often criticized for its soft, multilateral approach to foreign affairs, which according to its critics was being carried out at the expense of the defense of more vital Spanish security interests. Furthermore, Zapatero's dialogue-based approach was seen as carrying the unnecessary risk of making unnecessary concessions to non-democratic leaders all over the world. What this political, and to a large extent also academic discussion, comes down to is the basic question of where the "national interest" lies, and how it is most effectively defended.

Without doubt, the Zapatero government saw multilateral collaborations as the most efficient means to counter threats stemming from abroad, whether economic meltdowns, migration flows, climate change, religious conflicts, famine or war. Its doctrine of effective multilateralism offered a new kind of political realism which tried to redefine the Spanish national interest from a global and multilateral perspective. The fact that Spain was able to stimulate dialogue across civilizations in order to increase domestic security, promote development plans for Africa which radically diminished the migration pressure on Spain, or join the G20, thereby being able to influence economic decisions which affect the lives of all Spanish citizens, can be seen as important arguments in Zapatero's favor. What his government also demonstrated from April 2004 to November 2011 was a simple truth which had been largely forgotten during the run-up to the US intervention in Iraq: Diplomacy and international cooperation actually work, even in areas of great political and socioeconomic transformation, and with relatively modest means, diplomacy can be surprisingly effective.

Many more episodes could easily have been included in this book in order to underline the success of this approach from 2004 to 2011. In fact, as part of the ongoing attempts to foster effective multilateralism, the Zapatero government also gave a strong impetus to the Group of Friends for the Reform of the United Nations, just as it contributed to innovative UN programmes for health care, development and women's rights. Official Development Assistance funds were, in fact, doubled, and Spain actually became the sixth biggest donor in the United Nations system during the period Moratinos served as foreign minister of Spain.[5]

With regard to other, and perhaps more "domestic" issues, remarkable improvements were also achieved. For example, on 21 July 2009, Moratinos visited Gibraltar as the first Spanish Foreign Minister. As could be expected, the trip was fiercely criticized by the Spanish right, and one newspaper even baptized the picture of Moratinos, Chief Minister of Gibraltar Peter Caruana and Foreign Secretary David Miliband shaking hands "the photo of shame."[6] After a series of secret meetings with Caruana in 2004, the three parties struck the so-called Córdoba Agreement, which constituted the basis for what came to be publicly known as the "tripartite forum." Importantly, it was not a forum for negotiation, it was a "Moratinian" forum of dialogue and it was about Gibraltar, and therefore, not

---

[5] For further references to statistics, see Moratinos' personal web site: www.miguelangelmoratinos.com.

[6] On these polemics, see: "Moratinos, tras la polémica sobre Gibraltar: 'Rajoy ha sido desleal'," *El Mundo*, July 26, 2009. http://www.elmundo.es/elmundo/2009/07/26/espana/1248595317.html. The best survey in English on the Gibraltar question remains Chris Grocott and Gareth Stockey, *Gibraltar: A Modern History* (Cardiff: University of Wales Press, 2012).

about Spain or the concessions that Madrid might or might not be willing to make.[7] For the first time, it was now possible to exchange opinions on matters ranging from the environment to energy. What the Zapatero government actually did, on this occasion as well, was to coolly review the situation in light of what had been done and what needed to be done in light of the complete breakdown in the negotiations between London and Madrid in 2002.[8] After a meeting in the forum in September 2006, Moratinos was able to announce that Britain would grant €100 million to 5700 former Spanish workers who had not been paid adequately during the last 18 years.[9] This was the actual background for "the photo of shame."

Perhaps one day, when the effects of the financial crisis have eventually died out, people in Spain will begin to remember the Zapatero government not only for its handling of the economic crisis, but also for the many important initiatives described in this book, which no doubt contributed to bringing peace and stability to a world in constant change, to the benefit of all Spanish people. This is in no small part what foreign policy is about.

[7] Moratinos Files: Interview, José Pons.

[8] Peter Hain, the former British minister of state for Europe, accounts very accurately for these failed negotiations in his splendid memoirs, *Outside In*. He narrates how Aznar suddenly backtracked, after his foreign minister, Piqué, and his British counterpart, Jack Straw, had actually reached an historic agreement for shared sovereignty over Gibraltar. The British government had indeed invested a lot of political capital in the agreement, and therefore, as soon as Aznar backed out, the bilateral negotiations over Gibraltar soured. It was against this background that in 2004 the Zapatero government decided to implement an entirely new approach. Moratinos learned about the details of these negotiations from his predecessor Piqué in 2004, years before Hain's memoirs were published. The two versions coincide.Cf. Peter Hain, *Outside In* (London: Biteback Publishing, 2012), 274–285; Cf. Moratinos Files: Interview, Moratinos; José Pons.

[9] "Moratinos anuncia que los ex trabajadores y pensionistas españoles de Gibraltar cobrarán 'toda la cantidad' en abril de 2007," *La Vanguardia*, October 3, 2006. https://www.lavanguardia.com/politica/20061003/51285870508/moratinos-anuncia-que-los-ex-trabajadores-y-pensionistas-espanoles-de-gibraltar-cobraran-toda-la-ca.html.

A Bibliographical Endnote

Before concluding this book, I would like to acknowledge my intellectual debt to a number of works, scholars or institutions which are not cited directly or are only cited to a limited extent in this monograph, but which were nevertheless of great use to me during the first phase of my research. Above all, I would like to stress the usefulness of what I consider to be the best historical handbook on Spanish foreign policy, edited by Juan Carlos Pereira.[1] Also crucial were numerous articles and books published by three of Spain's most interesting research institutes, the *Barcelona Centre for International Affairs* (CIDOB), the *Elcano Royal Institute* and *Fundación Alternativas*. Above all, the yearbooks of CIDOB provide a formidable chronological overview of Spanish and international politics.[2] Without this tool, the preparation of my interviews would have been much more difficult. In addition, the yearbooks' critical analysis of Spanish foreign policy and international relations, offered by a different scholar each year, stimulated my initial thoughts on this project.[3] Several short articles

---

[1] Juan Carlos Pereira, *La política exterior de España. De 1800 hasta hoy*, second edition (Barcelona: Ariel, 2010).

[2] Cf. the yearbooks (*Anuario Internacional CIDOB*) available on https://www.cidob.org/publicaciones/(filter)/54483.

[3] In particular, I found the 2004 and 2005 surveys by Felipe Sahagún and Esther Barbé respectively, inspiring and helpful in the beginning of my research. Cf. Felipe Sahagún,

© The Editor(s) (if applicable) and The Author(s), under exclusive license to Springer Nature Switzerland AG 2019
M. Heiberg, *Spain and the Wider World since 2000*,
Security, Conflict and Cooperation in the Contemporary World,
https://doi.org/10.1007/978-3-030-27343-9

on all sorts of questions published in the monthly *Ari* journals of the Elcano Royal Institute for the period treated in this book were also helpful as background information. The same applies to a number of policy papers of the *Observatorio de Política Exterior* (OPEX) of the Fundación Alternativas. Finally, the seven volumes published by the Spanish foreign ministry containing Moratinos' official speeches and interventions were of great help in understanding the new direction of Spanish foreign policy, although I only quote this seven-volume publication on limited occasions.[4]

"Política exterior y de seguridad de España en 2004," in *Claves para interpretar la Política Exterior Española y las Relaciones Internacionales 2004. Anuario Internacional CIDOB 2004* (2005 edition). https://www.cidob.org/es/media2/publicacions/anuario_cidob/2004/18_articulo_sahagun; Esther Barbé, "Disenso y adversidad: la política exterior y de seguridad de España en 2005," in *Claves para interpretar la Política Exterior Española y las Relaciones Internacionales 2005. Anuario Internacional CIDOB 2005* (2006 edition). See https://www.cidob.org/es/media2/publicacions/anuario_cidob/2005/18_articulo_barbe.

[4] *Discursos y declaraciones del Ministro de Asuntos Exteriores y de Cooperacion, D. Miguel Angel Moratinos Cuyaube, 2004–2010* (Madrid: Ministerio de Asuntos Exteriores y de Cooperación, Oficina de Información Diplomatica, 2005–2011).

Sources and Bibliography

Primary Sources

Oral interviews ("The Moratinos Files")

Brufau, Antonio
Chaves, Manuel
Fernández de la Vega, María Teresa
March, Juan Antonio
Møller, Per Stig
Moratinos, Miguel Ángel
Pajín, Leire
Pons, José
Rodríguez Zapatero, José Luis
Salarich, José Eugenio
Sancho, Javier
Santamaría, Julián
Santos Maraver, Agustín
Villarino, Camilo

Published Sources

Spanish Official Sources

Cortes Generales:

Diario de sesiones del Congreso de Los Diputados, Pleno y Diputación Permanente.
Diario de Sesiones del Congreso de los Diputados, Comisiones, Asuntos Exteriores.

© The Editor(s) (if applicable) and The Author(s), under exclusive license to Springer Nature Switzerland AG 2019
M. Heiberg, *Spain and the Wider World since 2000*,
Security, Conflict and Cooperation in the Contemporary World,
https://doi.org/10.1007/978-3-030-27343-9

Ministerio de Asuntos Exteriores y de Cooperacion:

Discursos y declaraciones del Ministro de Asuntos Exteriores y de Cooperacion, D. Miguel Angel Moratinos Cuyaube, 2004. Madrid: Ministerio de Asuntos Exteriores y de Cooperación, Oficina de Informacion Diplomatica, 2005.

Discursos y declaraciones del Ministro de Asuntos Exteriores y de Cooperacion, D. Miguel Angel Moratinos Cuyaube, 2005. Madrid: Ministerio de Asuntos Exteriores y de Cooperación, Oficina de Informacion Diplomatica, 2006.

Discursos y declaraciones del Ministro de Asuntos Exteriores y de Cooperacion, D. Miguel Angel Moratinos Cuyaube, 2006. Madrid: Ministerio de Asuntos Exteriores y de Cooperación, Oficina de Informacion Diplomatica, 2007.

Discursos y declaraciones del Ministro de Asuntos Exteriores y de Cooperacion, D. Miguel Angel Moratinos Cuyaube, 2007. Madrid: Ministerio de Asuntos Exteriores y de Cooperación, Oficina de Informacion Diplomatica, 2008.

Discursos y declaraciones del Ministro de Asuntos Exteriores y de Cooperacion, D. Miguel Angel Moratinos Cuyaube, 2008. Madrid: Ministerio de Asuntos Exteriores y de Cooperación, Oficina de Informacion Diplomatica, 2009.

Discursos y declaraciones del Ministro de Asuntos Exteriores y de Cooperacion, D. Miguel Angel Moratinos Cuyaube, 2009. Madrid: Ministerio de Asuntos Exteriores y de Cooperación, Oficina de Informacion Diplomatica, 2010.

Discursos y declaraciones del Ministro de Asuntos Exteriores y de Cooperacion, D. Miguel Angel Moratinos Cuyaube, 2010. Madrid: Ministerio de Asuntos Exteriores y de Cooperación, Oficina de Informacion Diplomatica, 2011.

España hacia Asia y el Pacífico. Plan de acción 2005–2008. Madrid: Ministerio de Asuntos Exteriores y de Cooperación, Subsecretaría, Secretaría General Técnica, Área de Documentación y Publicaciones, October 2005.

Ministerio de Interior:

Inmigración irregular. Balance 2015. Lucha contra la inmigración regular. Madrid: Ministerio de Interior, 2015.

Banco de España:

Informe sobre la Crisis financiera y bancaria en España, 2008–2014. Madrid: Banco de España, May 2017.

Spanish Miscellaneous Sources

La política exterior de España: balance y debates parlamentarios (2004–2008). Madrid: Real Instituto Elcano de Estudios Internacionales y Estratégicos, 2007.

Anuario Internacional CIDOB. Barcelona: Barcelona Centre for International Affairs, 2004–2010.

Balance del primer año de Gobierno socialista. Brussels: Foro Europeo de Progreso, 2005.

Merecemos una España mejor. Programa Electora. Elecciones Generales. Madrid: PSOE, 2004.
Motivos. Madrid: PSOE, 2008.

US Official Sources

US Department of State, Online Archive:

Press Interviews

"A Review of U.S. Policy Toward Venezuela—November 2001–April 2002." OIG Report No. 02-OIG-003, July 2002.
Wikileaks (intercepted governments documents released through own website or *El País*).

Official Inquiries/Source Collections Regarding the War in Iraq and the War on Terror

The Iraq Study Group Report. New York: Vintage Books, 2006.
Alleged Secret Detentions and Unlawful Inter-State Transfers of Detainees Involving Council of Europe Member States. Parliamentary Assembly, Council of Europe, Doc. 10957, June 12, 2006.
The Report of the Iraq Inquiry. Executive Summary. London: House of Commons, July 6, 2016.
John Ehrenberg, Patrice McSherry, José Ramón Sánchez, and C.M. Caroleen Sayej. (2010). *The Iraq Papers.* New York: Oxford University Press, 2010.
Heiberg, Morten. *Et jura at forstå, et andet land at føre: Undersøgelse af en række spørgsmål vedrørende 2008-redegørelsen om påståede hemmelige CIA-flyvninger over og i Grønland samt dansk bistand hertil.* Copenhagen: DIIS, 2012.

United Nations

UN Security Council Resolutions, 1441, 1483, 1511, 1530, 1546
Security Council, Press Releases
Noticias ONU
Charter of the United Nations
Statements, United Nations General Assembly
MINURSO
Special Tribunal for Lebanon

European Union/European Communities

Communication from the Commission to the European Council: A European Economic Recovery Plan. Brussels, November 26, 2008.
European Council, Council of the European Union, Council Meeting, General Affairs and External Relations, General Affairs, Brussels.
European Council, Council of the European Union, Press releases.

Decision of the Council of the European Communities of 22 January 1972 Concerning the Accession of the Kingdom of Denmark, Ireland, the Kingdom of Norway, and the United Kingdom of Great Britain and Northern Ireland to the European Coal and Steel Community.

Common Position of 2 December 1996 Defined by the Council on the Basis of Article J.2 of the Treaty on European Union, on Cuba (96/697/CFSP).

The Treaty of Lisbon Amending the Treaty on European Union and the Treaty Establishing the European Community (2007/C 306/01).

Newspapers, Magazines, Press Agencies, News Websites

ABC (Australia)
ABC
Al-Jazeera.com
Associated Press
BBC news
Berlingske
Canarias
Diario Córdoba
EFE
El Confidencial
El Día de Córdoba
El Diario
El Diario Exterior
El Mundo
El País
El Periodico
elcorreo.com
Euobserver
Europa Press
exteriores.gob.es
Gramma International
GQ Magazine
Kurier
La Razón
La Vanguardia
Libertad Digital
miguelangelmoratinos.com
New York Times
Reuters
The Christian Science Monitor
The Jerusalem Post
The Times

Venezuelaanalysis.com
Wall Street Journal

Encyclopedias and Media Facilities

Youtube.com

Miscellaneous International Organizations:

Committee to Protect Journalists
Cornell Center on the Death Penalty Worldwide
G20
OECD
SIPRI
IPI Global Observatory
The World Bank

Diaries, Memoirs and Interview Books

Arias, Inocencio. *Confesiones de un diplomático. Del 11-S a 11-M*. Barcelona: Planeta, 2006.
Aznar, José María. *El compromiso de poder. Memoria II*. Barcelona: Planeta, 2013.
Aznar, José María. *Ocho años de gobierno: Una visión personal de España*. Barcelona: Planeta, 2005.
Bernanke, Ben S. *The Courage to Act. A Memoir of a Crisis and Its Aftermath*. New York and London: W. W. Norton, 2015.
Bono, José. *Diario de un ministro. De la tragedia del 11M al desafío independista catalán*. Barcelona: Planeta, 2016.
Bush, George W. *Decision Points*. New York: Crown Publishers, 2010.
Cuenca, José. *De Suárez a Gorbachov. Testimonios y confidencias de un embajador*. Madrid: Plaza y Valdés Editores, 2014.
Dezcallar, Jorge. *El anticuario de Teherán: historia de una vida diplomática*. Barcelona: Ediciones Península, 2018.
Dezcallar, Jorge. *Valió la pena: una vida entre diplomáticos y espías*. Barcelona: Península, 2015.
Hain, Peter. *Outside In*. London: Biteback Publishing, 2012
Morán, Fernando. *España en su sitio*. Barcelona: Plaza & Janes, Cambio, 1990.
Møller, Per Stig. *Udenrigsminister i krig og fred*. Copenhagen: Gyldendal, 2006.
Navarro, Julia. *El Nuevo socialismo. La vision de José Luis Rodríguez Zapatero*. Barcelona: Temas de Hoy, 2001.
Ortega, Jaime. *Encuentro, diálogo y acuerdo: el papa Francisco, Cuba y Estados Unidos*. Madrid: San Pablo, 2017.
Paulson, Henry M., Jr. *On the Brink. Inside the Race to Stop the Collapse of the Global Financial System*. New York and Boston: Business Plus, 2010.

Rice, Condoleezza. *No Higher Honor. A Memoir of My Years in Washington.* New York: Broadway Books, 2011.

Rodríguez Zapatero. José Luis, *El dilema. 600 días de vértigo.* Barcelona: Planeta, 2013.

Rumsfeld, Donald. *Known and Unknown. A Memoir.* London: Allen Lane, 2013.

Rupérez, Javier. *La Mirada sin ira. Memoria de política, diplomacia y vida en la España contemporánea.* Córdoba: Almuzara, 2016.

Rupérez, Javier. *Memoria de Washington. Embajador de España en la capital del imperio.* Madrid: La esfera de los libros, 2011.

Solbes, Pedro. *Recuerdos: 40 años de servicio público.* Barcelona: Ediciones Deusto, 2013.

Valenzuela, Javier. *Viajando con ZP.* Barcelona: Debate, 2007.

Villar, Francisco. *La Transición exterior de España: del aislamiento a la influencia (1976–1996).* Madrid: Marcial Pons, 2016.

SECONDARY SOURCES

Monographs, PhD-Theses and Collective Books

Arenal, Celestino. *Política exterior de España y relaciones con America Latina. Iberoamericanidad, Europeización y Atlantismo en la política exterior español.* Madrid: Fundación Carolina, 2011.

Cajal, Máximo. *Ceuta, Melilla, Olivenza y Gibraltar: ¿dónde acaba España?* Madrid: Siglo XXI de España, 2003.

Cajal, Máximo. *La Alianza de Civilizaciones de las Naciones Unidas: una mirada al futuro.* Madrid: Biblioteca Nueva, 2011.

Carvajal Arroyo, Ingrid, ed. *Memorias de un golpe de Estado. Cronología 11, 12, 13 y 14 2002.* Caracas: Gobierno Bolivariano de Venezuela/Ministerio de Poder Popular para la Comunicación y la Información, 2012.

Cembrero, Ignacio. *Vecinos alejados: Los secretos de la crisis entre España y Marruecos.* Barcelona: Galaxia Gutenberg, 2006.

Conrad, Sebastian. *What Is Global History?* Princeton, NJ: Princeton University Press, 2016.

Crespo Palomares, Cristina. *La alianza americana. La estrategia antiterrorista española y las relaciones hispano-norte-americanas (1996–2004).* Madrid: Catarata, 2016.

Dinan, Desmond. *Europe Recast. A History of the European Union.* Boulder, CO: Lynne Rienner, 2014.

Fernández de Miguel, Daniel. *El enemigo yanqui. Las raíces conservadores del antiamericanismo español.* Zaragoza, Spain: Genueve Ediciones, 2012.

Fernández-Molina, Irene. *Moroccan Foreign Policy Under Mohammed VI, 1999–2014.* London and New York: Routledge, 2016.

González Madriz, Yelitza. *Por qué el Estado es débil? El caso de Venezuela.* Granada: Editorial Comares, 2015.

Grocott, Chris, and Gareth Stockey. *Gibraltar: A Modern History.* Cardiff: University of Wales Press, 2012.

Hahn, Gordon M. *Ukraine over the Edge. Russia, the West and the New Cold War.* Jefferson: McFarland & Company, Inc., Publishers, 2018.

Heiberg, Morten. *US-Spanish Relations After Franco. Will of the Weak,* Vol. of Harvard Cold War Studies Book Series. Lanham, MD: Lexington Books, 2018.

Herro Curiel, Eva. "Periodistas y redes sociales en España. Del 11M al 15M (2004–2011)." Ph.D. diss., Universidad Carlos III de Madrid, 2013.

Iglesias-Cavicchioli, Manuel. *Aznar y los 'Neocons'. El impacto del neoconservadurismo en la política exteriror de España.* Barcelona: Huygens, 2017.

Jiménez Redondo, Juan Carlos. *De Suárez a Rodríguez Zapatero. La política exterior de la España democrática.* Paracuellos de Jarama, Madrid: Editorial Dilex, 2006.

Kennedy, Paul. *Nemesis, Economic Policy Under the PSOE and the Road to Defeat.* Manchester, UK: Manchester University Press, 2015.

Lemus, Encarnación. *Estados Unidos y la Transición Española. Entre la Revolución de los Claveles y la Marcha Verde.* Madrid: Silex, 2011.

LeoGrande, William M., and Peter Kornbluh. *Back Channel to Cuba: The Hidden History of Negotiations Between Washington and Havana.* Chapel Hill: The University of North Carolina Press, 2014.

Magone, José M. *Contemporary European Politics. A Comparative Introduction.* New York: Routledge, 2011.

Magone, José M. *Contemporary Spanish Politics,* second edition. New York: Routledge, 2009.

Mofette, David. *Governing Irregular Migration. Bordering Culture, Labour, and Security in Spain.* Vancouver and Toronto: UBC Press, 2018.

Muñoz, Antonio. *El amigo alemán. el SPD y el PSOE de la dictadura a la democracia.* Barcelona: RBA Libros, 2012.

Muñoz, Antonio. *Von der Franco-Diktatur zur Demokratie. Die Tätigkeit der Friedrich-Ebert-Stiftung in Spanien.* Bonn: Dietz, 2013.

Pereira, Juan Carlos. *La política exterior de España. De 1800 hasta hoy.* Barcelona: Ariel, 2010.

Powell, Charles. *El amigo americano. España y Estados Unidos: de la dictadura a la democracia.* Barcelona: Galaxia Gutenberg, 2011.

Reinares, Fernando. *Al-Qaeda's Revenge: The 2004 Madrid Train Bombings.* Washington: Woodrow Wilson Center Press, 2016.

Rekalde, Anjel, Santiago Alba Rico, Rui Pereira, Giovanni Giacopuzzi, and Jabier Salutregi. *11-M. Tres días que engañaron al mundo.* Tafalla, Spain: Txalaparta, 2004.

Rodríguez Jiménez, José Luis. *Agonía, traición, huida. El final del Sahara Español.* Barcelona, Spain: Critica, 2015.

Royo, Sebastian, *Lessons from the Economic Crisis in Spain*. New York: Palgrave Macmillan, 2013.

Sanchis i Marco, Manuel. *El fracaso de las élites. Cómo reparar los daños de la Gran Recesión*. Barcelona: Pasado & Presente, 2014.

Sanz Díaz, Carlos. "España y la República Federal de Alemania (1949–1966): política, economía y emigración, entre la guerra fría y la distensión." Ph.D. diss., Universidad Complutense de Madrid, 2005.

Segell, Glen. *Axis of Evil and Rogue States. The Bush Administration 2000–2004*. London: Glen Segell, 2005.

Staten, Clifford L. *The History of Cuba*. Santa Barbara, CA: Greenwood, 2015.

Stent, Angela E. *The Limits of Partnership. US-Russian Relations in the Twenty-First Century*. Princeton, NJ: Princeton University Press, 2013.

Villarino, Camilo. *Un Mundo en cambio. Perspectivas de la política exterior de la Unión Europea*. Barcelona: Icaria Antrazyt, 2009.

Viñas, Ángel. *Al servicio de Europa. Innovación y crisis en la Comisión Europea*. Madrid: Editorial Complutense, 2004.

Viñas, Ángel. *En las garras del águila. Los pactos con Estados Unidos, de Francisco Franco a Felipe González (1945–1995)*. Barcelona: Crítica, 2003.

Woodworth, Paddy. *Guerra sucia, manos limpias. ETS, el GAL y la democracia española*. Barcelona: Crítica, 2002.

Articles in Journals and Book Chapters

Adagio, Carmelo. "Youth Protests and the End of the Zapatero Government." In *Politics and Society in Contemporary Spain. From Rajoy to Zapatero*, edited by Bonnie N. Field and Alfonso Botti. New York: Palgrave Macmillan, 2013.

Arteaga Martín, Félix. "La política europea de seguridad y defensa." *Cuadernos de estrategia*, no. 145 (2010).

Ayuso Pozo, Anna. "The Recent History of Spain-Latin American Relations." In *Contemporary Spanish Foreign Policy*, edited by David García Cantalapiedra and Ramón Pacheco Pardo. Abingdon and New York: Routledge, 2014.

Barrios Fernández, Cristina. "Spain and Sub-Saharan Africa. Toward a Strategic Approach." In *Contemporary Spanish Foreign Policy*, edited by David García Cantalapiedra and Ramón Pacheco Pardo. Abingdon and New York: Routledge, 2014.

Barbé, Esther. "Disenso y adversidad: la política exterior y de seguridad de España en 2005." In *Claves para interpretar la Política Exterior Española y las Relaciones Internacionales 2005. Anuario Internacional CIDOB 2005*. Barcelona: CIDOB, 2006.

Barbé, Esther, and Elisabeth Johansson-Nogués. "The EU as a Modest 'Force for Good': The European Neighbourhood Policy." *International Affairs*, vol. 84, no. 1 (2008).

Barbé, Esther, and Laia Mestres. "La España de Zapatero en Europa. El aprendizaje de la negociación en una Unión Europea en crisis." *Quórum. Revista de pensamiento iberoamericano*, no. 19 (2007).

Bosco, Anna. "The Long Adiós: The PSOE and the End of the Zapatero Era." In *Politics and Society in Contemporary Spain. From Rajoy to Zapatero*, edited by Bonnie N. Field and Alfonso Botti. New York: Palgrave Macmillan, 2013.

Clement, Christopher I. "Confronting Hugo Chávez." In *Venezuela: Hugo Chavez and the Decline of an "Exceptional Democracy"*, edited by Steve Ellner and Miguel Tinker Salas. Lanham, MD: Rowman & Littlefield, 2007.

de Larramendi H.M. "The Mediterranean Policy of Spain." In *Mediterranean Policies from Above and Below*, edited by I. Schäfer and O. Henry. Baden-Baden: Nomos Publishers, 2009.

Eiermann, Martin, Yascha Mounk, and Limor Gultchin. "Populism: Trends, Threats and Future Prospects." *Report of the Tony Blair Institute for Global Change* (December 2017).

Erisman, H. Michael. "Cuba's International Economic Relations. A Macroperspective on Performance and Challenges." In *Cuban Foreign Policy Transformation Under Raúl Castro*, edited by H. Michael Erisman and John M. Kirk. Lanham, Boulder, New York, and London: Rowman & Littlefield, 2018.

Esteban, Mario. "Spain's Relations with China: Friends but Not Partners." *Chinese Political Science Review*, vol. 1, no. 2 (June 2016).

Fernández Pasarín, A., and F. Morata. "Spain at the Helm. The Spanish Presidencies of the Council of the European Union." *International Journal of Iberian Studies*, vol. 28, no. 2 and 3 (2015).

Font, Joan, and Araceu Mateos. "La participación electoral." In *Elecciones Generales 2004*, edited by José Ramón Montero, Ignacio Lago, and Mariano Torcal. Madrid: Centro de Investigaciones Sociológicas, 2007.

Forsberg, Tuomas, and Antti Seppo. "The Russo-Georgian War and EU Mediation." In *Russian Foreign Policy in the 21st Century*, edited by Roger E. Kanet. Houndsmill, Basingstoke, Hampshire: Palgrave Macmillan, 2011.

García Cantalapiedra, David. "Spanish Foreign Policy, the United States and *Soft* Bandwagoning." In *Contemporary Spanish Foreign Policy*, edited by David García Cantalapiedra and Ramón Pacheco Pardo. Abingdon and New York: Routledge, 2014.

García Pérez, Rafael. "España en un mundo en cambio: A la búsqueda de la influencia internacional (1986–2010)." In *La Política exterior de España. De 1800 hasta hoy*, second edition, edited by Juan Carlos Pereira. Barcelona: Ariel, 2010.

Gerbasi, Fernando. "La política exterior de la Revolución Bolivariana y Colombia." In *Hugo Chávez: Una década en el poder*, edited by Francesca Ramos Pismataro, Carlos A. Romero, and Hugo Eduardo Ramírez Arcos. Bogotá: Universidad del Rosario, 2010.

Gillespie, Richard. "'This Stupid Island': A Neighbourhood Confrontation in the Western Mediterranean." *International Politics*, no. 43 (2006).

Gratius, Susanne. "Cuba and the European Union." In *Cuban Foreign Policy Transformation Under Raúl Castro*, edited by H. Michael Erisman and John M. Kirk. Lanham, Boulder, New York, and London: Rowman & Littlefield, 2018.

Grau I Segú, Martí. "Voluntarismo o legado? El proceso de Barcelona y las alusiones históricas en la justificación de la política mediterránea de España (1995–2011)." *Studia Histórica Contemporáneai*, no. 34 (2016).

Gursch-Adam, Ruth, and Lívia Benková. "The Impact of Demographic Developments in Africa and Europe." *European View*, vol. 15, no. 2 (December 2016).

Heywood, Paul M. "Spain's EU Presidency: Ambitions Beyond Capacity?" *Journal of Common Market Studies*, vol. 49 (2011).

Hitchcock, William I. "The Ghost of Crises Past. The Troubled Alliance in Historical Perspective." In *The End of the West? Crisis and Change in the Atlantic Order*, edited by Jeffrey J. Anderson, G. John Ikenberry, and Thomas Risse. Ithaca, NY: Cornell University Press 2008.

Iglesias-Cavicchioli, Manuel. "A Period of Turbulent Change: Spanish-US Relations Since 2002." *The Whitehead Journal of Diplomacy and International Relations*, vol. 8 (Summer/Fall 2007).

Kirk, John M. "Historical Introduction to Foreign Policy Under Raúl Castro." In *Cuban Foreign Policy Transformation Under Raúl Castro*, edited by H. Michael Erisman and John M. Kirk. Lanham, Boulder, New York, and London: Rowman & Littlefield, 2018.

López Maya, Margarita. "Venezuela: Hugo Chávez y el bolivarianismo." *Revista Venezolana de Economía y Ciencias Sociales*, vol. 14, no. 3 (September–December 2008).

Martí, Francisco, and Javier J. Pérez. "Spanish Public Finances Through the Financial Crisis." *Documentos de Trabajo*, no. 1620 (Madrid, Banco de España, 2016).

Mestres, Laia. "Bilateralism in the Spanish Presidencies of the European Union: Alliances for the Development of European Foreign Policy." *International Journal of Iberian Studies*, vol. 28, no. 2 and 3 (2015).

Molina, Ignacio. "The 2010 Spanish EU Presidency. Trying to Innovate Europe in Troubled Times." *Swedish Institute for European Policy Studies*, 1op (2010).

Montero, José Ramón, and Ignacio Lago. "Del 11-M a 14-M: terrorismo, gestión del gobierno y rendición de cuentas." In *Elecciones Generales 2004*, edited by José Ramón Montero, Ignacio Lago, and Mariano Torcal. Madrid: Centro de Investigaciones Sociológicas, 2007.

Moratinos, Miguel Angel. "An Ethical and Political Commitment to Africa." Text published by the Real Instituto El Cano, Madrid, December 2005.

Morillas i Bassedas, Pol, and Carlos Carnicero Urabayen. "Europa y EE UU: hacia una relación pragmática." *Política exterior*, vol. 25, no. 139 (Extra) (2011).

Navajas Zubeldia, Carlos. "Democratization and Professionalism. Security and Defence Policy in Contemporary Spain." In *Contemporary Spanish Foreign Policy*, edited by David García Cantalapiedra and Ramón Pacheco Pardo. Abingdon and New York: Routledge, 2014.

Nye, Joseph. "Get Smart. Combining Hard and Soft Power." *Foreign Affairs*, July–August 2009.

Ortiz de Zárate, Roberto. "José Luis Rodríguez Zapatero." Biography Series of CIDOB. Barcelona: Barcelona Centre for International Affairs, 2017.

Pacheco Pardo, Ramón. "Spain and Asia. Towards a Closer Relationship." In *Contemporary Spanish Foreign Policy*, edited by David García Cantalapiedra and Ramón Pacheco Pardo. Abingdon and New York: Routledge, 2014.

Pérez Herrero, Pedro. "Las relaciones de España con América Latina (1810–2010): discursos, políticas, realidades." In *La política exterior de España. De 1800 hasta hoy*, edited by Juan Carlos Pereira. Barcelona: Ariel, 2010.

Pérez Viejo, Tomás. "El encuentro/desencuentro con la España democrática." In *Historia de la nación y del nacionalismo español*, edited by Antonio Morales Moya, Juan Pablo Fusi Aizpurúa, and Andrés de Blas Guerrero. Barcelona: Galaxia Gutenberg, 2013.

Priego Moreno, Alberto. "Spanish Soft Power and Its Structural (Non-traditional) Model of Diplomacy." In *Contemporary Spanish Foreign Policy*, edited by David García Cantalapiedra and Ramón Pacheco Pardo. Abingdon and New York: Routledge, 2014.

Powell, Charles. "A Second Transition, or More of the Same? Spanish Foreign Policy Under Zapatero." In *Spain's 'Second Transition'? The Socialist Government of José Luis Rodríguez Zapatero*, edited by Bonnie N. Field. London and New York: Routledge, 2001.

Romero, Carlos A. "Venezuela and Cuba." In *Cuban Foreign Policy Transformation Under Raúl Castro*, edited by H. Michael Erisman and John M. Kirk. Lanham, Boulder, New York, and London: Rowman & Littlefield, 2018.

Sahagún, Felipe. "Política exterior y de seguridad de España en 2004." In *Claves para interpretar la Política Exterior Española y las Relaciones Internacionales 2004. Anuario Internacional CIDOB 2004*. Barcelona: Barcelona Centre for International Affairs, 2005.

Sampedro, Victor, Óscar García Luengo, and José Manuel Sánchez Duarte. "Agendas electorales y medias de comunicación en la campaña de 2004." In *Elecciones Generales 2004*, edited by José Ramón Montero, Ignacio Lago, and Mariano Torcal. Madrid: Centro de Investigaciones Sociológicas, 2007.

Santamaría, Julián. "El azar y el contexto. Las elecciones generales de 2004." *Claves de razón práctica*, vol. 146 (2004).

Santamaría, Julián. "Las elecciones generales de 2004 en su contexto." In *Elecciones Generales 2004*, edited by José Ramón Montero, Ignacio Lago, and Mariano Torcal. Madrid: Centro de Investigaciones Sociológicas, 2007.

Sorroza Blanco, Alicia. "Spain and the European Union." In *Contemporary Spanish Foreign Policy*, edited by David García Cantalapiedra and Ramón Pacheco Pardo. Abingdon and New York: Routledge, 2014.

Torreblanca, José Ignacio. "La insoportable levedad de la política europea de España (2008–2011)." In *España en crisis. Balance de la segunda legislatura de Rodríguez Zapatero*, edited by César Colino y Ramón Cotarelo. Valencia: Tirant Humanidades, 2012.

Vaquer I Fanes. Jordi. "Spain in the Mediterranean and the Middle East. The Quest for Security and Status." In *Contemporary Spanish Foreign Policy*, edited by David García Cantalapiedra and Ramón Pacheco Pardo. Abingdon and New York: Routledge, 2014.

Viñas, Angel. "Años de Gloria. Años de sombra, tiempos de crisis." In *40 años con Franco*, edited by Julián Casanova. Barcelona: Crítica, 2015.

Viñas, Angel. "Negotiating the US-Spanish Agreement, 1953–1988: A Spanish Perspective." *Jean Monnet/Robert Schuman Paper Series*, vol. 3, no. 7 (September 2003).

Viñas, Ángel. "Los pactos con los Estados Unidos en el despertar de la España democrática, 1975–1995." In *España y Estados Unidos en el siglo XX*, edited by Lorenzo Delgado and Maria Dolres Elizalde. Madrid: CSIC, 2005.

Weeks, Gregory, "Soft Power, and the Obama Doctrine in Cuba." *The Latin Americanist*, vol. 60, no. 4 (December 2016).

Index